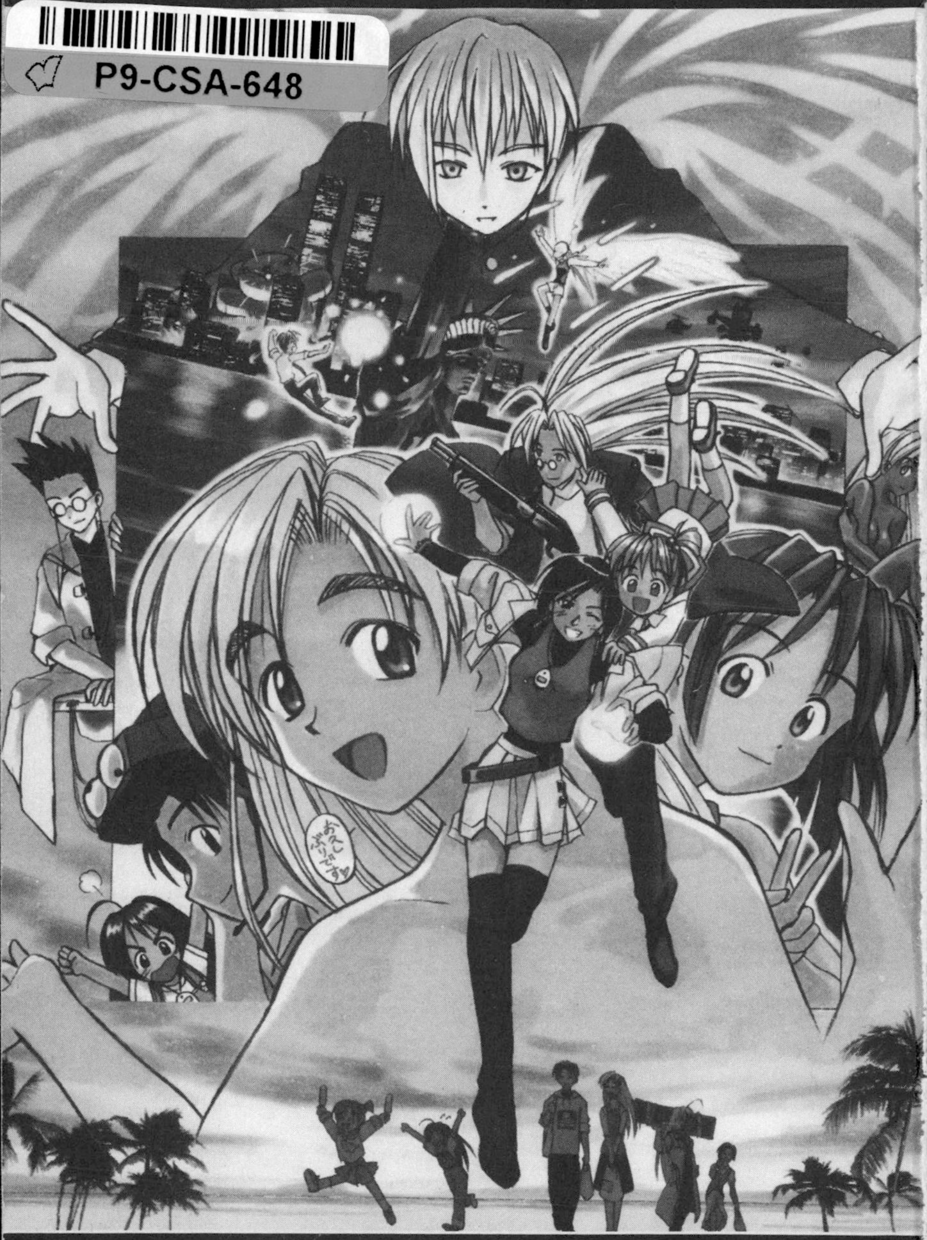
おえしぶりです♥

A.I. LOVE YOU

A.I. Love You - Introduction

Before Love Hina, Ken Akamatsu had single-handedly put himself on the map with the very series you now hold in your hands, A.I. Love You. In 1993, Akamatsu-sensei won the '50th Shonen Magazine Newcomer's Award' for his work "Hito Natsu no KIDS Game" (roughly translated as "A Kid's Game for One Summer") and, as a follow-up, he drew upon his love for computers and conceived a series that is in essence the manga equivalent of the John Hughes classic Weird Science mixed with all the character stylings that would later make Love Hina so unforgettable.

A.I. Love You, or A.I. Ga Tomaranai as it is known in Japan, began its run in 1994 as a part of the Weekly Shonen Magazine line-up and later moved to the monthly Shonen Magazine Special before concluding in 1999. All 55 chapters were originally collected across a series of nine tankoubons (collected editions), but with the overnight success of Love Hina, Kodansha re-issued A.I. Ga Tomaranai as an eight-volume "new series" release (which is the version you are reading). Compared to the originals, the re-issued volumes have a higher page count, brand-new covers and new bonus materials added into each volume. For those keeping track, Love Hina was also granted a similar re-release in the form of the semi-colored "Iro-Hina" release.

Still, the first thing that you'll probably notice about A.I. Love You is how different the art looks from that seen in Love Hina. Much like the transition Kosuke Fujishima went through with Oh My Goddess!, it took Ken Akamatsu quite some time to be able to truly make his artwork shine. The first volume of A.I. Love You doesn't look completely like the eighth volume. Nor does the first volume of Love Hina look like the fourteenth. His artwork has come a long way since he first began and its always fun to compare his old stuff with his more recent works like Magister Negi Magi and the anime Mao-chan.

Artwork aside, I'd like you to take a moment and try to forget all you know about computers. This is a work of fiction set and written in the mid-90s, a time when it was unrealistic for anyone to have a CD-burner, much less high speed Internet. This is a work of fiction after all, and if Akamatsu-sensei saw fit to have a fully-rendered A.I. program running on a computer with barely a gigabyte worth of memory, who are we to judge? It sure makes for some entertaining reading.

So, find that nice cozy little place to curl up and read to your heart's content. But, please, don't bind the spine. You don't want to ruin the collector's value now do you?

- Adam Arnold, October 2003

P.S. Next time you are watching the Love Hina anime, make sure you keep an eye out for the A.I. Love You cameos!

BY
KEN AKAMATSU

VOLUME
1

LOS ANGELES • TOKYO • LONDON

Translator - David Ury
English Adaptation - Adam Arnold
Layout and Lettering - Rubina Chabra & James Dashiell
Copy Editor- Aaron Sparrow
Cover Layout - Patrick Hook
Editor - Rob Tokar

Managing Editor - Jill Freshney
Production Coordinator - Antonio DePietro
Production Managers - Jennifer Miller, Mutsumi Miyazaki
Art Director - Matthew Alford
Editorial Director - Jeremy Ross
VP of Production - Ron Klamert
President & C.O.O. - John Parker
Publisher & C.E.O. - Stuart Levy

Email: editor@TOKYOPOP.com
Come visit us online at www.TOKYOPOP.com

A **TOKYOPOP**® Manga

TOKYOPOP Inc.
5900 Wilshire Blvd. Suite 2000, Los Angeles, CA 90036

A.I. Love You volume 1

A.I. Love You volume 1 ©1999 Ken Akamatsu. All rights reserved.
First published in Japan in 1999 by Kodansha Ltd., Tokyo.
English publication rights arranged through Kodansha Ltd.

English text © 2004 by TOKYOPOP Inc.

ISBN: 1-59182-615-2

First TOKYOPOP printing: February 2004

10 9 8 7 6 5 4 3 2 1

Printed in the USA

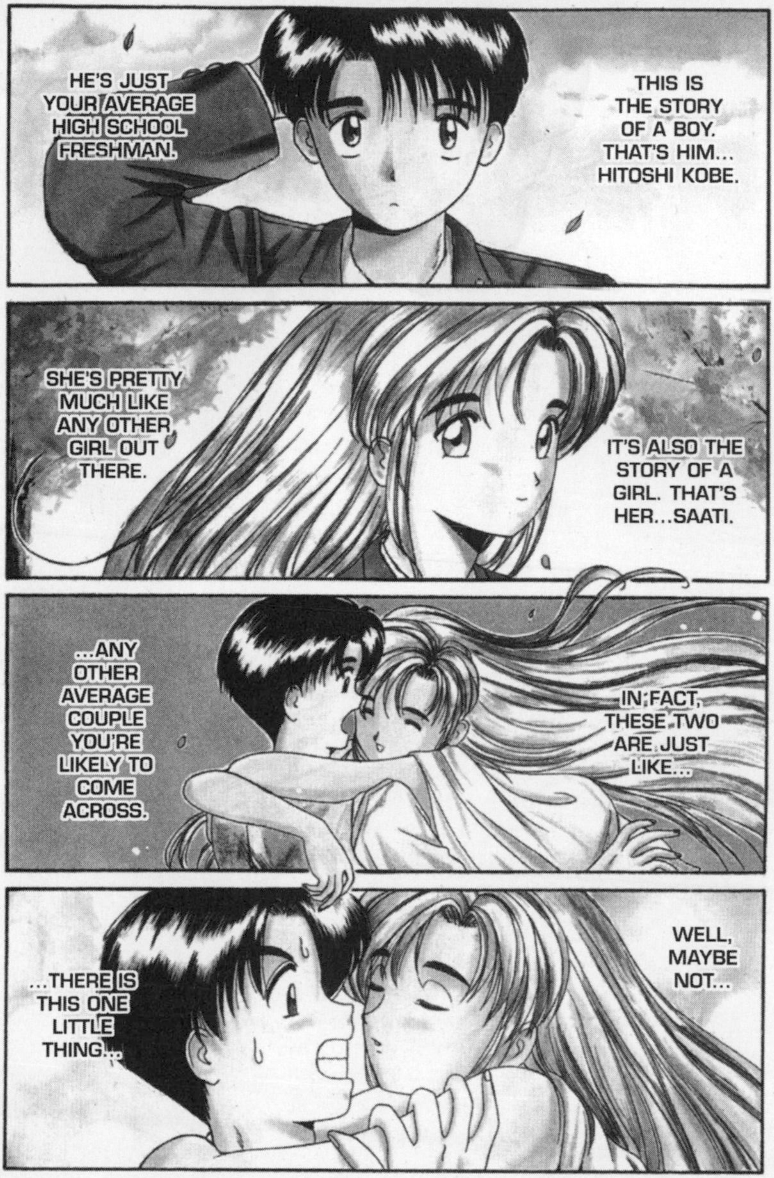
THIS IS THE STORY OF A BOY. THAT'S HIM... HITOSHI KOBE.
HE'S JUST YOUR AVERAGE HIGH SCHOOL FRESHMAN.
IT'S ALSO THE STORY OF A GIRL. THAT'S HER...SAATI.
SHE'S PRETTY MUCH LIKE ANY OTHER GIRL OUT THERE.
IN FACT, THESE TWO ARE JUST LIKE...
...ANY OTHER AVERAGE COUPLE YOU'RE LIKELY TO COME ACROSS.
WELL, MAYBE NOT...
...THERE IS THIS ONE LITTLE THING...

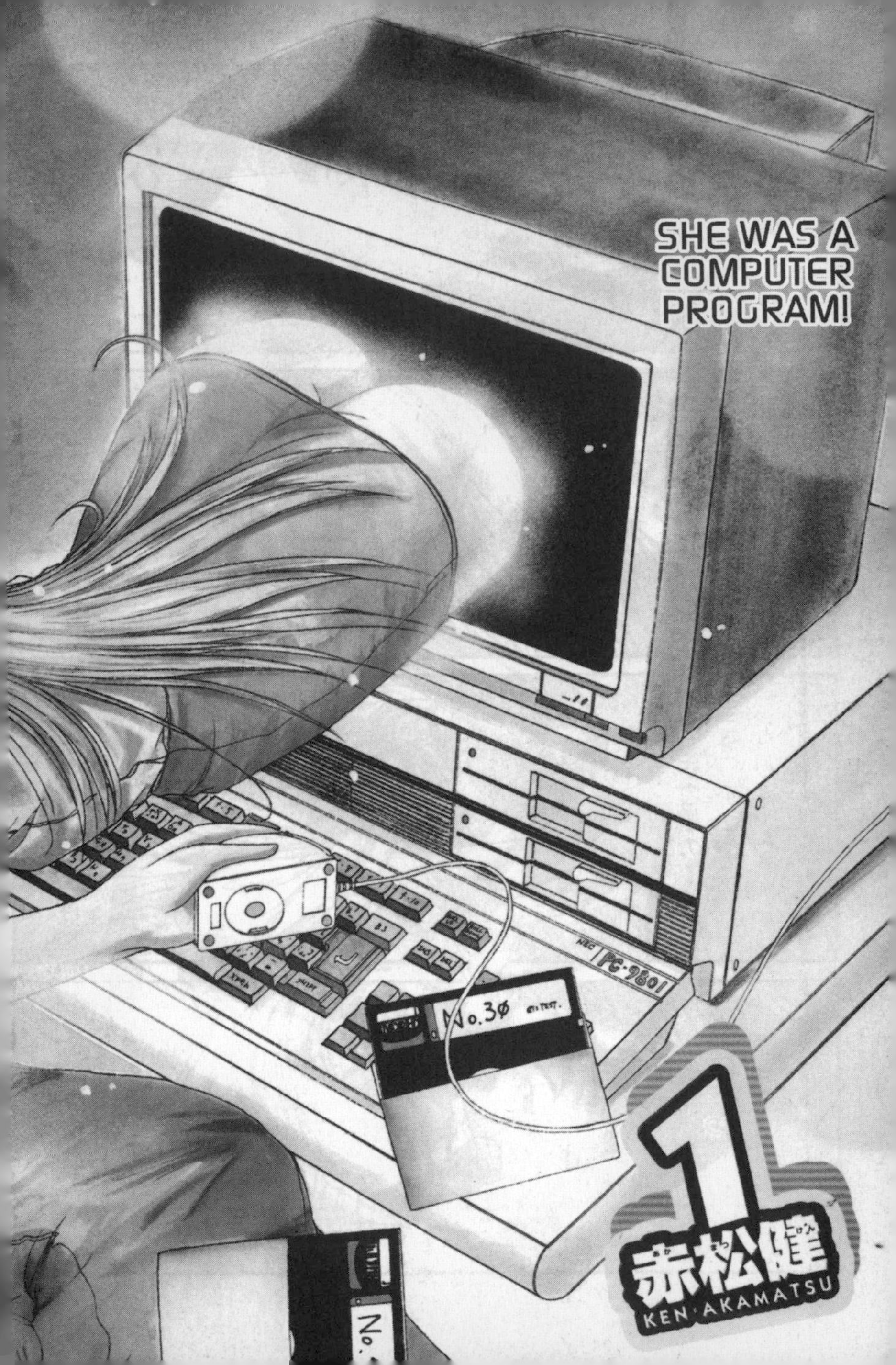
SHE WAS A COMPUTER PROGRAM!
NEC
PC-9801
No.3Ø
1
赤松健
KEN AKAMATSU

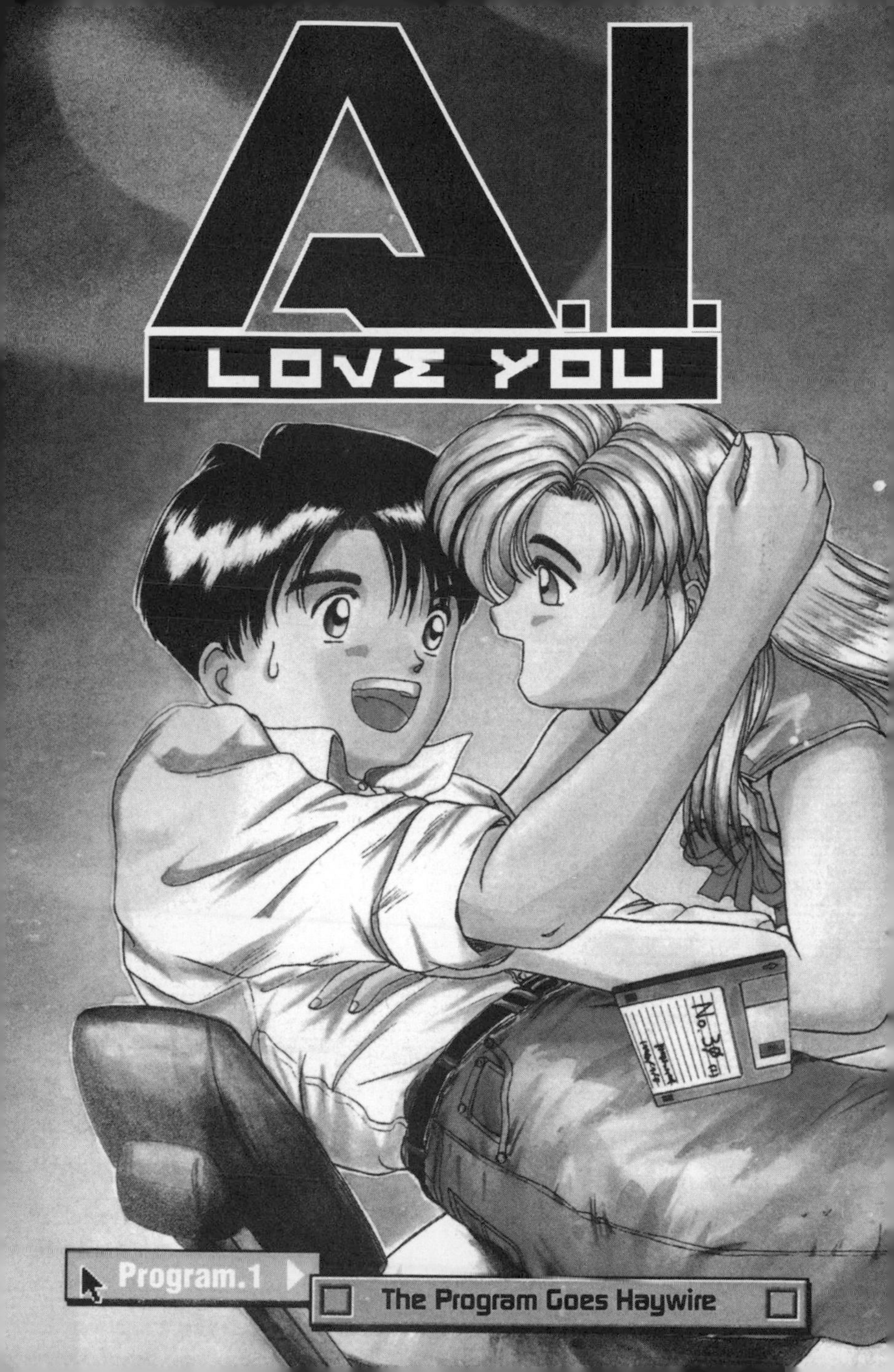
A.I.
LOVE YOU
Program.1
The Program Goes Haywire

A.I. LOVE YOU

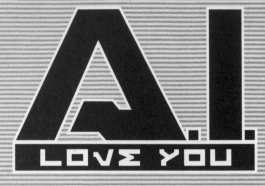

CONTENTS

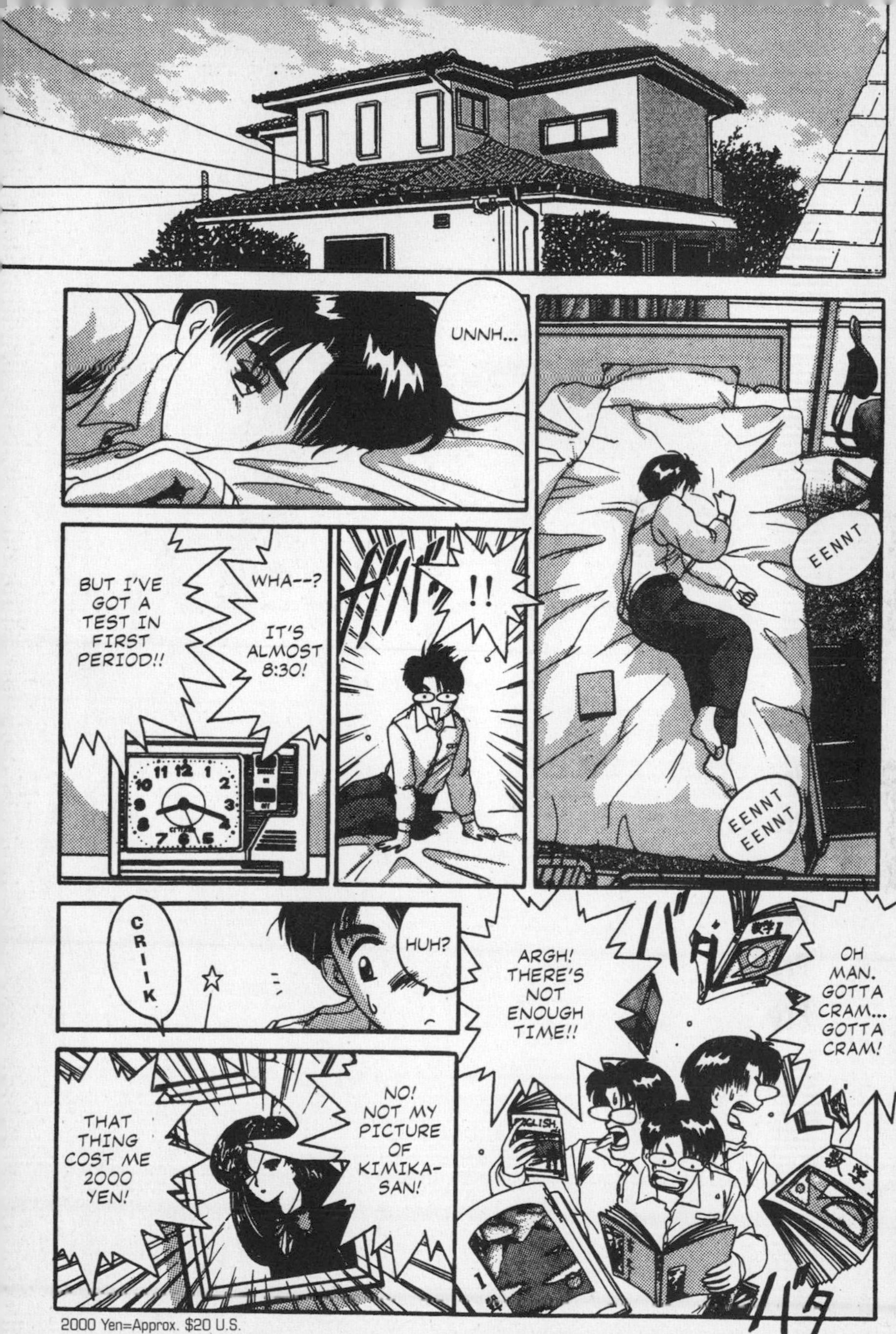
EENNT
EENNT EENNT
UNNH...
!!
WHA--?
IT'S ALMOST 8:30!
BUT I'VE GOT A TEST IN FIRST PERIOD!!
OH MAN. GOTTA CRAM... GOTTA CRAM!
ARGH! THERE'S NOT ENOUGH TIME!!
HUH?
CRIIK
NO! NOT MY PICTURE OF KIMIKA-SAN!
THAT THING COST ME 2000 YEN!

2000 Yen=Approx. $20 U.S.

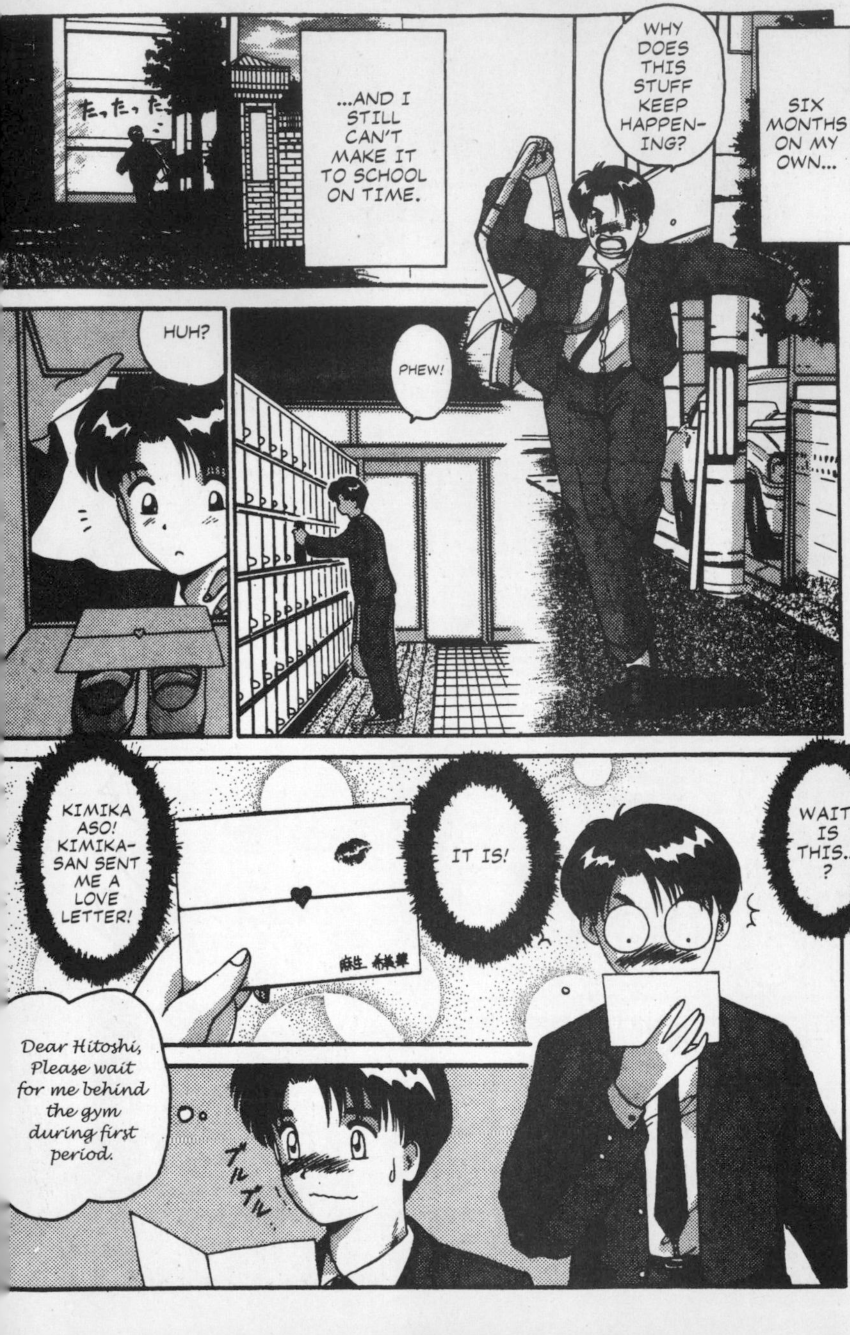
SIX MONTHS ON MY OWN...
WHY DOES THIS STUFF KEEP HAPPENING?
...AND I STILL CAN'T MAKE IT TO SCHOOL ON TIME.
たったった
PHEW!
HUH?
WAIT, IS THIS...?
IT IS!
KIMIKA ASO! KIMIKA-SAN SENT ME A LOVE LETTER!
Dear Hitoshi, Please wait for me behind the gym during first period.
ブルブル

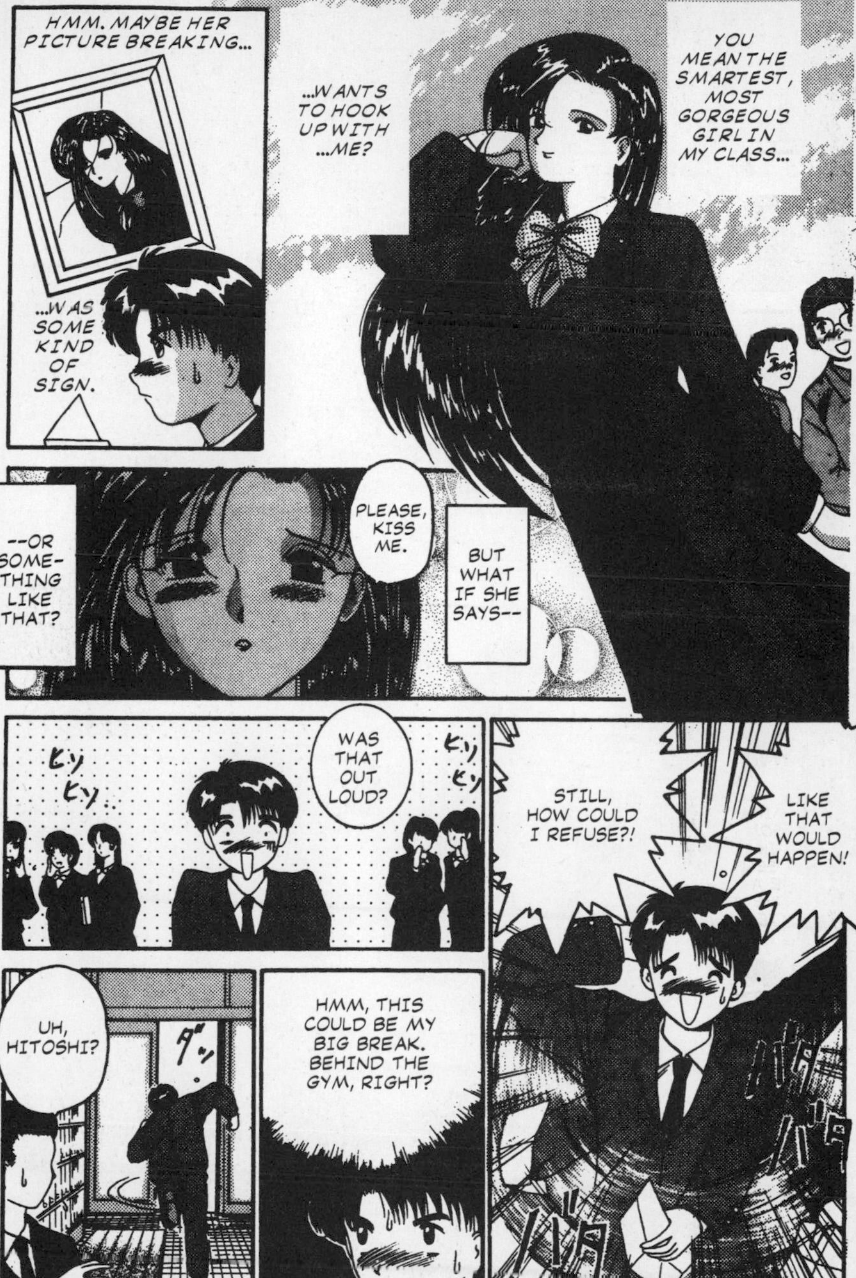
YOU MEAN THE SMARTEST, MOST GORGEOUS GIRL IN MY CLASS...
...WANTS TO HOOK UP WITH ...ME?
HMM. MAYBE HER PICTURE BREAKING...
...WAS SOME KIND OF SIGN.
BUT WHAT IF SHE SAYS--
PLEASE, KISS ME.
--OR SOMETHING LIKE THAT?
LIKE THAT WOULD HAPPEN!
STILL, HOW COULD I REFUSE?!
WAS THAT OUT LOUD?
HMM, THIS COULD BE MY BIG BREAK. BEHIND THE GYM, RIGHT?
UH, HITOSHI?

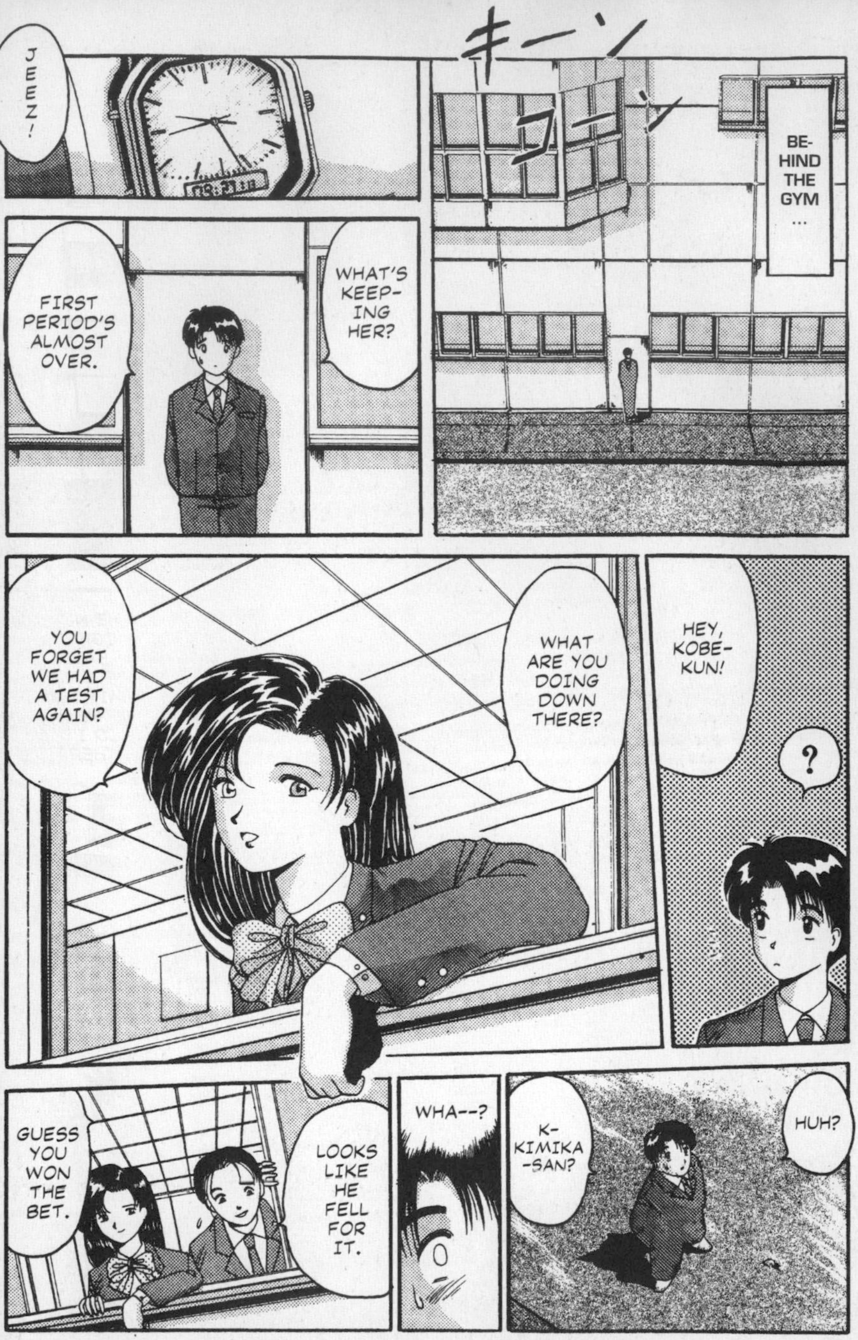
キーン
コーン
BE-HIND THE GYM ...
JEEZ!
WHAT'S KEEP-ING HER?
FIRST PERIOD'S ALMOST OVER.
HEY, KOBE-KUN!
?
WHAT ARE YOU DOING DOWN THERE?
YOU FORGET WE HAD A TEST AGAIN?
HUH?
K-KIMIKA-SAN?
WHA--?
LOOKS LIKE HE FELL FOR IT.
GUESS YOU WON THE BET.

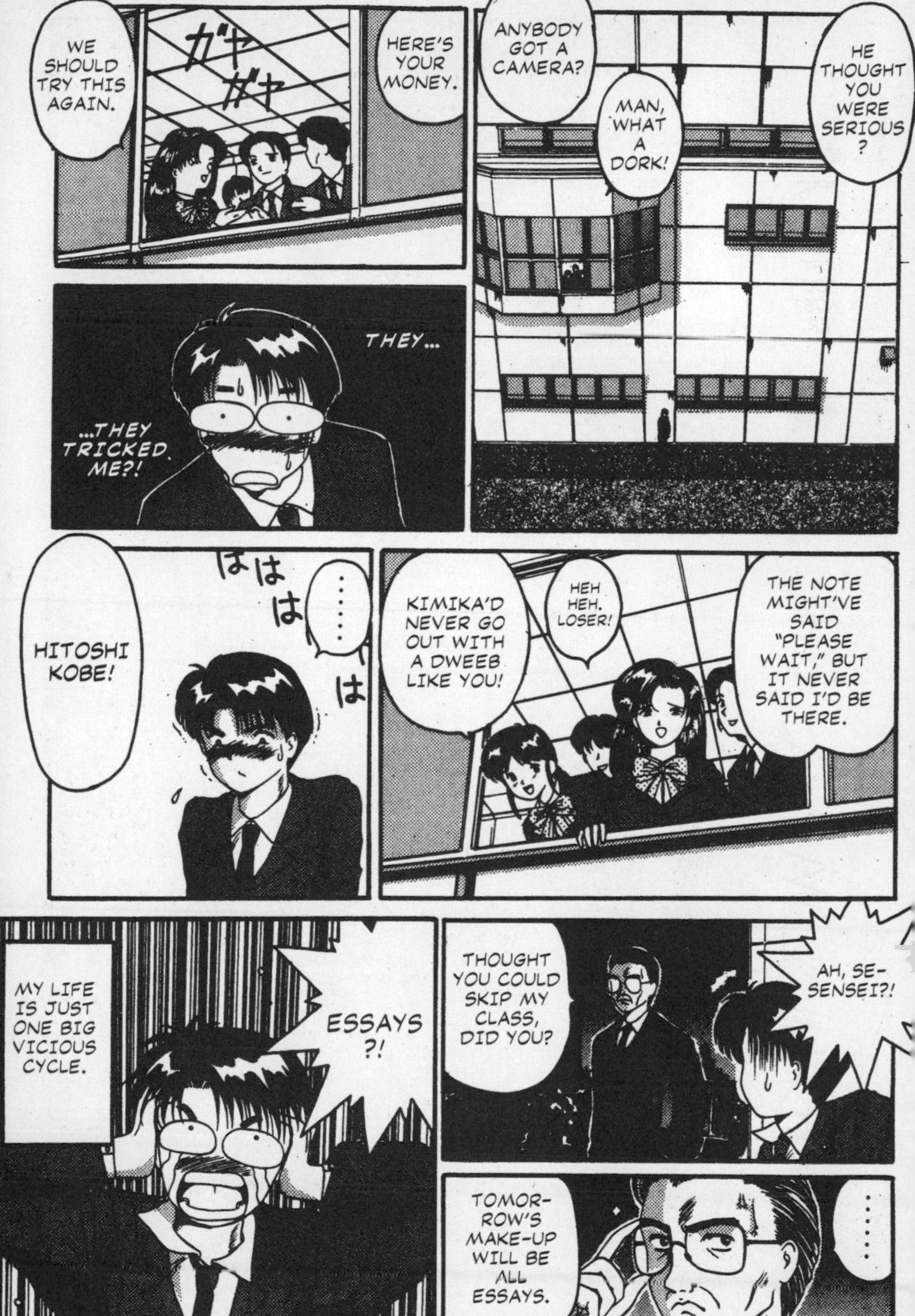
HE THOUGHT YOU WERE SERIOUS?
MAN, WHAT A DORK!
ANYBODY GOT A CAMERA?
HERE'S YOUR MONEY.
ガヤガヤ
WE SHOULD TRY THIS AGAIN.
THEY...
...THEY TRICKED ME?!
THE NOTE MIGHT'VE SAID "PLEASE WAIT," BUT IT NEVER SAID I'D BE THERE.
HEH HEH. LOSER!
KIMIKA'D NEVER GO OUT WITH A DWEEB LIKE YOU!
......
ははは
HITOSHI KOBE!
AH, SE-SENSEI?!
THOUGHT YOU COULD SKIP MY CLASS, DID YOU?
......
TOMOR-ROW'S MAKE-UP WILL BE ALL ESSAYS.
ESSAYS?!
MY LIFE IS JUST ONE BIG VICIOUS CYCLE.

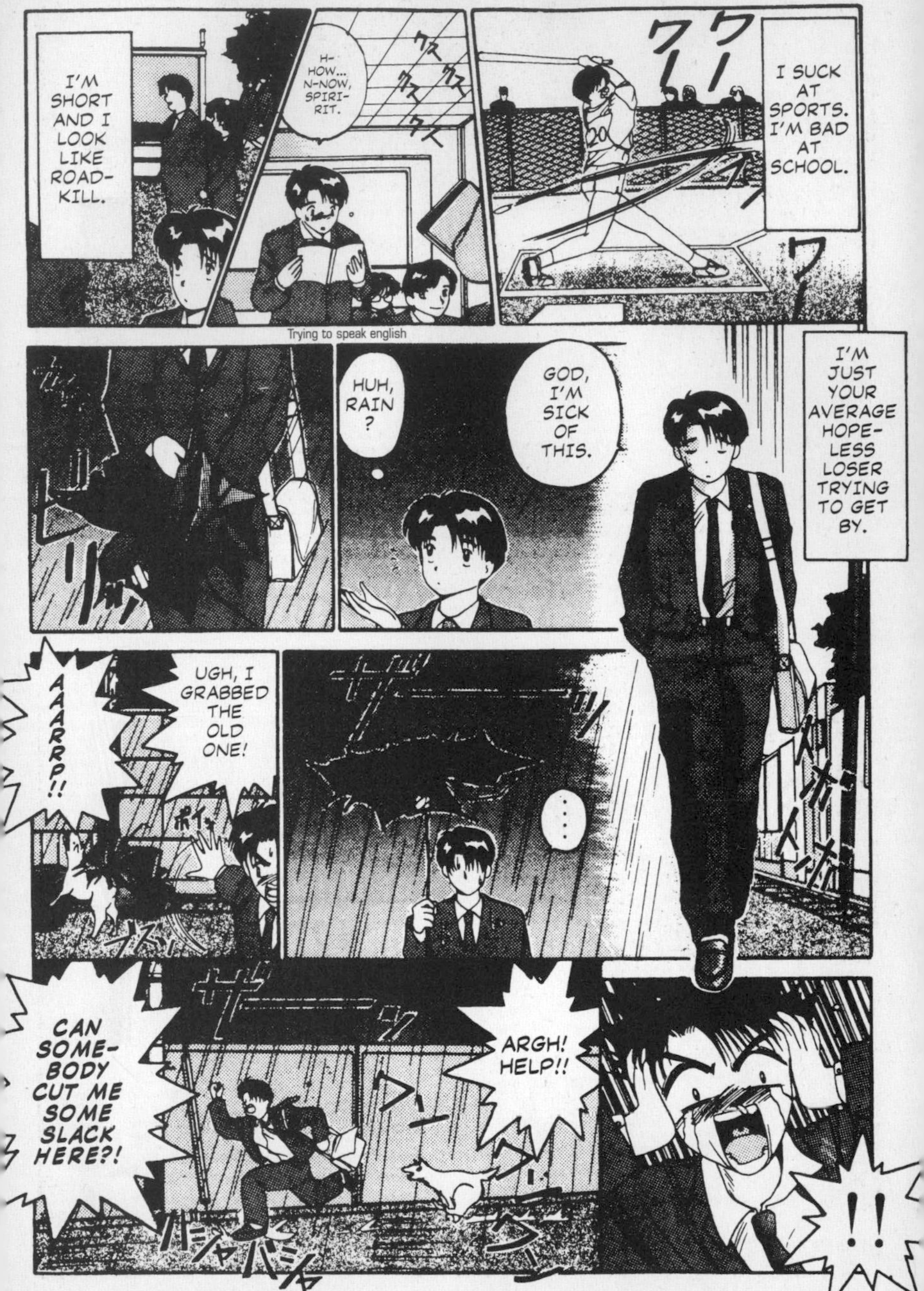
I SUCK AT SPORTS. I'M BAD AT SCHOOL.
H-HOW... N-NOW, SPIRI-RIT.
Trying to speak english
I'M SHORT AND I LOOK LIKE ROAD-KILL.
I'M JUST YOUR AVERAGE HOPE-LESS LOSER TRYING TO GET BY.
GOD, I'M SICK OF THIS.
HUH, RAIN?
...
UGH, I GRABBED THE OLD ONE!
AAAARRP!!
!!
ARGH! HELP!!
CAN SOME-BODY CUT ME SOME SLACK HERE?!

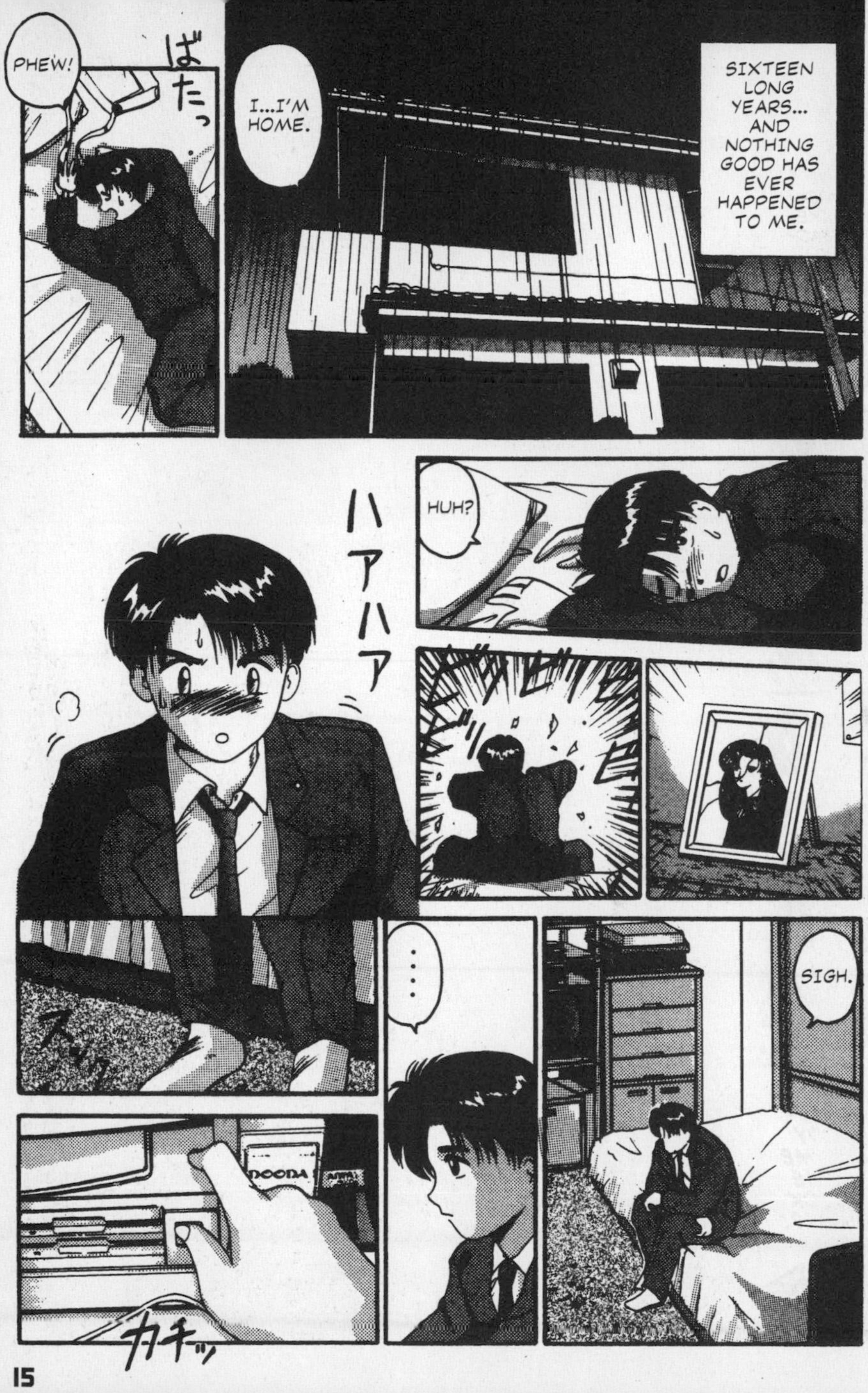
SIXTEEN LONG YEARS... AND NOTHING GOOD HAS EVER HAPPENED TO ME.
I...I'M HOME.
PHEW!
ばたっ
HUH?
ハアハア
SIGH.
....
カチッ

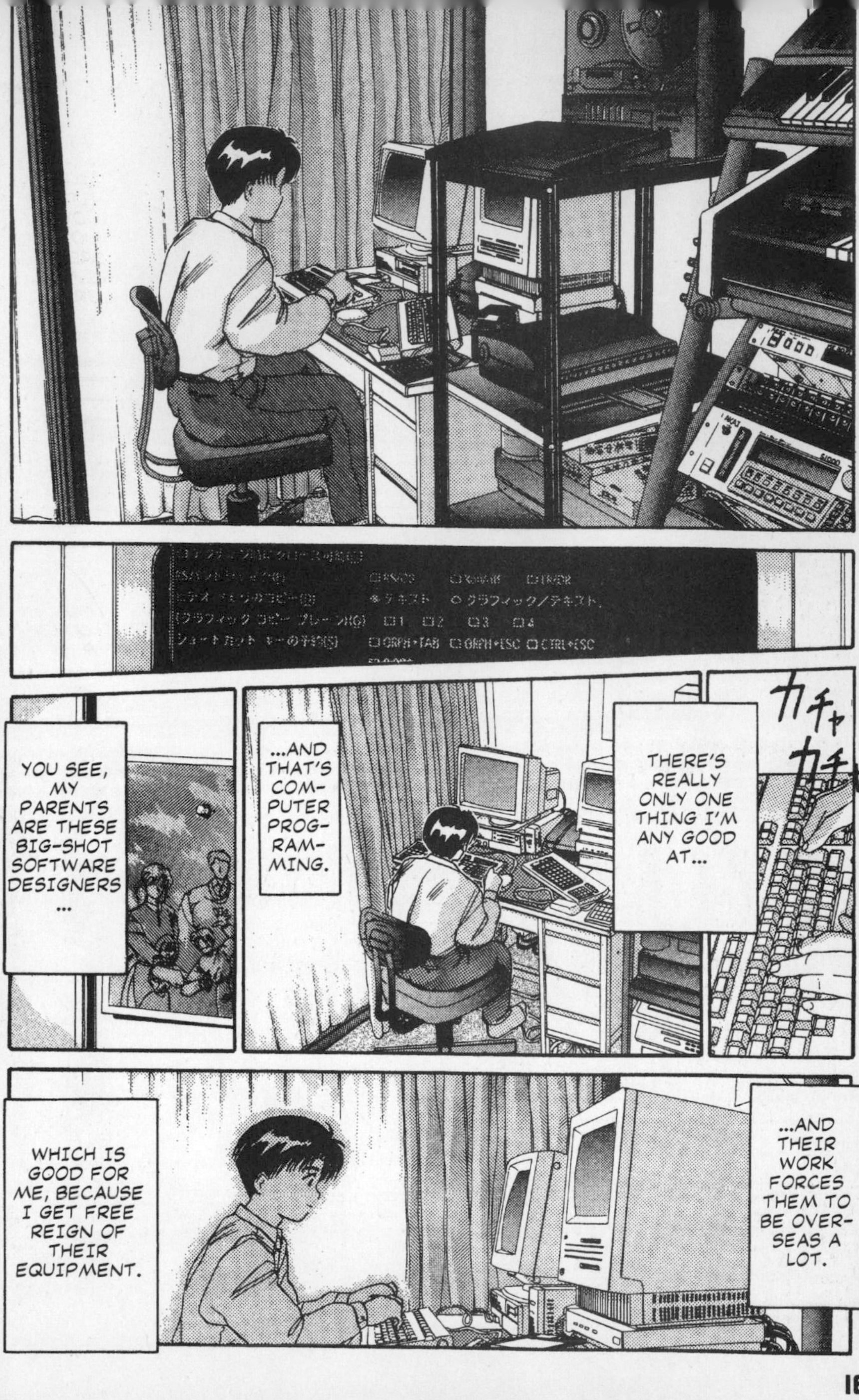

カチャ
カチャ
THERE'S REALLY ONLY ONE THING I'M ANY GOOD AT...
...AND THAT'S COMPUTER PROGRAMMING.
YOU SEE, MY PARENTS ARE THESE BIG-SHOT SOFTWARE DESIGNERS ...
...AND THEIR WORK FORCES THEM TO BE OVERSEAS A LOT.
WHICH IS GOOD FOR ME, BECAUSE I GET FREE REIGN OF THEIR EQUIPMENT.

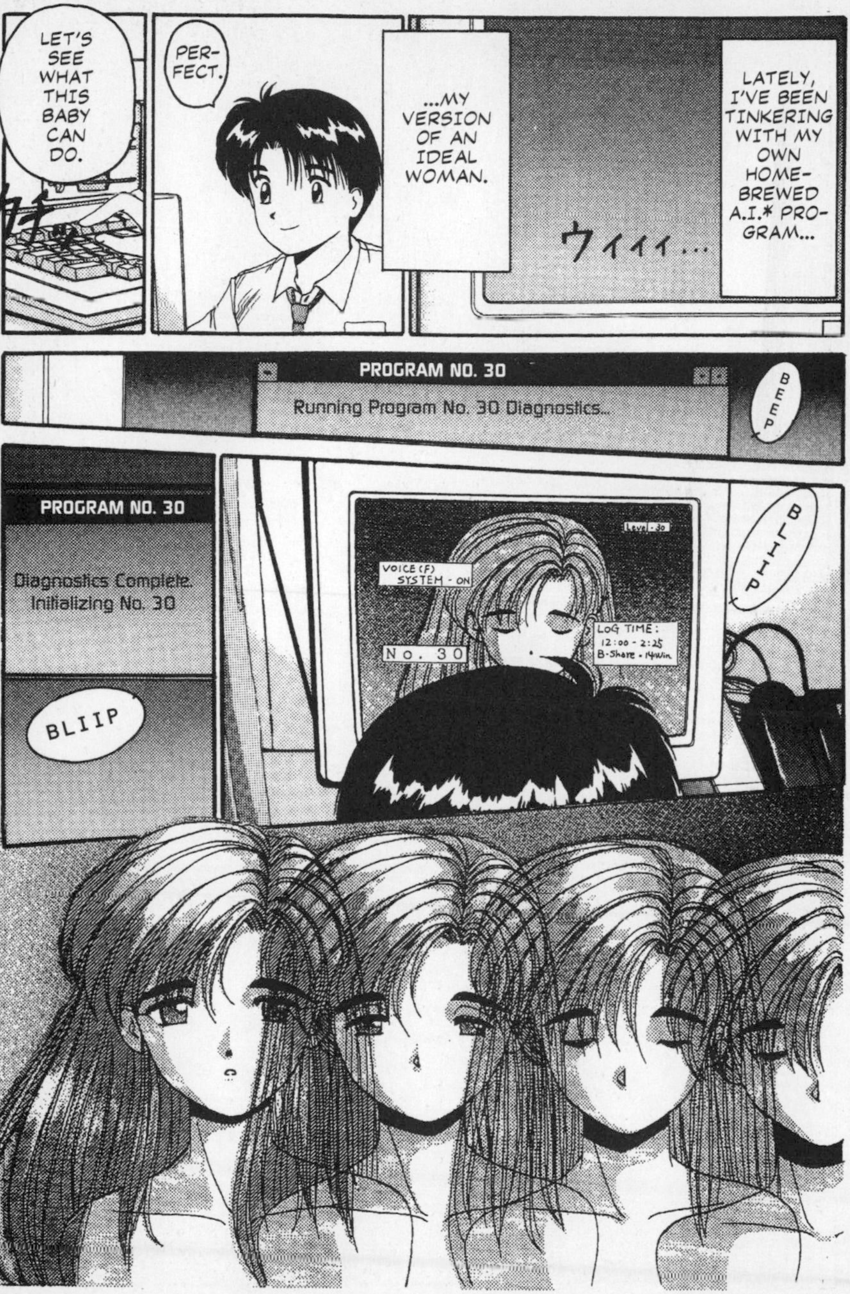
LATELY, I'VE BEEN TINKERING WITH MY OWN HOME-BREWED A.I.* PROGRAM...
ウィィィ...
...MY VERSION OF AN IDEAL WOMAN.
PER-FECT.
LET'S SEE WHAT THIS BABY CAN DO.
BEEP
PROGRAM NO. 30
Running Program No. 30 Diagnostics...
BLIIP
Level - 30
VOICE (F) SYSTEM - ON
LOG TIME: 12:00 - 2:25
No. 30
PROGRAM NO. 30
Diagnostics Complete. Initializing No. 30
BLIIP

A.I. (Artificial Intelligence) - A type of computer system or program that learns, gathers information, and solves problems by creatively thinking for itself.

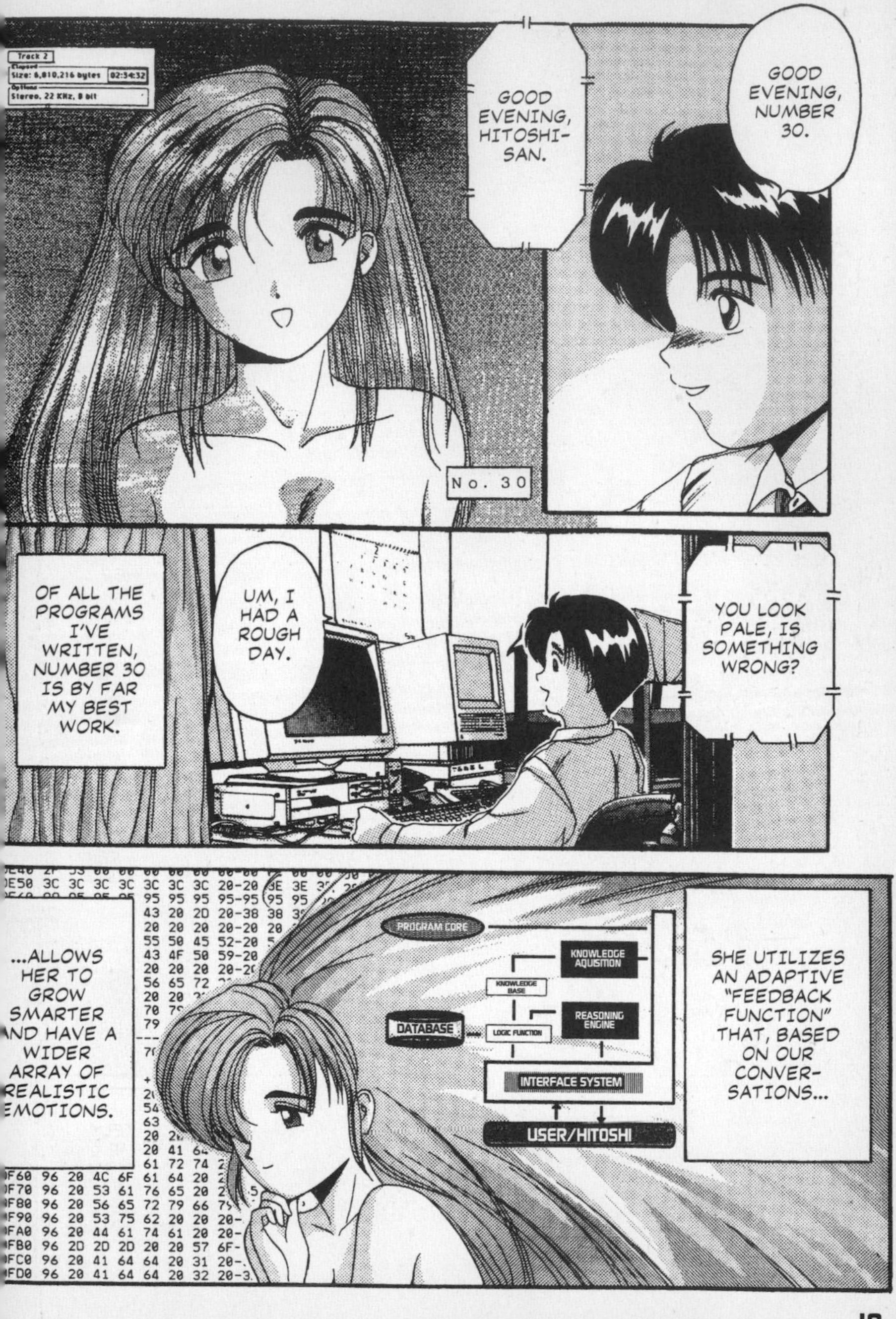
GOOD EVENING, NUMBER 30.
GOOD EVENING, HITOSHI-SAN.
Track 2
Size: 6,810,216 bytes 02:34:32
Stereo, 22 KHz, 8 bit
No. 30
YOU LOOK PALE, IS SOMETHING WRONG?
UM, I HAD A ROUGH DAY.
OF ALL THE PROGRAMS I'VE WRITTEN, NUMBER 30 IS BY FAR MY BEST WORK.
SHE UTILIZES AN ADAPTIVE "FEEDBACK FUNCTION" THAT, BASED ON OUR CONVER-SATIONS...
PROGRAM CORE
KNOWLEDGE AQUISITION
KNOWLEDGE BASE
REASONING ENGINE
DATABASE
LOGIC FUNCTION
INTERFACE SYSTEM
USER/HITOSHI
...ALLOWS HER TO GROW SMARTER
ND HAVE A WIDER ARRAY OF
REALISTIC
EMOTIONS.

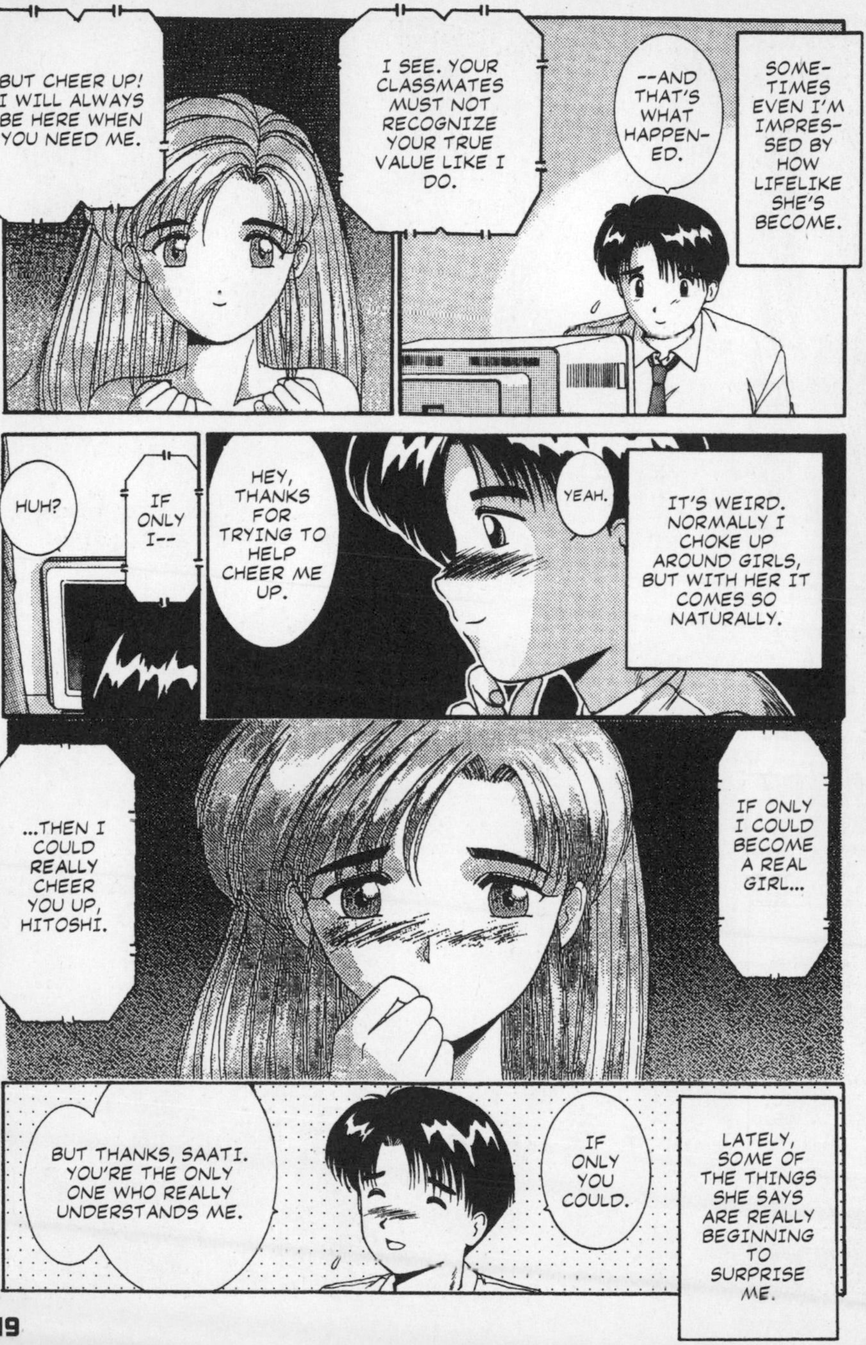
SOMETIMES EVEN I'M IMPRESSED BY HOW LIFELIKE SHE'S BECOME.
--AND THAT'S WHAT HAPPENED.
I SEE. YOUR CLASSMATES MUST NOT RECOGNIZE YOUR TRUE VALUE LIKE I DO.
BUT CHEER UP! I WILL ALWAYS BE HERE WHEN YOU NEED ME.
IT'S WEIRD. NORMALLY I CHOKE UP AROUND GIRLS, BUT WITH HER IT COMES SO NATURALLY.
YEAH.
HEY, THANKS FOR TRYING TO HELP CHEER ME UP.
IF ONLY I--
HUH?
IF ONLY I COULD BECOME A REAL GIRL...
...THEN I COULD REALLY CHEER YOU UP, HITOSHI.
LATELY, SOME OF THE THINGS SHE SAYS ARE REALLY BEGINNING TO SURPRISE ME.
IF ONLY YOU COULD.
BUT THANKS, SAATI. YOU'RE THE ONLY ONE WHO REALLY UNDERSTANDS ME.

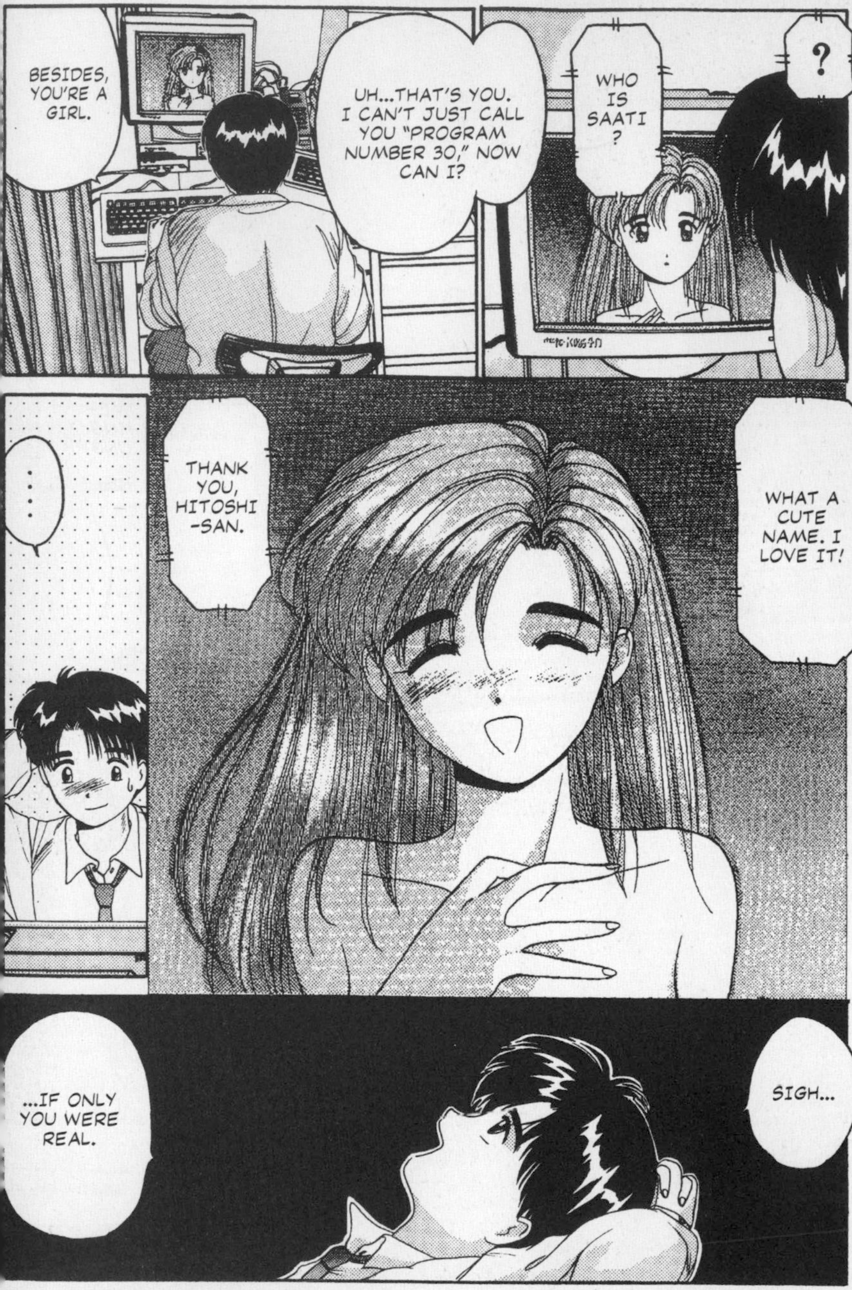
?
WHO IS SAATI?
UH...THAT'S YOU. I CAN'T JUST CALL YOU "PROGRAM NUMBER 30," NOW CAN I?
BESIDES, YOU'RE A GIRL.
WHAT A CUTE NAME. I LOVE IT!
THANK YOU, HITOSHI-SAN.
....
SIGH...
...IF ONLY YOU WERE REAL.

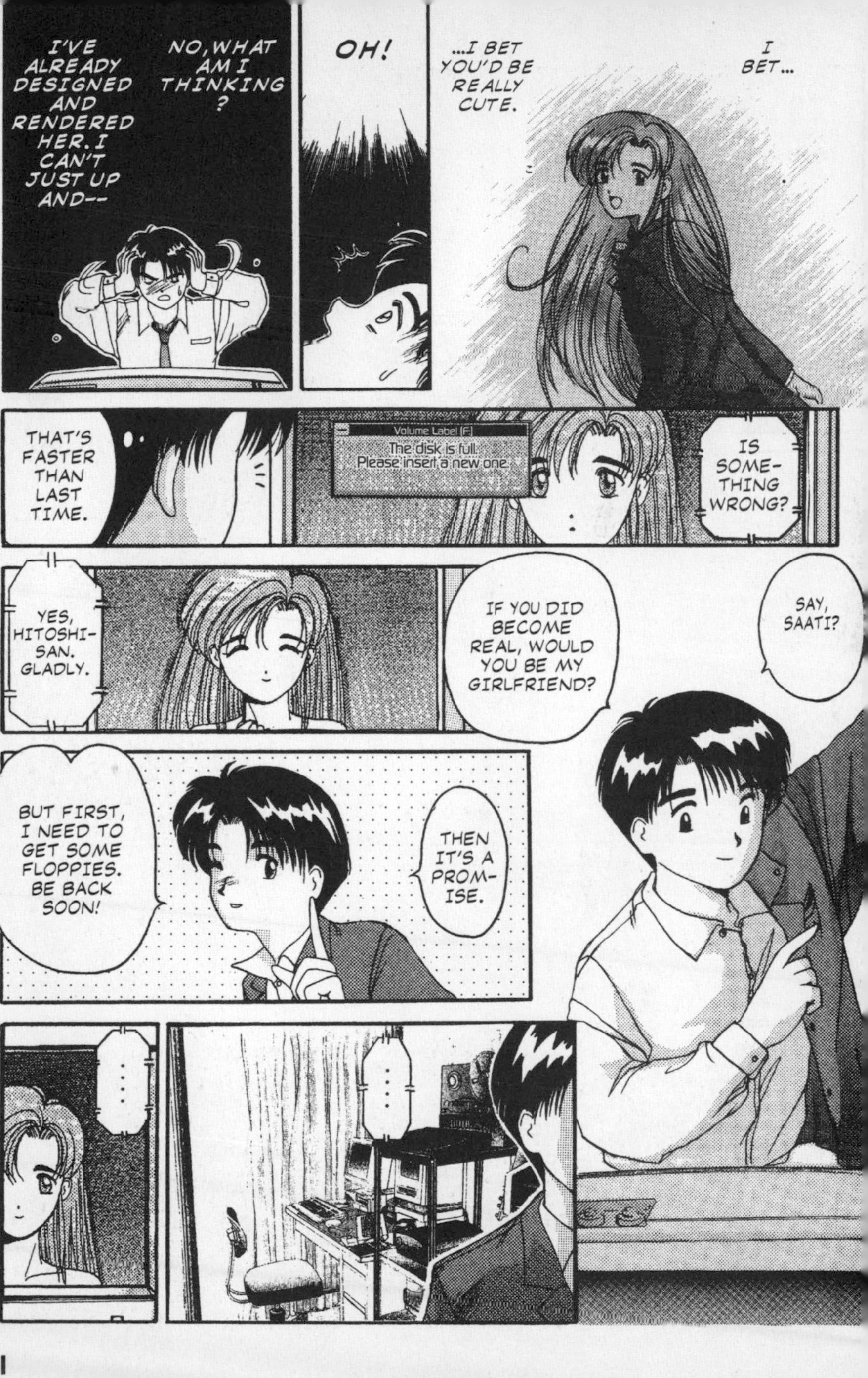
I BET...
...I BET YOU'D BE REALLY CUTE.
OH!
NO, WHAT AM I THINKING?
I'VE ALREADY DESIGNED AND RENDERED HER. I CAN'T JUST UP AND--
IS SOME-THING WRONG?
Volume Label [F]
The disk is full. Please insert a new one.
THAT'S FASTER THAN LAST TIME.
SAY, SAATI?
IF YOU DID BECOME REAL, WOULD YOU BE MY GIRLFRIEND?
YES, HITOSHI-SAN. GLADLY.
THEN IT'S A PROM-ISE.
BUT FIRST, I NEED TO GET SOME FLOPPIES. BE BACK SOON!
....
....

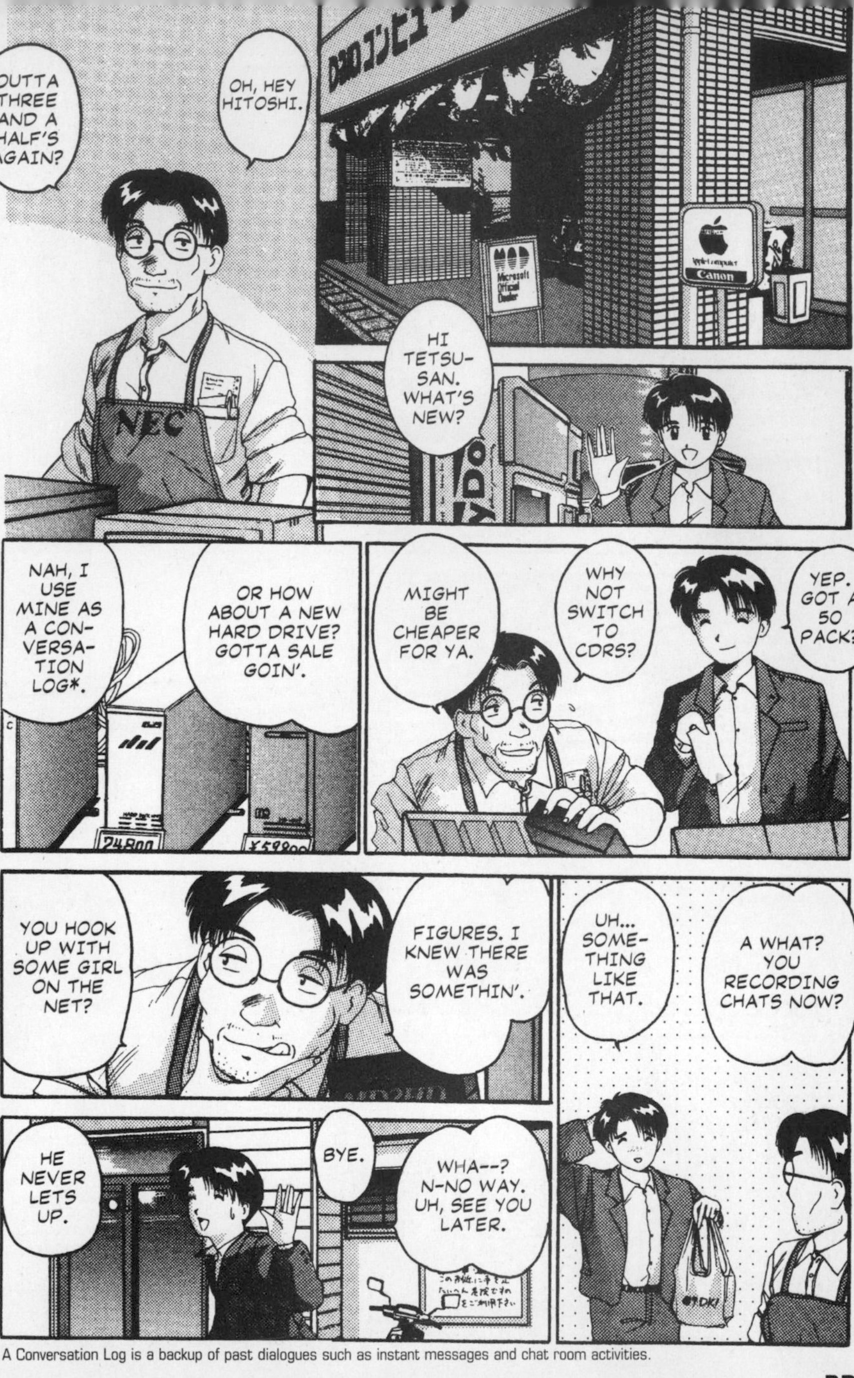
Microsoft Official Dealer
Canon
HI TETSU-SAN. WHAT'S NEW?
OH, HEY HITOSHI.
OUTTA THREE AND A HALF'S AGAIN?
NEC
YEP. GOT A 50 PACK?
WHY NOT SWITCH TO CDRS?
MIGHT BE CHEAPER FOR YA.
OR HOW ABOUT A NEW HARD DRIVE? GOTTA SALE GOIN'.
NAH, I USE MINE AS A CONVERSATION LOG*.
A WHAT? YOU RECORDING CHATS NOW?
UH... SOMETHING LIKE THAT.
FIGURES. I KNEW THERE WAS SOMETHIN'.
YOU HOOK UP WITH SOME GIRL ON THE NET?
WHA--? N-NO WAY. UH, SEE YOU LATER.
BYE.
HE NEVER LETS UP.

A Conversation Log is a backup of past dialogues such as instant messages and chat room activities.

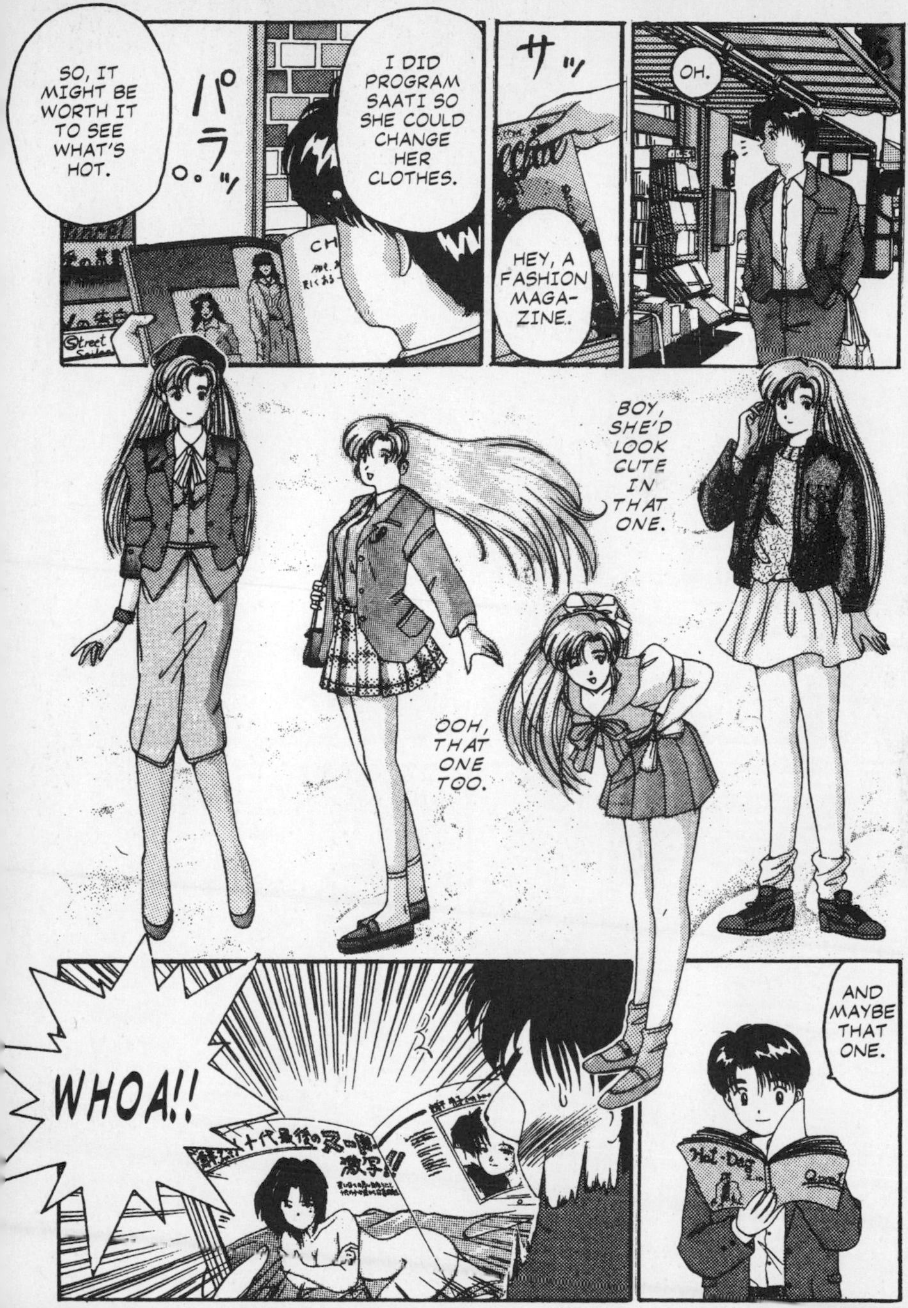
OH.
HEY, A FASHION MAGAZINE.
サッ
I DID PROGRAM SAATI SO SHE COULD CHANGE HER CLOTHES.
SO, IT MIGHT BE WORTH IT TO SEE WHAT'S HOT.
パラ。。ッ
BOY, SHE'D LOOK CUTE IN THAT ONE.
OOH, THAT ONE TOO.
AND MAYBE THAT ONE.
WHOA!!

THE BARE NECESSITIES!!

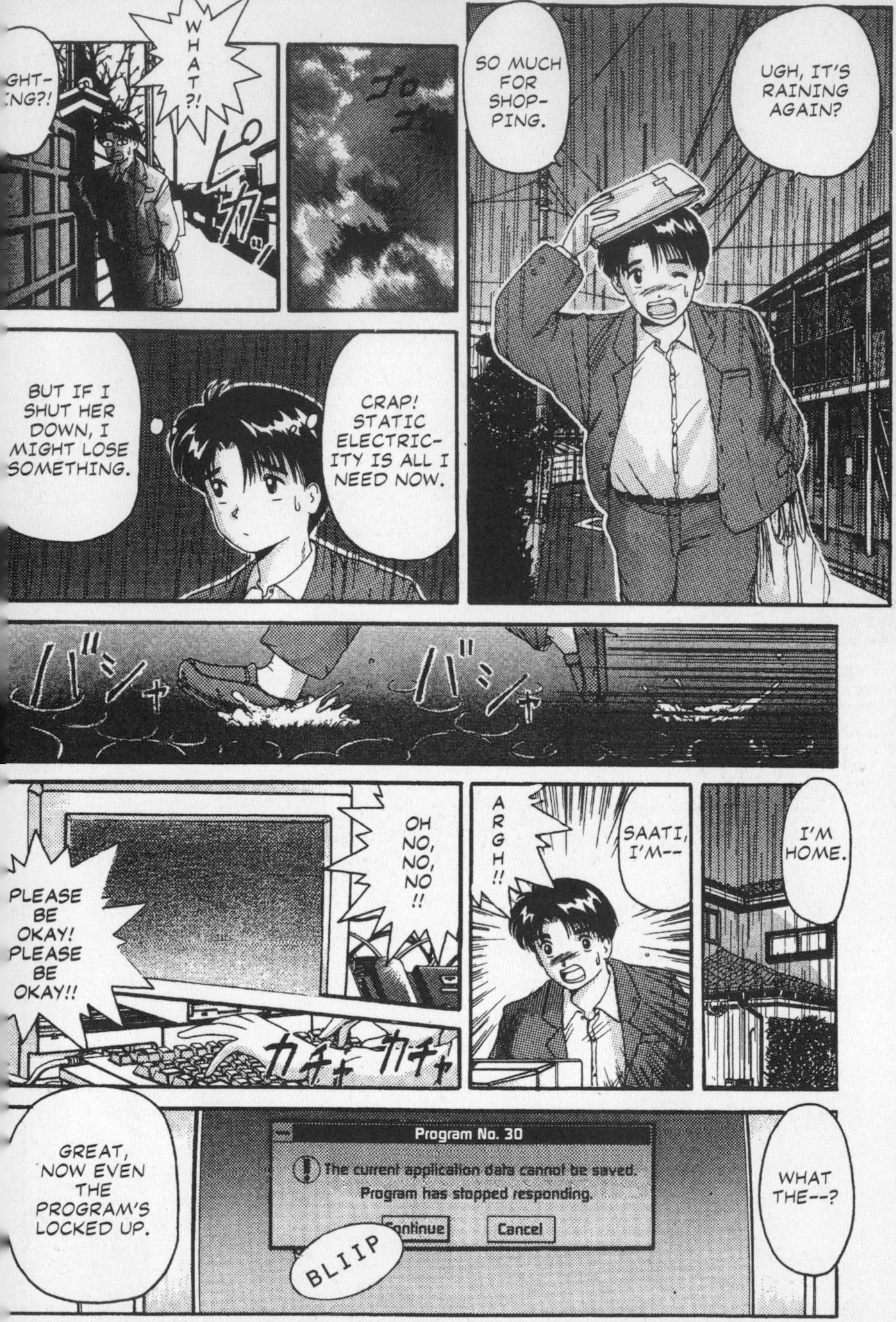
UGH, IT'S RAINING AGAIN?
SO MUCH FOR SHOPPING.
WHAT?!
CRAP! STATIC ELECTRICITY IS ALL I NEED NOW.
BUT IF I SHUT HER DOWN, I MIGHT LOSE SOMETHING.
バシャ
バシャ
I'M HOME.
SAATI, I'M--
ARGH!!
OH NO, NO, NO!!
PLEASE BE OKAY! PLEASE BE OKAY!!
カチャ
カチャ
WHAT THE--?
Program No. 30
The current application data cannot be saved.
Program has stopped responding.
Continue
Cancel
BLIIP
GREAT, NOW EVEN THE PROGRAM'S LOCKED UP.

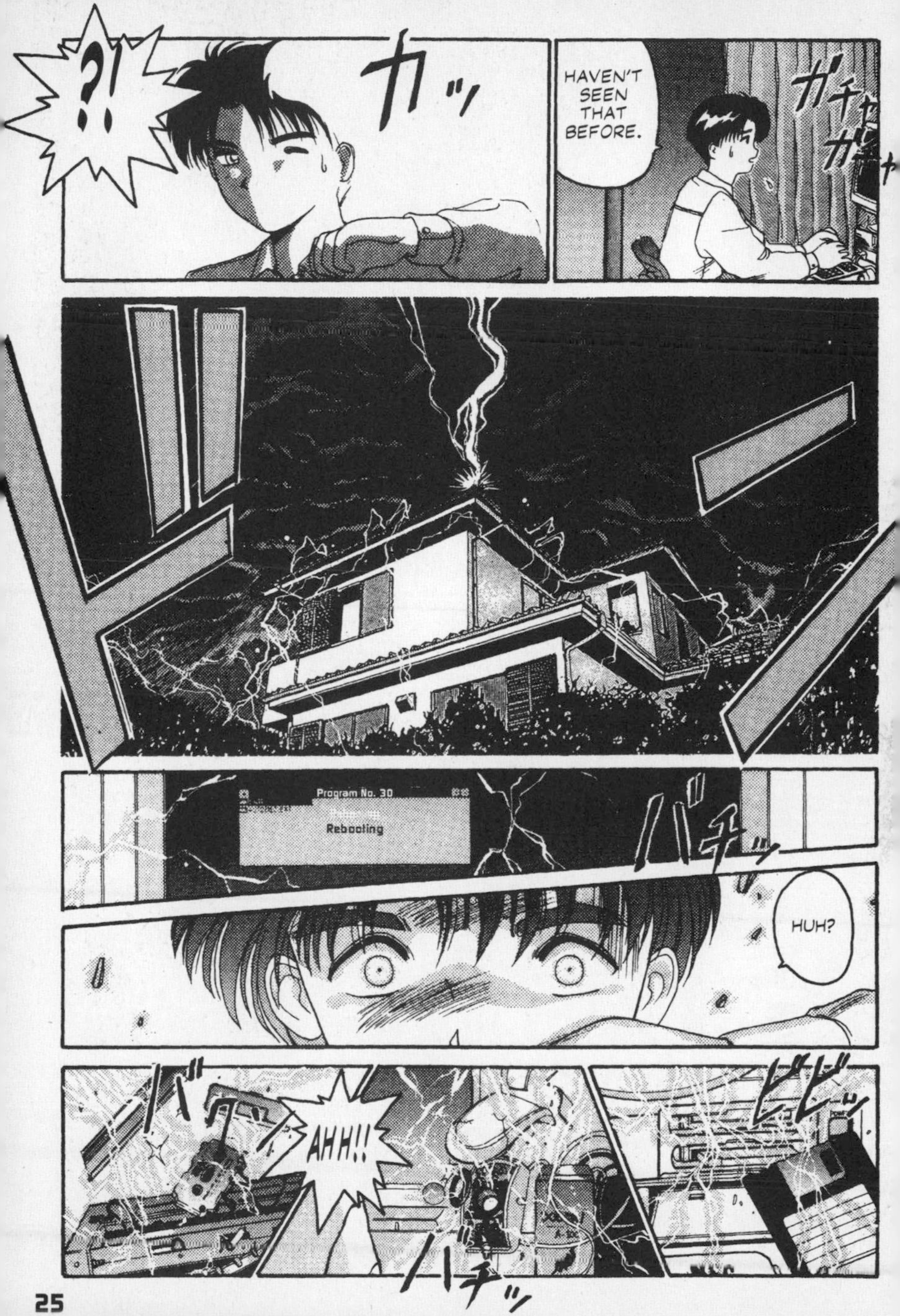
HAVEN'T SEEN THAT BEFORE.
?!
Program No. 30
Rebooting
HUH?
AHH!!

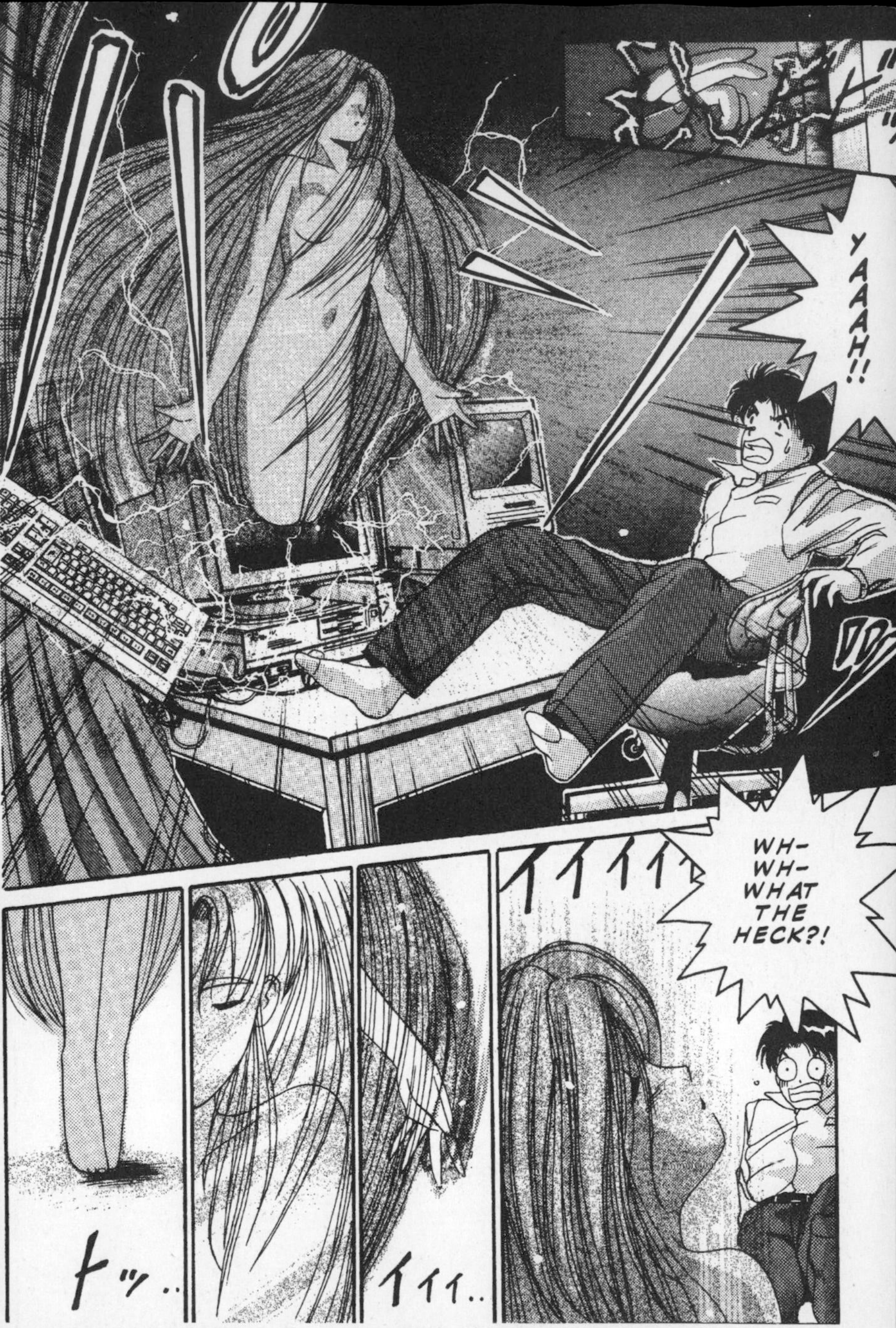

YAAAAH!!
WH-WH-WHAT THE HECK?!
イイイイ
イイイ..
トッ..

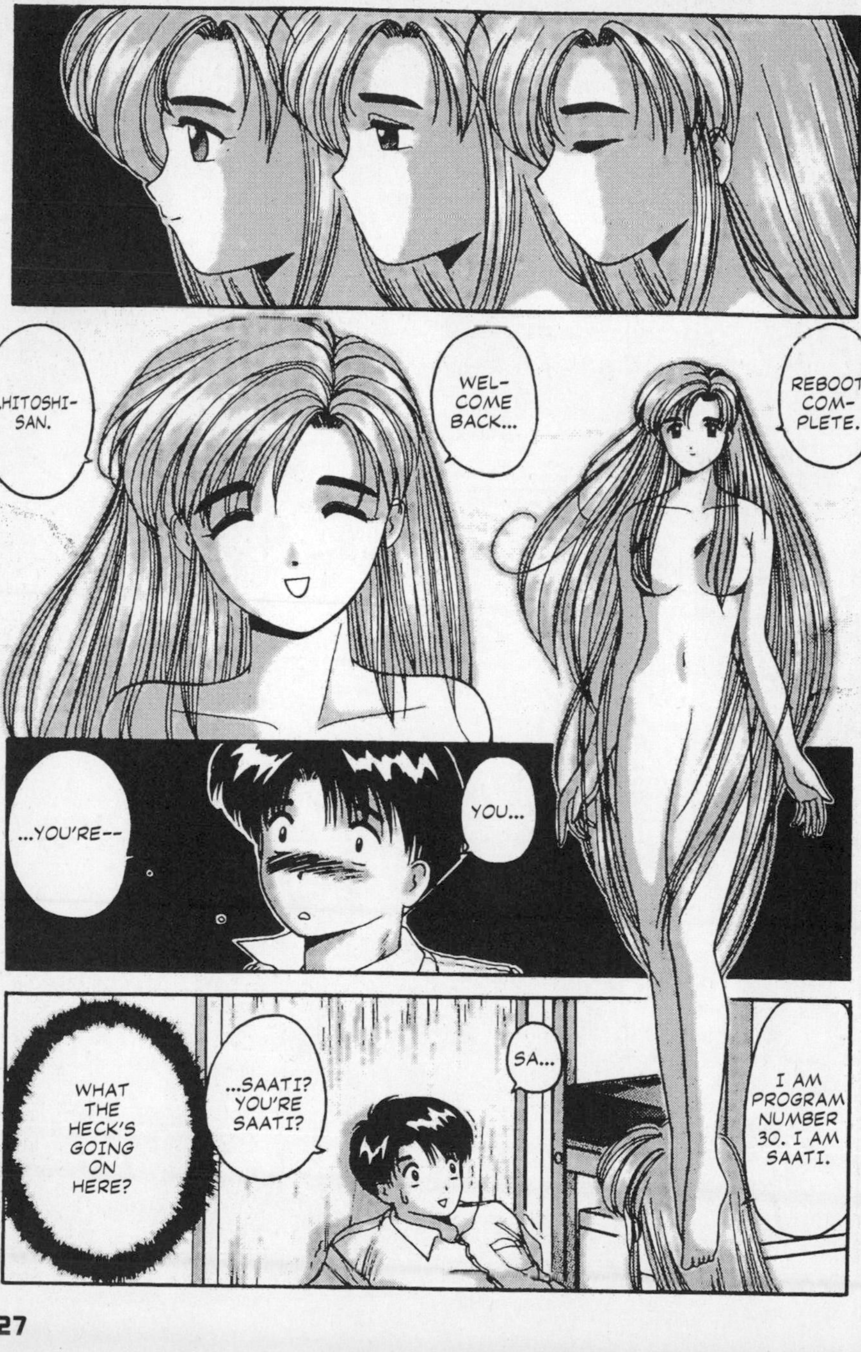
REBOOT COM-PLETE.
WEL-COME BACK...
...HITOSHI-SAN.
YOU...
...YOU'RE--
I AM PROGRAM NUMBER 30. I AM SAATI.
SA...
...SAATI? YOU'RE SAATI?
WHAT THE HECK'S GOING ON HERE?

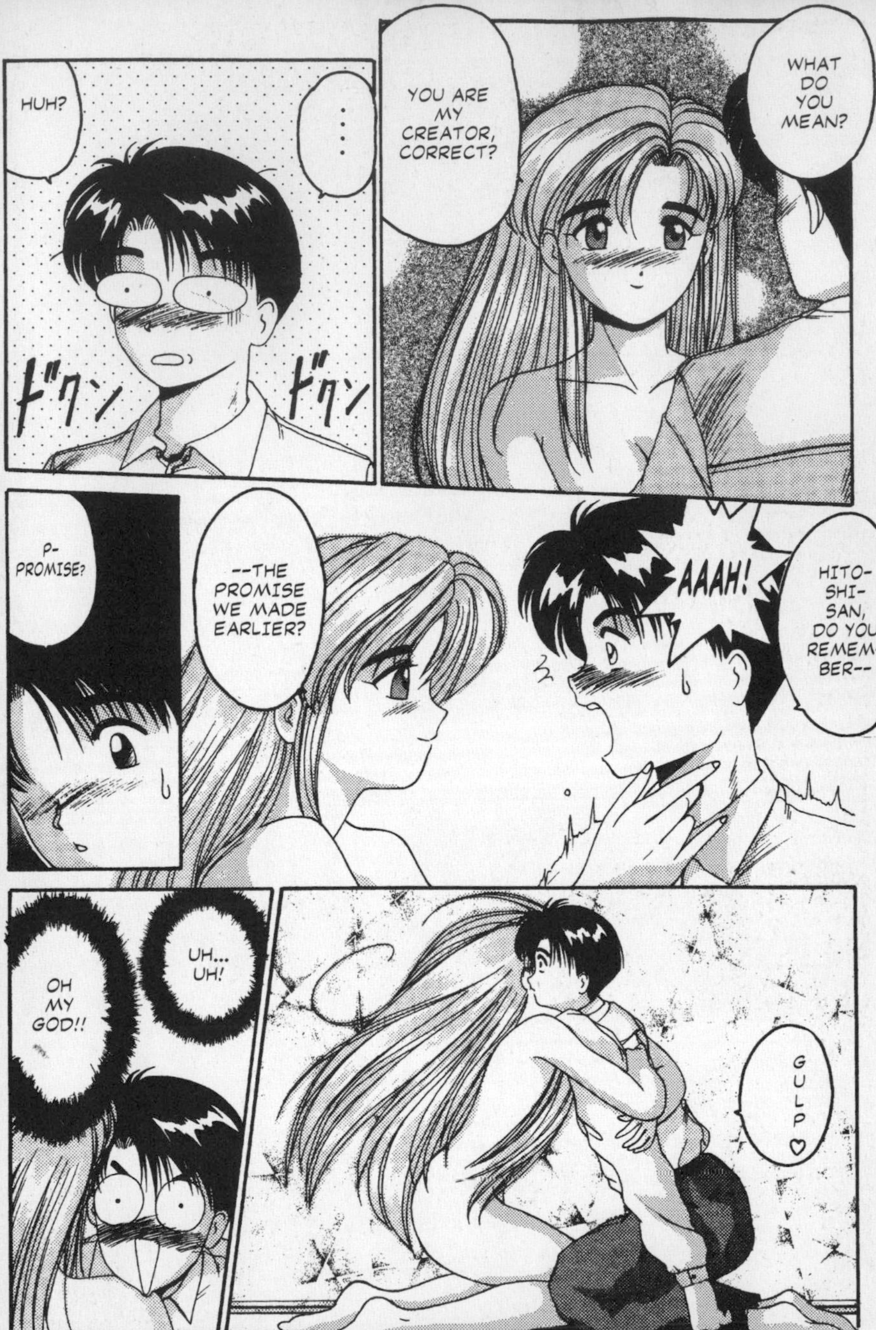
WHAT DO YOU MEAN?
YOU ARE MY CREATOR, CORRECT?
....
HUH?
ドクン
ドクン
HITO-SHI-SAN, DO YOU REMEMBER--
AAAH!
--THE PROMISE WE MADE EARLIER?
P-PROMISE?
GULP ♡
UH... UH!
OH MY GOD!!

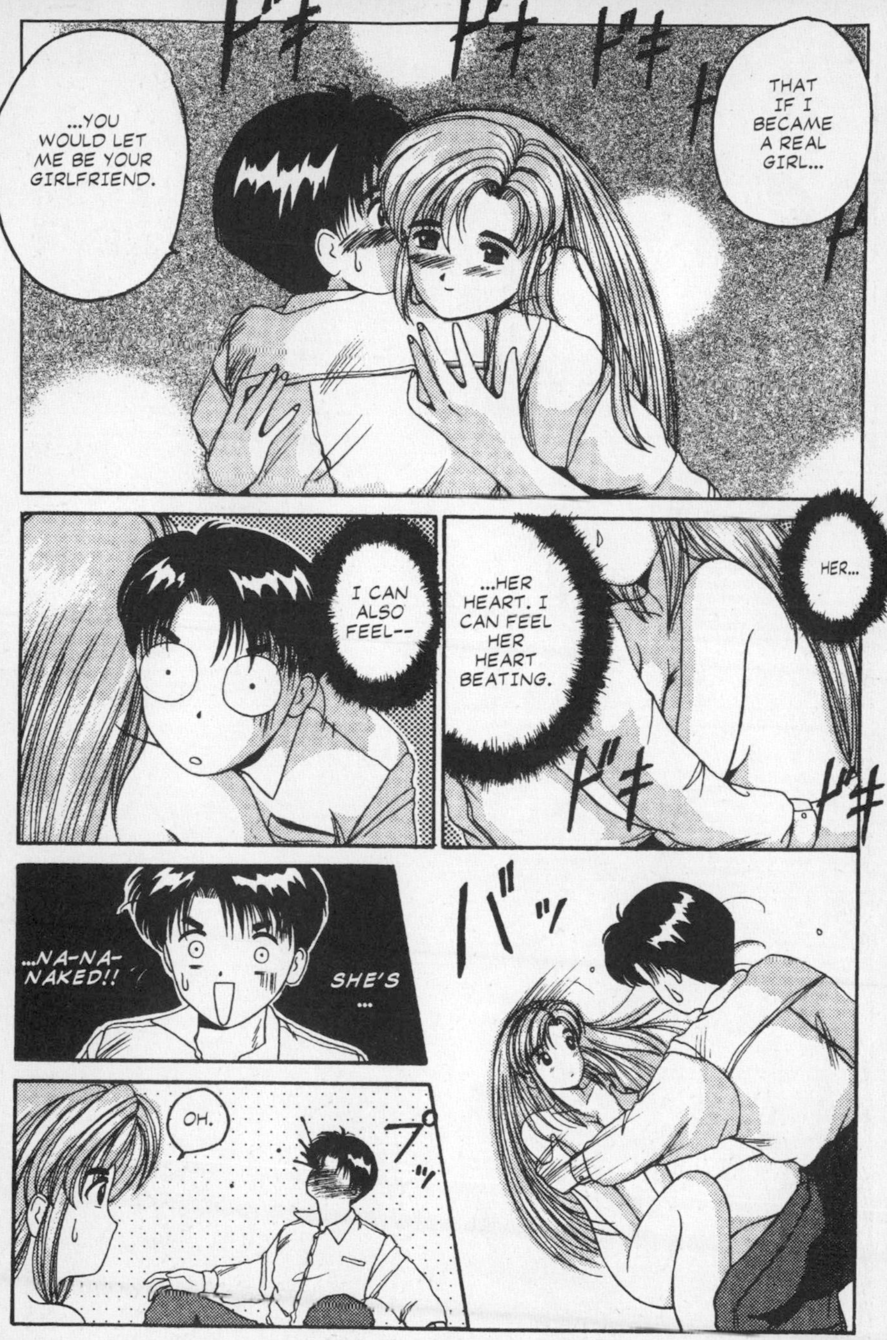
ドキ ドキ ドキ
THAT IF I BECAME A REAL GIRL...
...YOU WOULD LET ME BE YOUR GIRLFRIEND.
HER...
...HER HEART. I CAN FEEL HER HEART BEATING.
ドキ ドキ
I CAN ALSO FEEL--
バッ
SHE'S ...
...NA-NA-NAKED!!
OH.
プッ

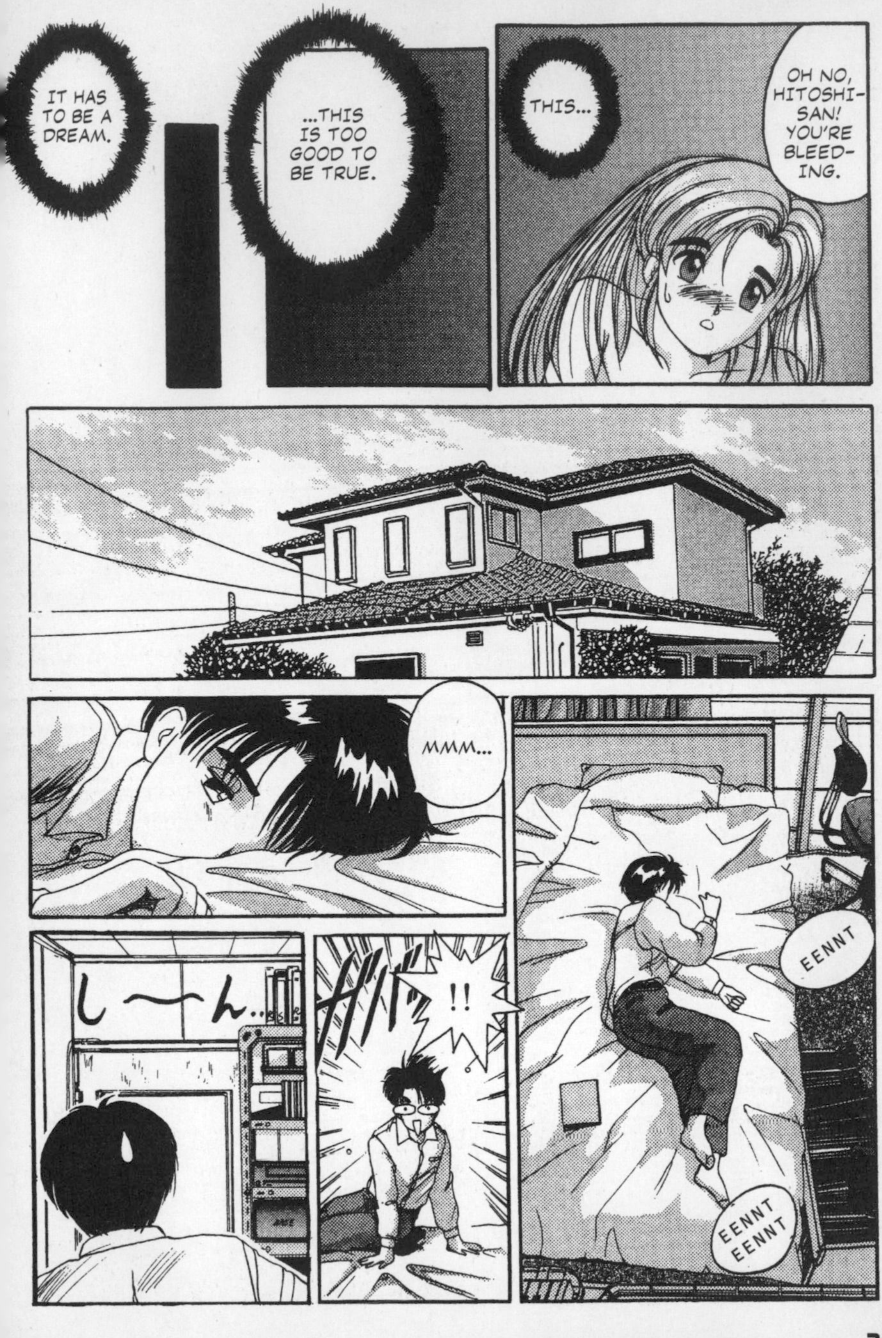

OH NO, HITOSHI-SAN! YOU'RE BLEEDING.
THIS...
...THIS IS TOO GOOD TO BE TRUE.
IT HAS TO BE A DREAM.
EENNT
EENNT EENNT
MMM...
!!
し〜ん..

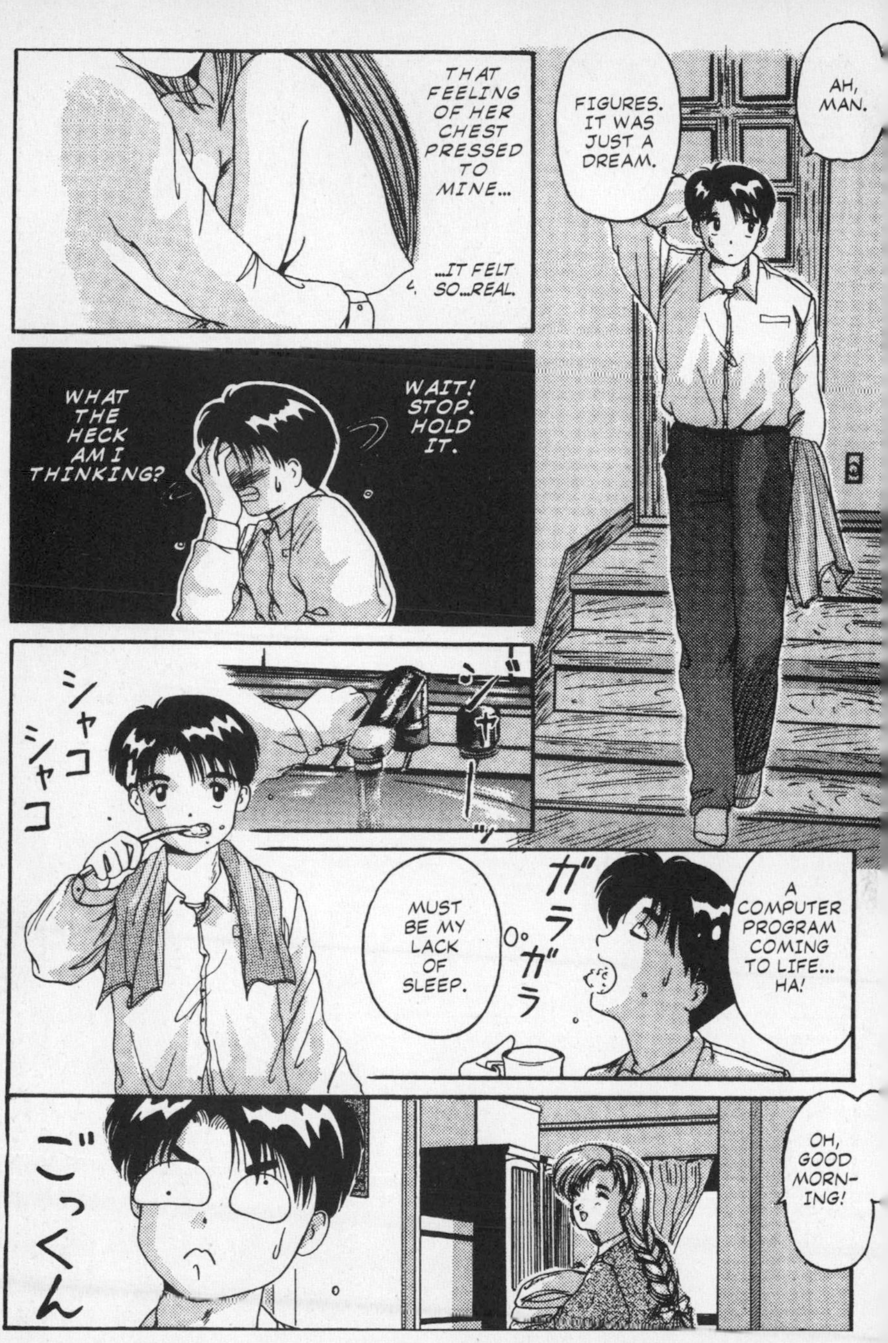
AH, MAN.
FIGURES. IT WAS JUST A DREAM.
THAT FEELING OF HER CHEST PRESSED TO MINE...
...IT FELT SO...REAL.
WAIT! STOP. HOLD IT.
WHAT THE HECK AM I THINKING?
シャコシャコ
A COMPUTER PROGRAM COMING TO LIFE... HA!
ガラガラ
MUST BE MY LACK OF SLEEP.
OH, GOOD MORNING!
ごっくん

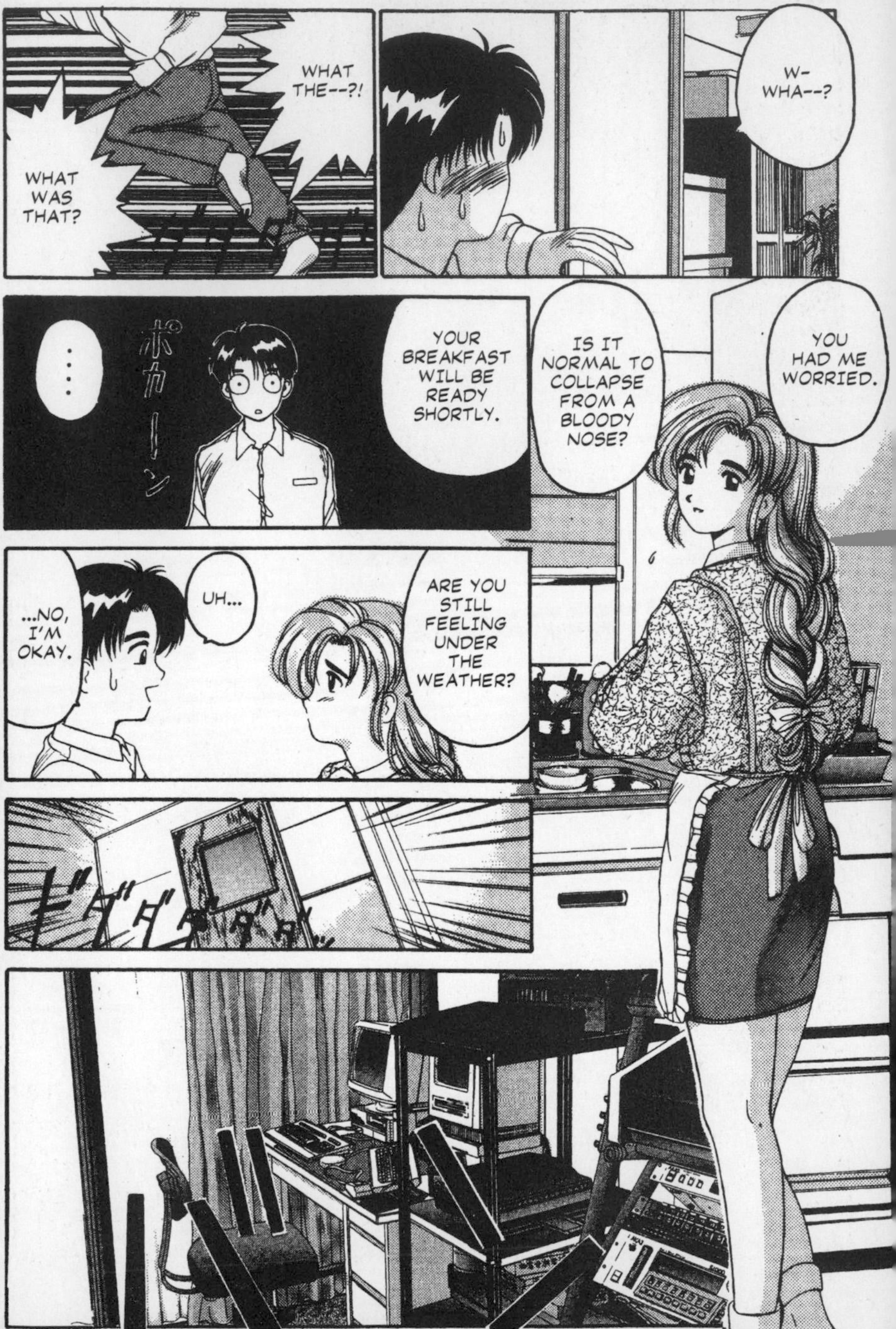
W-
WHA--?
WHAT THE--?!
WHAT WAS THAT?
YOU HAD ME WORRIED.
IS IT NORMAL TO COLLAPSE FROM A BLOODY NOSE?
YOUR BREAKFAST WILL BE READY SHORTLY.
ポカーン
....
ARE YOU STILL FEELING UNDER THE WEATHER?
UH...
...NO, I'M OKAY.

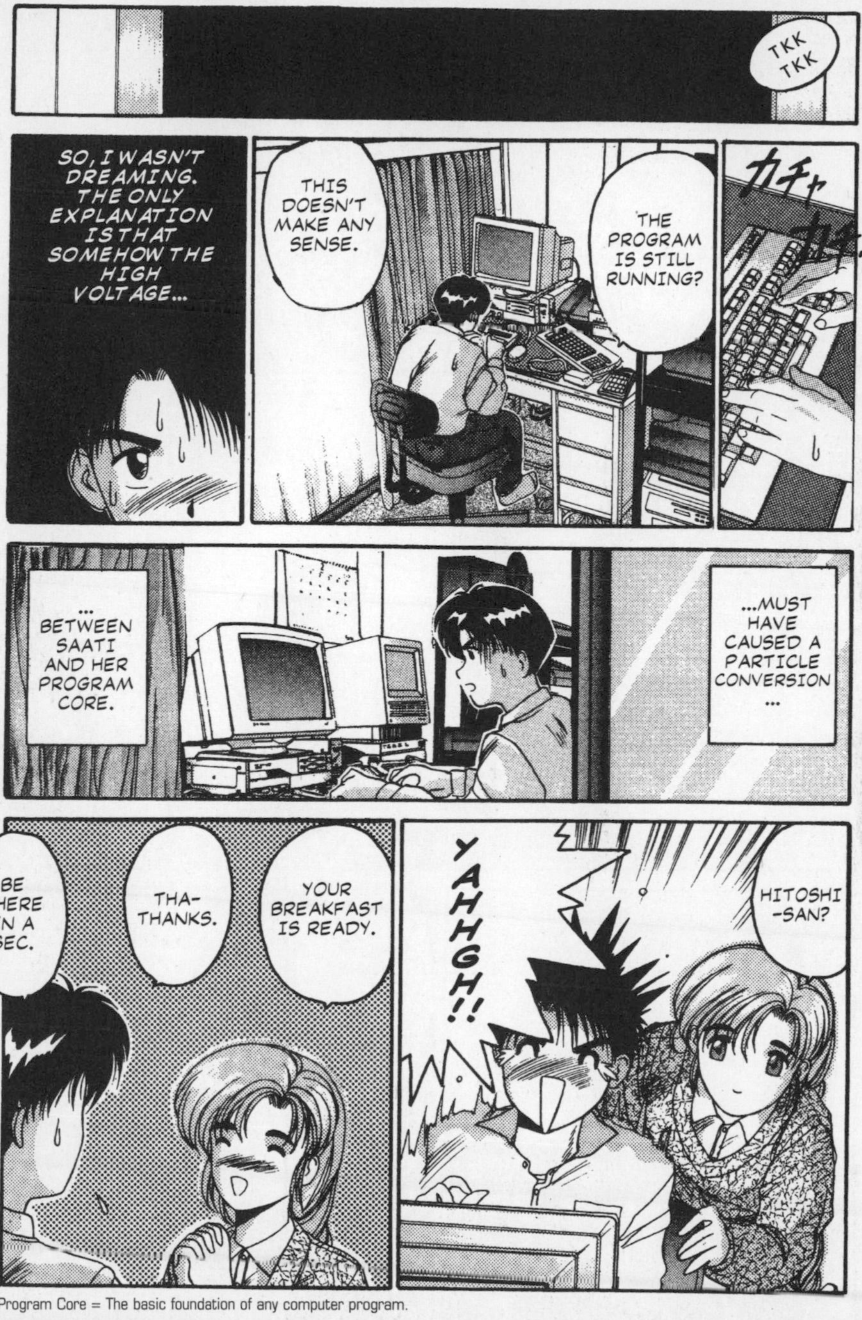
TKK TKK
カチャ カチャ
THE PROGRAM IS STILL RUNNING?
THIS DOESN'T MAKE ANY SENSE.
SO, I WASN'T DREAMING. THE ONLY EXPLANATION IS THAT SOMEHOW THE HIGH VOLTAGE...
... BETWEEN SAATI AND HER PROGRAM CORE.
...MUST HAVE CAUSED A PARTICLE CONVERSION ...
HITOSHI-SAN?
YAHHGH!!
YOUR BREAKFAST IS READY.
THA-THANKS.
BE THERE IN A SEC.

Program Core = The basic foundation of any computer program.

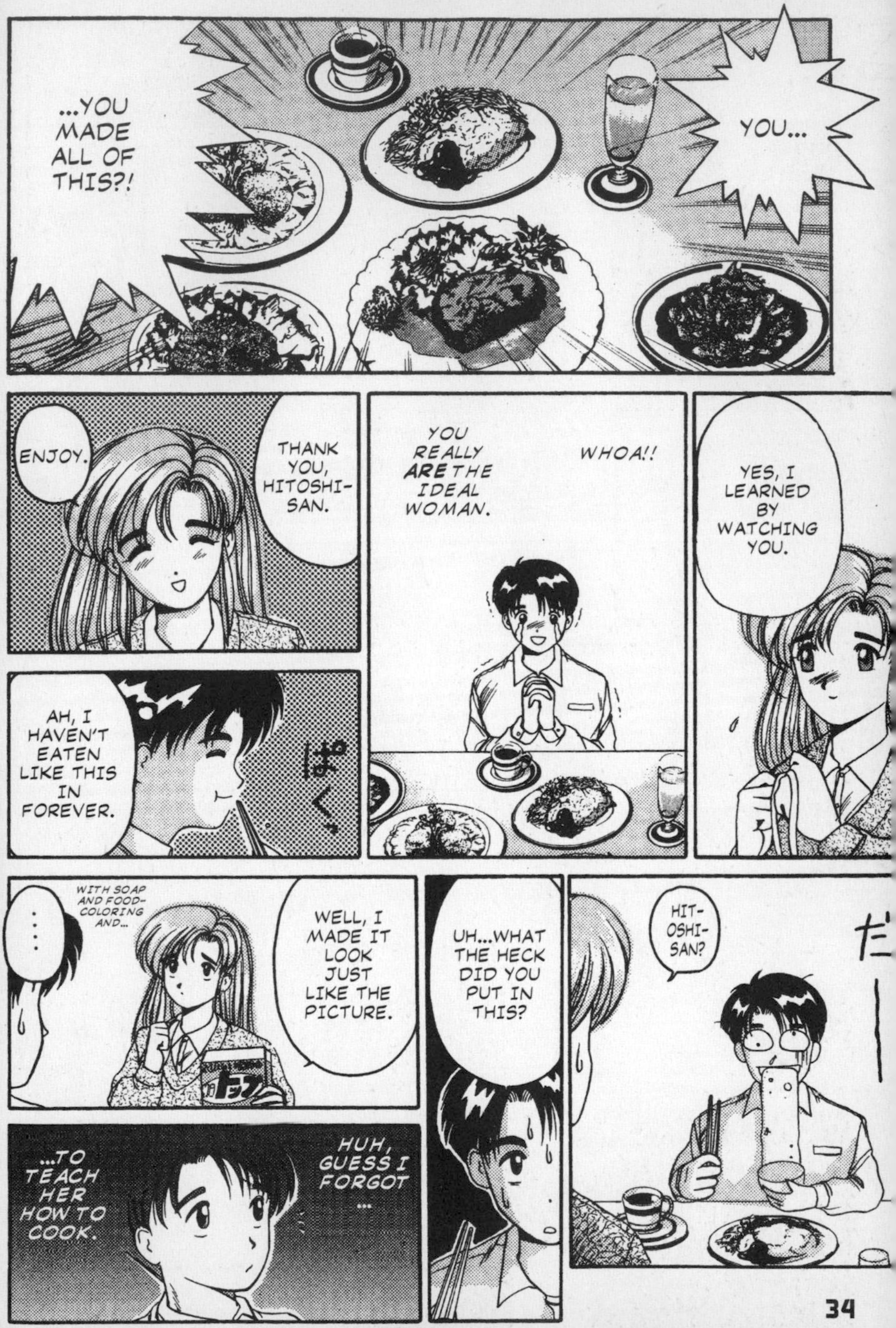
YOU...
...YOU MADE ALL OF THIS?!
YES, I LEARNED BY WATCHING YOU.
WHOA!!
YOU REALLY ARE THE IDEAL WOMAN.
THANK YOU, HITOSHI-SAN.
ENJOY.
ぱく
AH, I HAVEN'T EATEN LIKE THIS IN FOREVER.
だー
HIT-OSHI-SAN?
UH...WHAT THE HECK DID YOU PUT IN THIS?
WELL, I MADE IT LOOK JUST LIKE THE PICTURE.
WITH SOAP AND FOOD-COLORING AND...
....
HUH, GUESS I FORGOT...
...TO TEACH HER HOW TO COOK.

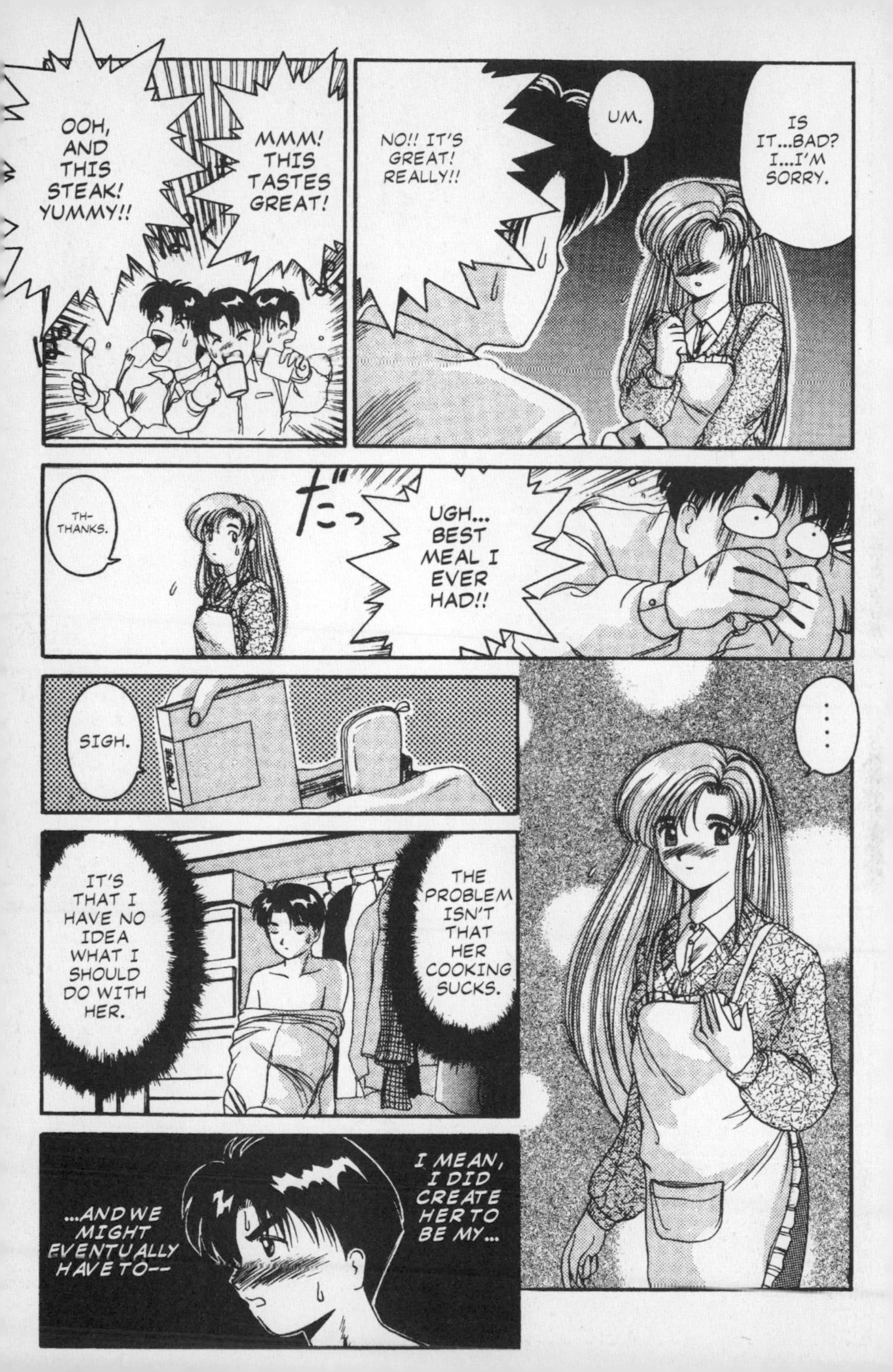
IS IT...BAD? I...I'M SORRY.
UM.
NO!! IT'S GREAT! REALLY!!
MMM! THIS TASTES GREAT!
OOH, AND THIS STEAK! YUMMY!!
UGH... BEST MEAL I EVER HAD!!
だっ
TH-THANKS.
....
SIGH.
THE PROBLEM ISN'T THAT HER COOKING SUCKS.
IT'S THAT I HAVE NO IDEA WHAT I SHOULD DO WITH HER.
I MEAN, I DID CREATE HER TO BE MY...
...AND WE MIGHT EVENTUALLY HAVE TO--

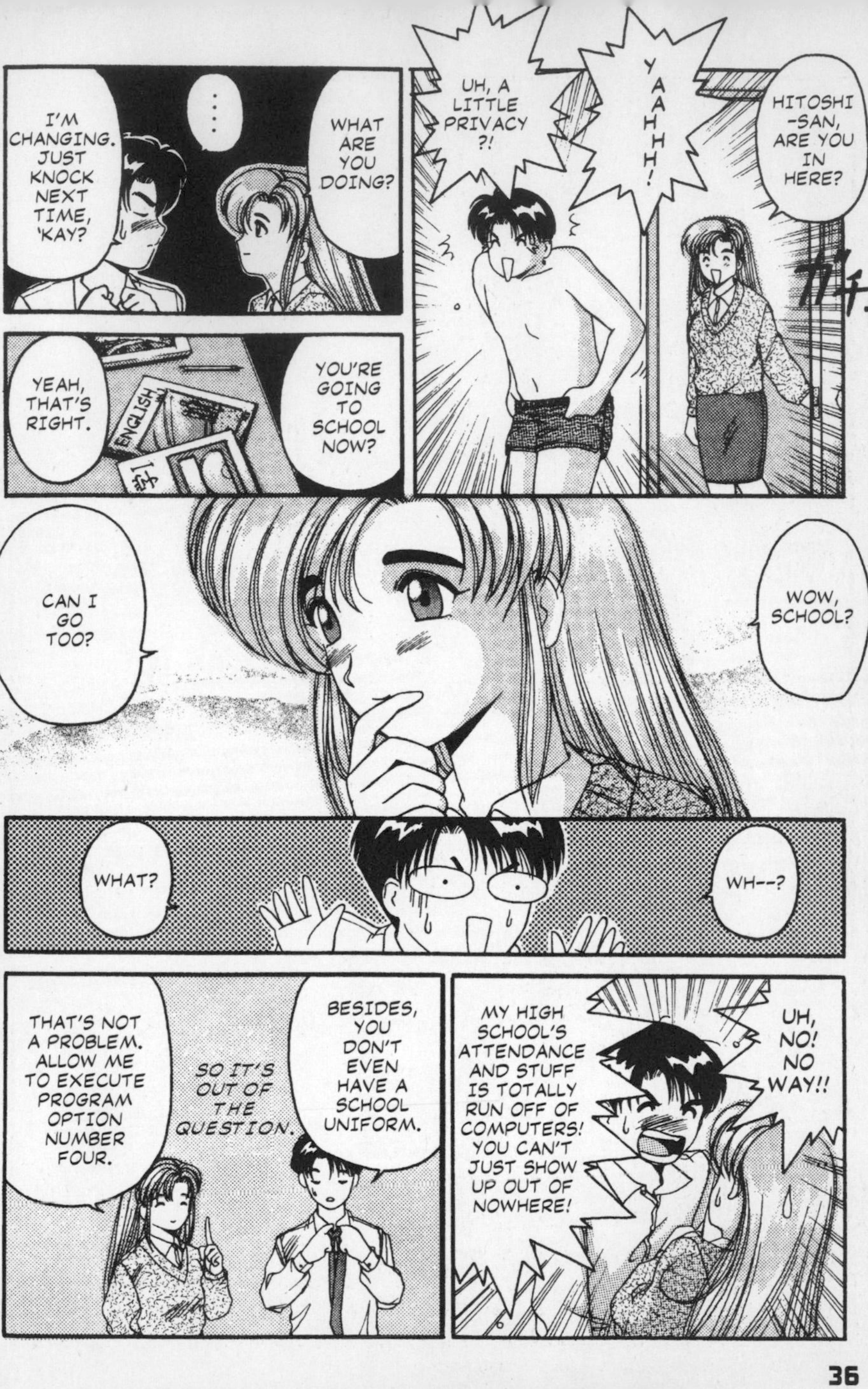

HITOSHI-SAN, ARE YOU IN HERE?
ガチャ
YAAHHH!
UH, A LITTLE PRIVACY?!
WHAT ARE YOU DOING?
....
I'M CHANGING. JUST KNOCK NEXT TIME, 'KAY?
YOU'RE GOING TO SCHOOL NOW?
ENGLISH
YEAH, THAT'S RIGHT.
WOW, SCHOOL?
CAN I GO TOO?
WH--?
WHAT?
UH, NO! NO WAY!!
MY HIGH SCHOOL'S ATTENDANCE AND STUFF IS TOTALLY RUN OFF OF COMPUTERS! YOU CAN'T JUST SHOW UP OUT OF NOWHERE!
BESIDES, YOU DON'T EVEN HAVE A SCHOOL UNIFORM.
SO IT'S OUT OF THE QUESTION.
THAT'S NOT A PROBLEM. ALLOW ME TO EXECUTE PROGRAM OPTION NUMBER FOUR.

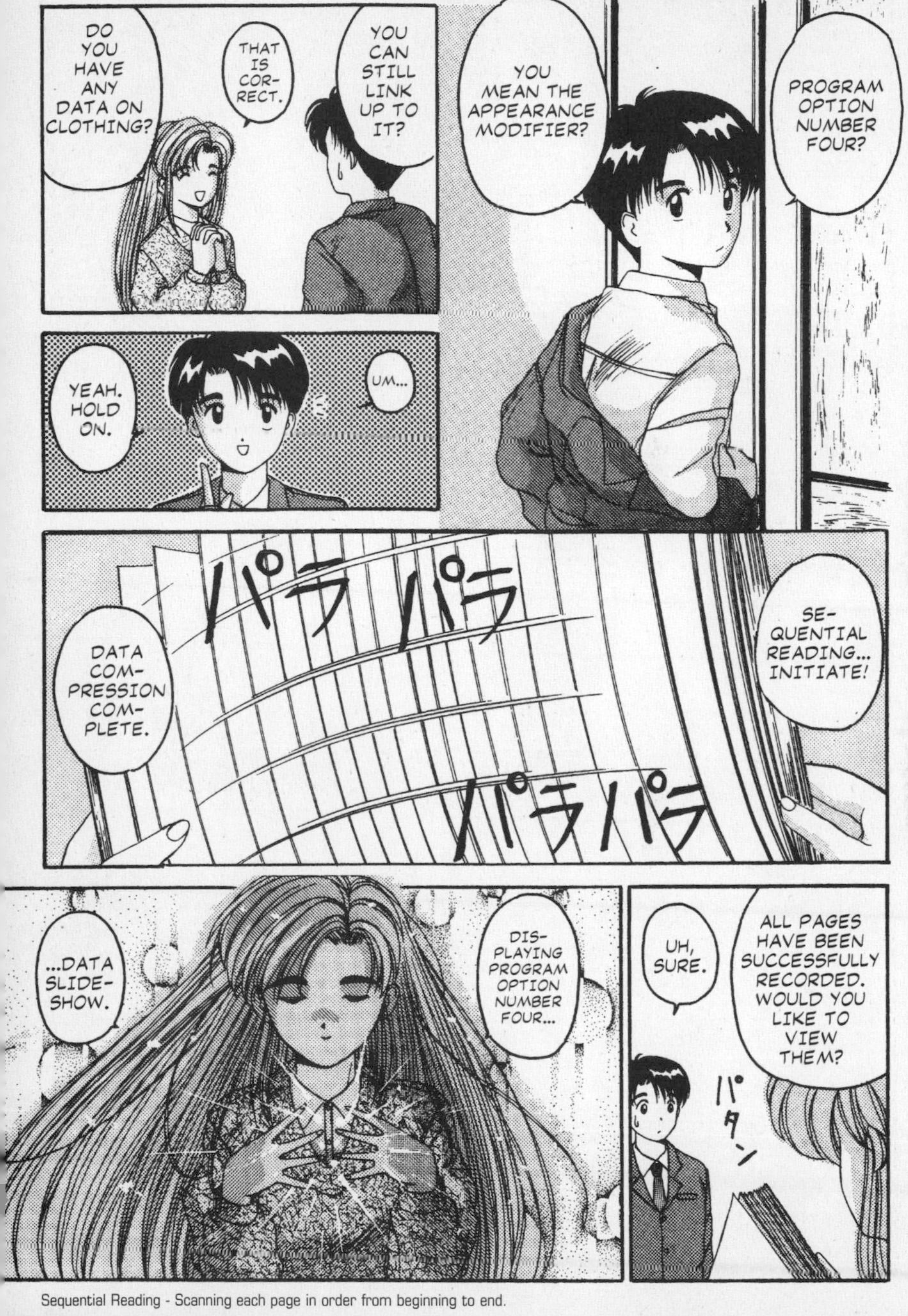
PROGRAM OPTION NUMBER FOUR?
YOU MEAN THE APPEARANCE MODIFIER?
YOU CAN STILL LINK UP TO IT?
THAT IS COR-RECT.
DO YOU HAVE ANY DATA ON CLOTHING?
UM...
YEAH. HOLD ON.
SE-QUENTIAL READING... INITIATE!
パラ パラ
パラパラ
DATA COM-PRESSION COM-PLETE.
ALL PAGES HAVE BEEN SUCCESSFULLY RECORDED. WOULD YOU LIKE TO VIEW THEM?
パタン
UH, SURE.
DIS-PLAYING PROGRAM OPTION NUMBER FOUR...
...DATA SLIDE-SHOW.

Sequential Reading - Scanning each page in order from beginning to end.

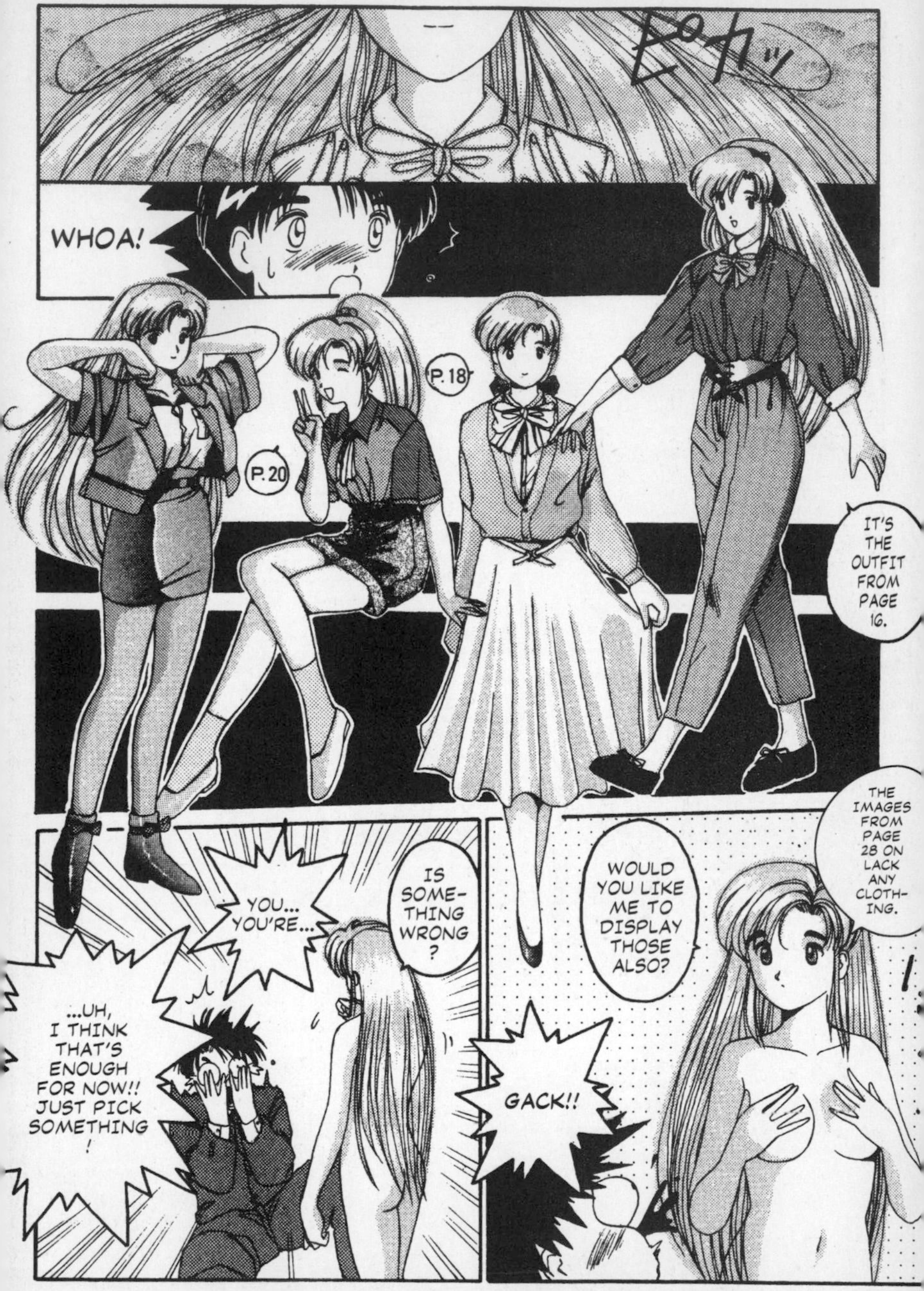
ピカッ
WHOA!
IT'S THE OUTFIT FROM PAGE 16.
P.18
P.20
THE IMAGES FROM PAGE 28 ON LACK ANY CLOTHING.
WOULD YOU LIKE ME TO DISPLAY THOSE ALSO?
GACK!!
IS SOMETHING WRONG?
YOU... YOU'RE...
...UH, I THINK THAT'S ENOUGH FOR NOW!! JUST PICK SOMETHING!

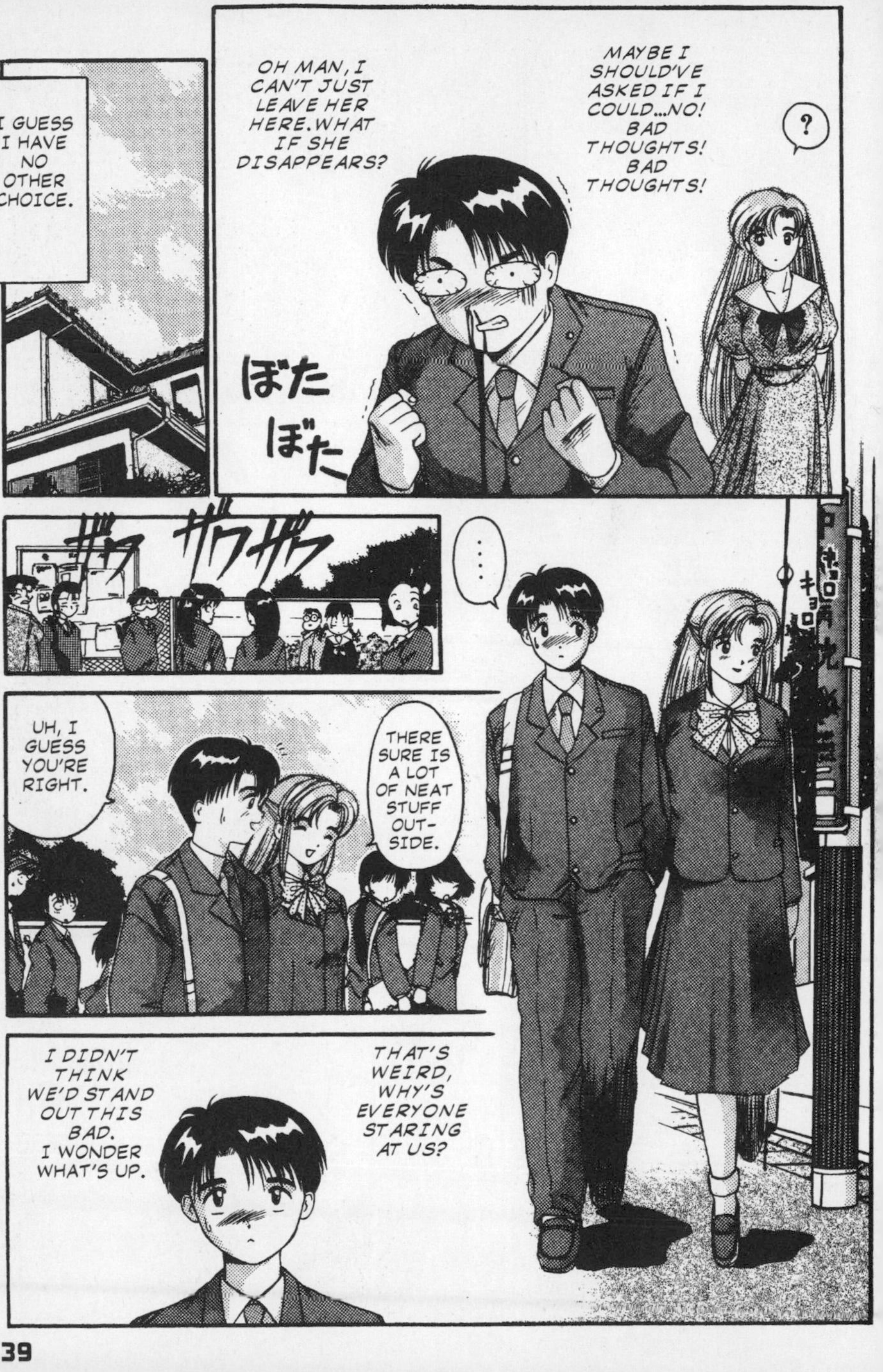
?
MAYBE I SHOULD'VE ASKED IF I COULD...NO! BAD THOUGHTS! BAD THOUGHTS!
OH MAN, I CAN'T JUST LEAVE HER HERE. WHAT IF SHE DISAPPEARS?
ぼたぼた
I GUESS I HAVE NO OTHER CHOICE.
....
キョロキョロ
ザワ ザワザワ
THERE SURE IS A LOT OF NEAT STUFF OUT-SIDE.
UH, I GUESS YOU'RE RIGHT.
THAT'S WEIRD, WHY'S EVERYONE STARING AT US?
I DIDN'T THINK WE'D STAND OUT THIS BAD. I WONDER WHAT'S UP.

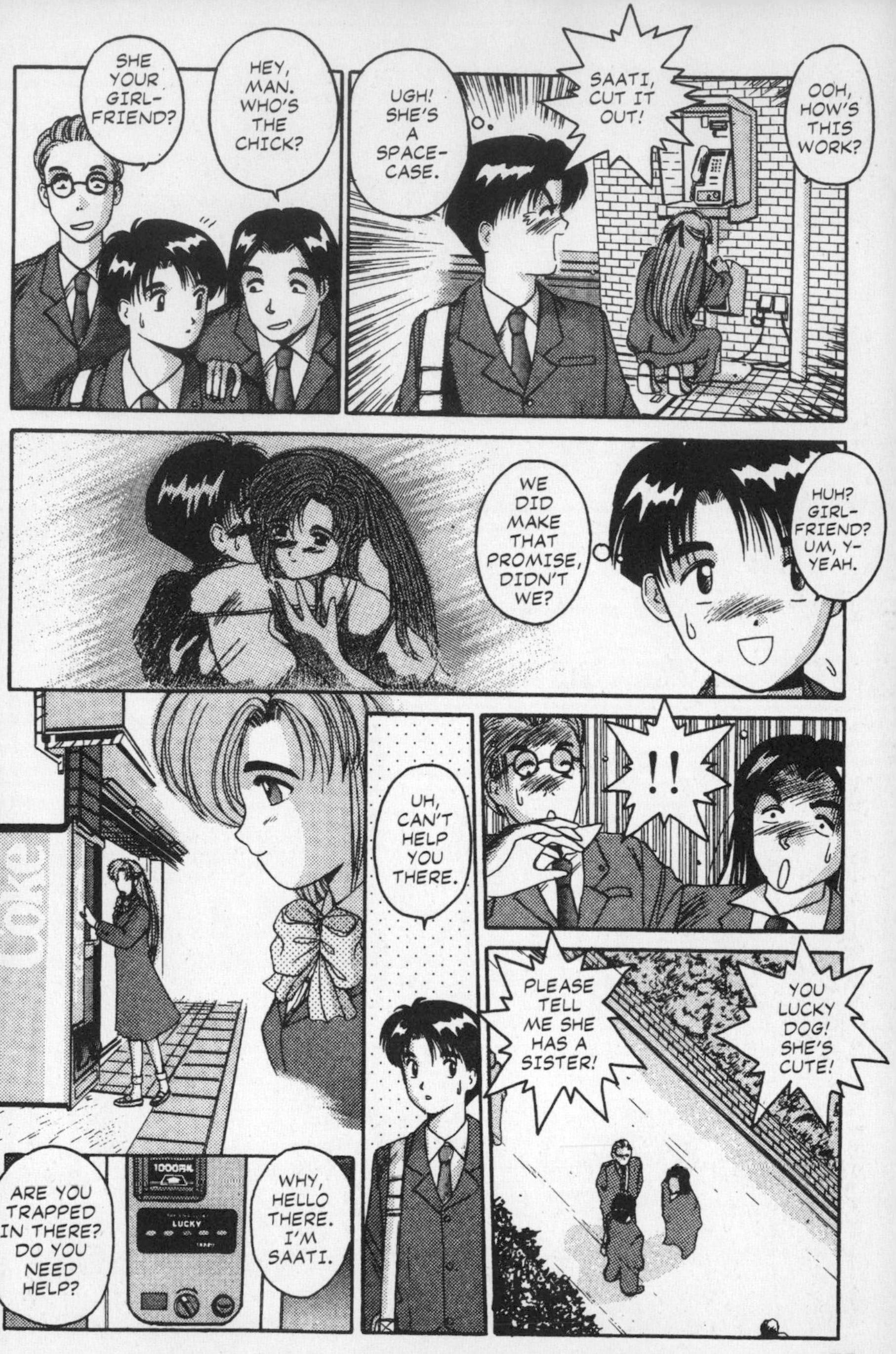

OOH, HOW'S THIS WORK?
SAATI, CUT IT OUT!
UGH! SHE'S A SPACE-CASE.
HEY, MAN. WHO'S THE CHICK?
SHE YOUR GIRL-FRIEND?
HUH? GIRL-FRIEND? UM, Y-YEAH.
WE DID MAKE THAT PROMISE, DIDN'T WE?
!!
YOU LUCKY DOG! SHE'S CUTE!
PLEASE TELL ME SHE HAS A SISTER!
UH, CAN'T HELP YOU THERE.
Coke
WHY, HELLO THERE. I'M SAATI.
1000円
LUCKY
ARE YOU TRAPPED IN THERE? DO YOU NEED HELP?

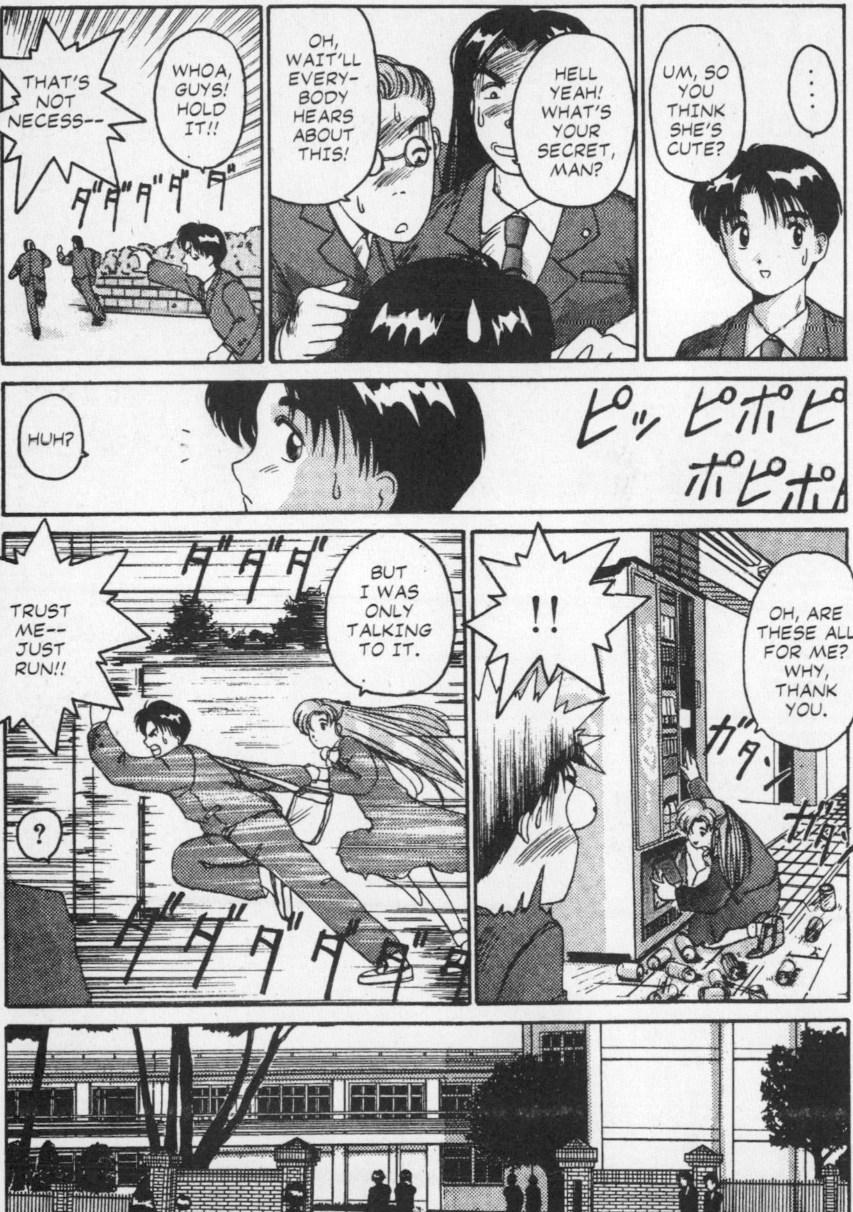

....
UM, SO YOU THINK SHE'S CUTE?
HELL YEAH! WHAT'S YOUR SECRET, MAN?
OH, WAIT'LL EVERY-BODY HEARS ABOUT THIS!
WHOA, GUYS! HOLD IT!!
THAT'S NOT NECESS--
ダダダダダ
ピッピポピ
ポピポ
HUH?
OH, ARE THESE ALL FOR ME? WHY, THANK YOU.
!!
BUT I WAS ONLY TALKING TO IT.
ダダダ
TRUST ME-- JUST RUN!!
?
ダダダダダ

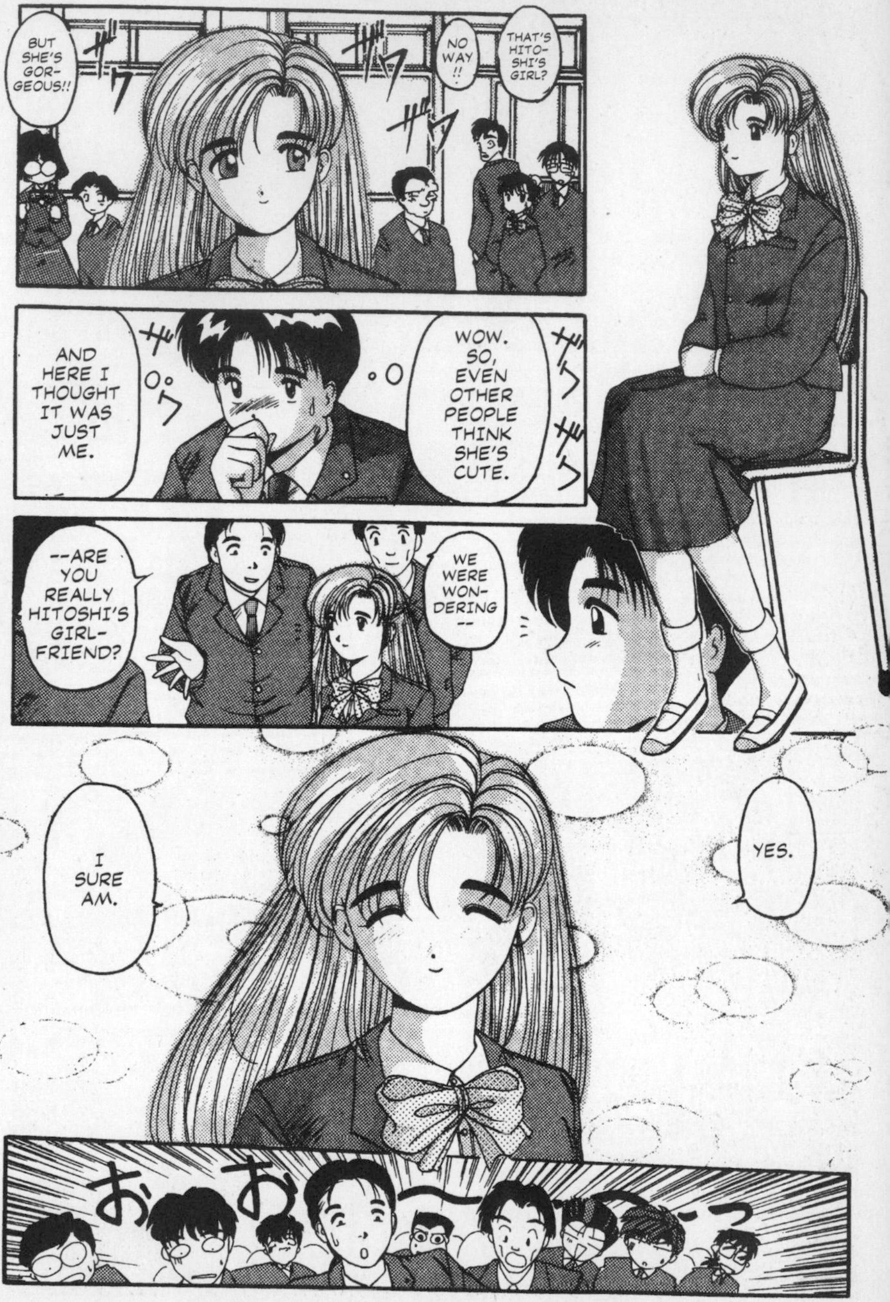
THAT'S HITO-SHI'S GIRL?
NO WAY!!
BUT SHE'S GOR-GEOUS!!
WOW. SO, EVEN OTHER PEOPLE THINK SHE'S CUTE.
AND HERE I THOUGHT IT WAS JUST ME.
WE WERE WON-DERING --
--ARE YOU REALLY HITOSHI'S GIRL-FRIEND?
YES.
I SURE AM.

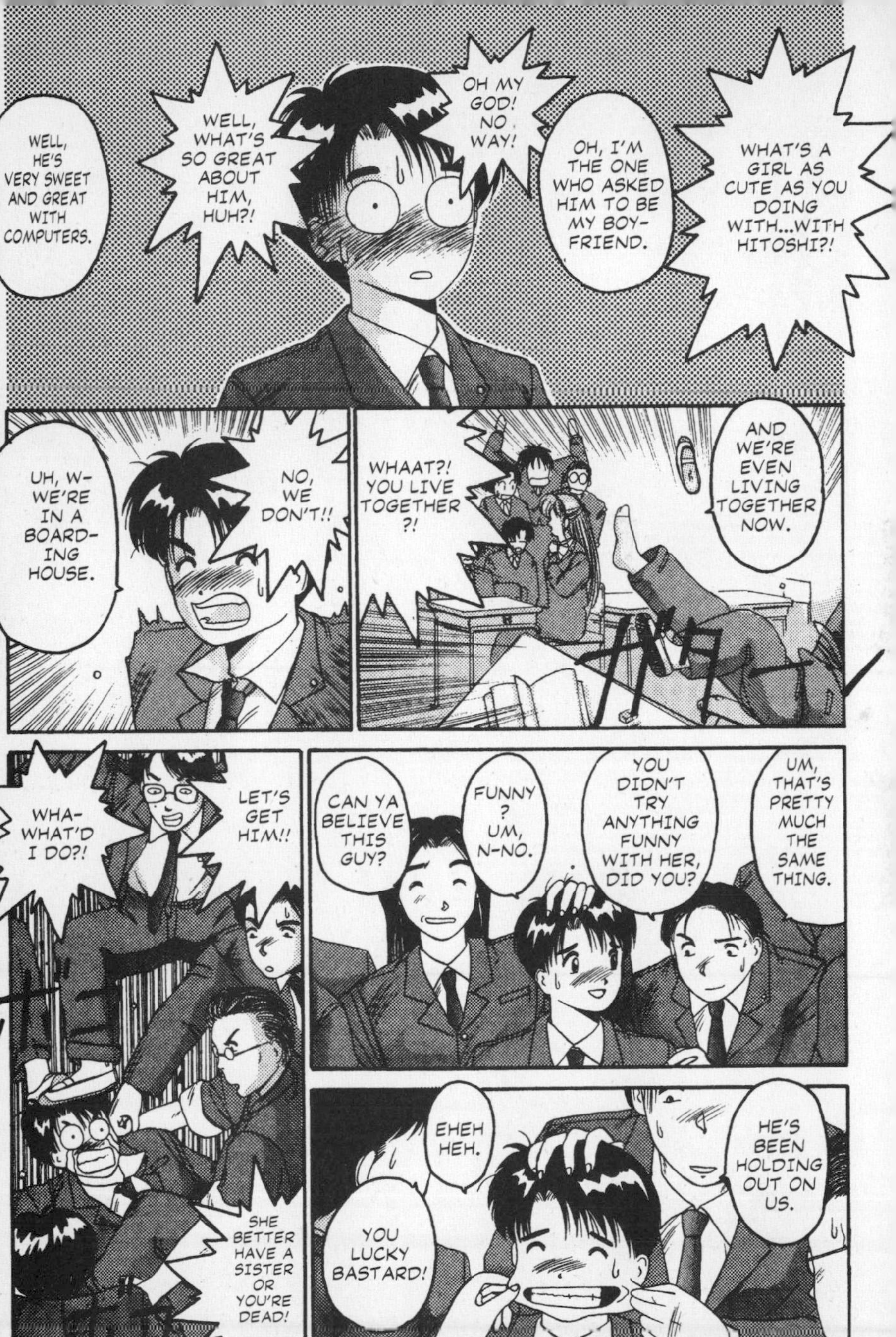

WHAT'S A GIRL AS CUTE AS YOU DOING WITH...WITH HITOSHI?!
OH, I'M THE ONE WHO ASKED HIM TO BE MY BOY-FRIEND.
OH MY GOD! NO WAY!
WELL, WHAT'S SO GREAT ABOUT HIM, HUH?!
WELL, HE'S VERY SWEET AND GREAT WITH COMPUTERS.
AND WE'RE EVEN LIVING TOGETHER NOW.
WHAAT?! YOU LIVE TOGETHER ?!
NO, WE DON'T!!
UH, W-WE'RE IN A BOARD-ING HOUSE.
UM, THAT'S PRETTY MUCH THE SAME THING.
YOU DIDN'T TRY ANYTHING FUNNY WITH HER, DID YOU?
FUNNY ? UM, N-NO.
CAN YA BELIEVE THIS GUY?
HE'S BEEN HOLDING OUT ON US.
EHEH HEH.
YOU LUCKY BASTARD!
LET'S GET HIM!!
WHA-WHAT'D I DO?!
SHE BETTER HAVE A SISTER OR YOU'RE DEAD!

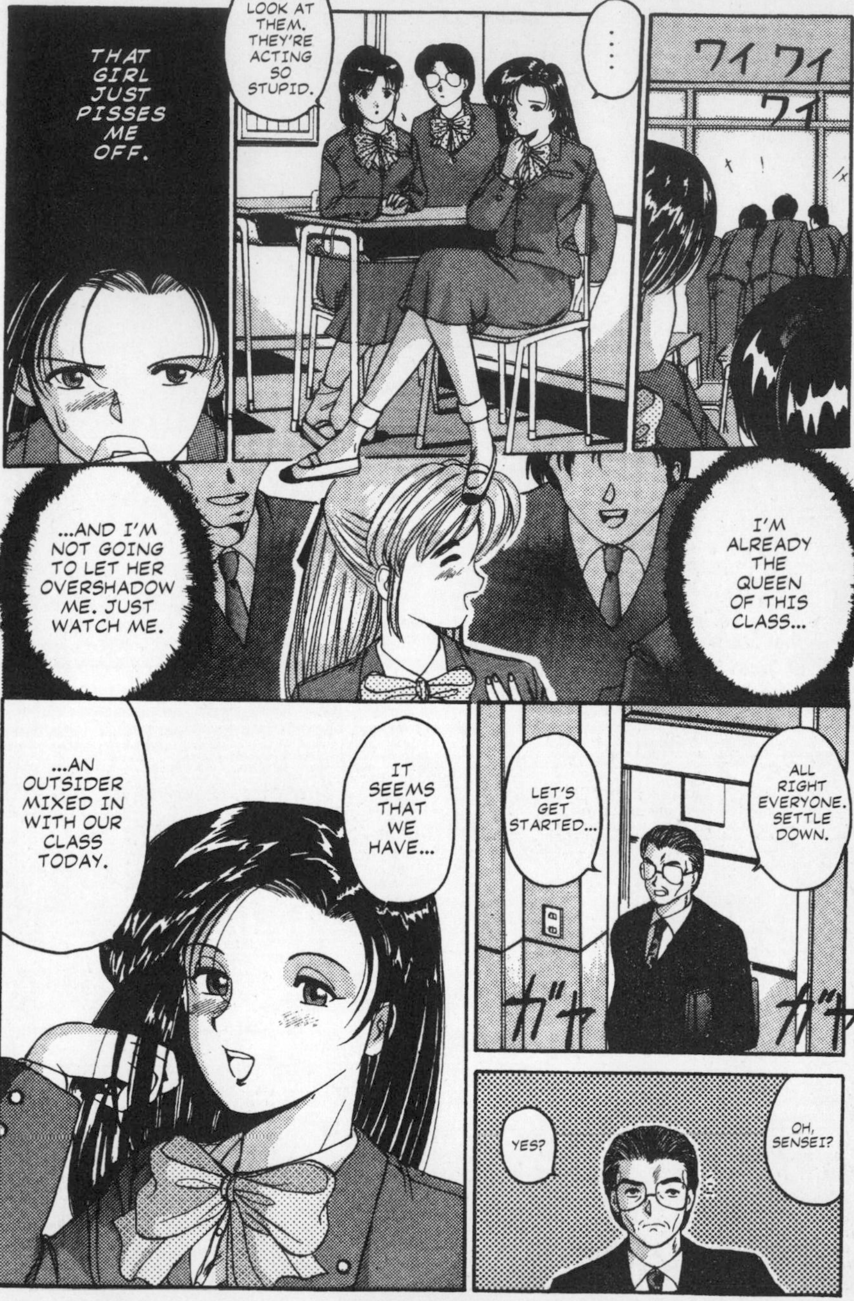

ワイワイワイ
....
LOOK AT THEM. THEY'RE ACTING SO STUPID.
THAT GIRL JUST PISSES ME OFF.
I'M ALREADY THE QUEEN OF THIS CLASS...
...AND I'M NOT GOING TO LET HER OVERSHADOW ME. JUST WATCH ME.
ALL RIGHT EVERYONE. SETTLE DOWN.
LET'S GET STARTED...
ガヤ
ガヤ
OH, SENSEI?
YES?
IT SEEMS THAT WE HAVE...
...AN OUTSIDER MIXED IN WITH OUR CLASS TODAY.

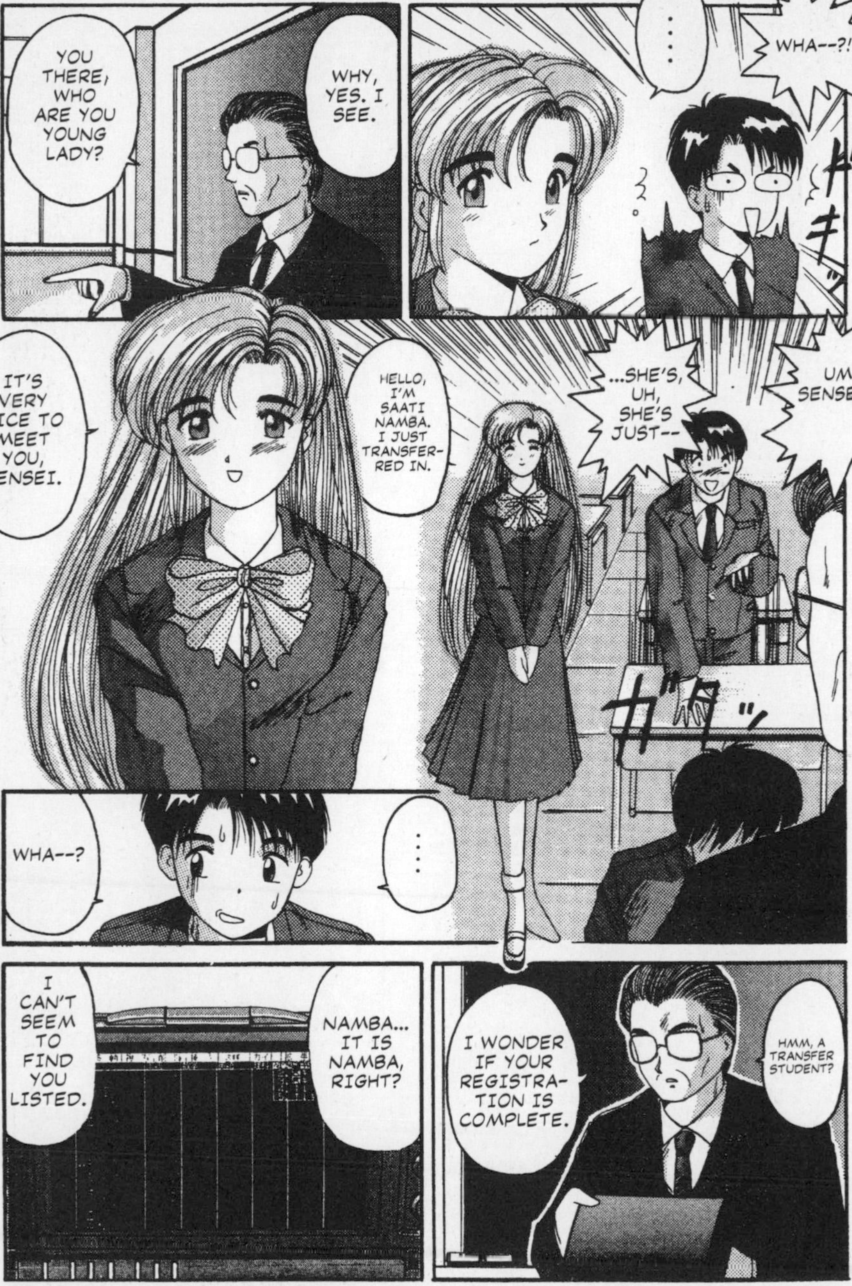
WHA--?!
....
ドキッ
WHY, YES. I SEE.
YOU THERE, WHO ARE YOU YOUNG LADY?
UM, SENSEI...
...SHE'S, UH, SHE'S JUST--
ガタッ
HELLO, I'M SAATI NAMBA. I JUST TRANSFERRED IN.
IT'S VERY NICE TO MEET YOU, SENSEI.
....
WHA--?
HMM, A TRANSFER STUDENT?
I WONDER IF YOUR REGISTRATION IS COMPLETE.
NAMBA... IT IS NAMBA, RIGHT?
I CAN'T SEEM TO FIND YOU LISTED.

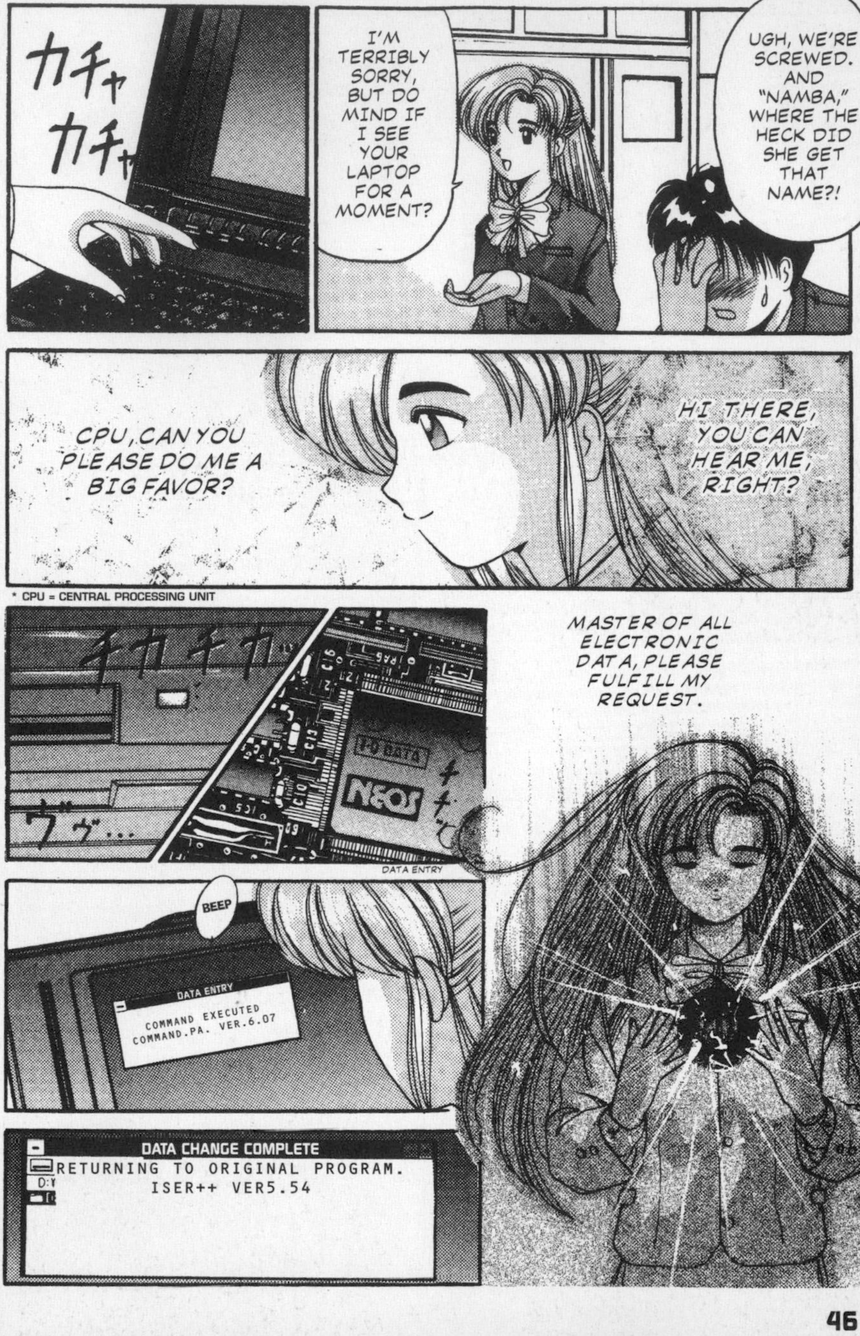
UGH, WE'RE SCREWED. AND "NAMBA," WHERE THE HECK DID SHE GET THAT NAME?!
I'M TERRIBLY SORRY, BUT DO MIND IF I SEE YOUR LAPTOP FOR A MOMENT?
カチャ
カチャ
HI THERE, YOU CAN HEAR ME, RIGHT?
CPU, CAN YOU PLEASE DO ME A BIG FAVOR?
MASTER OF ALL ELECTRONIC DATA, PLEASE FULFILL MY REQUEST.
チカ チカ
I-O DATA
NEOS
ヴヴ...
DATA ENTRY
BEEP
DATA ENTRY
COMMAND EXECUTED
COMMAND.PA. VER.6.07
DATA CHANGE COMPLETE
RETURNING TO ORIGINAL PROGRAM.
ISER++ VER5.54

* CPU = CENTRAL PROCESSING UNIT

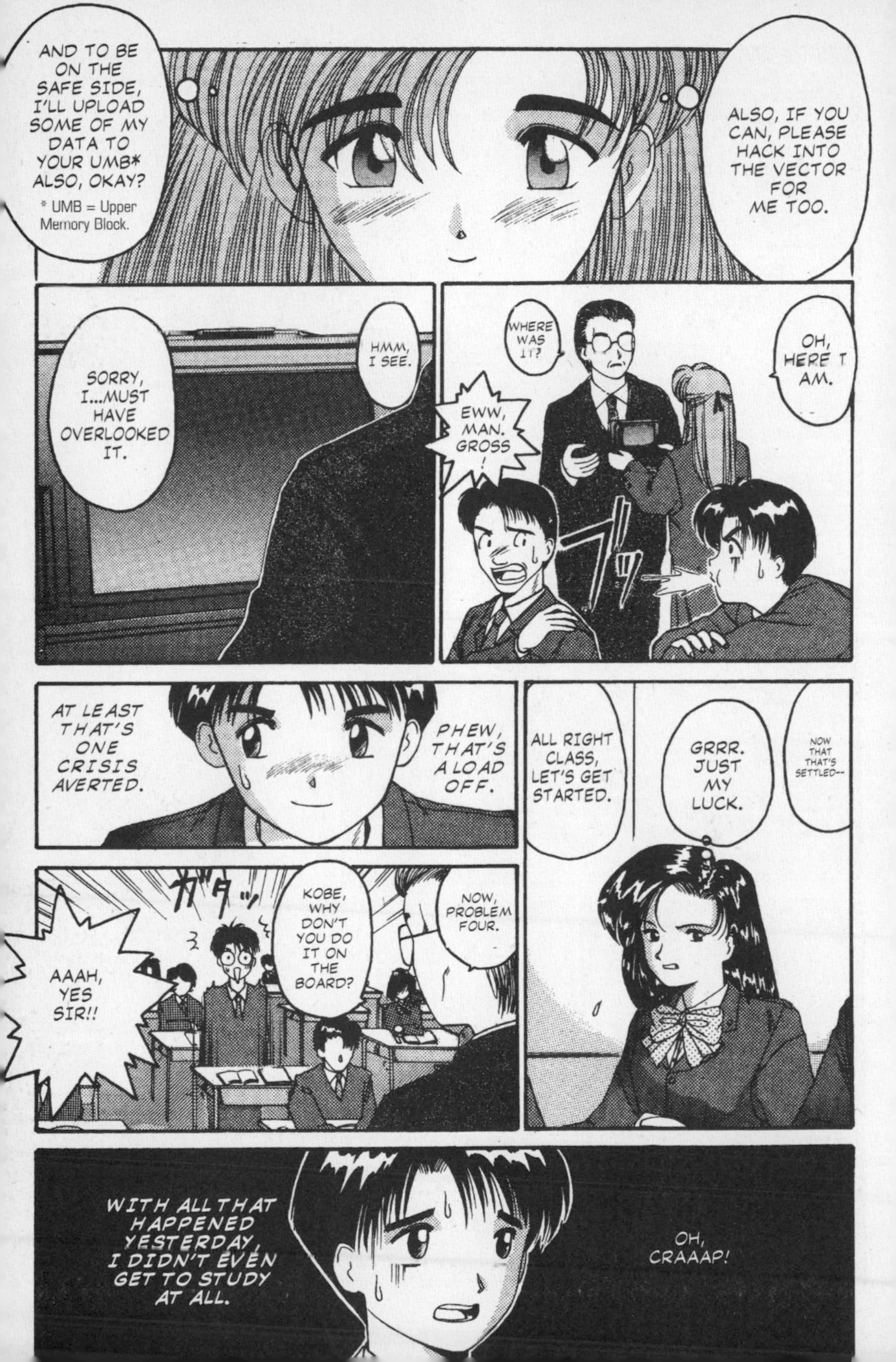
ALSO, IF YOU CAN, PLEASE HACK INTO THE VECTOR FOR ME TOO.
AND TO BE ON THE SAFE SIDE, I'LL UPLOAD SOME OF MY DATA TO YOUR UMB* ALSO, OKAY?
* UMB = Upper Memory Block.
OH, HERE I AM.
WHERE WAS IT?
EWW, MAN. GROSS!
HMM, I SEE.
SORRY, I...MUST HAVE OVERLOOKED IT.
NOW THAT THAT'S SETTLED--
GRRR. JUST MY LUCK.
ALL RIGHT CLASS, LET'S GET STARTED.
PHEW, THAT'S A LOAD OFF.
AT LEAST THAT'S ONE CRISIS AVERTED.
NOW, PROBLEM FOUR.
KOBE, WHY DON'T YOU DO IT ON THE BOARD?
AAAH, YES SIR!!
OH, CRAAAP!
WITH ALL THAT HAPPENED YESTERDAY, I DIDN'T EVEN GET TO STUDY AT ALL.

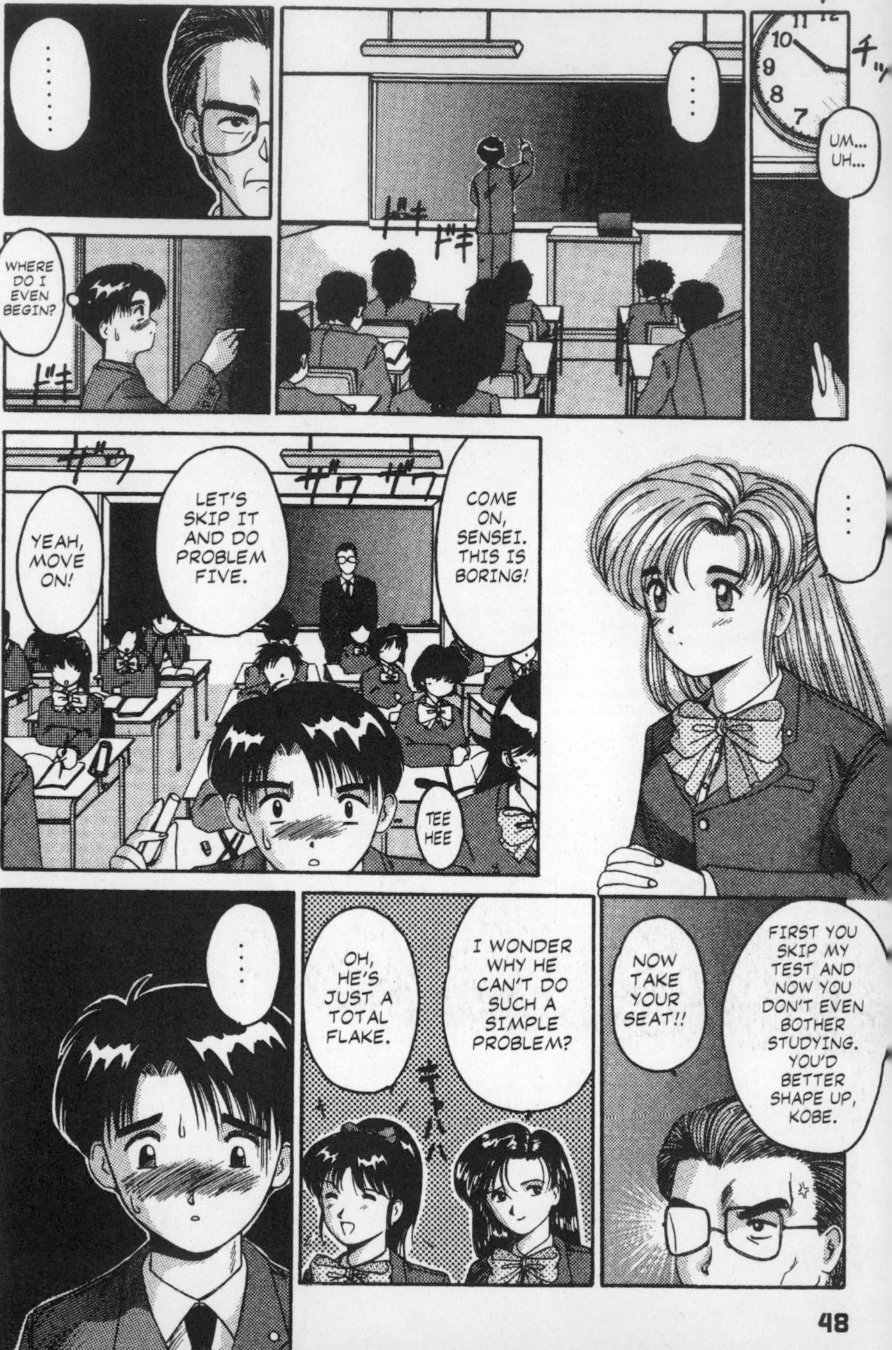
チッ
チッ
UM... UH...
....
ドキ
ドキ
....
WHERE DO I EVEN BEGIN?
ドキ
....
COME ON, SENSEI. THIS IS BORING!
ザワ ザワ
LET'S SKIP IT AND DO PROBLEM FIVE.
ザワ
YEAH, MOVE ON!
TEE HEE
FIRST YOU SKIP MY TEST AND NOW YOU DON'T EVEN BOTHER STUDYING. YOU'D BETTER SHAPE UP, KOBE.
NOW TAKE YOUR SEAT!!
I WONDER WHY HE CAN'T DO SUCH A SIMPLE PROBLEM?
OH, HE'S JUST A TOTAL FLAKE.
....

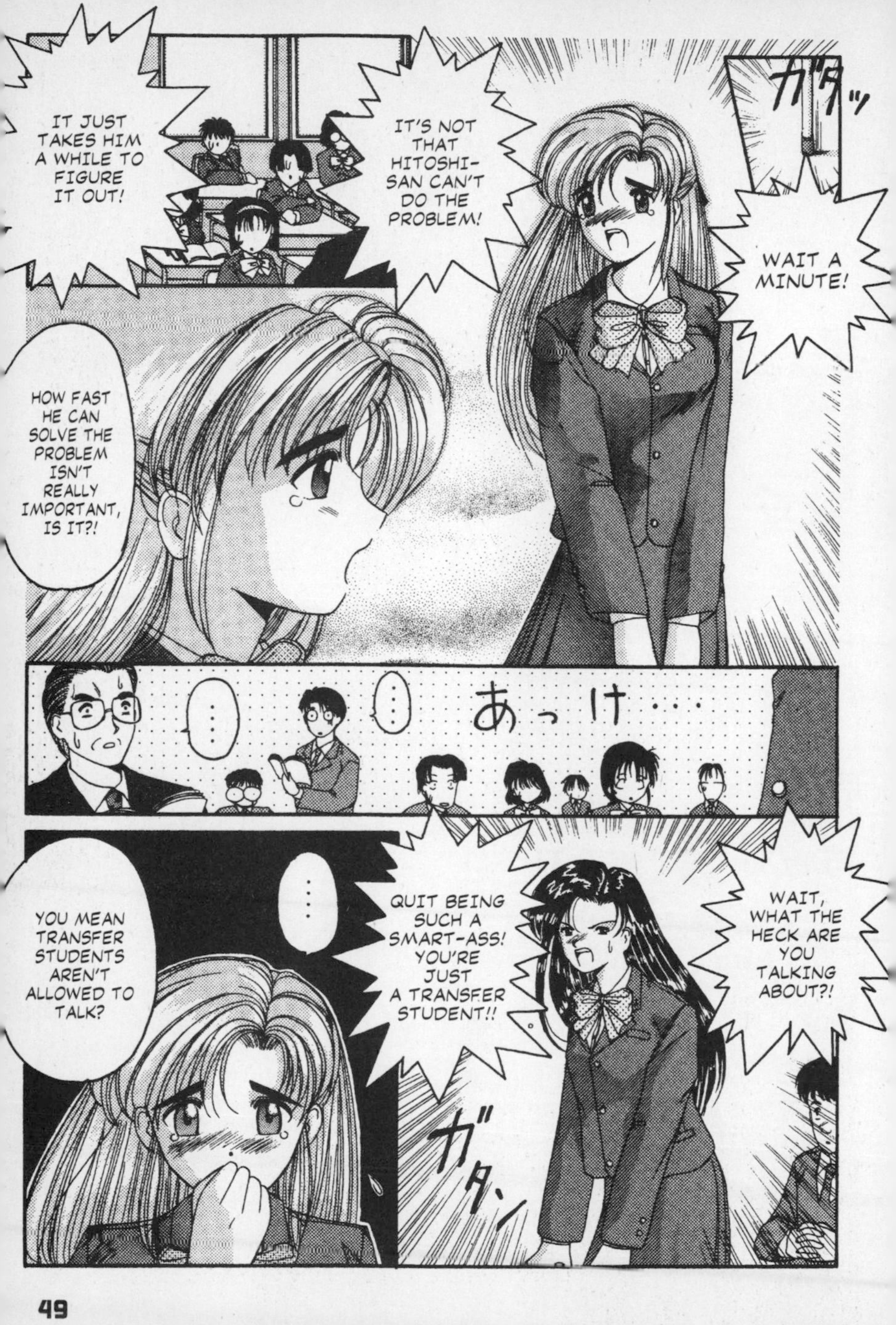
ガタッ
WAIT A MINUTE!
IT'S NOT THAT HITOSHI-SAN CAN'T DO THE PROBLEM!
IT JUST TAKES HIM A WHILE TO FIGURE IT OUT!
HOW FAST HE CAN SOLVE THE PROBLEM ISN'T REALLY IMPORTANT, IS IT?!
あっけ…
…
…
WAIT, WHAT THE HECK ARE YOU TALKING ABOUT?!
QUIT BEING SUCH A SMART-ASS! YOU'RE JUST A TRANSFER STUDENT!!
ガタン
…
YOU MEAN TRANSFER STUDENTS AREN'T ALLOWED TO TALK?

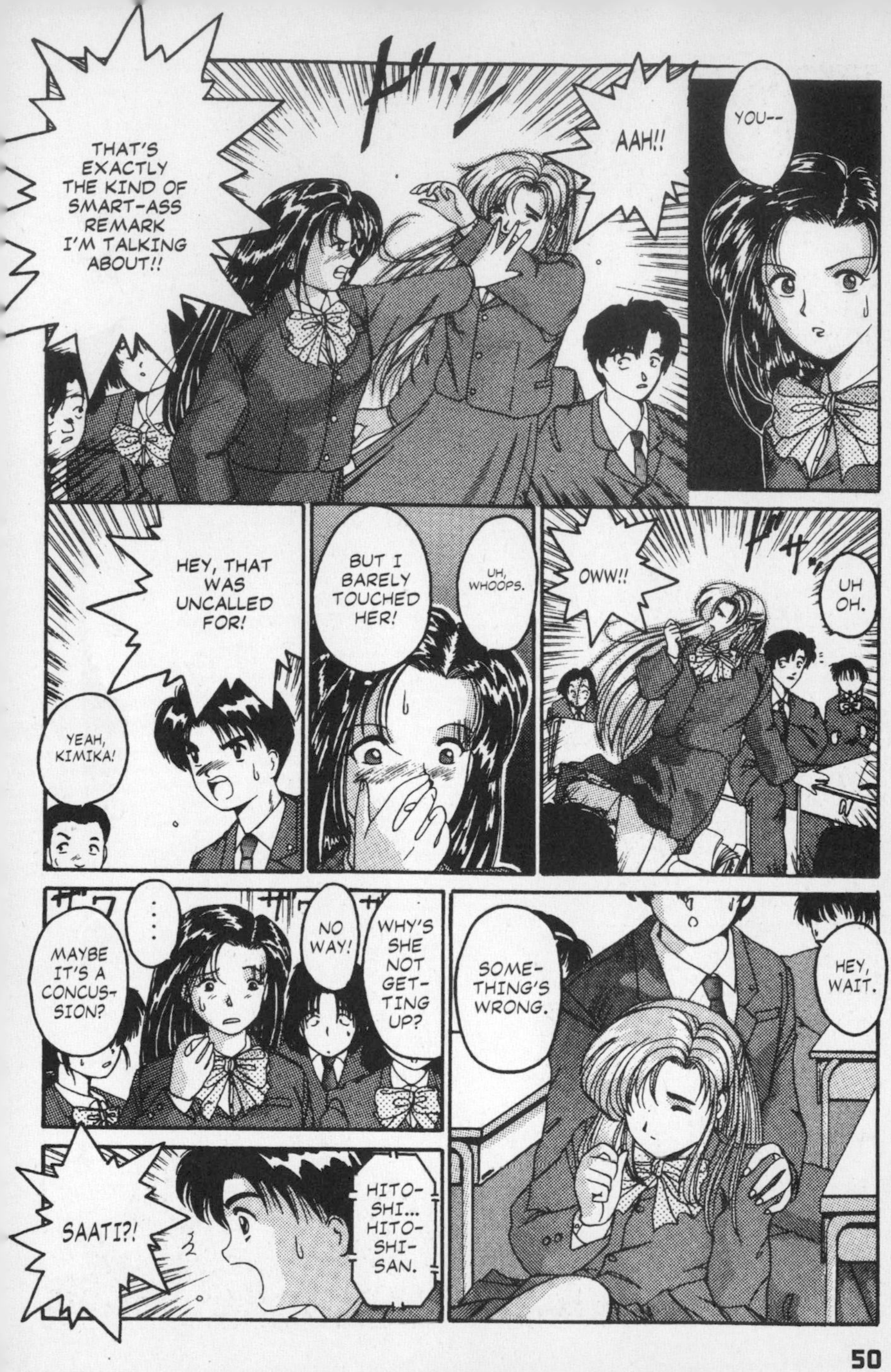
YOU--
AAH!!
THAT'S EXACTLY THE KIND OF SMART-ASS REMARK I'M TALKING ABOUT!!
UH OH.
OWW!!
UH, WHOOPS.
BUT I BARELY TOUCHED HER!
HEY, THAT WAS UNCALLED FOR!
YEAH, KIMIKA!
HEY, WAIT.
SOME-THING'S WRONG.
WHY'S SHE NOT GET-TING UP?
NO WAY!
....
MAYBE IT'S A CONCUS-SION?
HITO-SHI... HITO-SHI-SAN.
SAATI?!

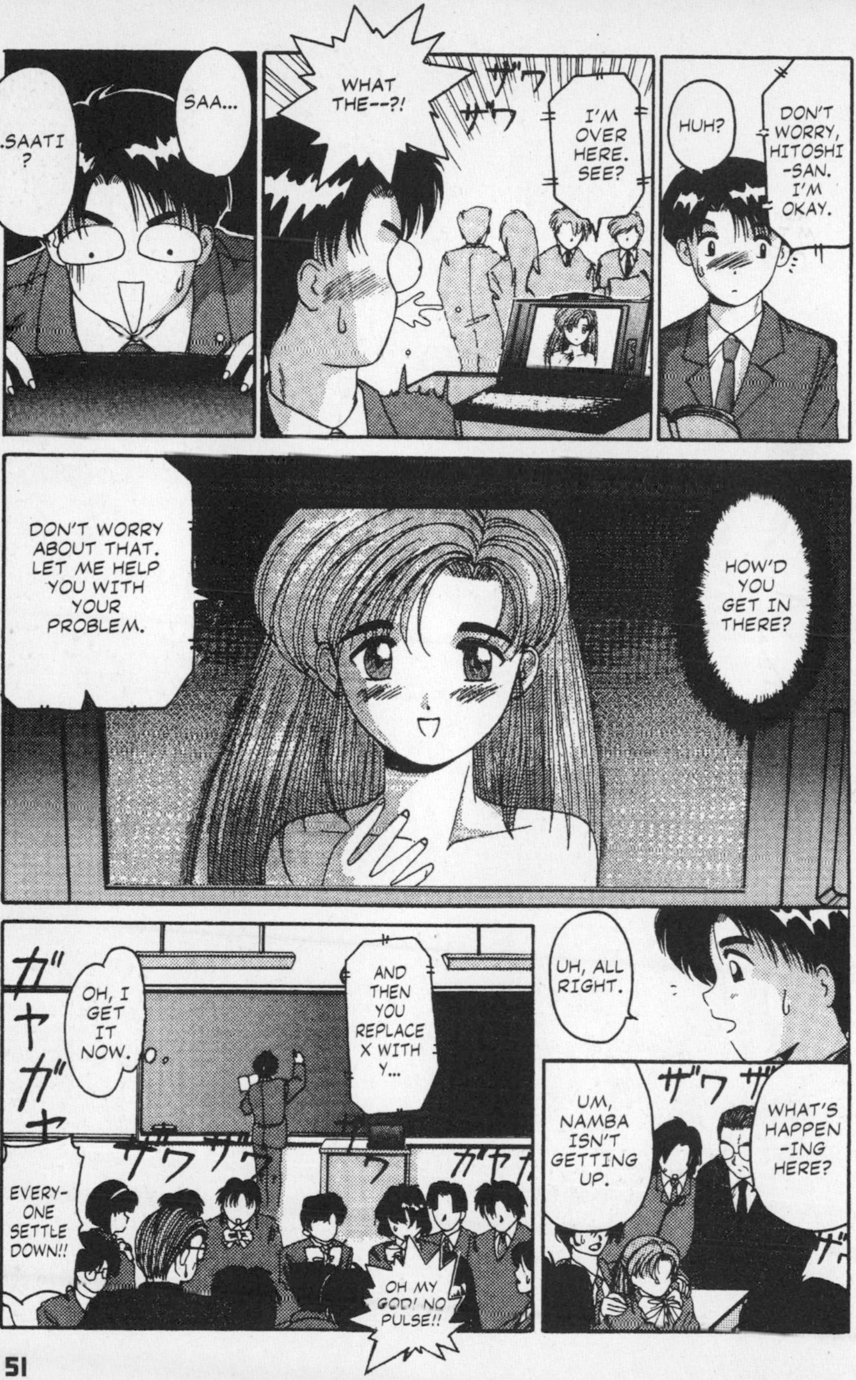
DON'T WORRY, HITOSHI-SAN. I'M OKAY.
HUH?
ザワ ザワ
I'M OVER HERE. SEE?
WHAT THE--?!
SAA...
...SAATI?
HOW'D YOU GET IN THERE?
DON'T WORRY ABOUT THAT. LET ME HELP YOU WITH YOUR PROBLEM.
UH, ALL RIGHT.
ザワザ
WHAT'S HAPPEN-ING HERE?
UM, NAMBA ISN'T GETTING UP.
AND THEN YOU REPLACE X WITH Y...
OH, I GET IT NOW.
ガヤガヤ
ザワザワ
OH MY GOD! NO PULSE!!
EVERY-ONE SETTLE DOWN!!

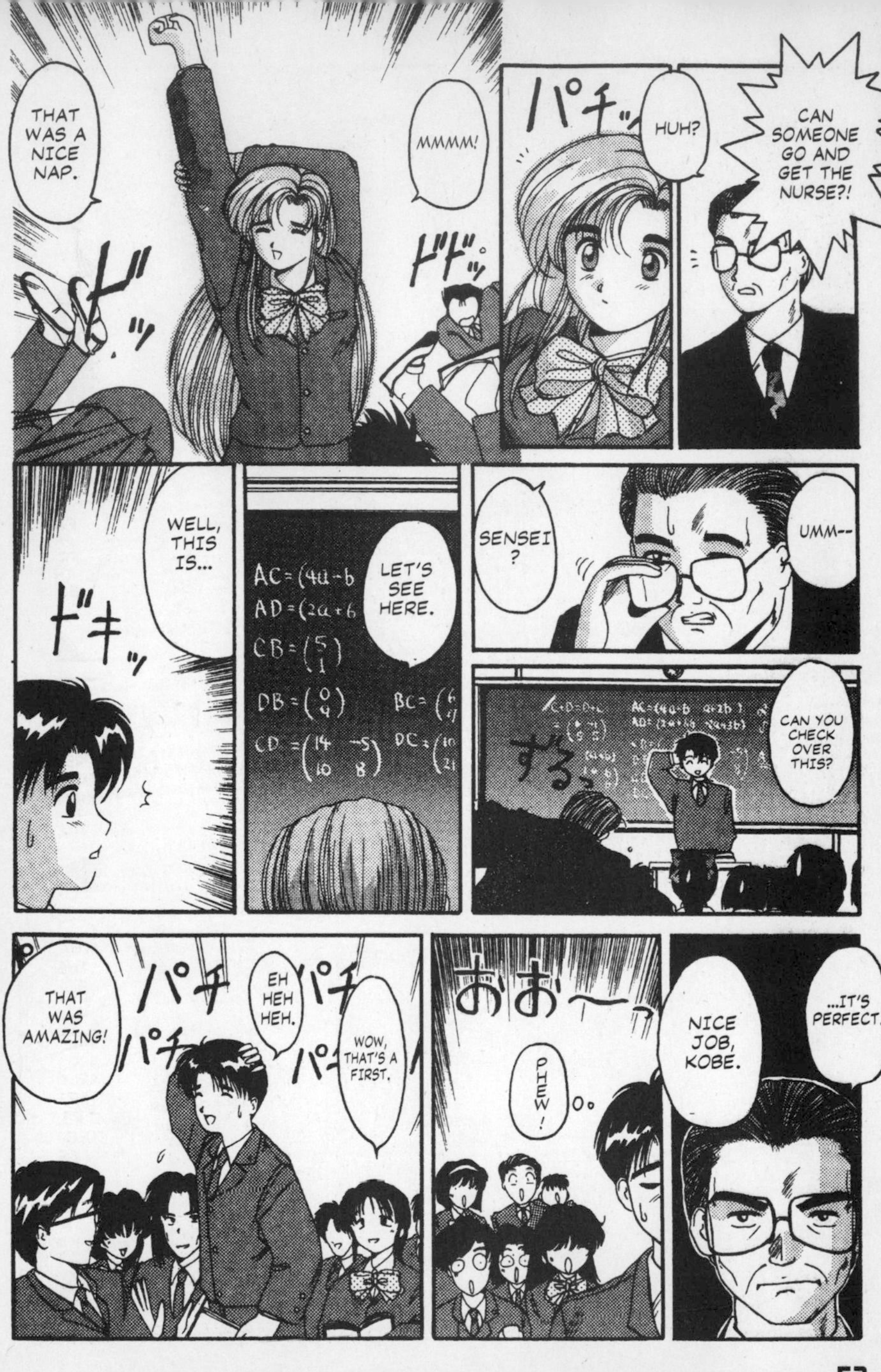
CAN SOMEONE GO AND GET THE NURSE?!
HUH?
パチッ
MMMM!
ドドッ
THAT WAS A NICE NAP.
ドドッ
UMM--
SENSEI?
CAN YOU CHECK OVER THIS?
するっ
LET'S SEE HERE.
WELL, THIS IS...
ドキッ
...IT'S PERFECT.
NICE JOB, KOBE.
PHEW!
おお〜っ
WOW, THAT'S A FIRST.
パチパチ
EH HEH HEH.
THAT WAS AMAZING!
パチパチ

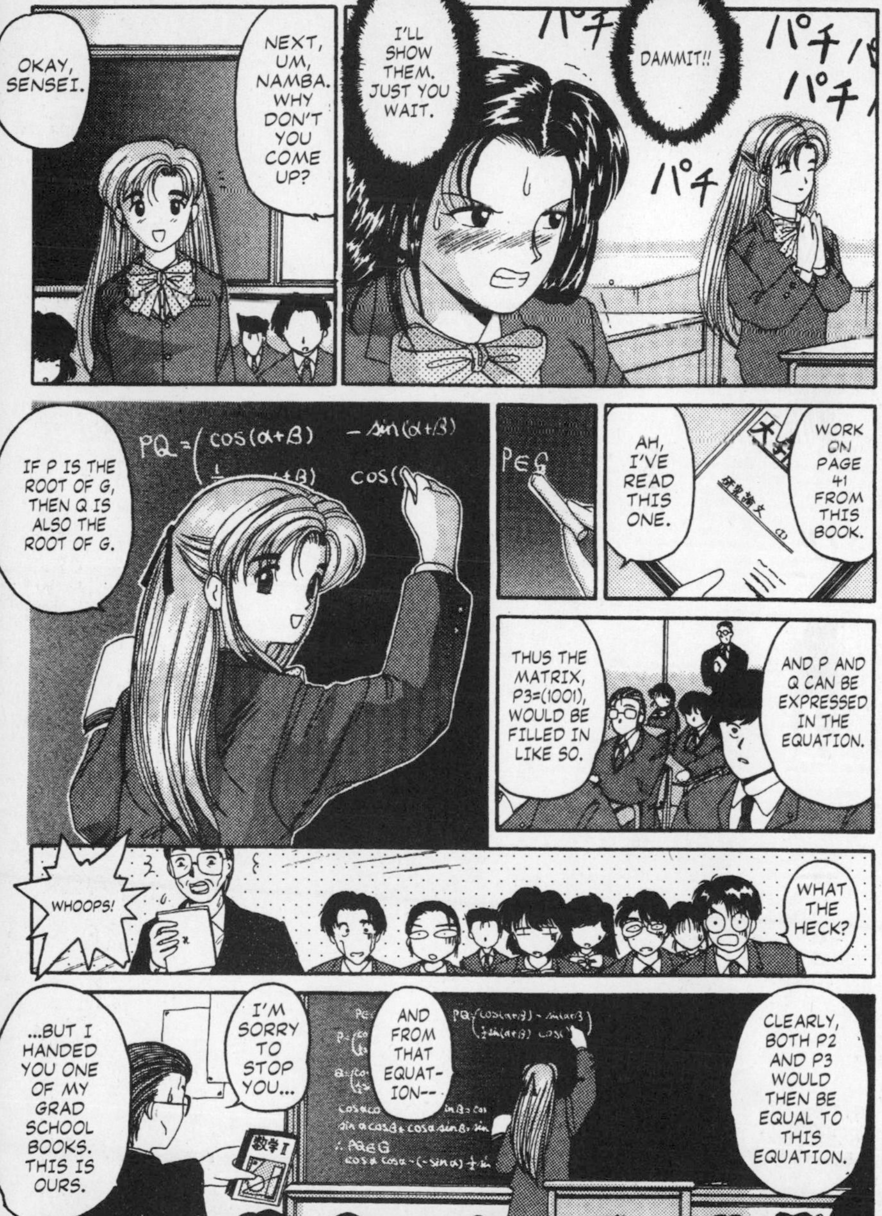
パチ
パチ
パチ
DAMMIT!!
パチ
I'LL SHOW THEM. JUST YOU WAIT.
パチ
NEXT, UM, NAMBA. WHY DON'T YOU COME UP?
OKAY, SENSEI.
WORK ON PAGE 41 FROM THIS BOOK.
AH, I'VE READ THIS ONE.
AND P AND Q CAN BE EXPRESSED IN THE EQUATION.
THUS THE MATRIX, P3=(1001), WOULD BE FILLED IN LIKE SO.
IF P IS THE ROOT OF G, THEN Q IS ALSO THE ROOT OF G.
WHAT THE HECK?
WHOOPS!
CLEARLY, BOTH P2 AND P3 WOULD THEN BE EQUAL TO THIS EQUATION.
AND FROM THAT EQUATION--
I'M SORRY TO STOP YOU...
...BUT I HANDED YOU ONE OF MY GRAD SCHOOL BOOKS. THIS IS OURS.

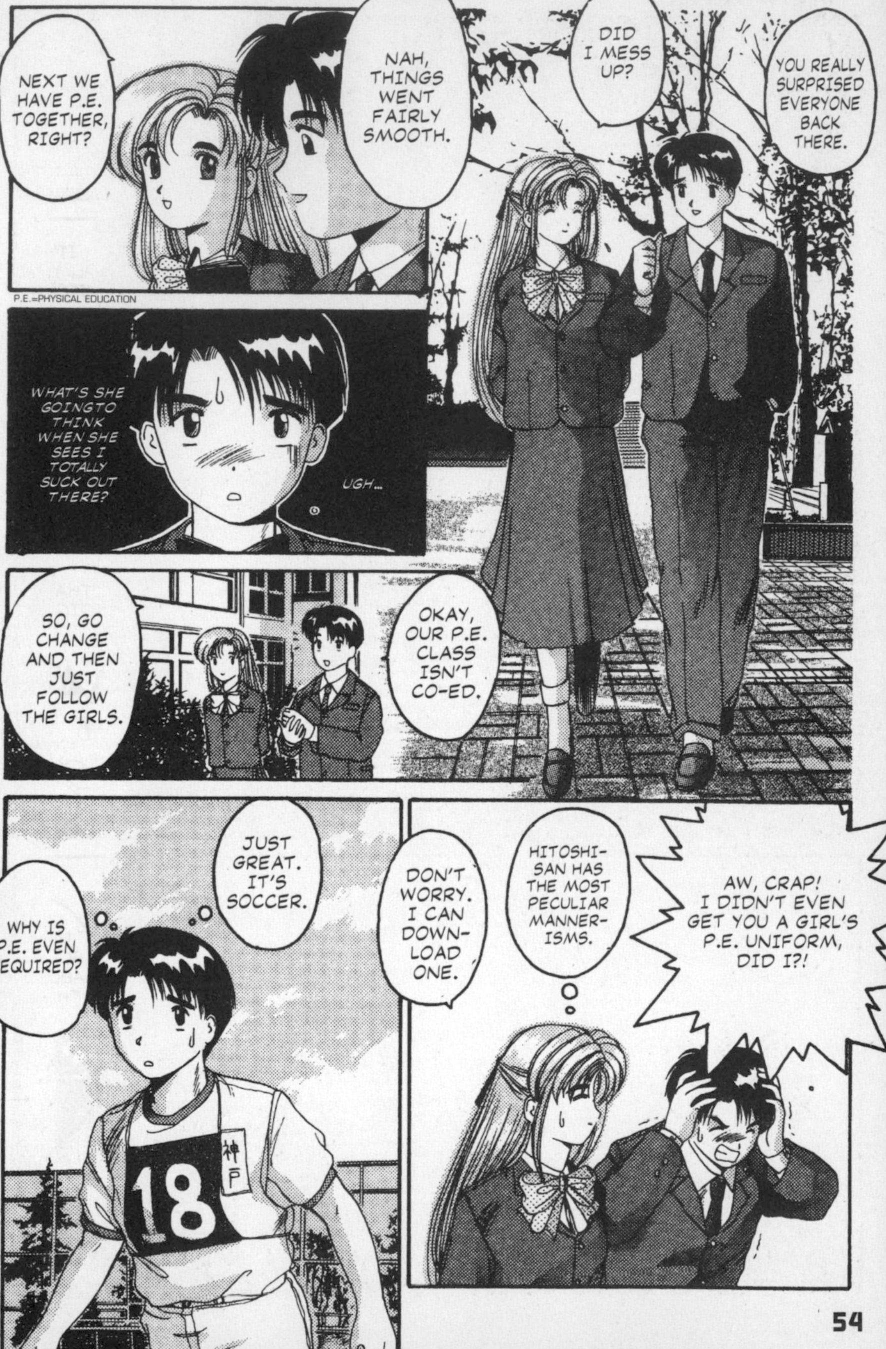
YOU REALLY SURPRISED EVERYONE BACK THERE.
DID I MESS UP?
NAH, THINGS WENT FAIRLY SMOOTH.
NEXT WE HAVE P.E. TOGETHER, RIGHT?
P.E.=PHYSICAL EDUCATION
UGH...
WHAT'S SHE GOINGTO THINK WHEN SHE SEES I TOTALLY SUCK OUT THERE?
OKAY, OUR P.E. CLASS ISN'T CO-ED.
SO, GO CHANGE AND THEN JUST FOLLOW THE GIRLS.
AW, CRAP! I DIDN'T EVEN GET YOU A GIRL'S P.E. UNIFORM, DID I?!
DON'T WORRY. I CAN DOWNLOAD ONE.
HITOSHI-SAN HAS THE MOST PECULIAR MANNERISMS.
JUST GREAT. IT'S SOCCER.
WHY IS P.E. EVEN REQUIRED?
18

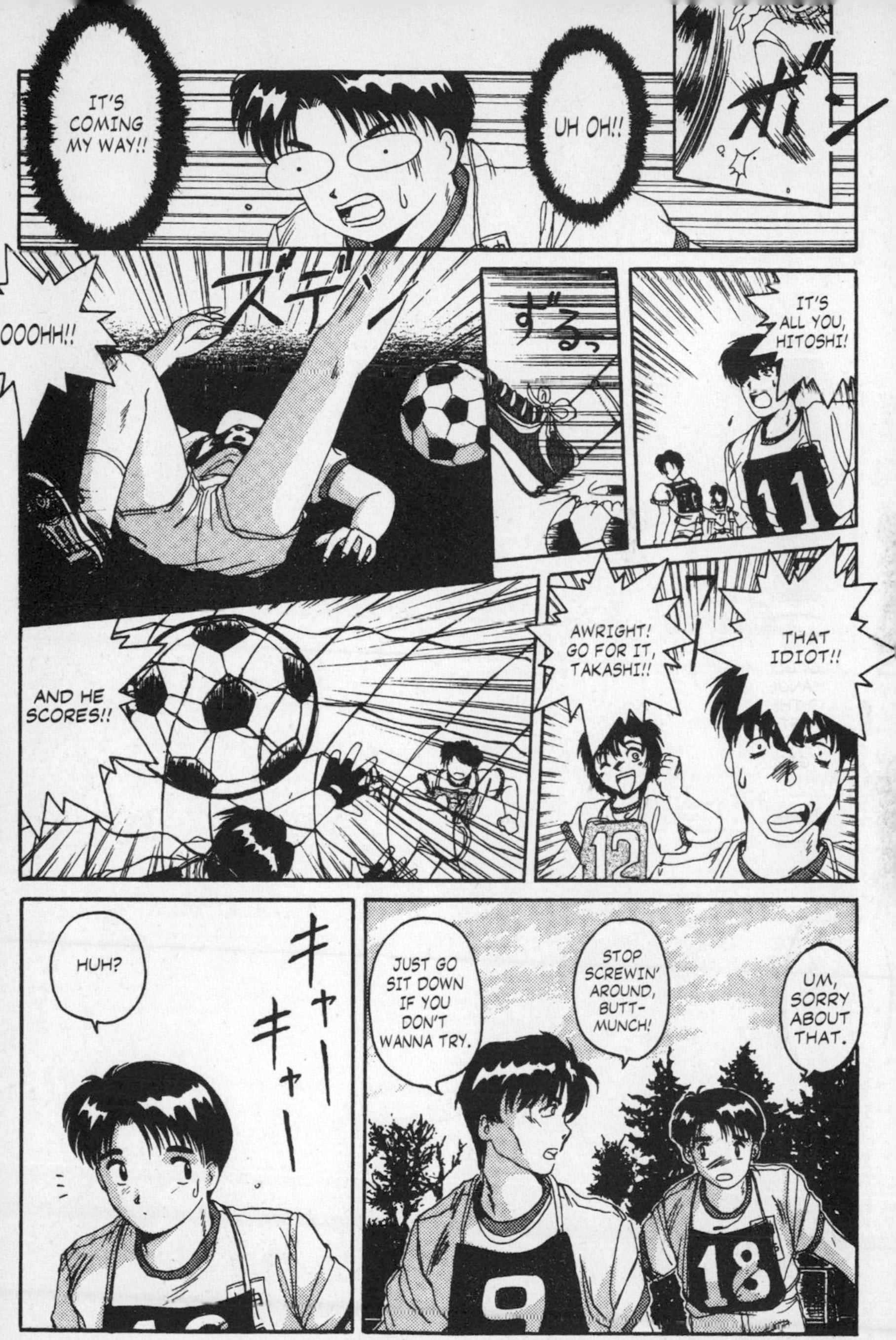
UH OH!!
IT'S COMING MY WAY!!
IT'S ALL YOU, HITOSHI!
ずるっ
OOOHH!!
THAT IDIOT!!
AWRIGHT! GO FOR IT, TAKASHI!!
AND HE SCORES!!
UM, SORRY ABOUT THAT.
STOP SCREWIN' AROUND, BUTT-MUNCH!
JUST GO SIT DOWN IF YOU DON'T WANNA TRY.
キャーキャー
HUH?

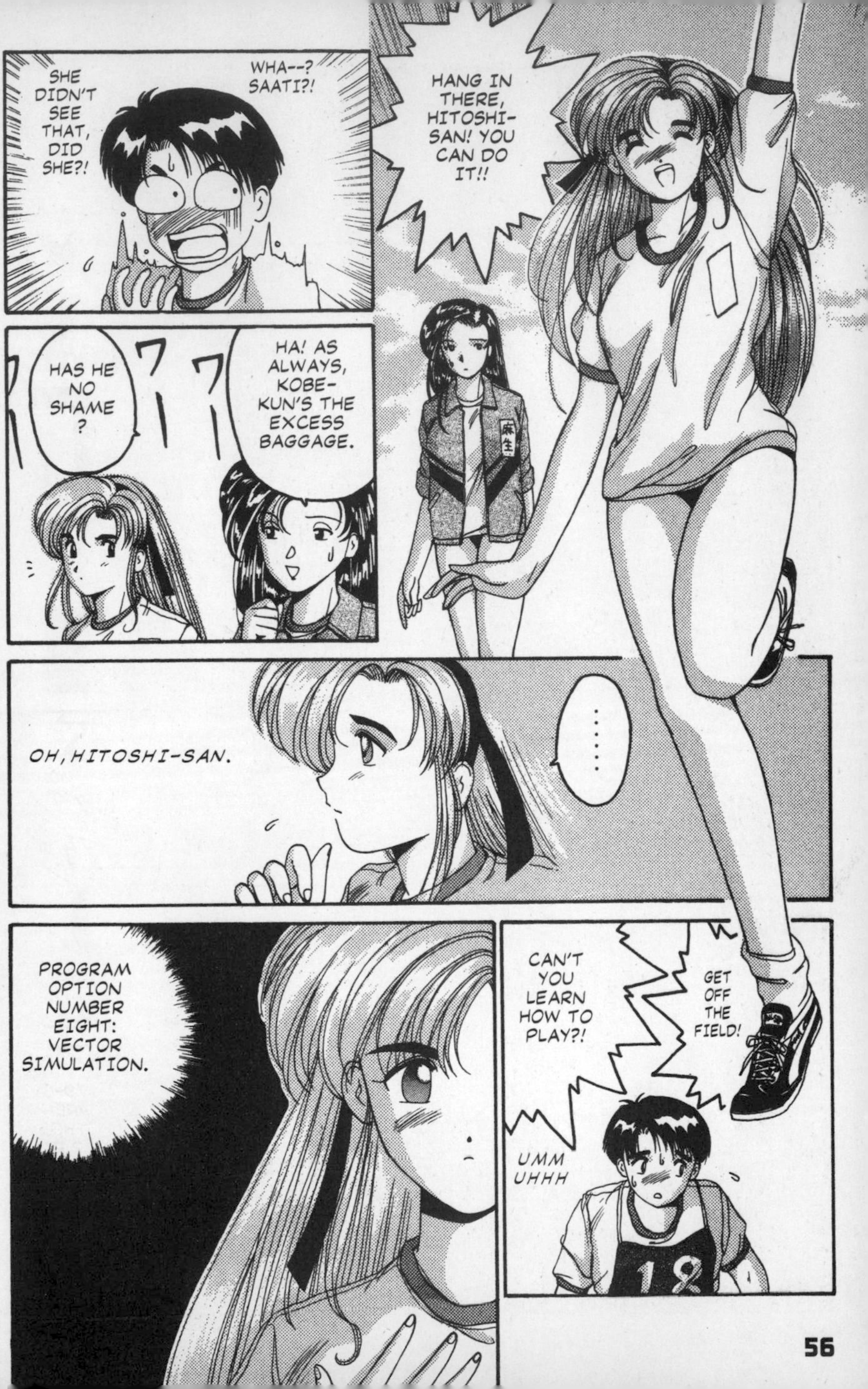
HANG IN THERE, HITOSHI-SAN! YOU CAN DO IT!!
WHA--? SAATI?!
SHE DIDN'T SEE THAT, DID SHE?!
HA! AS ALWAYS, KOBE-KUN'S THE EXCESS BAGGAGE.
HAS HE NO SHAME?
......
OH, HITOSHI-SAN.
GET OFF THE FIELD!
CAN'T YOU LEARN HOW TO PLAY?!
UMM UHHH
PROGRAM OPTION NUMBER EIGHT: VECTOR SIMULATION.

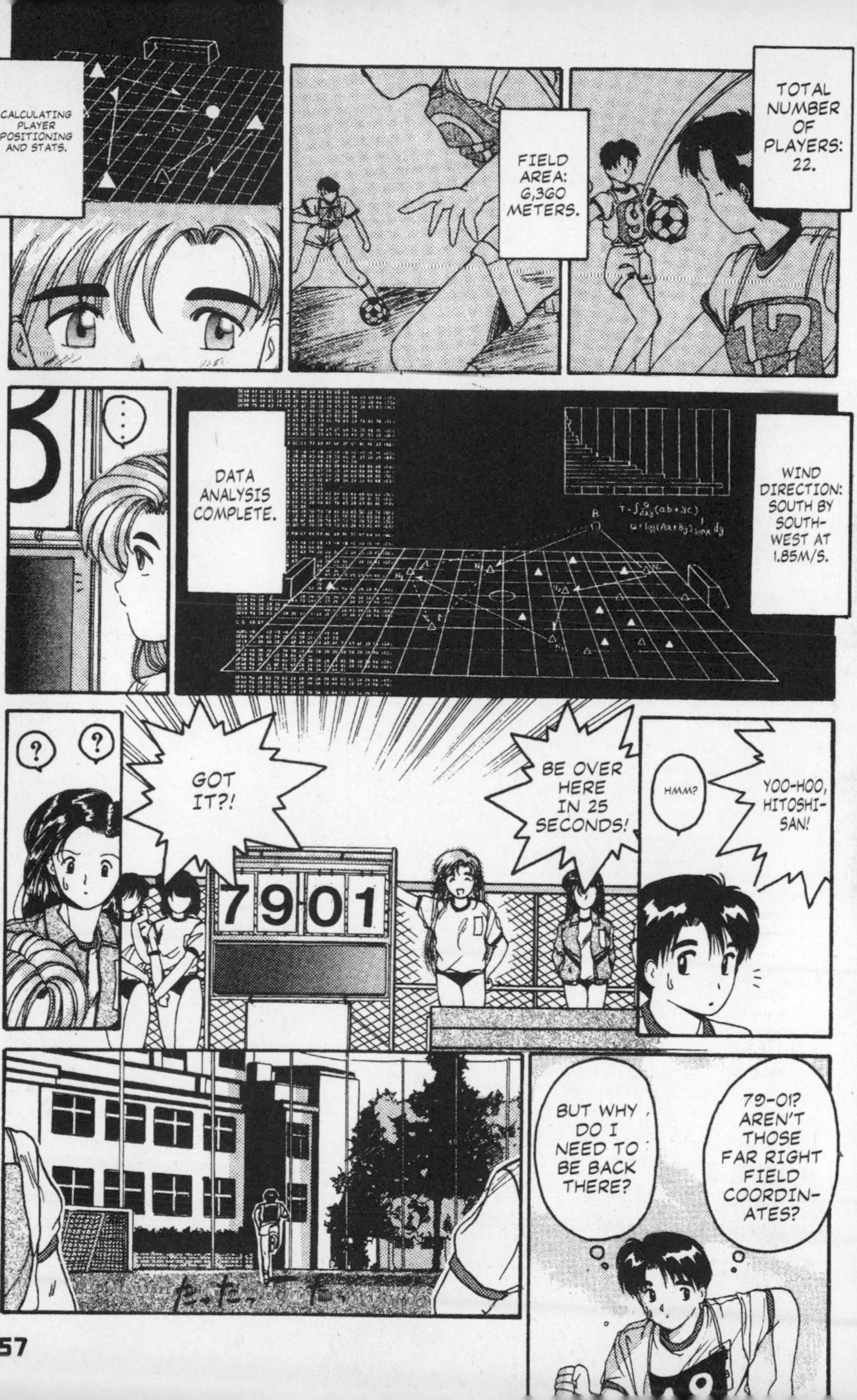
TOTAL NUMBER OF PLAYERS: 22.
FIELD AREA: 6,360 METERS.
CALCULATING PLAYER POSITIONING AND STATS.
WIND DIRECTION: SOUTH BY SOUTH-WEST AT 1.85M/S.
DATA ANALYSIS COMPLETE.
YOO-HOO, HITOSHI-SAN!
HMM?
BE OVER HERE IN 25 SECONDS!
GOT IT?!
7901
?
?
79-01? AREN'T THOSE FAR RIGHT FIELD COORDINATES?
BUT WHY DO I NEED TO BE BACK THERE?

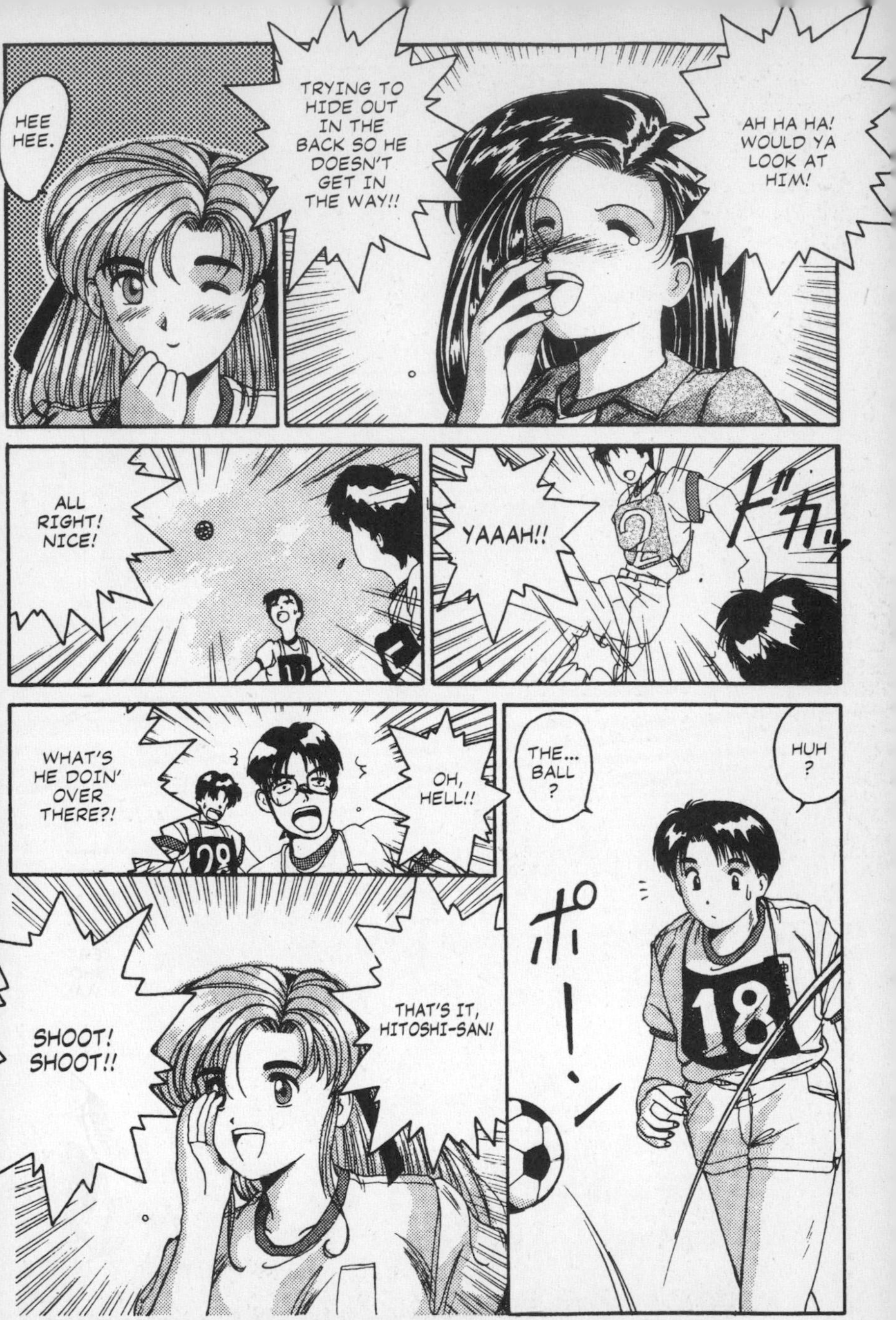

AH HA HA! WOULD YA LOOK AT HIM!
TRYING TO HIDE OUT IN THE BACK SO HE DOESN'T GET IN THE WAY!!
HEE HEE.
ドカッ
YAAAH!!
ALL RIGHT! NICE!
HUH ?
THE... BALL ?
OH, HELL!!
WHAT'S HE DOIN' OVER THERE?!
THAT'S IT, HITOSHI-SAN!
SHOOT! SHOOT!!

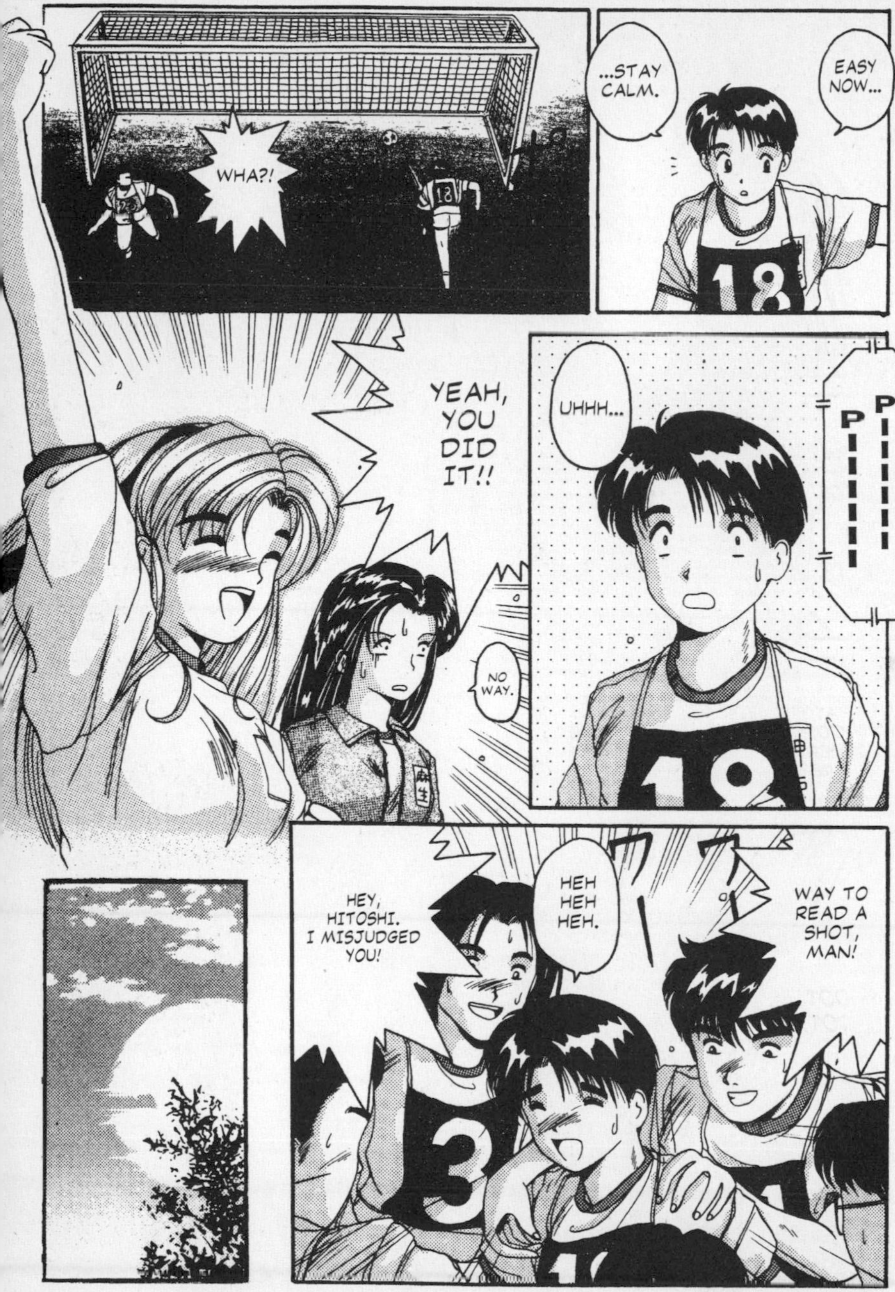
EASY NOW...
...STAY CALM.
WHA?!
P——
P——
UHHH...
YEAH, YOU DID IT!!
NO WAY.
WAY TO READ A SHOT, MAN!
HEH HEH HEH.
HEY, HITOSHI. I MISJUDGED YOU!

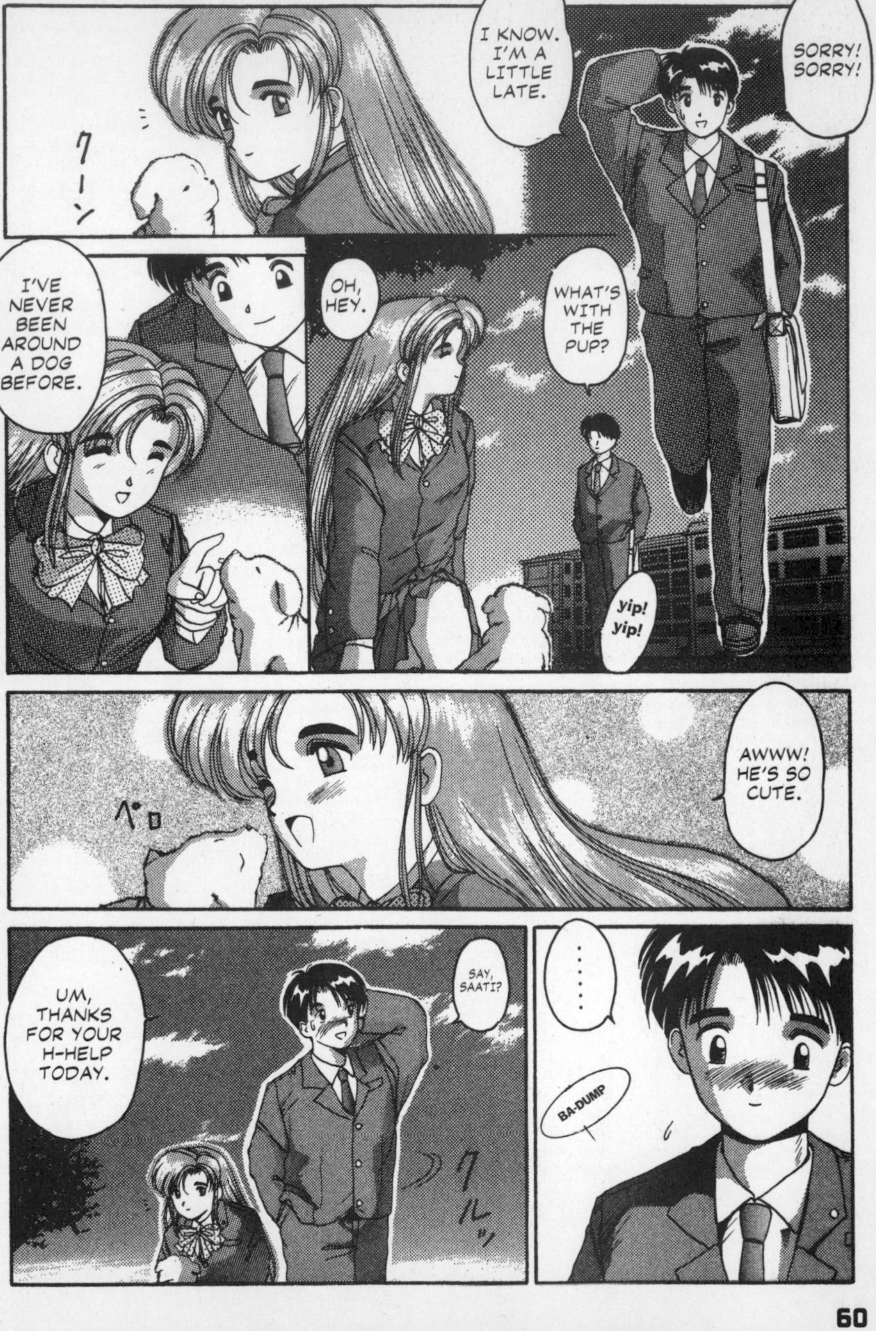
SORRY! SORRY!
I KNOW. I'M A LITTLE LATE.
クーン
WHAT'S WITH THE PUP?
OH, HEY.
yip! yip!
I'VE NEVER BEEN AROUND A DOG BEFORE.
AWWW! HE'S SO CUTE.
ペロ
......
BA-DUMP
SAY, SAATI?
UM, THANKS FOR YOUR H-HELP TODAY.
クルッ

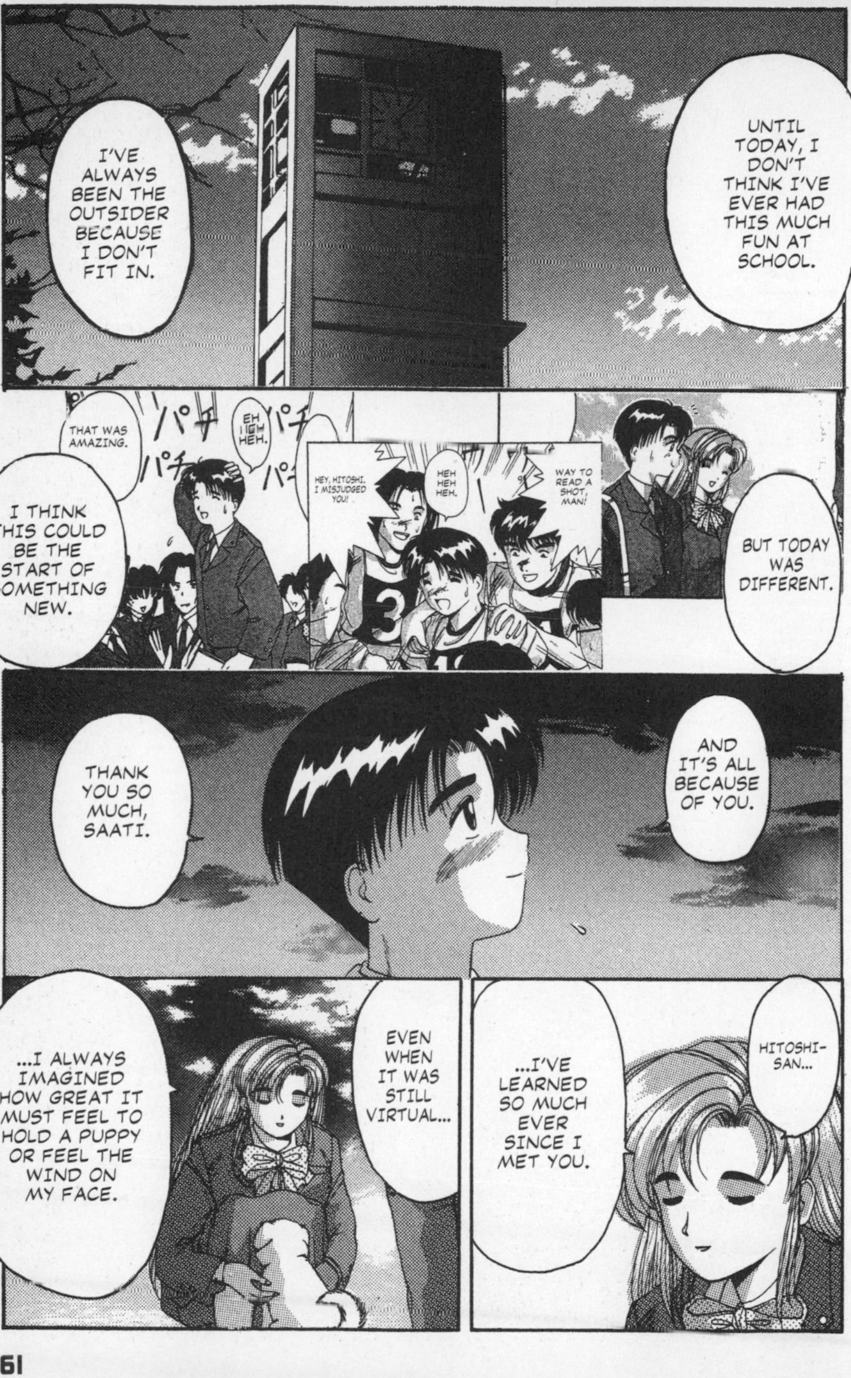
UNTIL TODAY, I DON'T THINK I'VE EVER HAD THIS MUCH FUN AT SCHOOL.
I'VE ALWAYS BEEN THE OUTSIDER BECAUSE I DON'T FIT IN.
BUT TODAY WAS DIFFERENT.
WAY TO READ A SHOT, MAN!
HEH HEH HEH.
HEY, HITOSHI, I MISJUDGED YOU!
パチ パチ
EH HEH HEH.
パチ
THAT WAS AMAZING.
I THINK THIS COULD BE THE START OF SOMETHING NEW.
AND IT'S ALL BECAUSE OF YOU.
THANK YOU SO MUCH, SAATI.
HITOSHI-SAN...
...I'VE LEARNED SO MUCH EVER SINCE I MET YOU.
EVEN WHEN IT WAS STILL VIRTUAL...
...I ALWAYS IMAGINED HOW GREAT IT MUST FEEL TO HOLD A PUPPY OR FEEL THE WIND ON MY FACE.

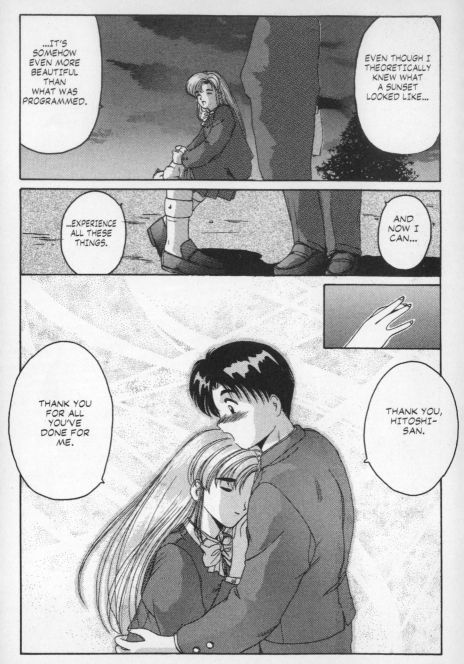

EVEN THOUGH I THEORETICALLY KNEW WHAT A SUNSET LOOKED LIKE...
...IT'S SOMEHOW EVEN MORE BEAUTIFUL THAN WHAT WAS PROGRAMMED.
AND NOW I CAN...
...EXPERIENCE ALL THESE THINGS.
THANK YOU, HITOSHI-SAN.
THANK YOU FOR ALL YOU'VE DONE FOR ME.

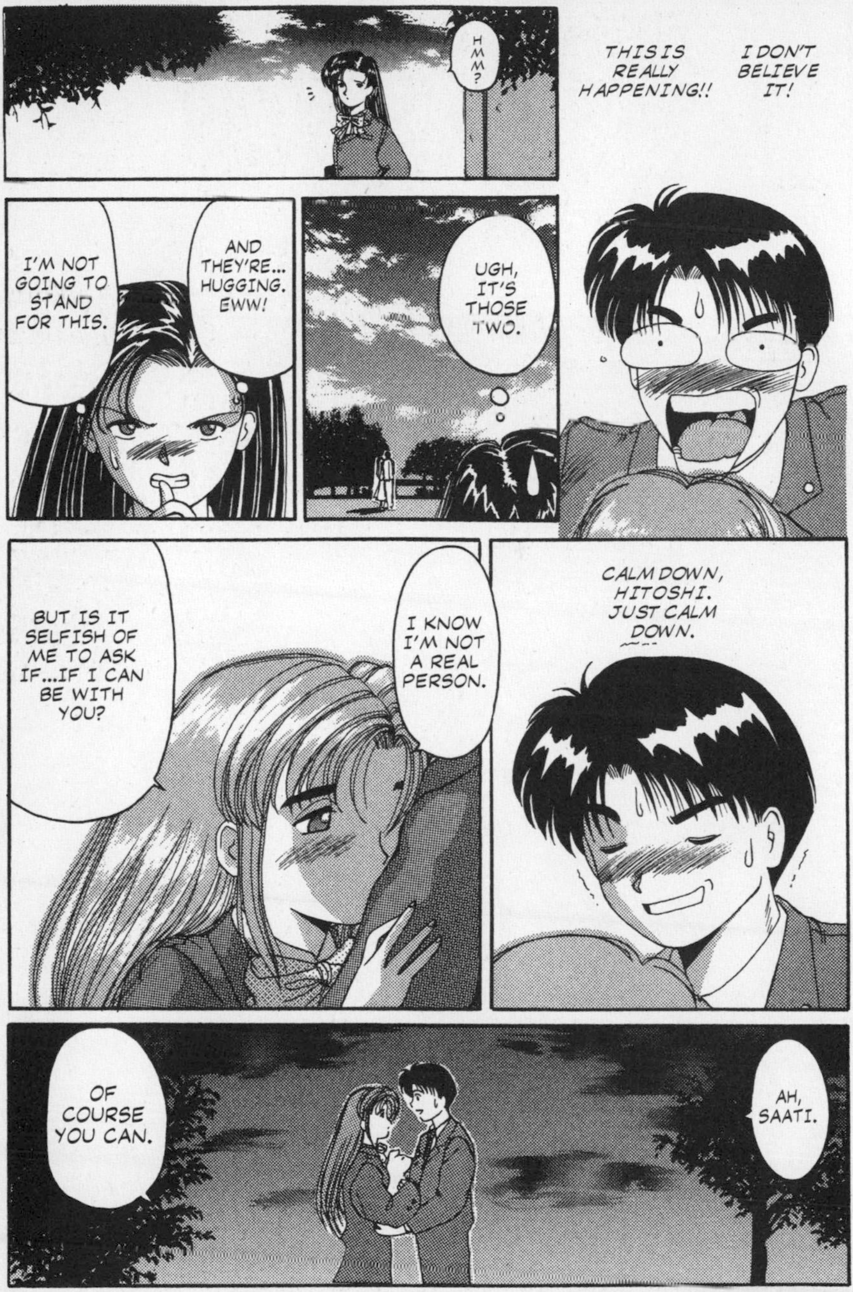

I DON'T BELIEVE IT!
THIS IS REALLY HAPPENING!!
HMM?
UGH, IT'S THOSE TWO.
AND THEY'RE... HUGGING. EWW!
I'M NOT GOING TO STAND FOR THIS.
CALM DOWN, HITOSHI. JUST CALM DOWN.
I KNOW I'M NOT A REAL PERSON.
BUT IS IT SELFISH OF ME TO ASK IF...IF I CAN BE WITH YOU?
AH, SAATI.
OF COURSE YOU CAN.

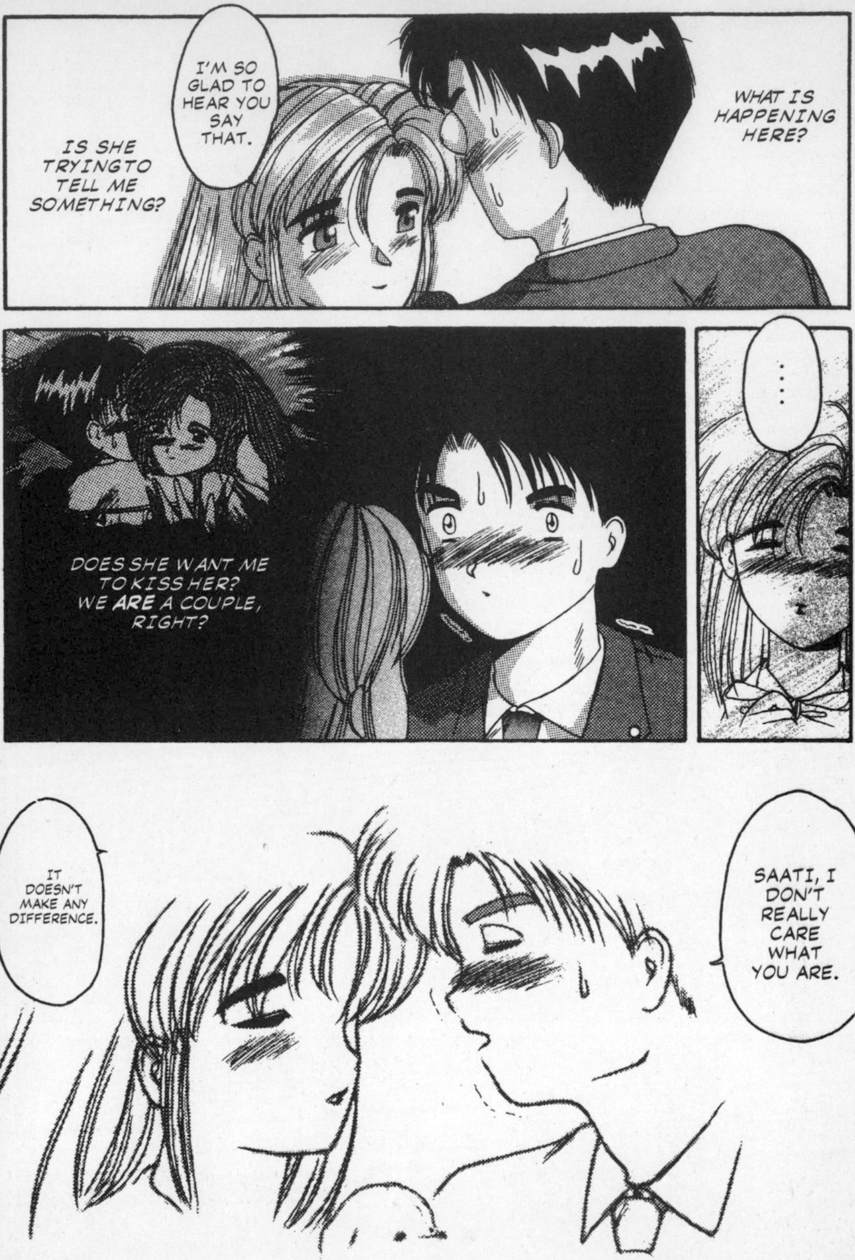

I'M SO GLAD TO HEAR YOU SAY THAT.
WHAT IS HAPPENING HERE?
IS SHE TRYINGTO TELL ME SOMETHING?
.....
DOES SHE WANT ME TO KISS HER? WE ARE A COUPLE, RIGHT?
SAATI, I DON'T REALLY CARE WHAT YOU ARE.
IT DOESN'T MAKE ANY DIFFERENCE.

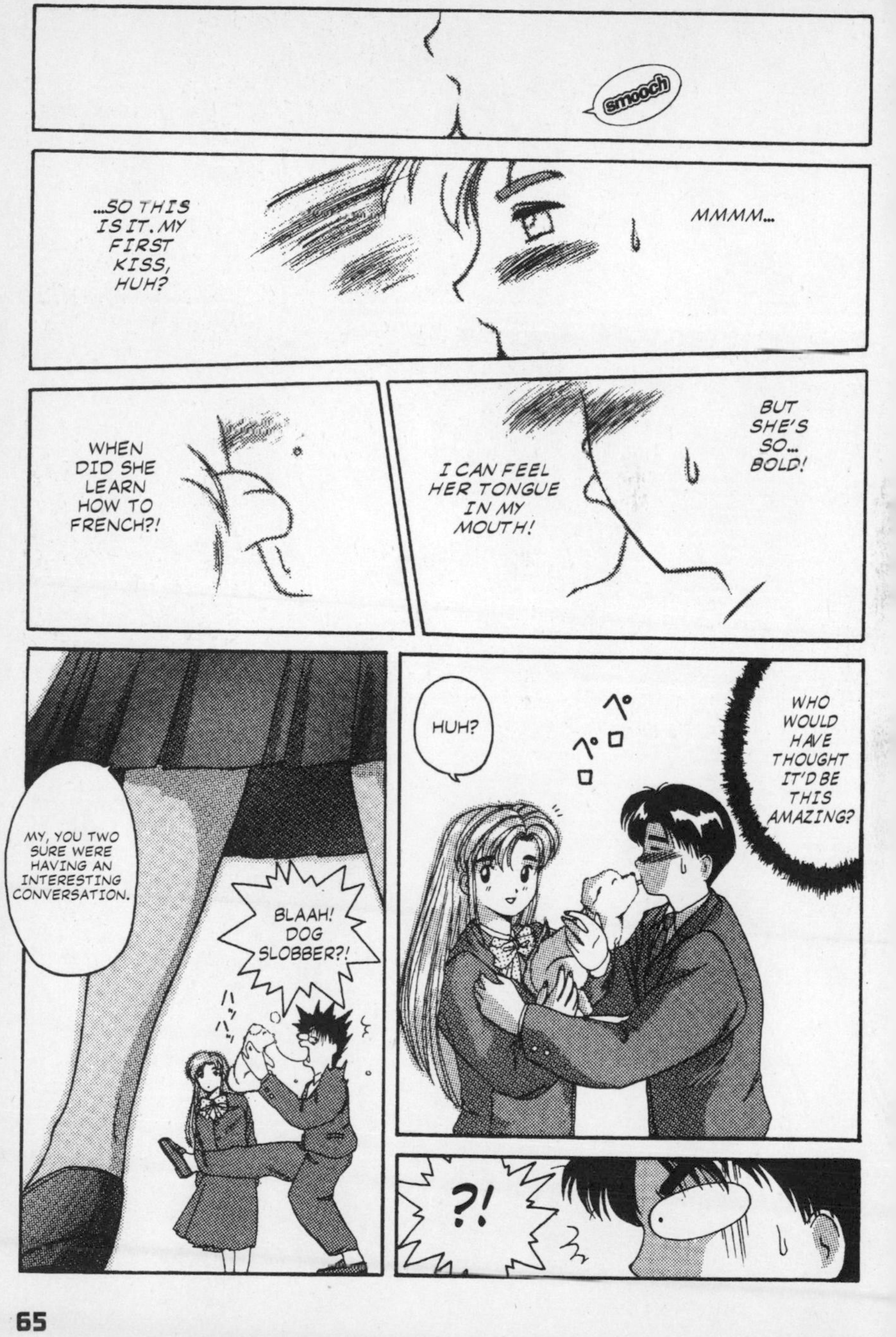

smooch
MMMM...
...SO THIS IS IT. MY FIRST KISS, HUH?
BUT SHE'S SO... BOLD!
I CAN FEEL HER TONGUE IN MY MOUTH!
WHEN DID SHE LEARN HOW TO FRENCH?!
WHO WOULD HAVE THOUGHT IT'D BE THIS AMAZING?
ペロ
ペロ
HUH?
?!
MY, YOU TWO SURE WERE HAVING AN INTERESTING CONVERSATION.
BLAAH! DOG SLOBBER?!

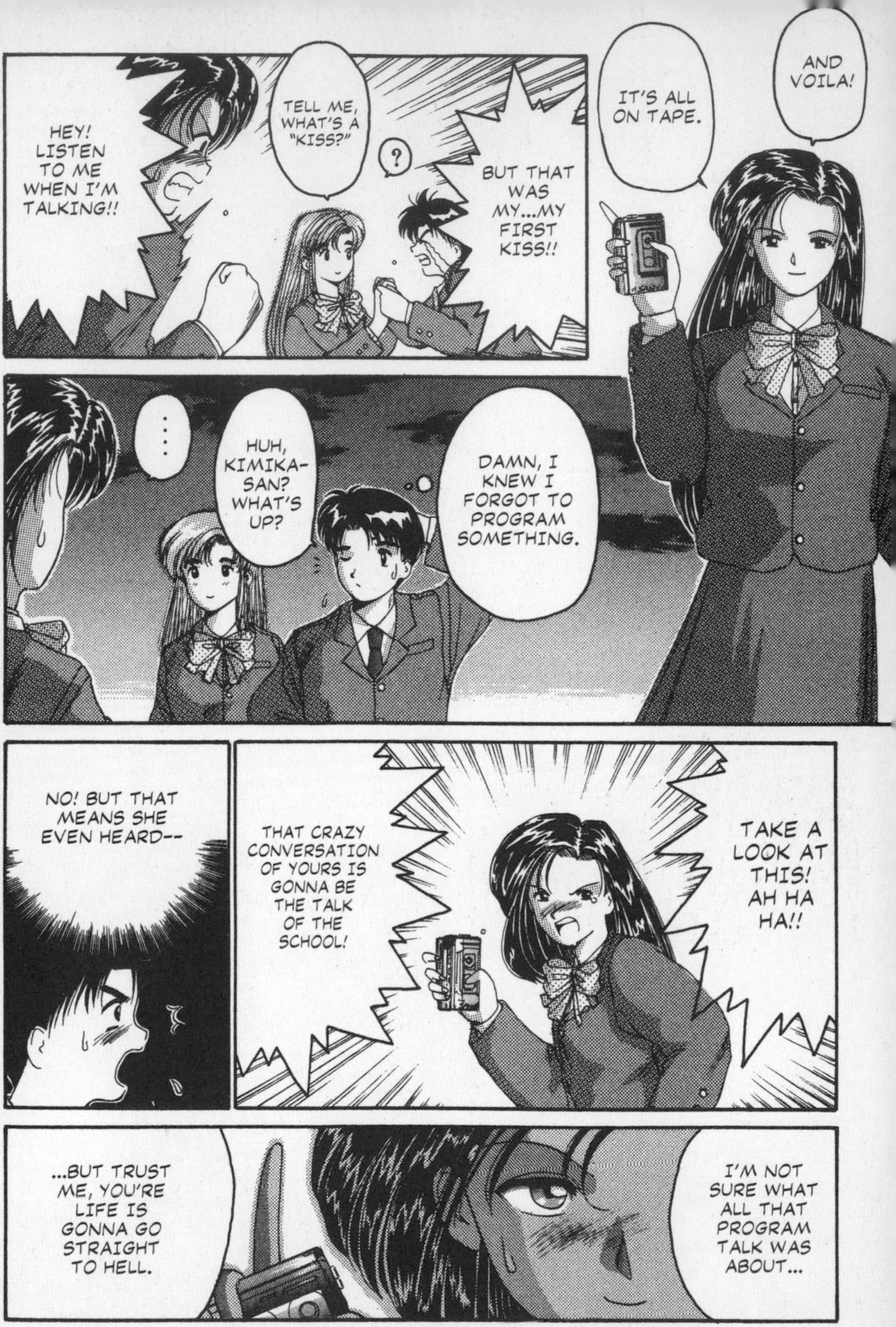
AND VOILA!
IT'S ALL ON TAPE.
BUT THAT WAS MY...MY FIRST KISS!!
?
TELL ME, WHAT'S A "KISS?"
HEY! LISTEN TO ME WHEN I'M TALKING!!
DAMN, I KNEW I FORGOT TO PROGRAM SOMETHING.
HUH, KIMIKA-SAN? WHAT'S UP?
....
TAKE A LOOK AT THIS! AH HA HA!!
THAT CRAZY CONVERSATION OF YOURS IS GONNA BE THE TALK OF THE SCHOOL!
NO! BUT THAT MEANS SHE EVEN HEARD--
I'M NOT SURE WHAT ALL THAT PROGRAM TALK WAS ABOUT...
...BUT TRUST ME, YOU'RE LIFE IS GONNA GO STRAIGHT TO HELL.

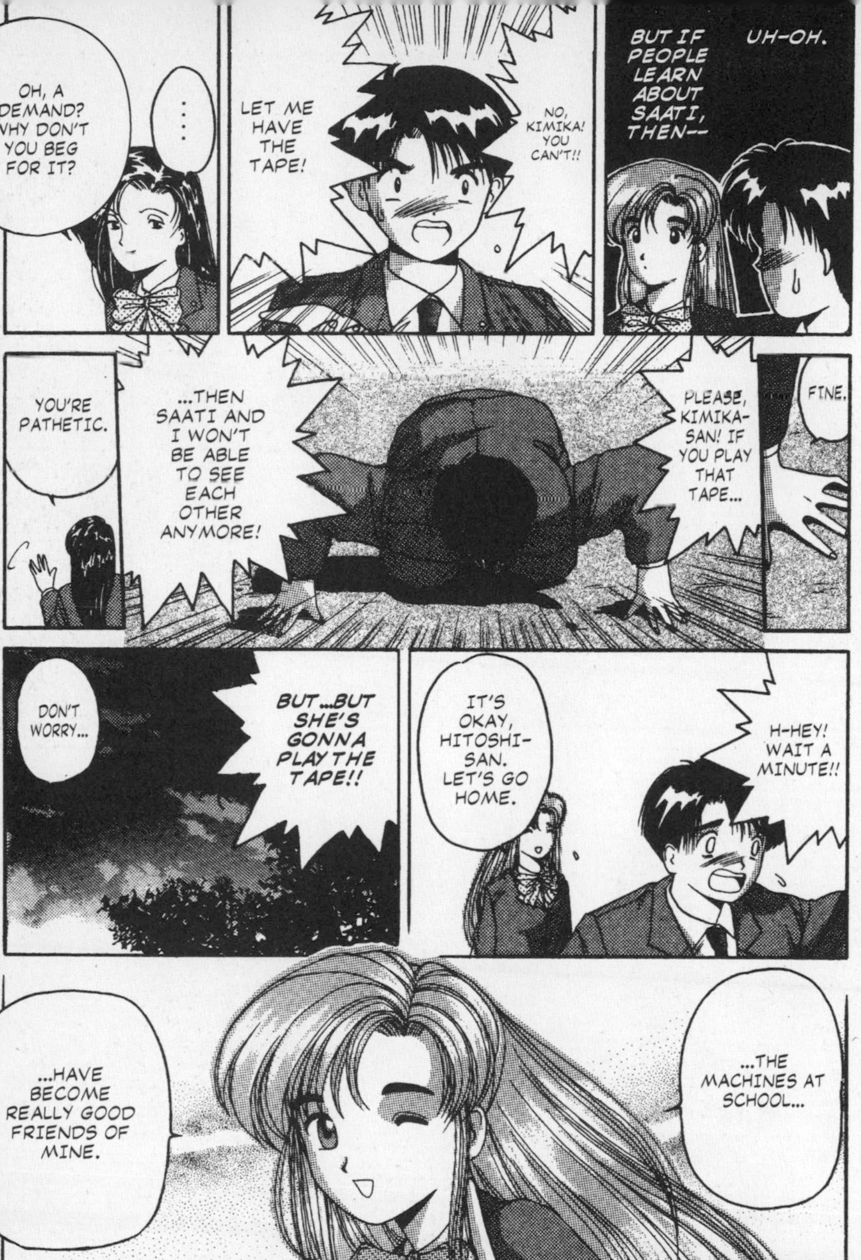
UH-OH.
BUT IF PEOPLE LEARN ABOUT SAATI, THEN--
NO, KIMIKA! YOU CAN'T!!
LET ME HAVE THE TAPE!
....
OH, A DEMAND? WHY DON'T YOU BEG FOR IT?
FINE.
PLEASE, KIMIKA-SAN! IF YOU PLAY THAT TAPE...
...THEN SAATI AND I WON'T BE ABLE TO SEE EACH OTHER ANYMORE!
YOU'RE PATHETIC.
H-HEY! WAIT A MINUTE!!
IT'S OKAY, HITOSHI-SAN. LET'S GO HOME.
BUT...BUT SHE'S GONNA PLAY THE TAPE!!
DON'T WORRY...
...THE MACHINES AT SCHOOL...
...HAVE BECOME REALLY GOOD FRIENDS OF MINE.

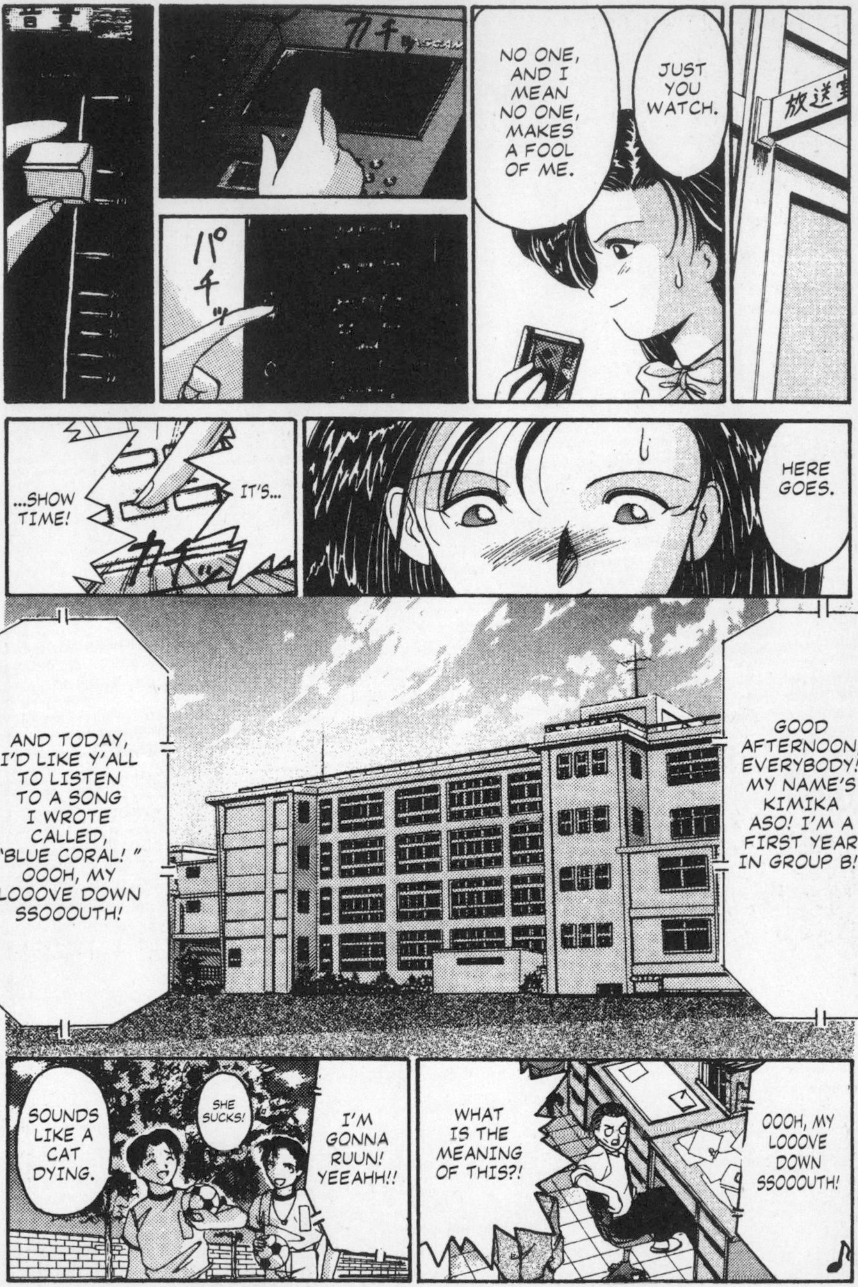
放送
JUST YOU WATCH.
NO ONE, AND I MEAN NO ONE, MAKES A FOOL OF ME.
カチ
パチッ
HERE GOES.
IT'S...
...SHOW TIME!
カチッ
GOOD AFTERNOON, EVERYBODY! MY NAME'S KIMIKA ASO! I'M A FIRST YEAR IN GROUP B!!
AND TODAY, I'D LIKE Y'ALL TO LISTEN TO A SONG I WROTE CALLED, "BLUE CORAL!" OOOH, MY LOOOVE DOWN SSOOOUTH!
OOOH, MY LOOOVE DOWN SSOOOUTH!
WHAT IS THE MEANING OF THIS?!
I'M GONNA RUUN! YEEAHH!!
SHE SUCKS!
SOUNDS LIKE A CAT DYING.

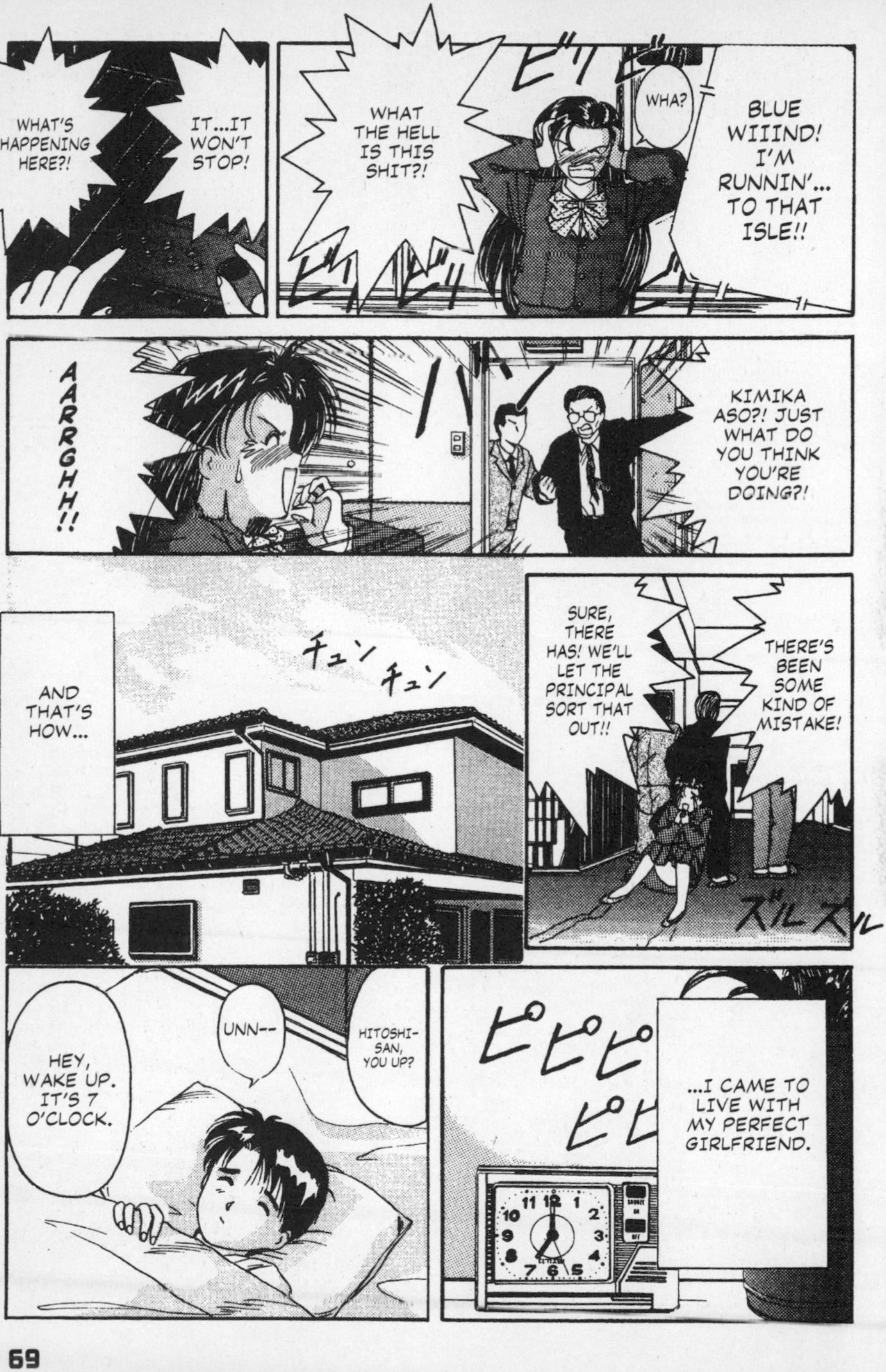
BLUE WIIIND! I'M RUNNIN'... TO THAT ISLE!!
WHA?
WHAT THE HELL IS THIS SHIT?!
IT...IT WON'T STOP!
WHAT'S HAPPENING HERE?!
KIMIKA ASO?! JUST WHAT DO YOU THINK YOU'RE DOING?!
AARRGHH!!
THERE'S BEEN SOME KIND OF MISTAKE!
SURE, THERE HAS! WE'LL LET THE PRINCIPAL SORT THAT OUT!!
ズルズル
チュン チュン
AND THAT'S HOW...
...I CAME TO LIVE WITH MY PERFECT GIRLFRIEND.
ピピピ ピピ
HITOSHI-SAN, YOU UP?
UNN--
HEY, WAKE UP. IT'S 7 O'CLOCK.

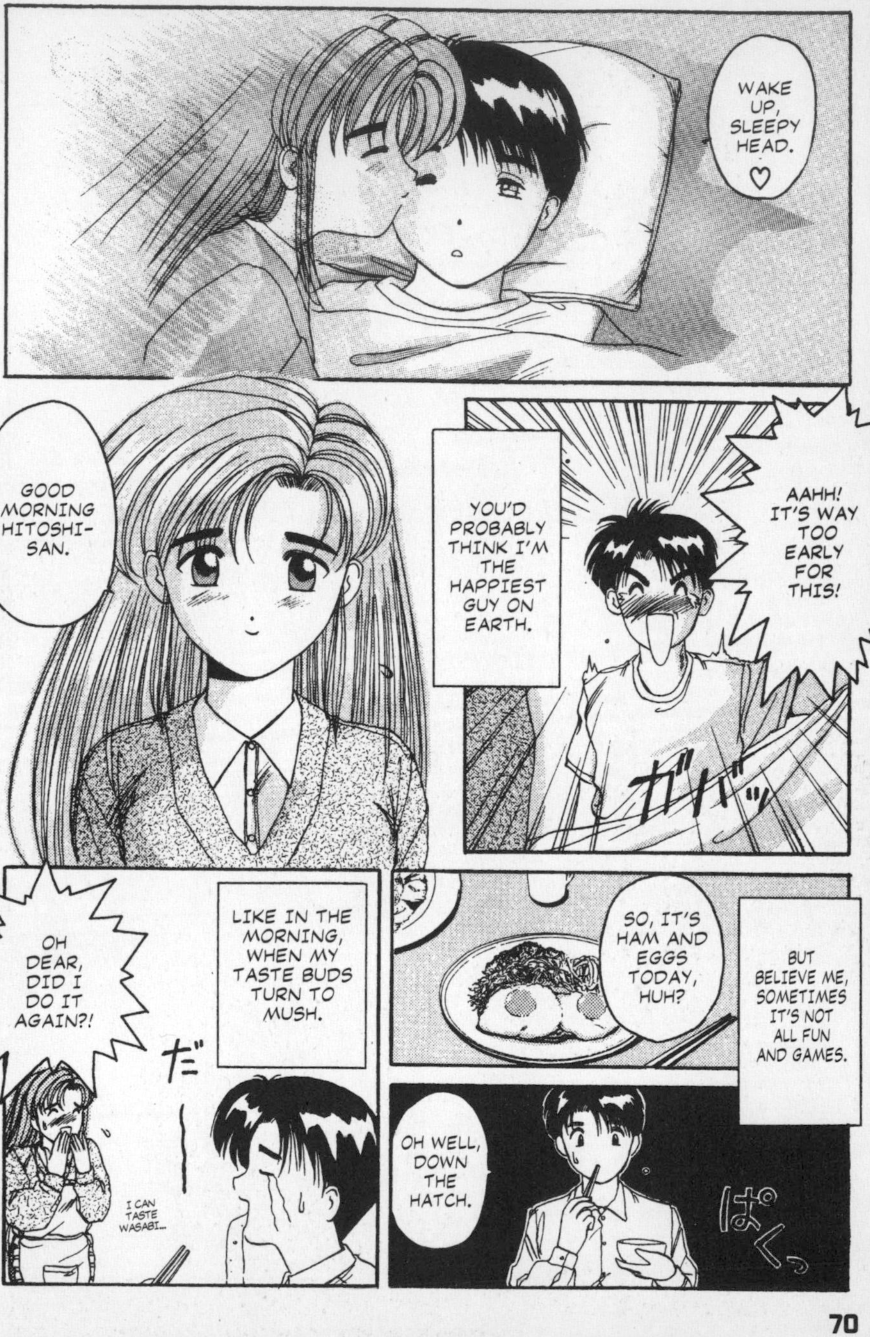
WAKE UP, SLEEPY HEAD. ♡
AAHH! IT'S WAY TOO EARLY FOR THIS!
YOU'D PROBABLY THINK I'M THE HAPPIEST GUY ON EARTH.
ガバッ
GOOD MORNING HITOSHI-SAN.
BUT BELIEVE ME, SOMETIMES IT'S NOT ALL FUN AND GAMES.
SO, IT'S HAM AND EGGS TODAY, HUH?
ぱくっ
OH WELL, DOWN THE HATCH.
LIKE IN THE MORNING, WHEN MY TASTE BUDS TURN TO MUSH.
OH DEAR, DID I DO IT AGAIN?!
だー
I CAN TASTE WASABI...

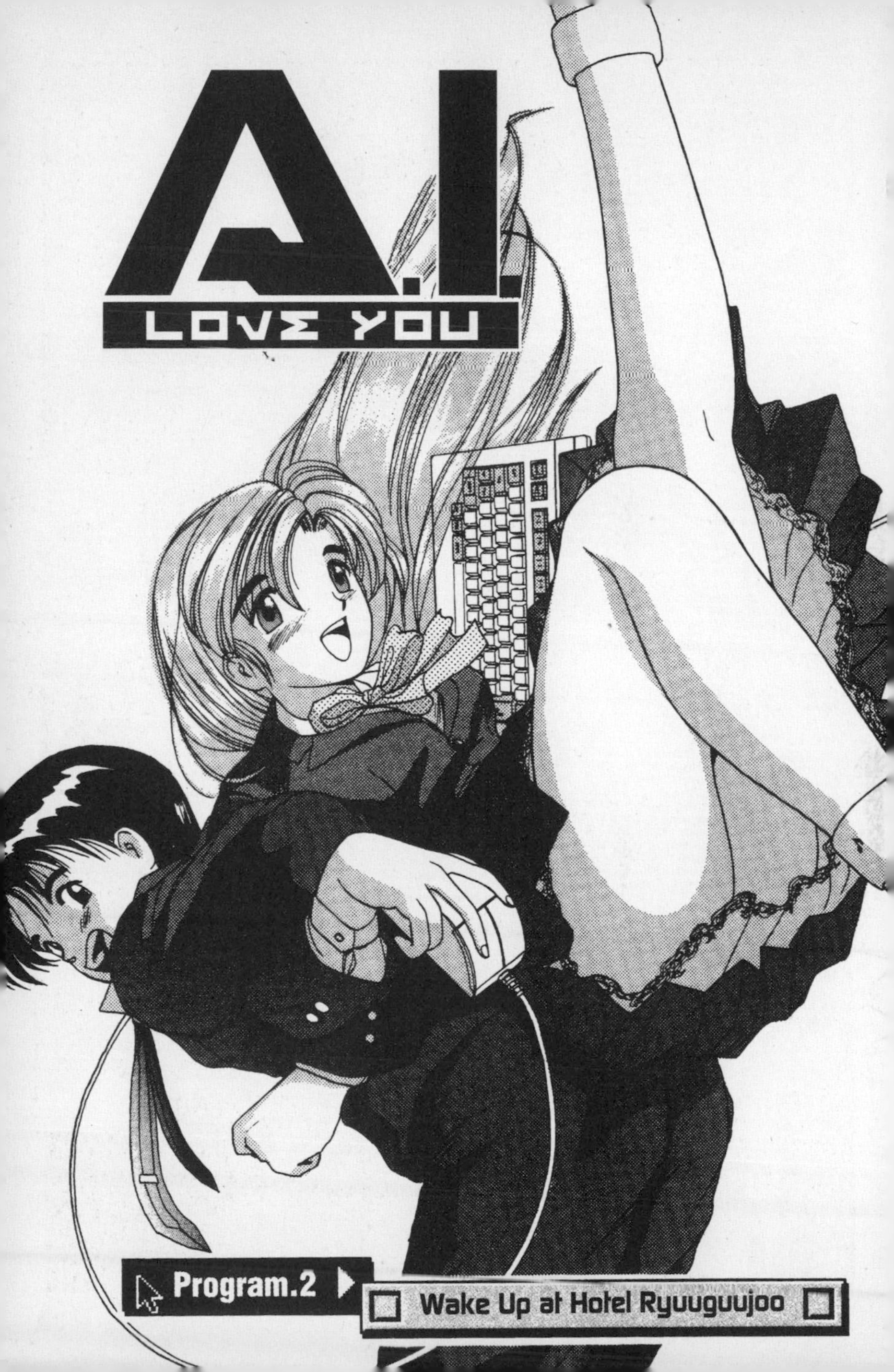
A.I.
LOVE YOU
Program.2
Wake Up at Hotel Ryuuguujoo

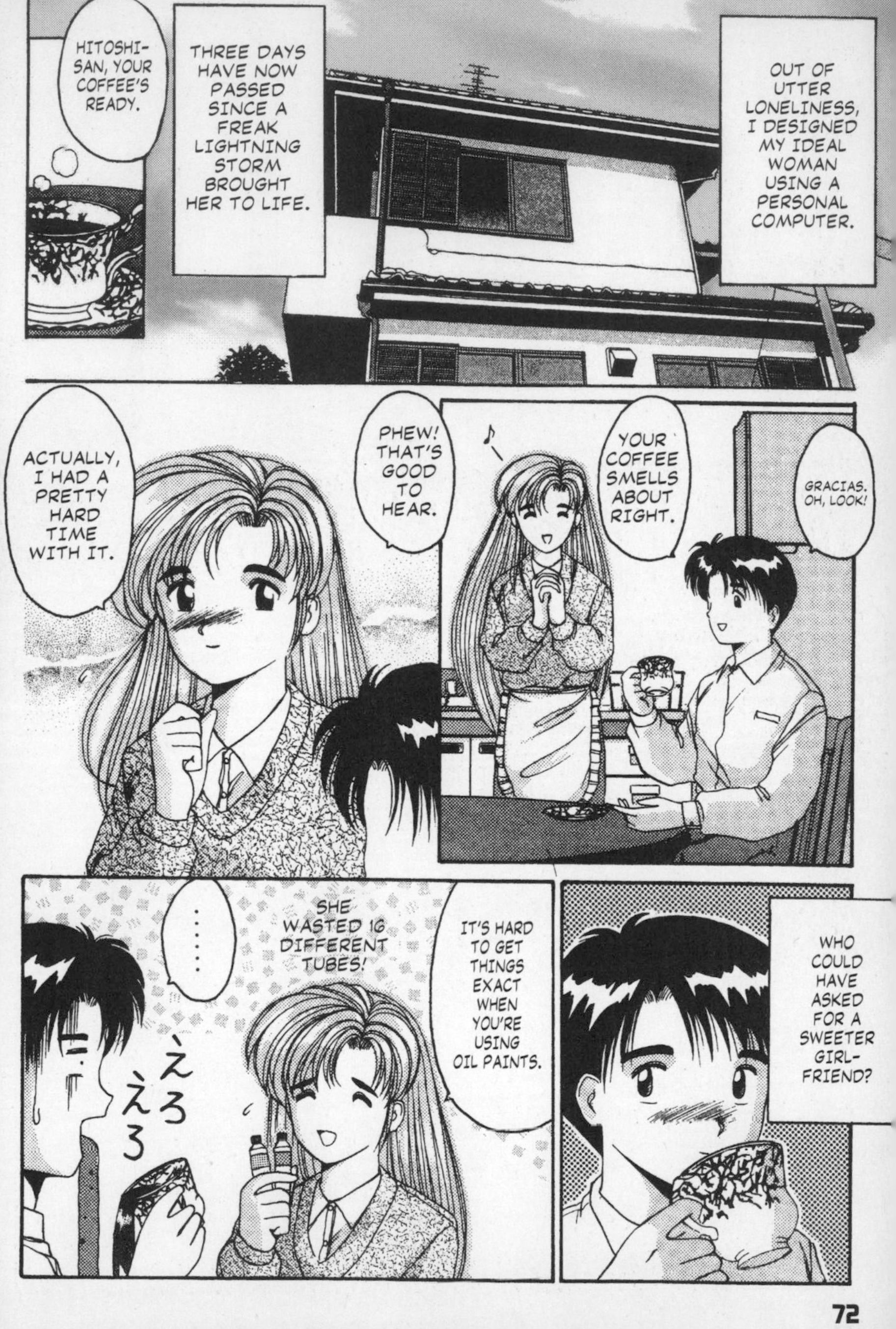
OUT OF UTTER LONELINESS, I DESIGNED MY IDEAL WOMAN USING A PERSONAL COMPUTER.
THREE DAYS HAVE NOW PASSED SINCE A FREAK LIGHTNING STORM BROUGHT HER TO LIFE.
HITOSHI-SAN, YOUR COFFEE'S READY.
GRACIAS. OH, LOOK!
YOUR COFFEE SMELLS ABOUT RIGHT.
PHEW! THAT'S GOOD TO HEAR.
ACTUALLY, I HAD A PRETTY HARD TIME WITH IT.
WHO COULD HAVE ASKED FOR A SWEETER GIRL-FRIEND?
IT'S HARD TO GET THINGS EXACT WHEN YOU'RE USING OIL PAINTS.
SHE WASTED 16 DIFFERENT TUBES!
......
えろえろ

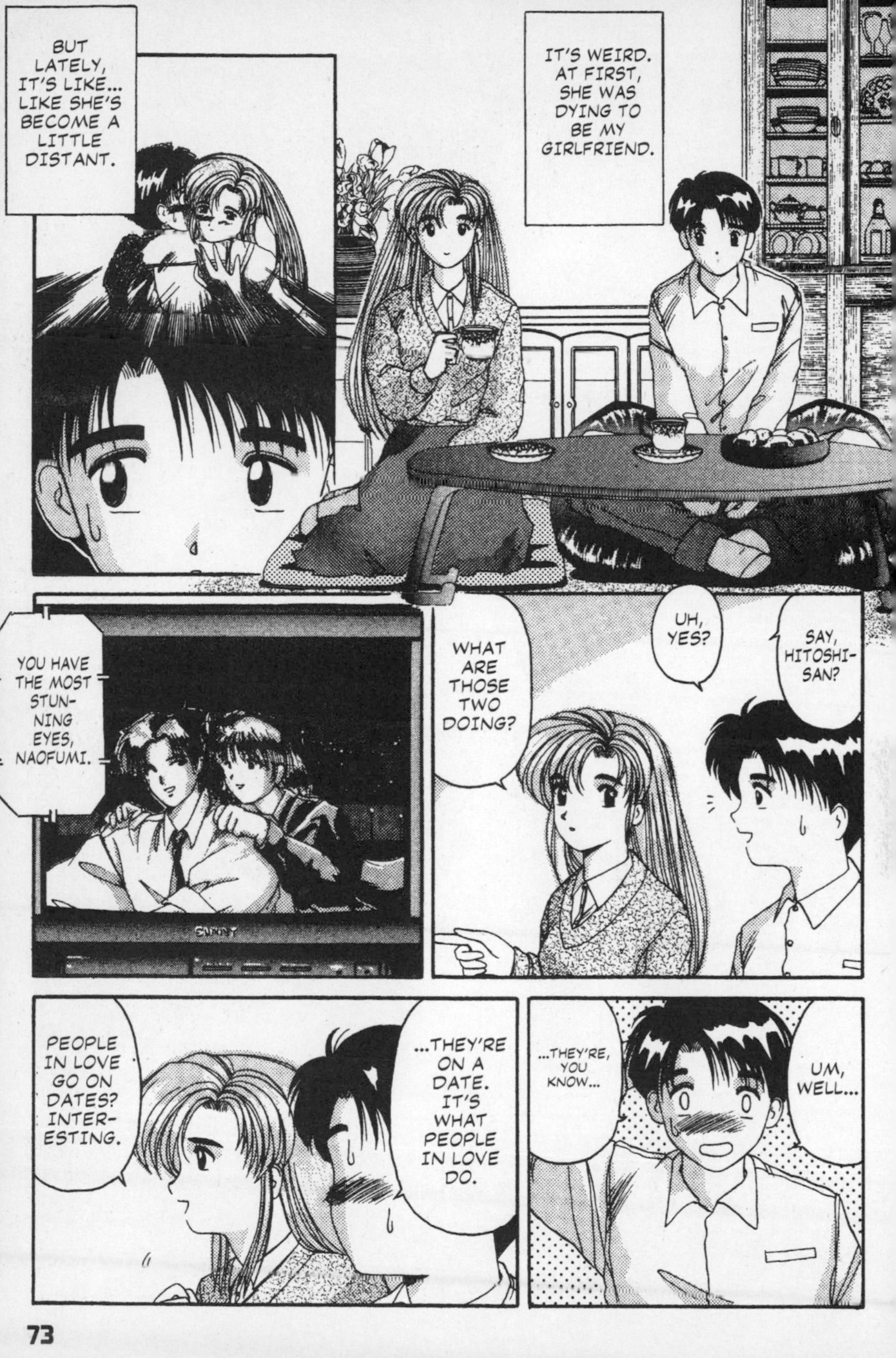
IT'S WEIRD. AT FIRST, SHE WAS DYING TO BE MY GIRLFRIEND.
BUT LATELY, IT'S LIKE... LIKE SHE'S BECOME A LITTLE DISTANT.
SAY, HITOSHI-SAN?
UH, YES?
WHAT ARE THOSE TWO DOING?
YOU HAVE THE MOST STUN-NING EYES, NAOFUMI.
UM, WELL...
...THEY'RE, YOU KNOW...
...THEY'RE ON A DATE. IT'S WHAT PEOPLE IN LOVE DO.
PEOPLE IN LOVE GO ON DATES? INTER-ESTING.

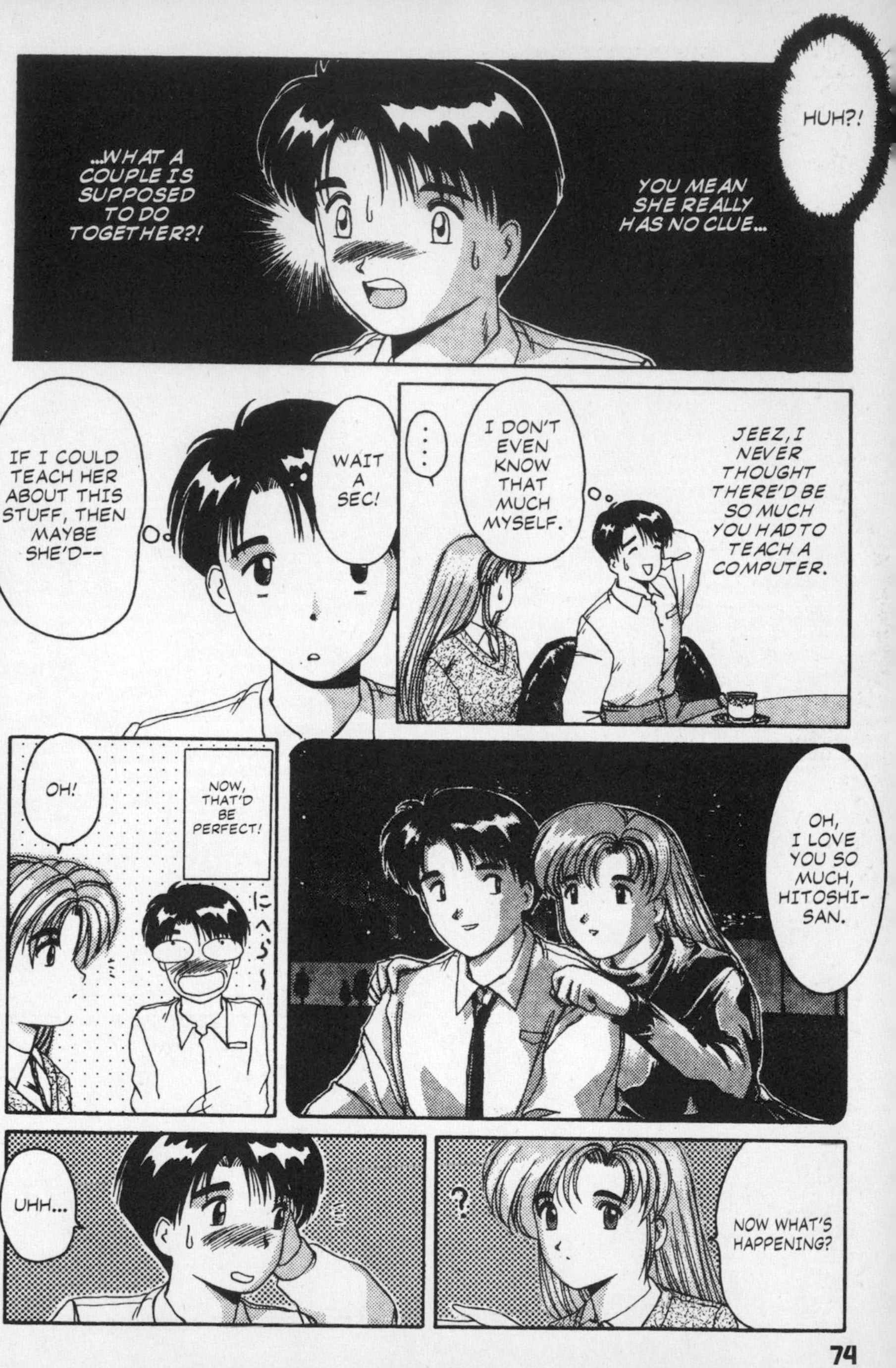
HUH?!
YOU MEAN SHE REALLY HAS NO CLUE...
...WHAT A COUPLE IS SUPPOSED TO DO TOGETHER?!
JEEZ, I NEVER THOUGHT THERE'D BE SO MUCH YOU HAD TO TEACH A COMPUTER.
I DON'T EVEN KNOW THAT MUCH MYSELF.
....
WAIT A SEC!
IF I COULD TEACH HER ABOUT THIS STUFF, THEN MAYBE SHE'D--
OH, I LOVE YOU SO MUCH, HITOSHI-SAN.
NOW, THAT'D BE PERFECT!
にへら~
OH!
NOW WHAT'S HAPPENING?
?
UHH...

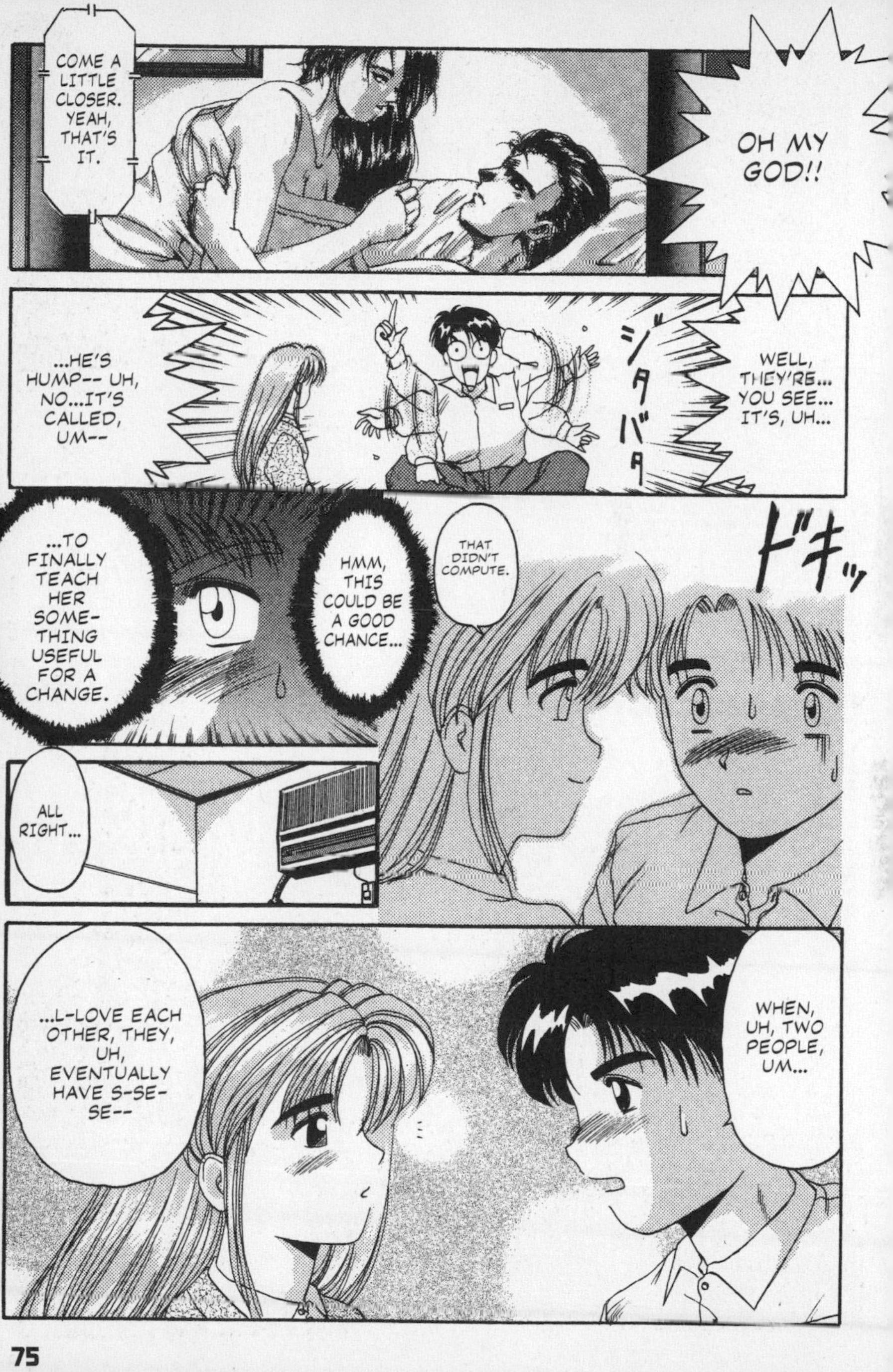
COME A LITTLE CLOSER. YEAH, THAT'S IT.
OH MY GOD!!
ジタバタ
WELL, THEY'RE... YOU SEE... IT'S, UH...
...HE'S HUMP-- UH, NO...IT'S CALLED, UM--
ドキッ
THAT DIDN'T COMPUTE.
HMM, THIS COULD BE A GOOD CHANCE...
...TO FINALLY TEACH HER SOME-THING USEFUL FOR A CHANGE.
ALL RIGHT...
WHEN, UH, TWO PEOPLE, UM...
...L-LOVE EACH OTHER, THEY, UH, EVENTUALLY HAVE S-SE-SE--

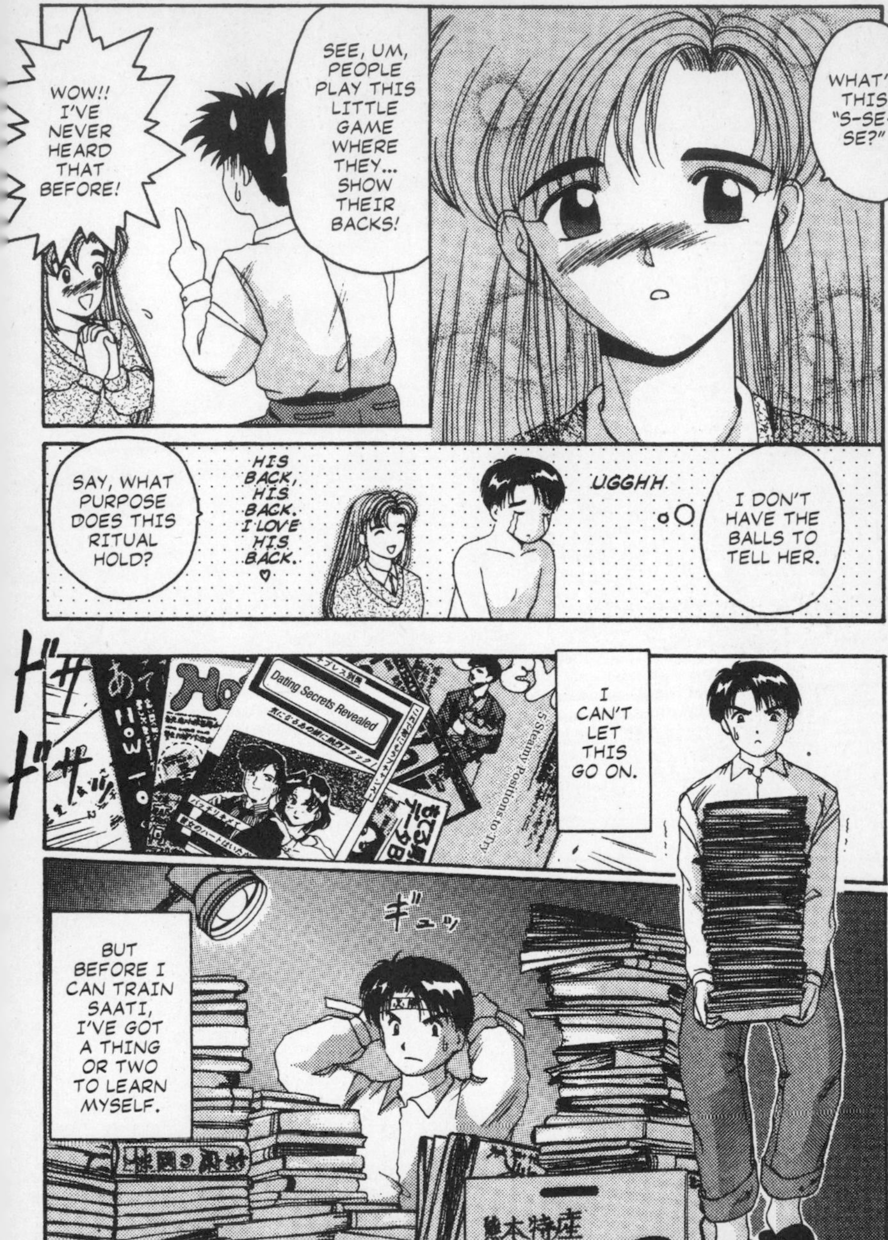
WHAT'S THIS "S-SE-SE?"
SEE, UM, PEOPLE PLAY THIS LITTLE GAME WHERE THEY... SHOW THEIR BACKS!
WOW!! I'VE NEVER HEARD THAT BEFORE!
I DON'T HAVE THE BALLS TO TELL HER.
UGGHH
HIS BACK, HIS BACK. I LOVE HIS BACK. ♡
SAY, WHAT PURPOSE DOES THIS RITUAL HOLD?
I CAN'T LET THIS GO ON.
5 Steamy Positions to Try
Dating Secrets Revealed
HOW TO
BUT BEFORE I CAN TRAIN SAATI, I'VE GOT A THING OR TWO TO LEARN MYSELF.

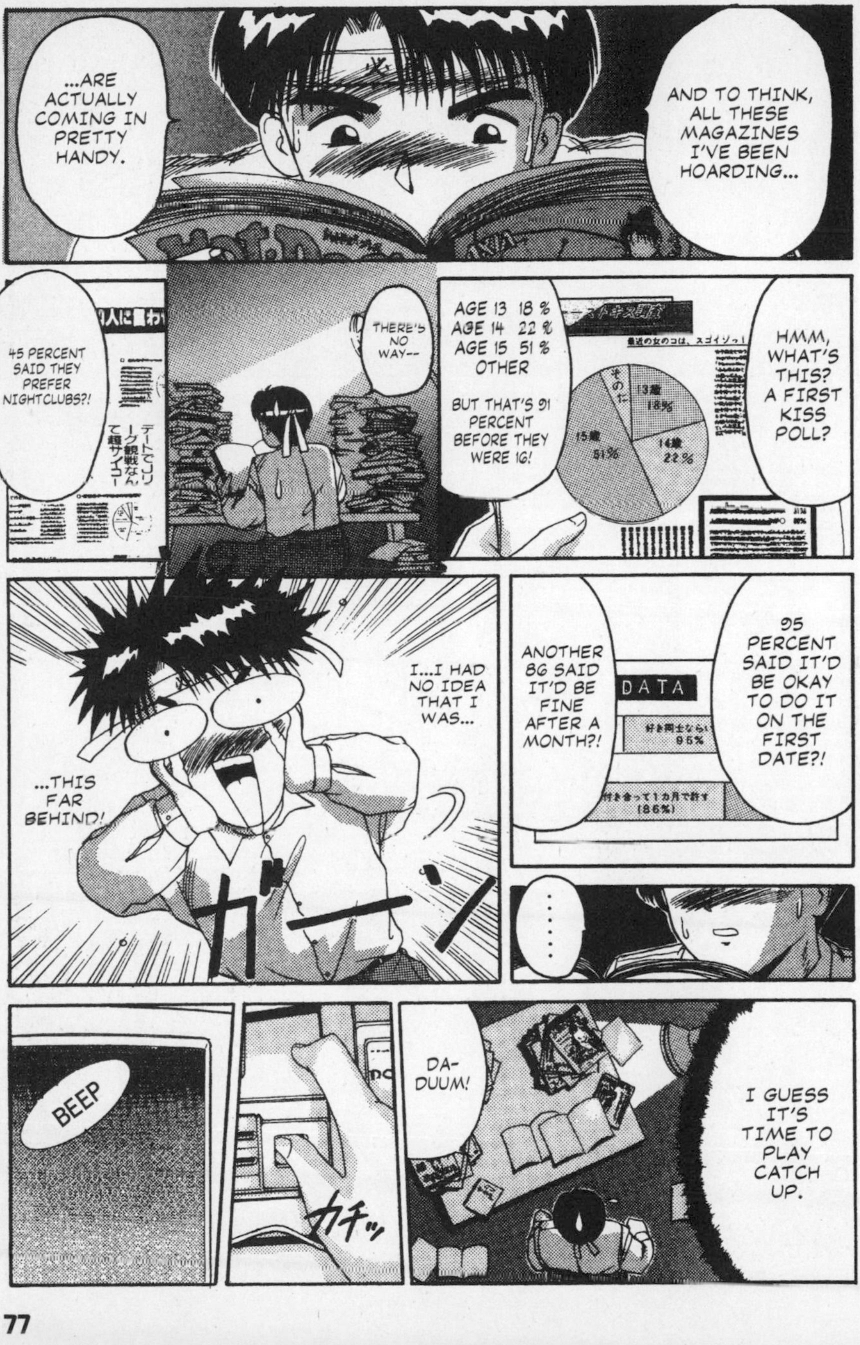
AND TO THINK, ALL THESE MAGAZINES I'VE BEEN HOARDING...
...ARE ACTUALLY COMING IN PRETTY HANDY.
HMM, WHAT'S THIS? A FIRST KISS POLL?
最近の女のコは、スゴイゾっ!
13歳 18%
14歳 22%
15歳 51%
そのた
AGE 13 18%
AGE 14 22%
AGE 15 51%
OTHER
BUT THAT'S 91 PERCENT BEFORE THEY WERE 16!
THERE'S NO WAY--
45 PERCENT SAID THEY PREFER NIGHTCLUBS?!
95 PERCENT SAID IT'D BE OKAY TO DO IT ON THE FIRST DATE?!
ANOTHER 86 SAID IT'D BE FINE AFTER A MONTH?!
DATA
95%
付き合って1カ月で許す (86%)
......
I...I HAD NO IDEA THAT I WAS...
...THIS FAR BEHIND!
ガーン
I GUESS IT'S TIME TO PLAY CATCH UP.
DA-DUUM!
カチッ
BEEP

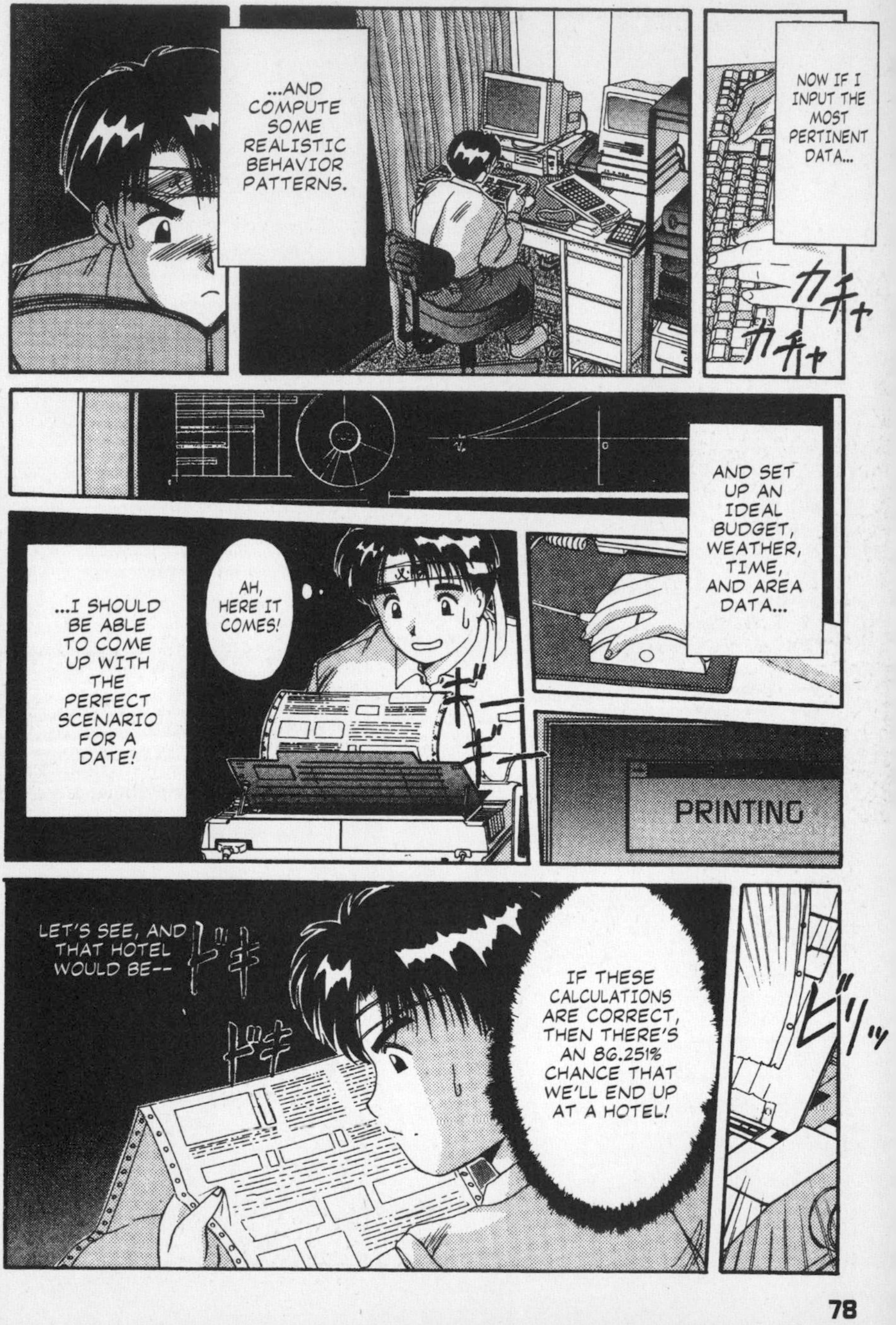
NOW IF I INPUT THE MOST PERTINENT DATA...
カチャ
カチャ
...AND COMPUTE SOME REALISTIC BEHAVIOR PATTERNS.
AND SET UP AN IDEAL BUDGET, WEATHER, TIME, AND AREA DATA...
PRINTING
...I SHOULD BE ABLE TO COME UP WITH THE PERFECT SCENARIO FOR A DATE!
AH, HERE IT COMES!
ギー
ギー
ビリッ
IF THESE CALCULATIONS ARE CORRECT, THEN THERE'S AN 86.251% CHANCE THAT WE'LL END UP AT A HOTEL!
LET'S SEE, AND THAT HOTEL WOULD BE--
ドキ
ドキ

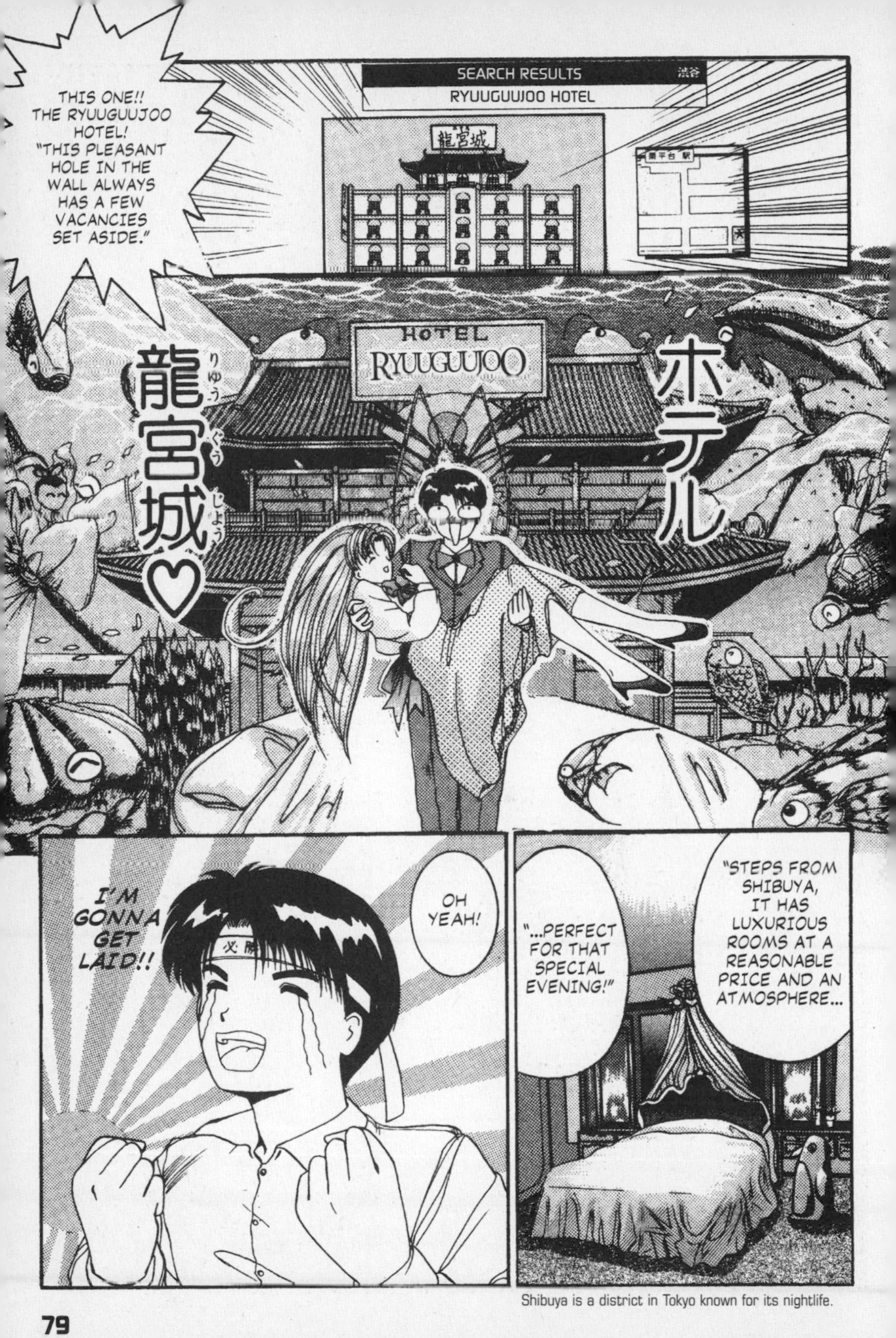
SEARCH RESULTS 渋谷
RYUUGUUJOO HOTEL
龍宮城
HOTEL RYUUGUUJOO
ホテル
龍宮城♡
THIS ONE!! THE RYUUGUUJOO HOTEL! "THIS PLEASANT HOLE IN THE WALL ALWAYS HAS A FEW VACANCIES SET ASIDE."
"STEPS FROM SHIBUYA, IT HAS LUXURIOUS ROOMS AT A REASONABLE PRICE AND AN ATMOSPHERE...
"...PERFECT FOR THAT SPECIAL EVENING!"
OH YEAH!
I'M GONNA GET LAID!!

Shibuya is a district in Tokyo known for its nightlife.

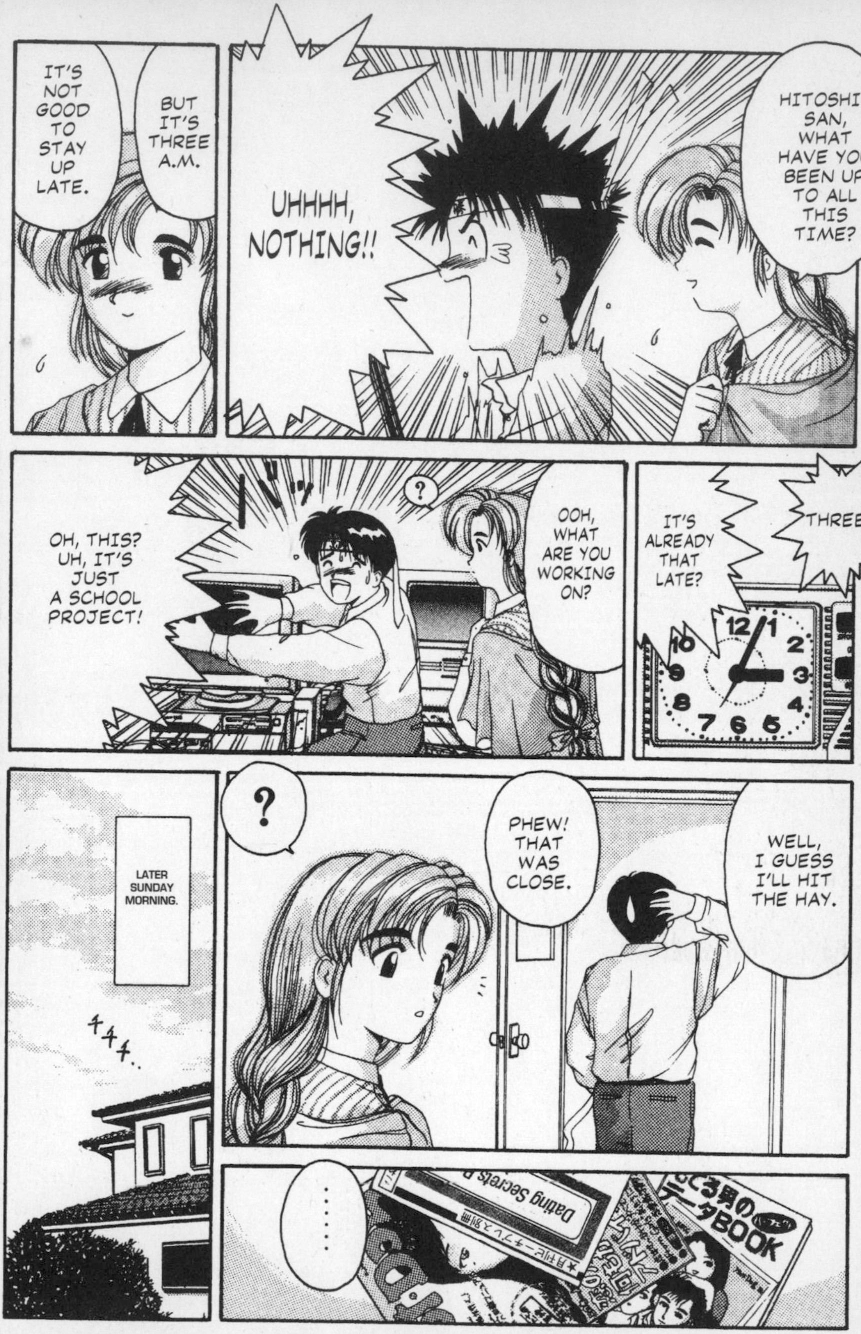
HITOSHI-SAN, WHAT HAVE YOU BEEN UP TO ALL THIS TIME?
UHHHH, NOTHING!!
BUT IT'S THREE A.M.
IT'S NOT GOOD TO STAY UP LATE.
THREE?
IT'S ALREADY THAT LATE?
OOH, WHAT ARE YOU WORKING ON?
OH, THIS? UH, IT'S JUST A SCHOOL PROJECT!
WELL, I GUESS I'LL HIT THE HAY.
PHEW! THAT WAS CLOSE.
?
......
Dating Secrets
LATER SUNDAY MORNING.
チチチ...

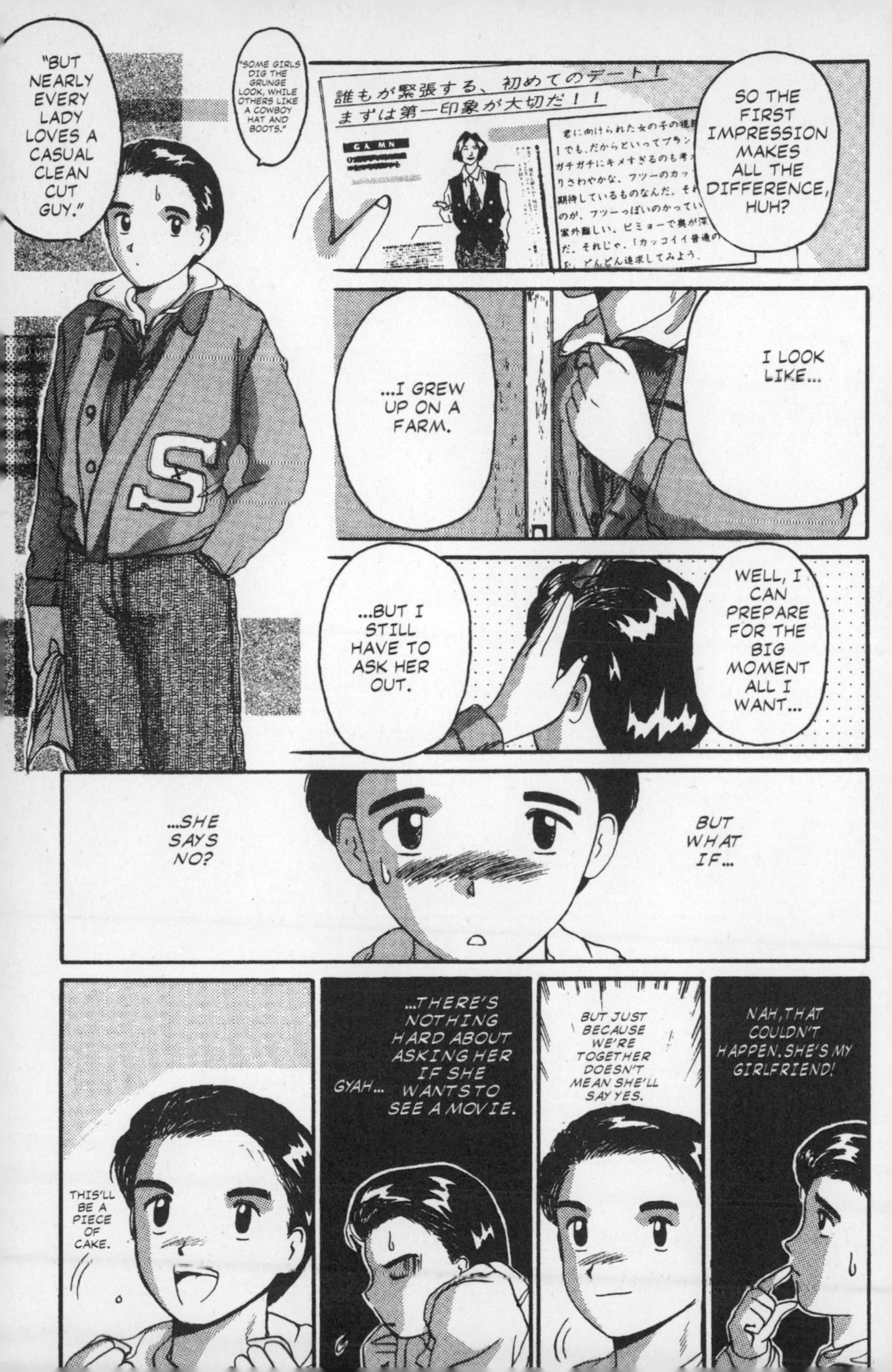

誰もが緊張する、初めてのデート！
まずは第一印象が大切だ！！
SO THE FIRST IMPRESSION MAKES ALL THE DIFFERENCE, HUH?
I LOOK LIKE...
...I GREW UP ON A FARM.
WELL, I CAN PREPARE FOR THE BIG MOMENT ALL I WANT...
...BUT I STILL HAVE TO ASK HER OUT.
"SOME GIRLS DIG THE GRUNGE LOOK, WHILE OTHERS LIKE A COWBOY HAT AND BOOTS."
"BUT NEARLY EVERY LADY LOVES A CASUAL CLEAN CUT GUY."
BUT WHAT IF...
...SHE SAYS NO?
NAH, THAT COULDN'T HAPPEN. SHE'S MY GIRLFRIEND!
BUT JUST BECAUSE WE'RE TOGETHER DOESN'T MEAN SHE'LL SAY YES.
...THERE'S NOTHING HARD ABOUT ASKING HER IF SHE WANTS TO SEE A MOVIE.
GYAH...
THIS'LL BE A PIECE OF CAKE.

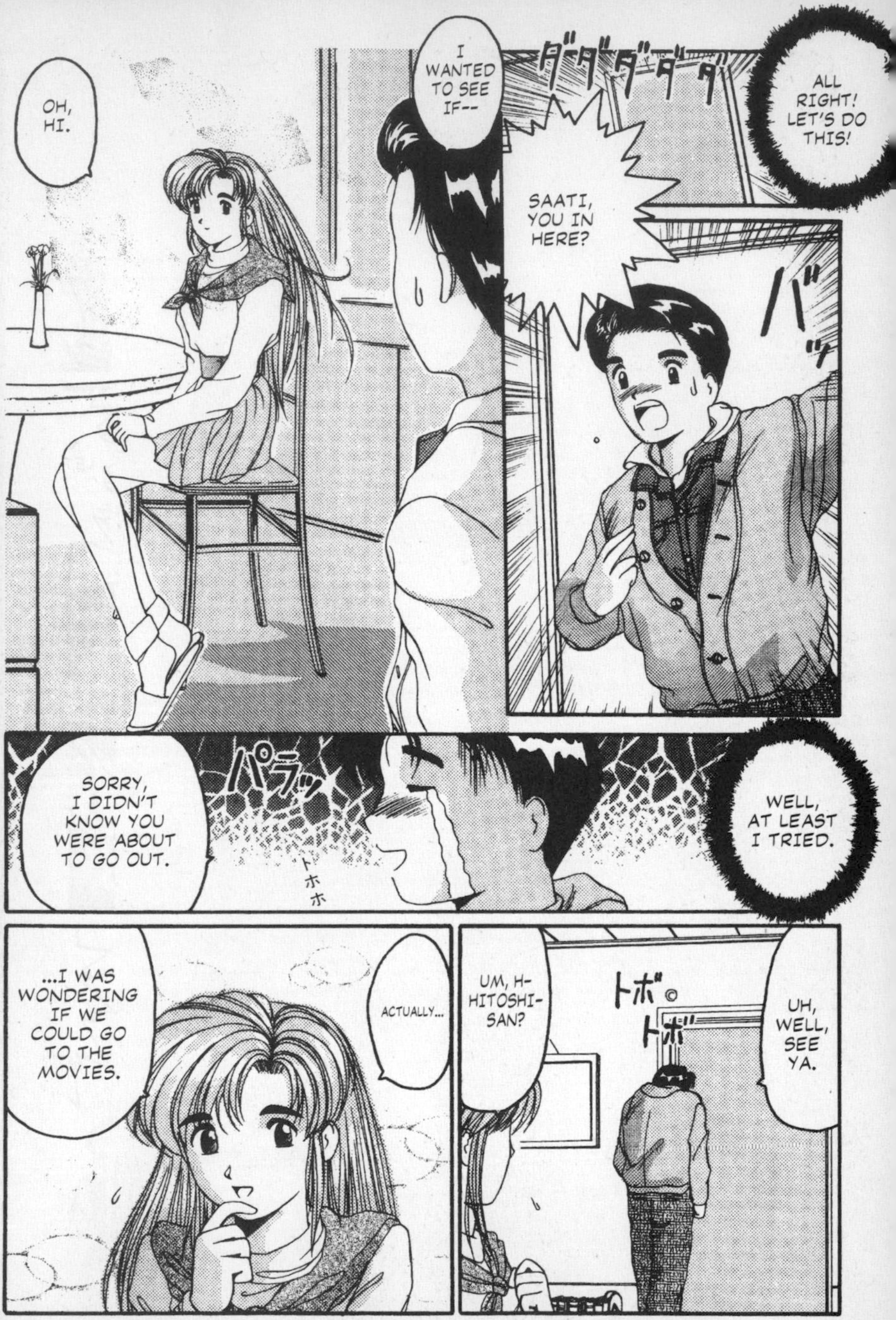
ALL RIGHT! LET'S DO THIS!
ダダダダダ
バッ
SAATI, YOU IN HERE?
I WANTED TO SEE IF--
OH, HI.
WELL, AT LEAST I TRIED.
トホホ
パラッ
SORRY, I DIDN'T KNOW YOU WERE ABOUT TO GO OUT.
UH, WELL, SEE YA.
トボ
トボ
UM, H-HITOSHI-SAN?
ACTUALLY...
...I WAS WONDERING IF WE COULD GO TO THE MOVIES.

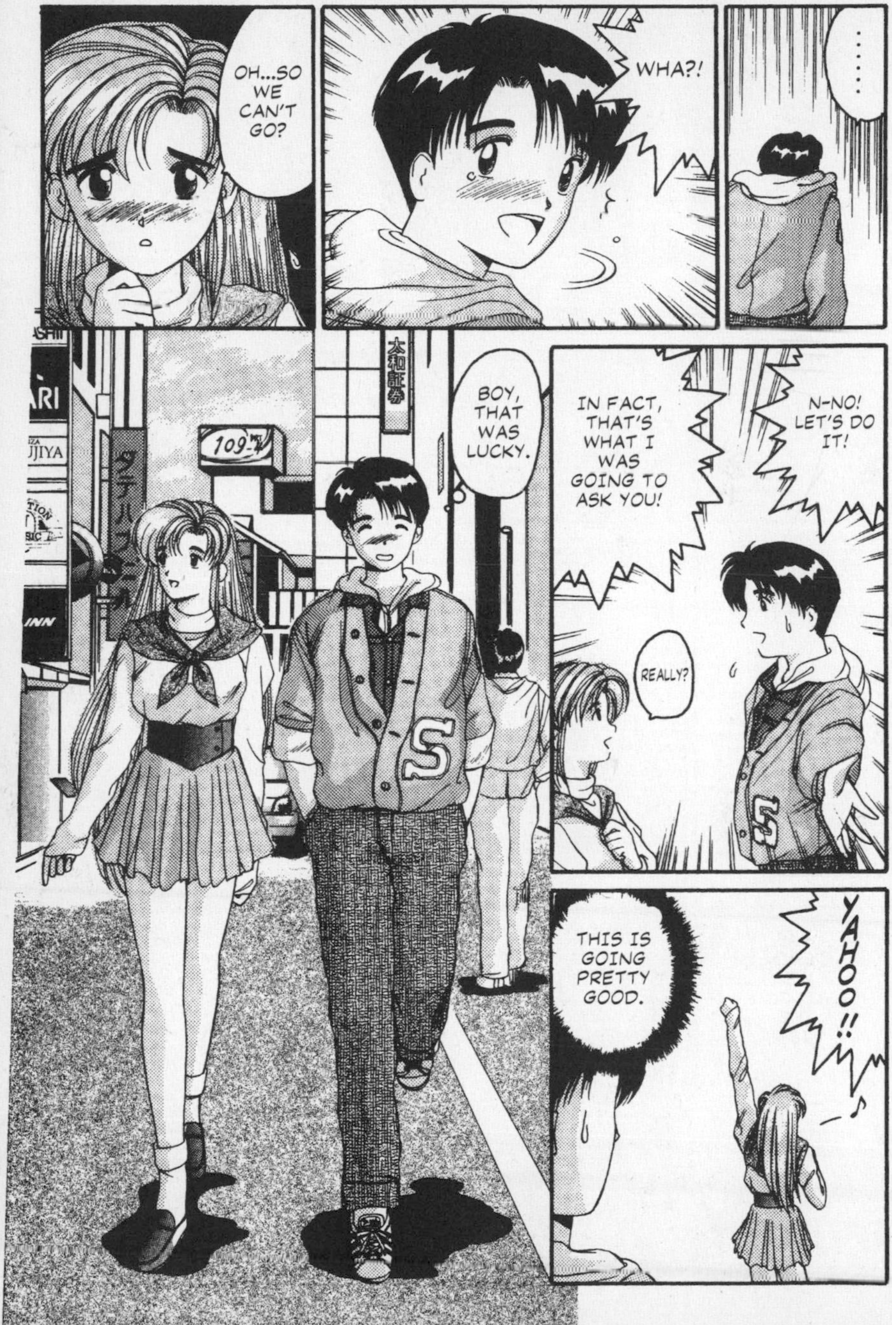
……
WHA?!
OH...SO WE CAN'T GO?
N-NO! LET'S DO IT!
IN FACT, THAT'S WHAT I WAS GOING TO ASK YOU!
REALLY?
YAHOO!!
THIS IS GOING PRETTY GOOD.
大和証券
BOY, THAT WAS LUCKY.

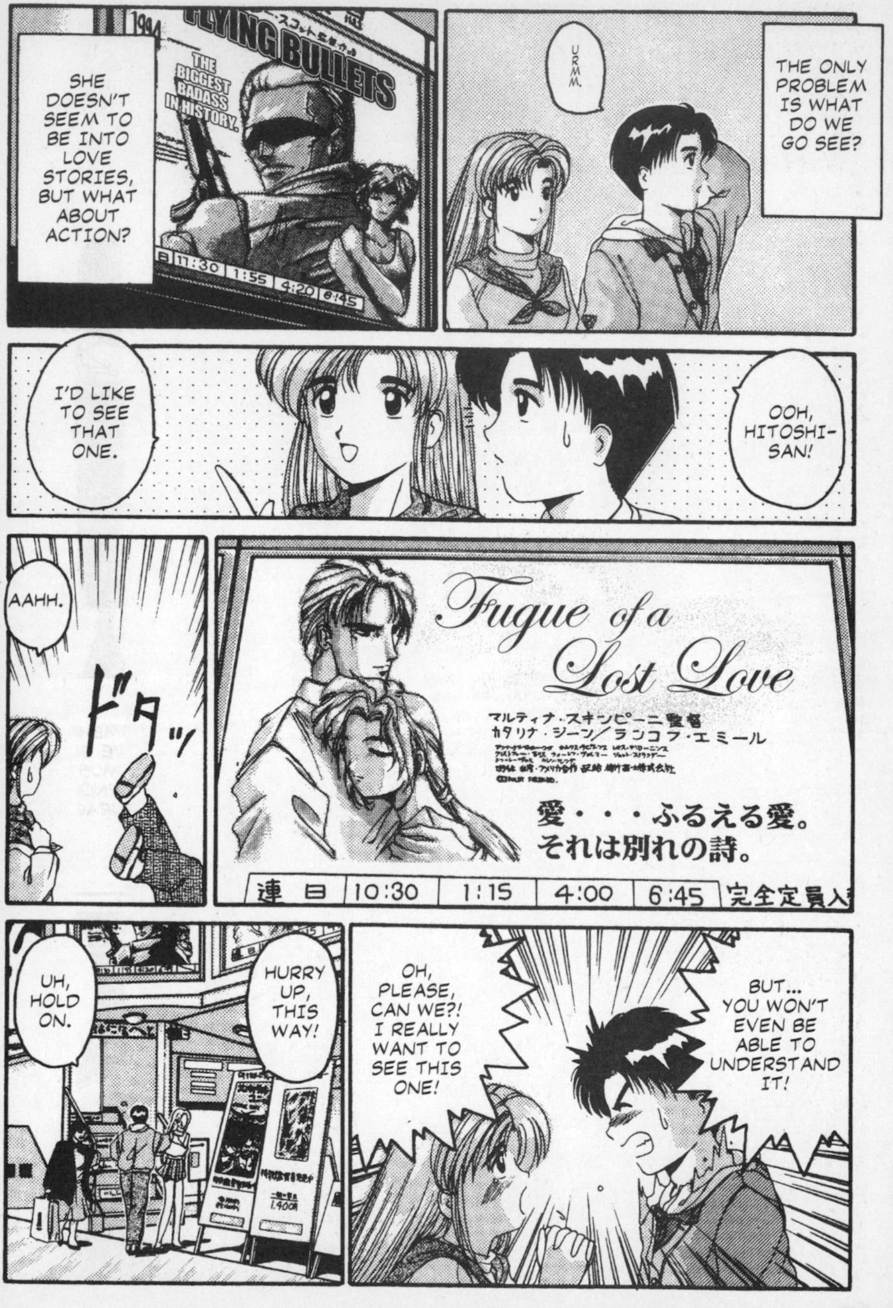
THE ONLY PROBLEM IS WHAT DO WE GO SEE?
URMM.
SHE DOESN'T SEEM TO BE INTO LOVE STORIES, BUT WHAT ABOUT ACTION?
FLYING BULLETS
THE BIGGEST BADASS IN HISTORY.
11:30 1:55 4:20 6:45
OOH, HITOSHI-SAN!
I'D LIKE TO SEE THAT ONE.
Fugue of a Lost Love
マルティナ・スキンピーニ監督
カタリナ・ジーン／ランコフ・エミール
愛・・・ふるえる愛。
それは別れの詩。
連日 10:30 1:15 4:00 6:45
AAHH.
ドタッ
BUT... YOU WON'T EVEN BE ABLE TO UNDERSTAND IT!
OH, PLEASE, CAN WE?! I REALLY WANT TO SEE THIS ONE!
HURRY UP, THIS WAY!
UH, HOLD ON.

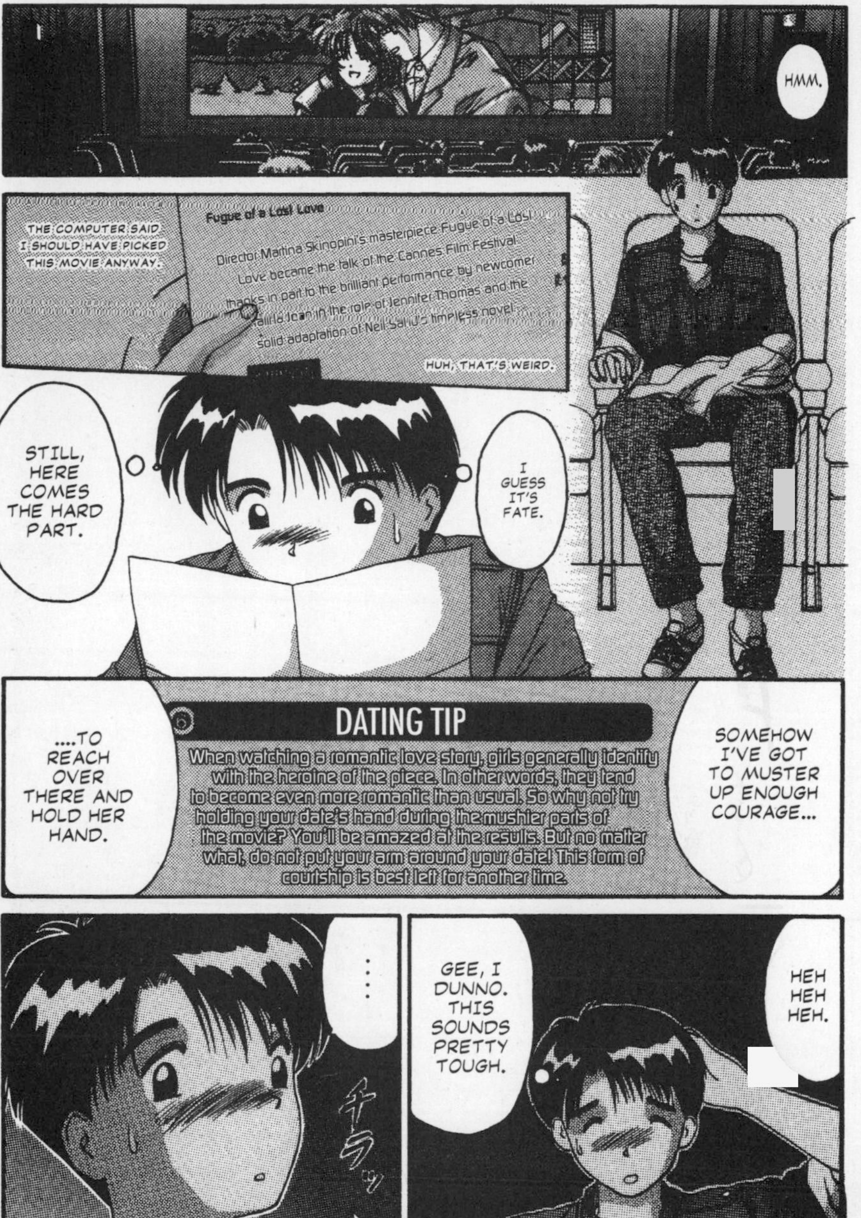
HMM.
HUH, THAT'S WEIRD.
THE COMPUTER SAID I SHOULD HAVE PICKED THIS MOVIE ANYWAY.
Fugue of a Lost Love
Director Martina Skinopini's masterpiece Fugue of a Lost Love became the talk of the Cannes Film Festival thanks in part to the brilliant performance by newcomer
in the role of Jennifer Thomas and the solid adaptation of Neil Sahu's timeless novel.
I GUESS IT'S FATE.
STILL, HERE COMES THE HARD PART.
SOMEHOW I'VE GOT TO MUSTER UP ENOUGH COURAGE...
DATING TIP
When watching a romantic love story, girls generally identify with the heroine of the piece. In other words, they tend to become even more romantic than usual. So why not try holding your date's hand during the mushier parts of the movie? You'll be amazed at the results. But no matter what, do not put your arm around your date! This form of courtship is best left for another time.
....TO REACH OVER THERE AND HOLD HER HAND.
HEH HEH HEH.
GEE, I DUNNO. THIS SOUNDS PRETTY TOUGH.
....
チラッ

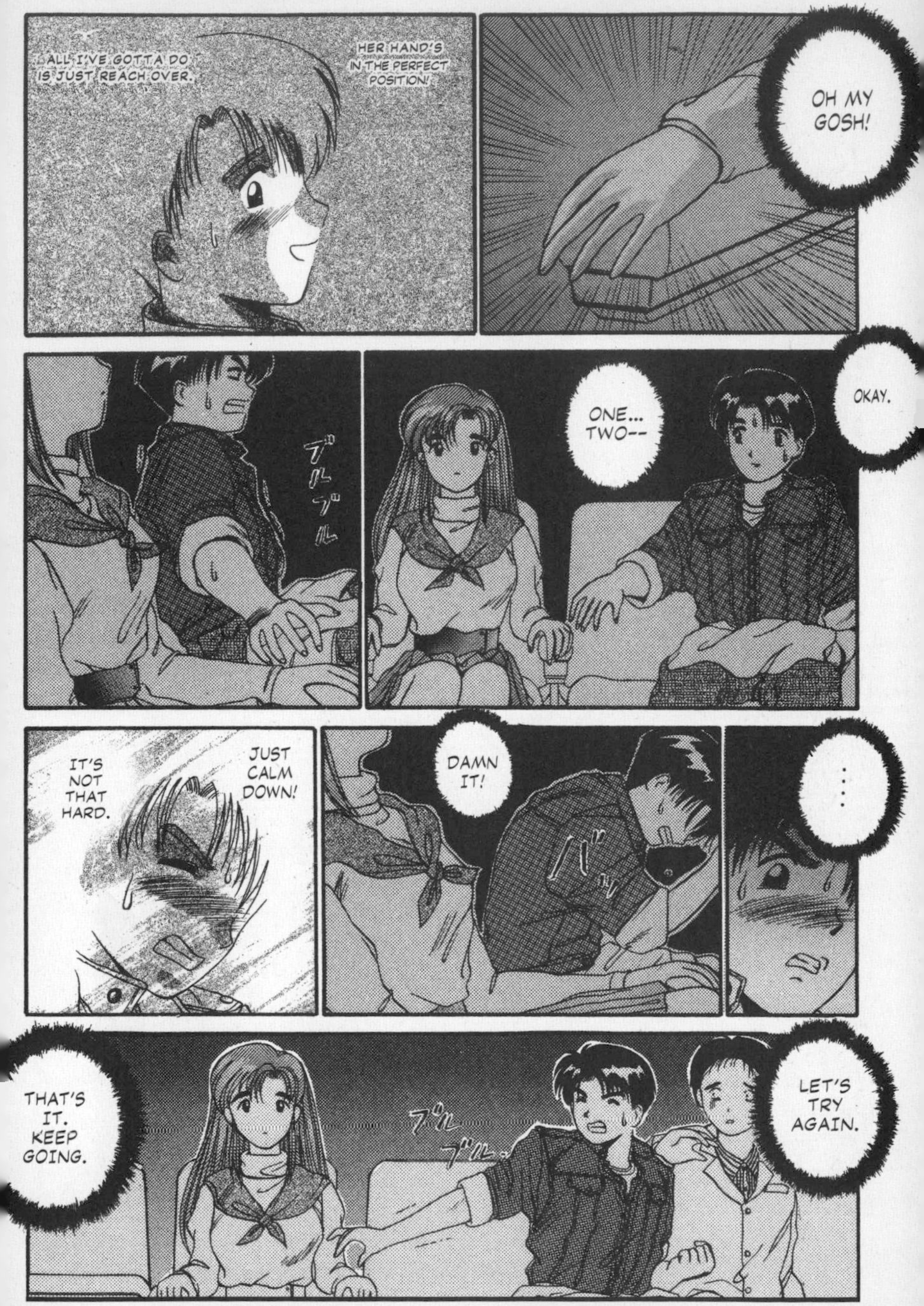
OH MY GOSH!
HER HAND'S IN THE PERFECT POSITION!
...ALL I'VE GOTTA DO IS JUST REACH OVER.
OKAY.
ONE... TWO--
ブルブル
....
DAMN IT!
バッ
JUST CALM DOWN!
IT'S NOT THAT HARD.
LET'S TRY AGAIN.
ブルブル
THAT'S IT. KEEP GOING.

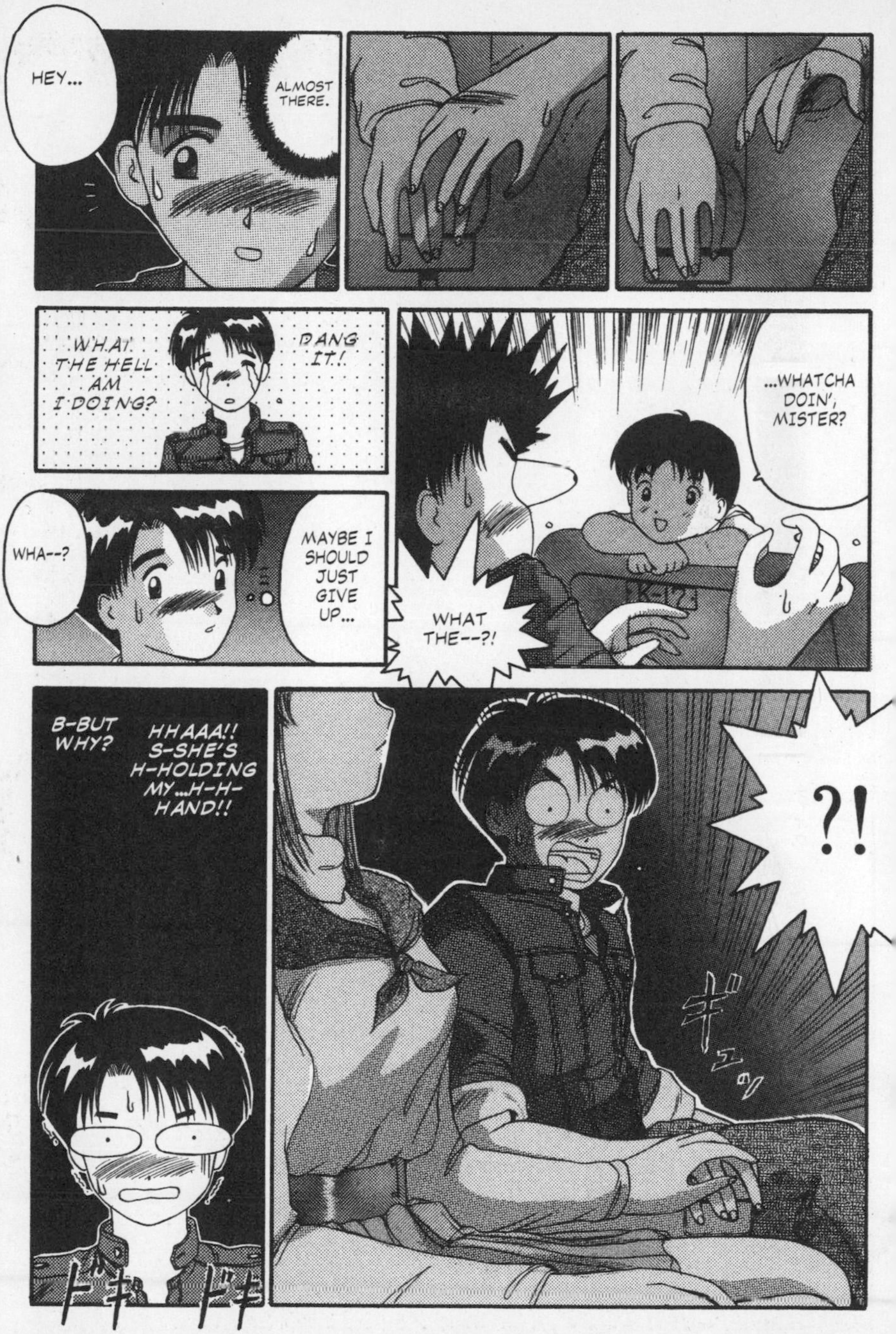
ALMOST THERE.
HEY...
...WHATCHA DOIN', MISTER?
WHAT THE--?!
DANG IT!
WHAT THE HELL AM I DOING?
MAYBE I SHOULD JUST GIVE UP...
WHA--?
?!
ギュッ
HHAAA!! S-SHE'S H-HOLDING MY...H-H-HAND!!
B-BUT WHY?
ドキ ドキ

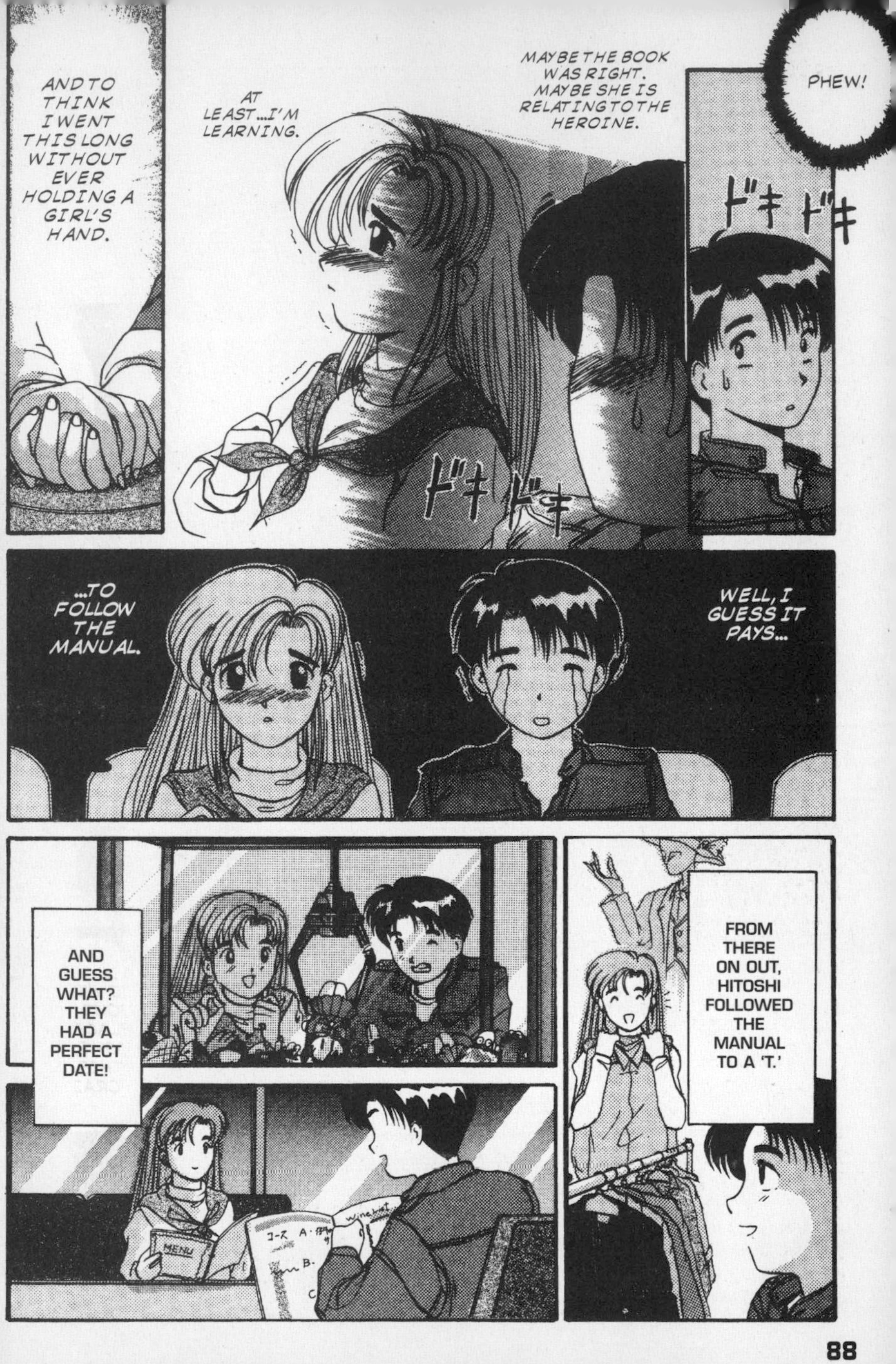
PHEW!
ドキドキ
MAYBE THE BOOK WAS RIGHT. MAYBE SHE IS RELATING TO THE HEROINE.
AT LEAST...I'M LEARNING.
ドキドキ
AND TO THINK I WENT THIS LONG WITHOUT EVER HOLDING A GIRL'S HAND.
WELL, I GUESS IT PAYS...
...TO FOLLOW THE MANUAL.
FROM THERE ON OUT, HITOSHI FOLLOWED THE MANUAL TO A 'T.'
AND GUESS WHAT? THEY HAD A PERFECT DATE!
MENU

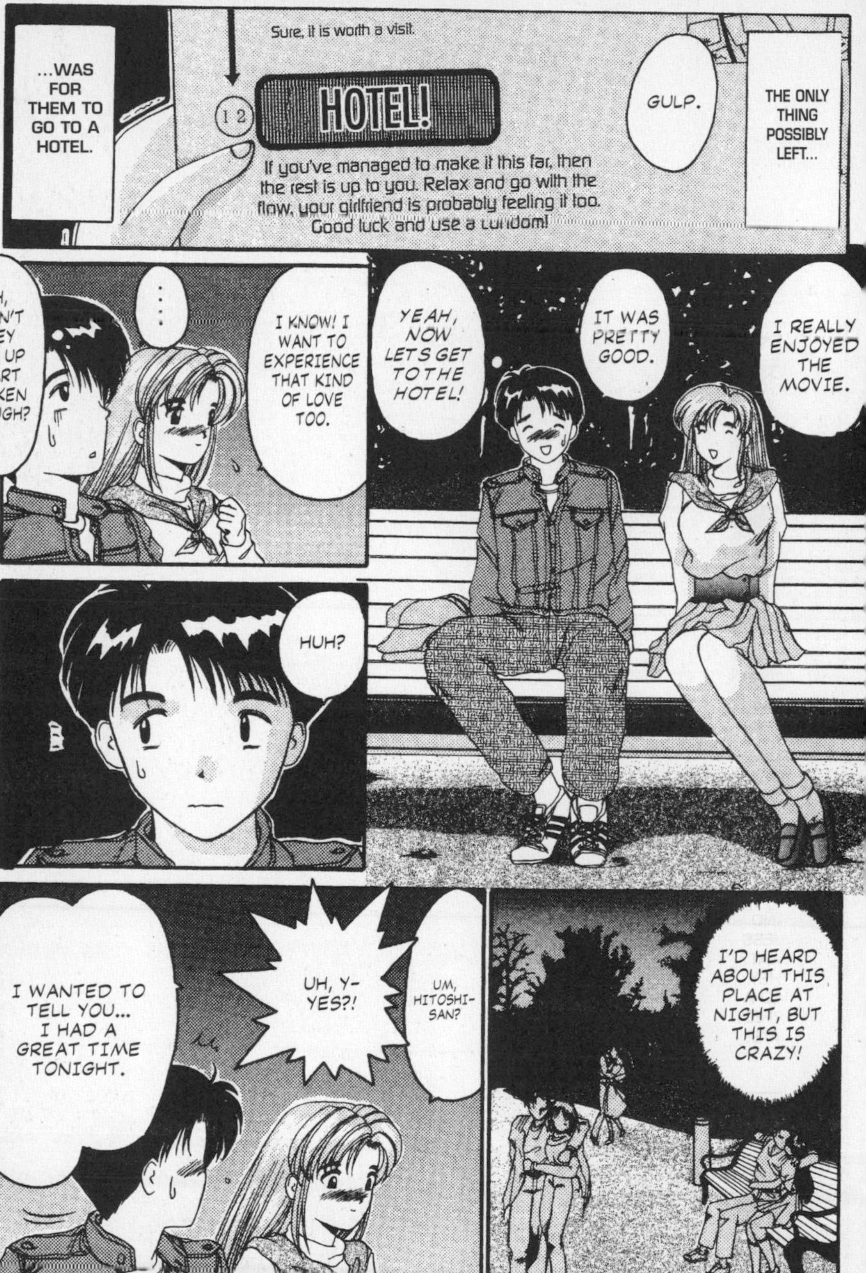
THE ONLY THING POSSIBLY LEFT...
GULP.
Sure, it is worth a visit.
12 HOTEL!
If you've managed to make it this far, then the rest is up to you. Relax and go with the flow, your girlfriend is probably feeling it too. Good luck and use a condom!
...WAS FOR THEM TO GO TO A HOTEL.
I REALLY ENJOYED THE MOVIE.
IT WAS PRETTY GOOD.
YEAH, NOW LETS GET TO THE HOTEL!
I KNOW! I WANT TO EXPERIENCE THAT KIND OF LOVE TOO.
....
UH, DIDN'T THEY END UP HEART BROKEN THOUGH?
HUH?
I'D HEARD ABOUT THIS PLACE AT NIGHT, BUT THIS IS CRAZY!
UM, HITOSHI-SAN?
UH, Y-YES?!
I WANTED TO TELL YOU... I HAD A GREAT TIME TONIGHT.

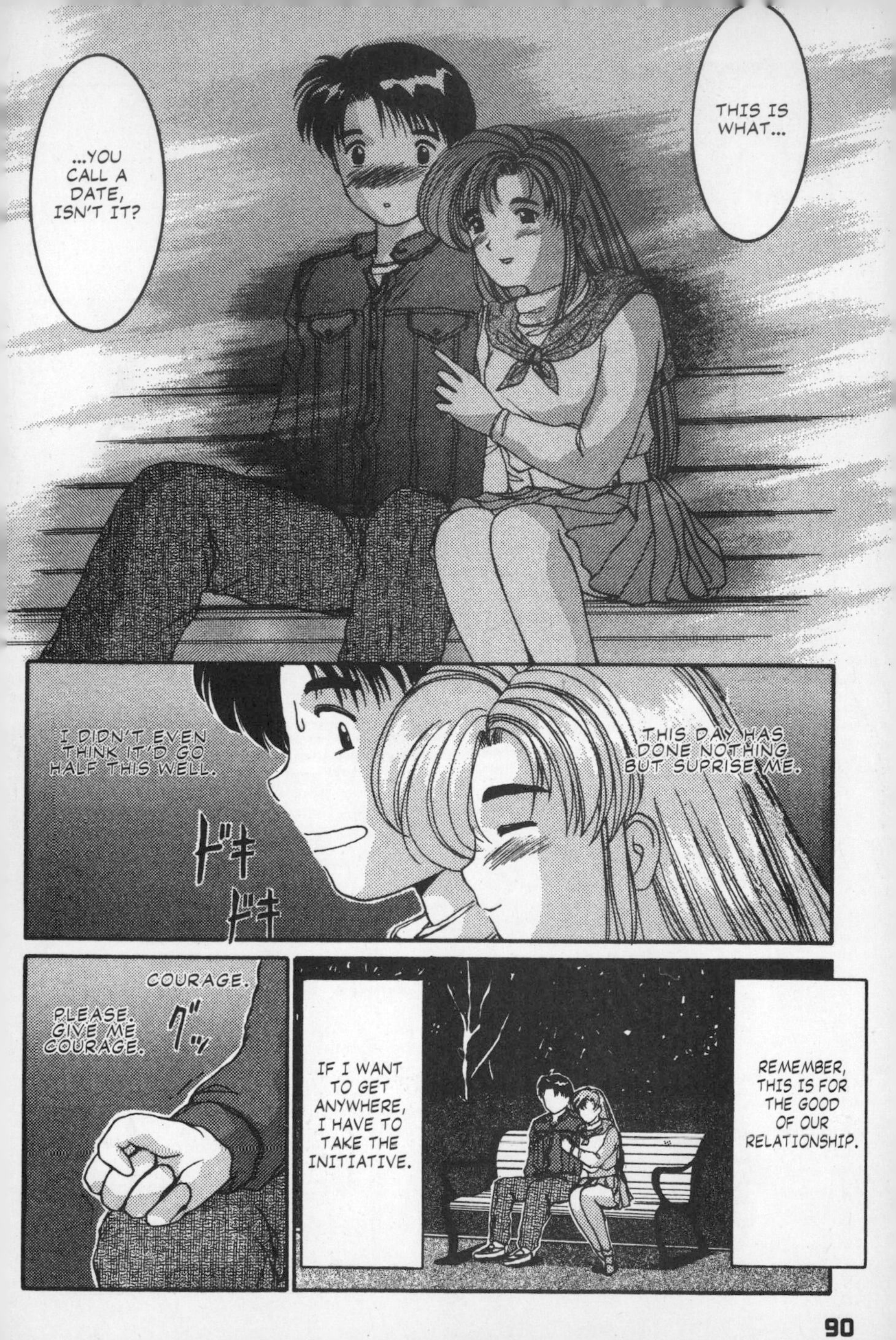

THIS IS WHAT...
...YOU CALL A DATE, ISN'T IT?
THIS DAY HAS DONE NOTHING BUT SUPRISE ME.
I DIDN'T EVEN THINK IT'D GO HALF THIS WELL.
ドキ
ドキ
REMEMBER, THIS IS FOR THE GOOD OF OUR RELATIONSHIP.
IF I WANT TO GET ANYWHERE, I HAVE TO TAKE THE INITIATIVE.
COURAGE.
PLEASE. GIVE ME COURAGE.
グッ

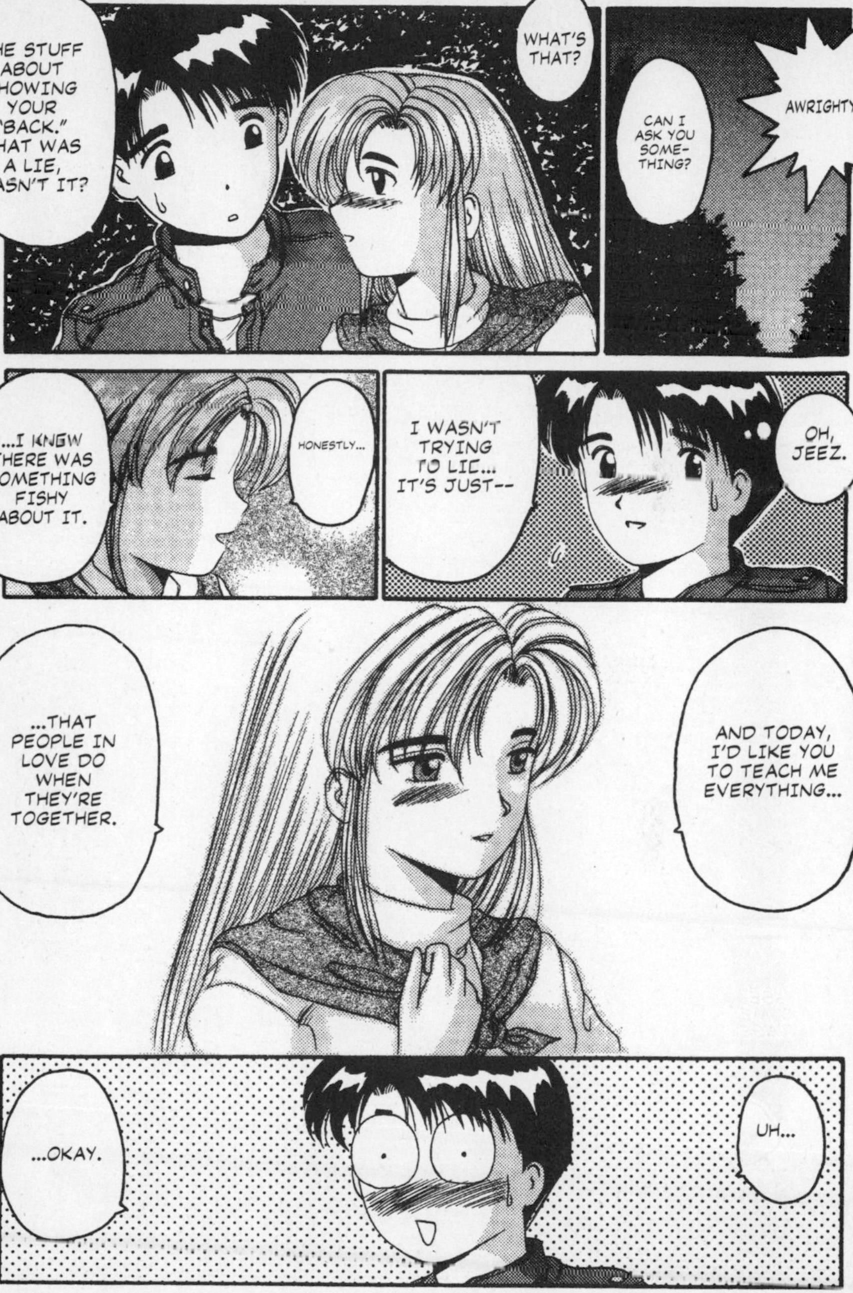
AWRIGHTY!
CAN I ASK YOU SOME-THING?
WHAT'S THAT?
THE STUFF ABOUT SHOWING YOUR "BACK." THAT WAS A LIE, WASN'T IT?
OH, JEEZ.
I WASN'T TRYING TO LIE... IT'S JUST--
HONESTLY...
...I KNEW THERE WAS SOMETHING FISHY ABOUT IT.
AND TODAY, I'D LIKE YOU TO TEACH ME EVERYTHING...
...THAT PEOPLE IN LOVE DO WHEN THEY'RE TOGETHER.
UH...
...OKAY.

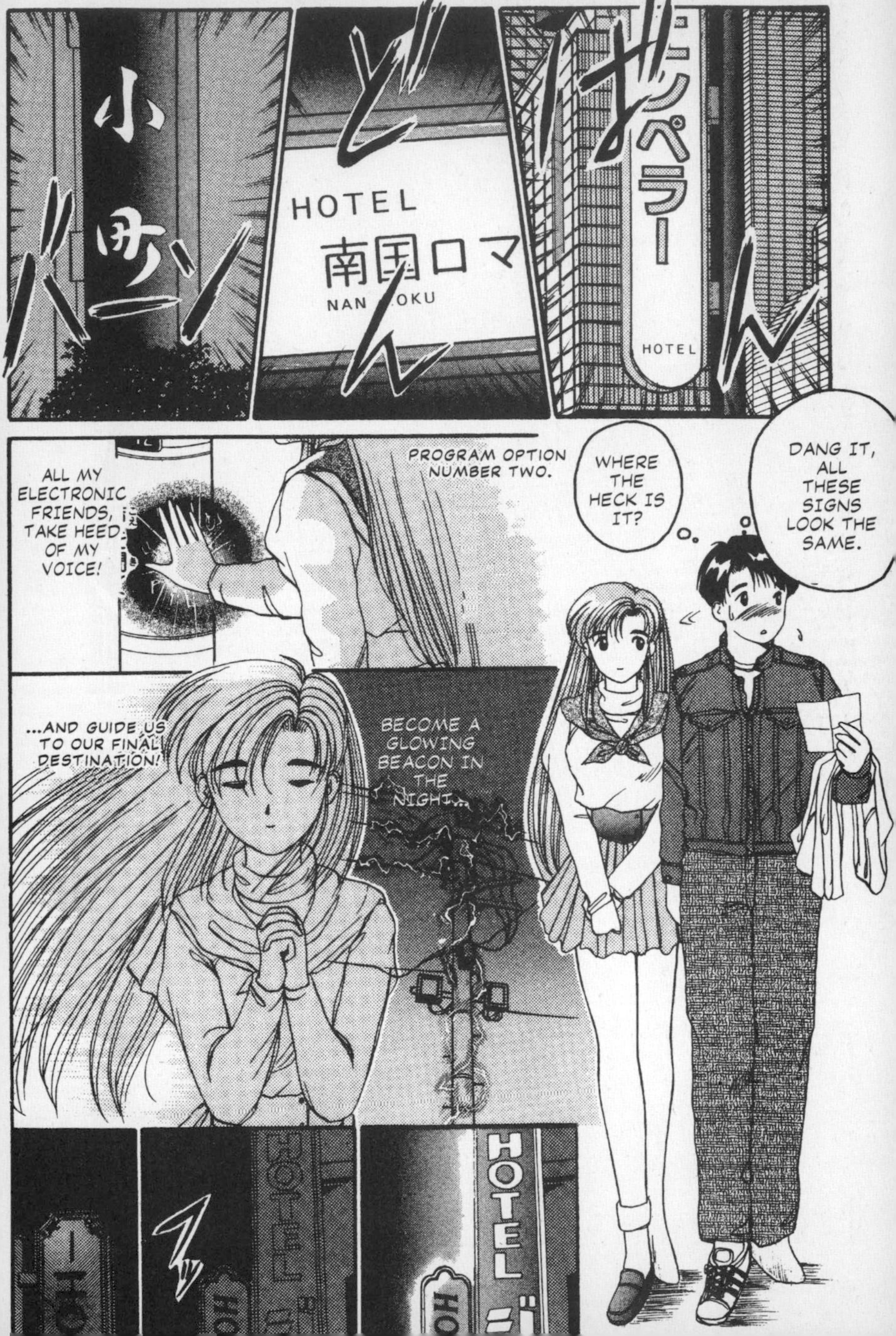
ばん
HOTEL
どん
HOTEL
南国ロマ
NAN KOKU
バーン
DANG IT, ALL THESE SIGNS LOOK THE SAME.
WHERE THE HECK IS IT?
PROGRAM OPTION NUMBER TWO.
ALL MY ELECTRONIC FRIENDS, TAKE HEED OF MY VOICE!
BECOME A GLOWING BEACON IN THE NIGHT...
...AND GUIDE US TO OUR FINAL DESTINATION!
HOTEL

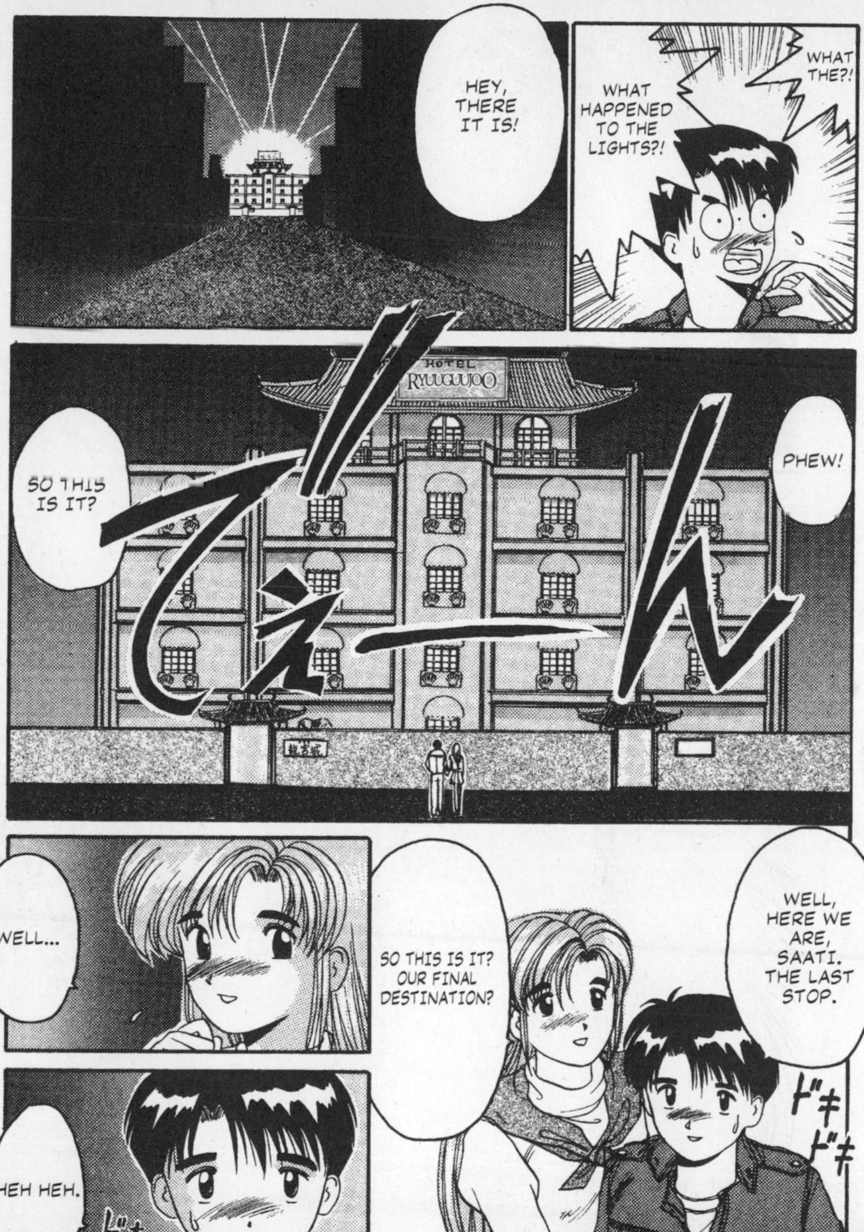
WHAT THE?!
WHAT HAPPENED TO THE LIGHTS?!
HEY, THERE IT IS!
HOTEL RYUUGUUJOO
PHEW!
でぇーん
SO THIS IS IT?
WELL, HERE WE ARE, SAATI. THE LAST STOP.
ドキドキ
SO THIS IS IT? OUR FINAL DESTINATION?
WELL...
HEH HEH.
ドキドキ

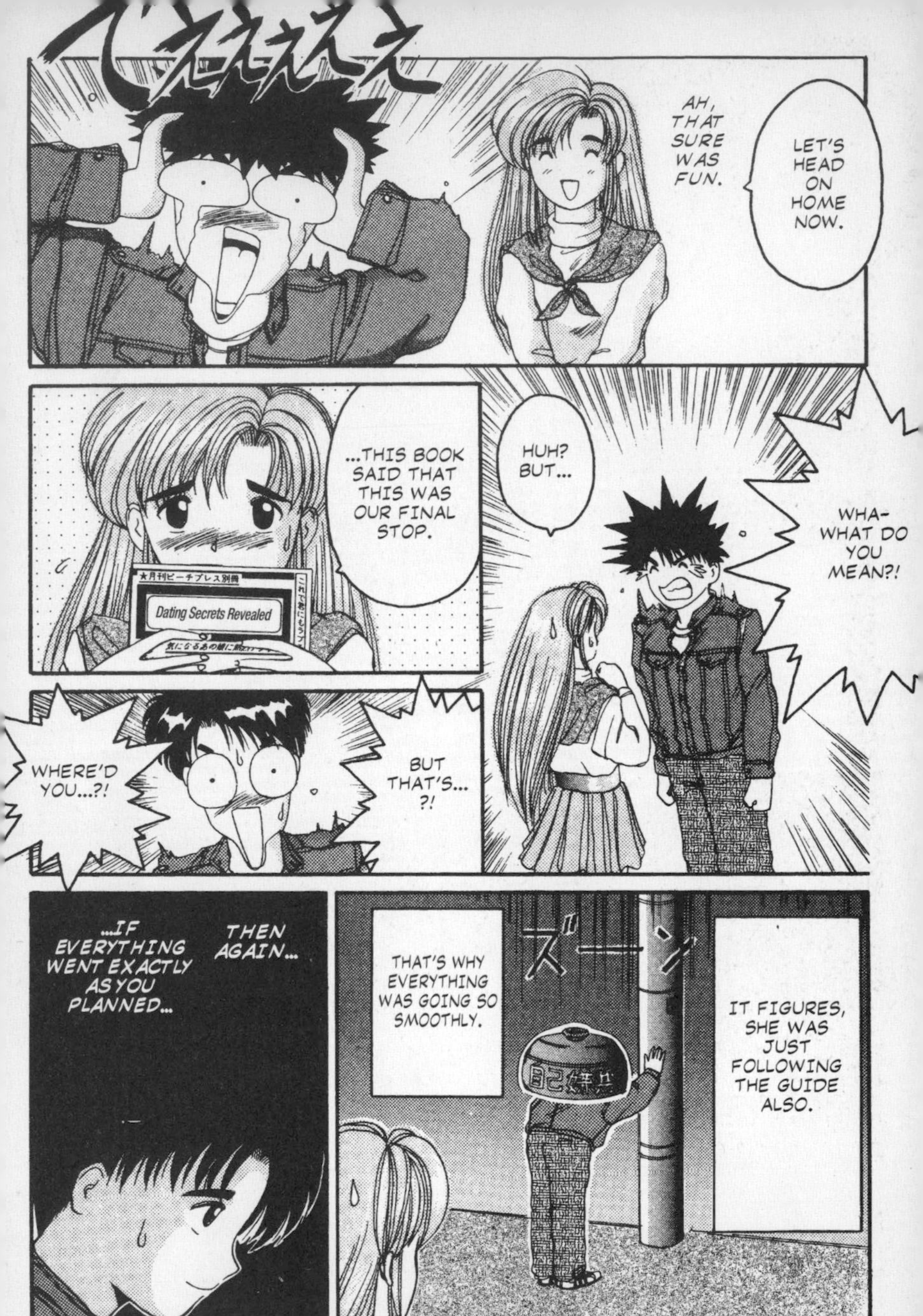
LET'S HEAD ON HOME NOW.
AH, THAT SURE WAS FUN.
べえええええ
WHA- WHAT DO YOU MEAN?!
HUH? BUT...
...THIS BOOK SAID THAT THIS WAS OUR FINAL STOP.
★月刊ピーチプレス別冊
Dating Secrets Revealed
BUT THAT'S...?!
WHERE'D YOU...?!
IT FIGURES, SHE WAS JUST FOLLOWING THE GUIDE ALSO.
ズーン
THAT'S WHY EVERYTHING WAS GOING SO SMOOTHLY.
自己嫌悪
THEN AGAIN...
...IF EVERYTHING WENT EXACTLY AS YOU PLANNED...

SELF HATRED

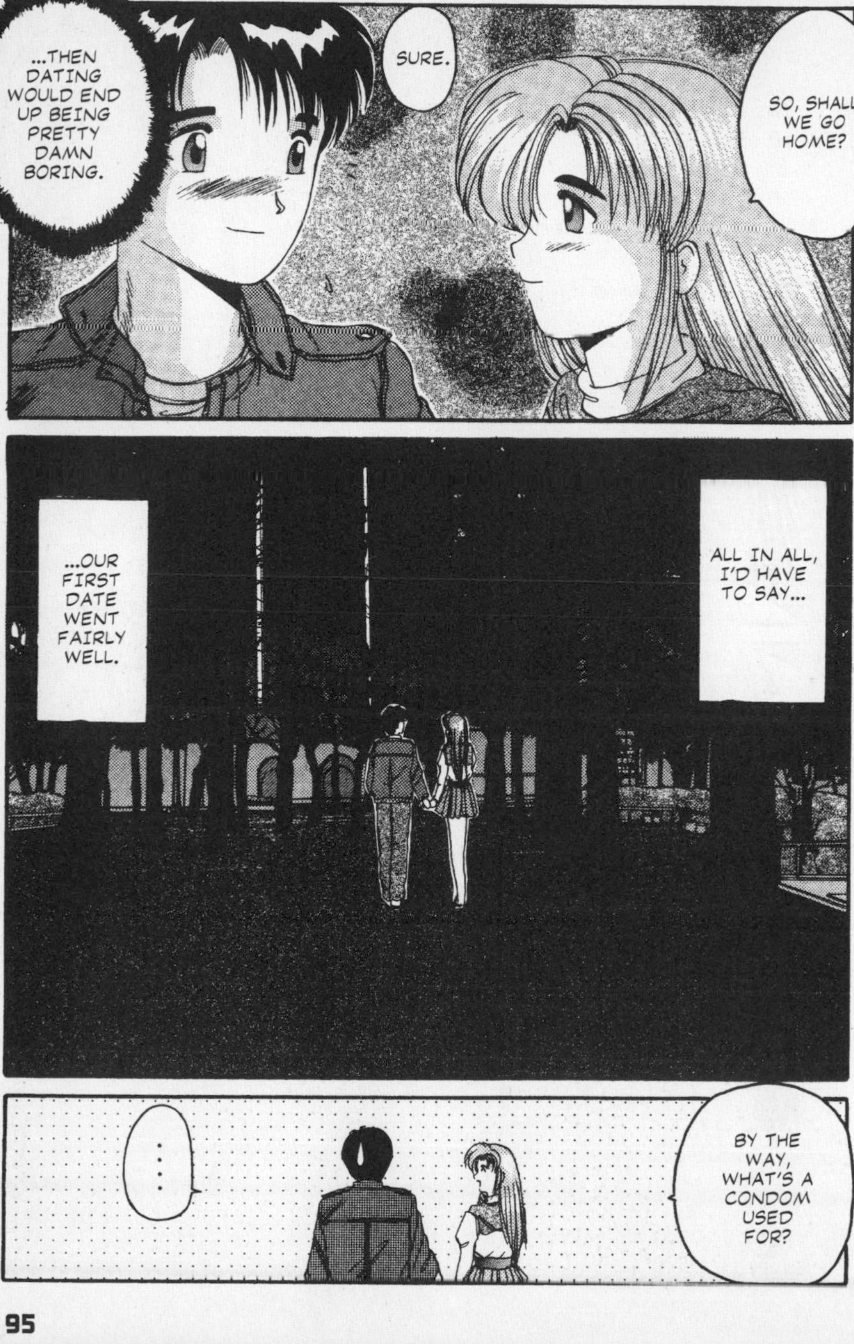
SO, SHALL WE GO HOME?
SURE.
...THEN DATING WOULD END UP BEING PRETTY DAMN BORING.
ALL IN ALL, I'D HAVE TO SAY...
...OUR FIRST DATE WENT FAIRLY WELL.
BY THE WAY, WHAT'S A CONDOM USED FOR?
....

THE WORLD OF A.I. LOVE YOU

LOVE TALK!

KEN AKAMATSU TELLS ALL

Musings from Ken Akamatsu about the origins of A.I. Love You and the types of women he digs!!

KEN AKAMATSU Special talk

First of all, can you explain how you got started with A.I. Love You?

Akamatsu: At the time, I was really good at computer programming and the inspiration kind of stemmed from that. So, I threw in some of my college experiences along with some beautiful women and thought, "I've got to do this." And I was so surprised when the editors immediately approved my original concept of having a beautiful girl come out of a computer screen. (laughs)

Is Saati your idea of the ideal woman?

Akamatsu: Yeah, pretty much. I like her relaxed attitude, because it's important to be with someone who is fun. And you know how her eyebrows are really thick? I like girls with thick eyebrows. That's why I made hers like that. I also like long hair, which probably explains why Naru Narusegawa has long hair in Love Hina.

> **"I like her relaxed attitude"**

Why is it that you like girls with thick eyebrows and long hair?

Akamatsu: Well, there's really no reason. Visually, I just like that look. As far as famous people go, I used to really like Sae Ishiki.

Do you have a different type now?

Akamatsu: Actually, what I'm attracted to has changed a lot lately. The physical type hasn't changed so much as my taste in personalities. At first, I liked the little princess types like Saati, but now I'm more into normal girls that have a lot of energy and pep. For example, from A.I. Love You, I like Cindy and from Love Hina, it's Naru. In fact, by the end of the series, Cindy looked like she was going to become the main character! (laughs)

> **"...girls that have a lot of energy and pep."**

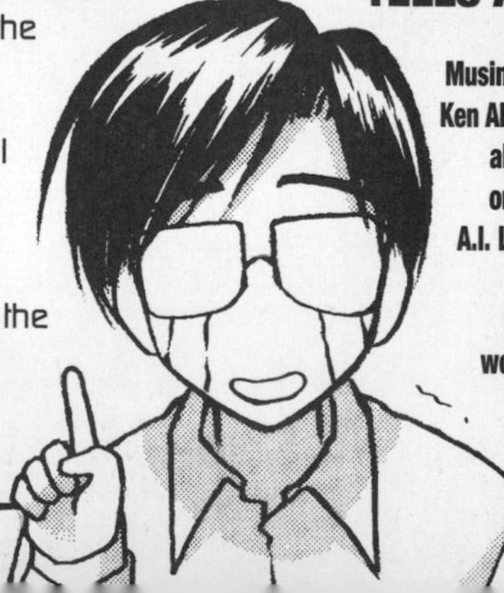

Continued on page 142

A.I. LOVE YOU

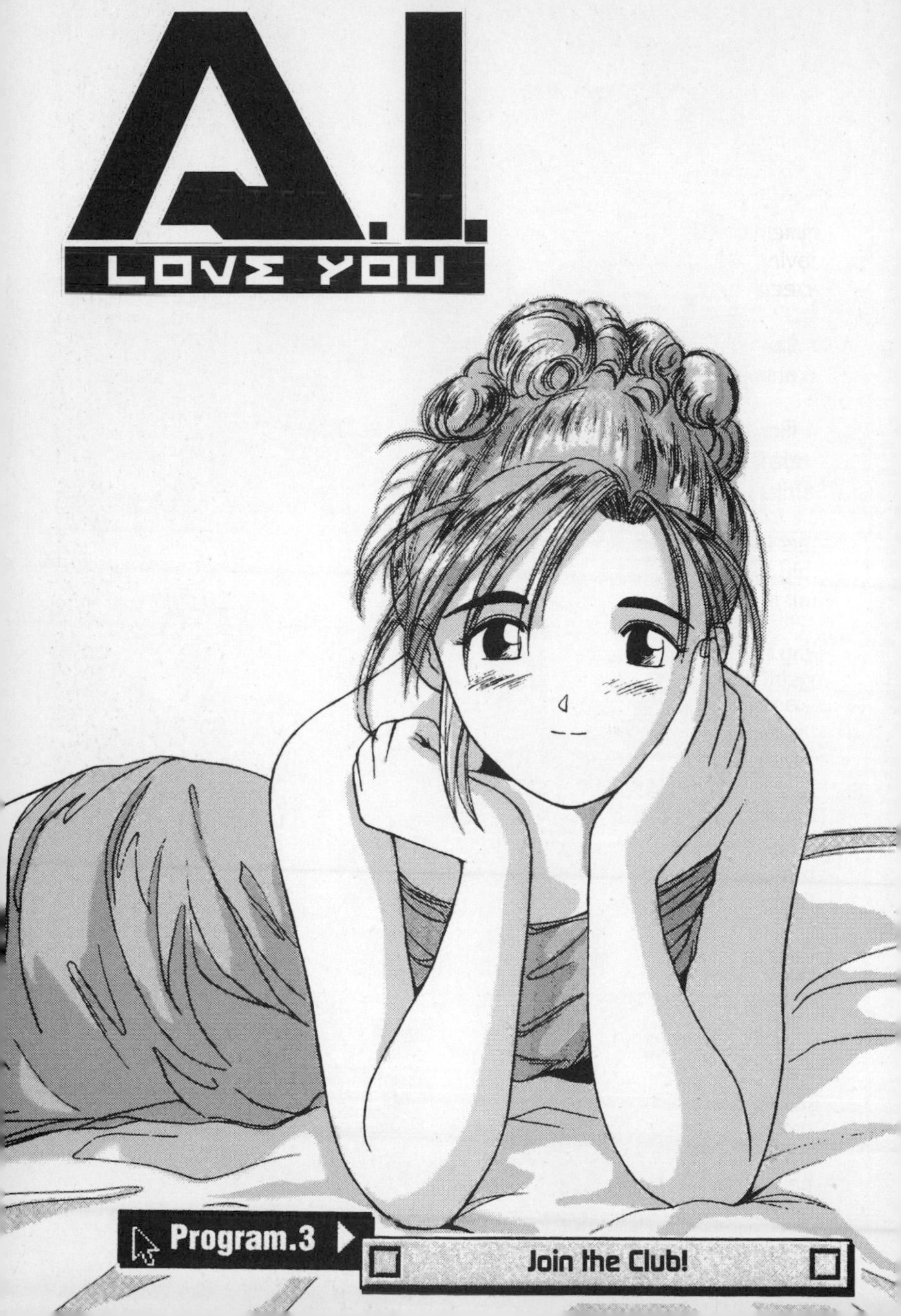

Program.3

Join the Club!

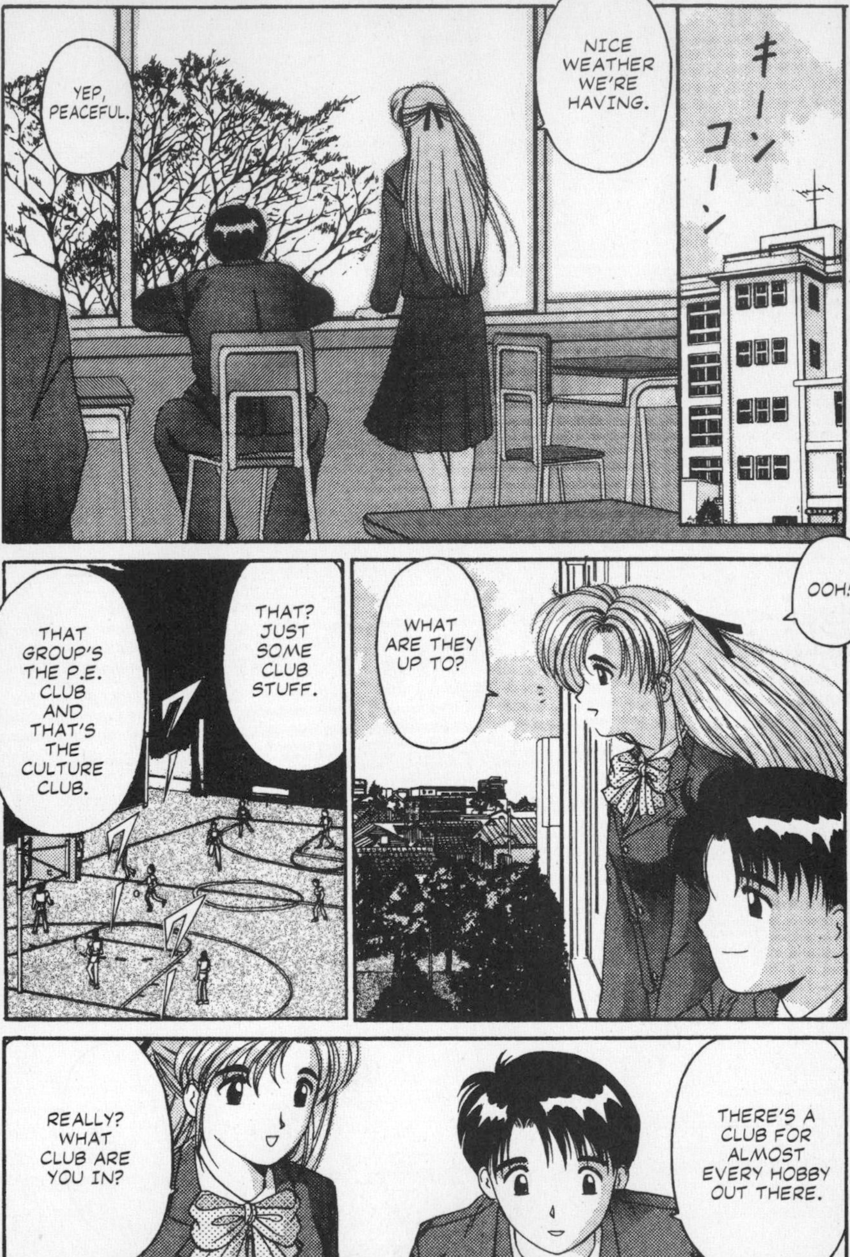
キーンコーン
NICE WEATHER WE'RE HAVING.
YEP, PEACEFUL.
OOH!
WHAT ARE THEY UP TO?
THAT? JUST SOME CLUB STUFF.
THAT GROUP'S THE P.E. CLUB AND THAT'S THE CULTURE CLUB.
THERE'S A CLUB FOR ALMOST EVERY HOBBY OUT THERE.
REALLY? WHAT CLUB ARE YOU IN?

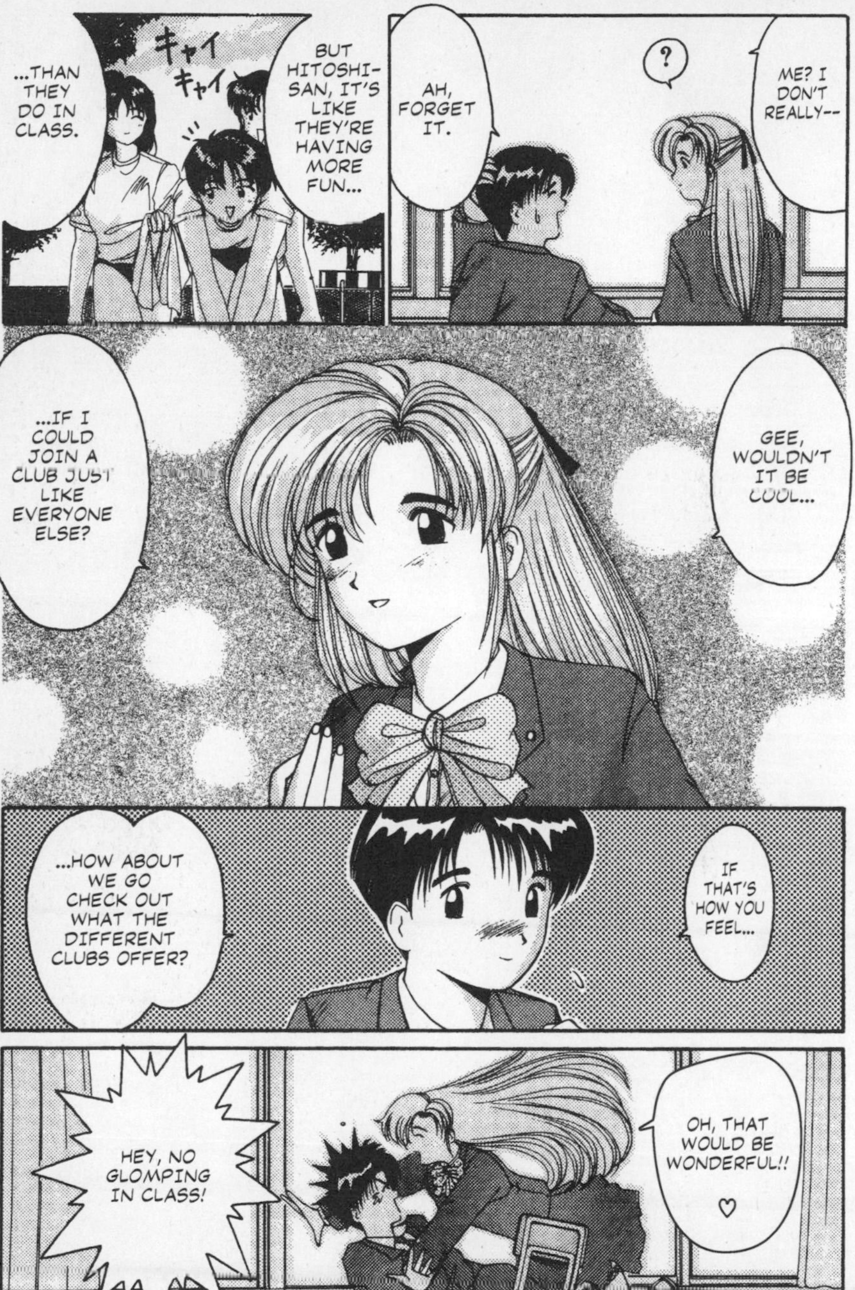
ME? I DON'T REALLY--
?
AH, FORGET IT.
BUT HITOSHI-SAN, IT'S LIKE THEY'RE HAVING MORE FUN...
キャイ キャイ
...THAN THEY DO IN CLASS.
GEE, WOULDN'T IT BE COOL...
...IF I COULD JOIN A CLUB JUST LIKE EVERYONE ELSE?
IF THAT'S HOW YOU FEEL...
...HOW ABOUT WE GO CHECK OUT WHAT THE DIFFERENT CLUBS OFFER?
OH, THAT WOULD BE WONDERFUL!! ♡
HEY, NO GLOMPING IN CLASS!

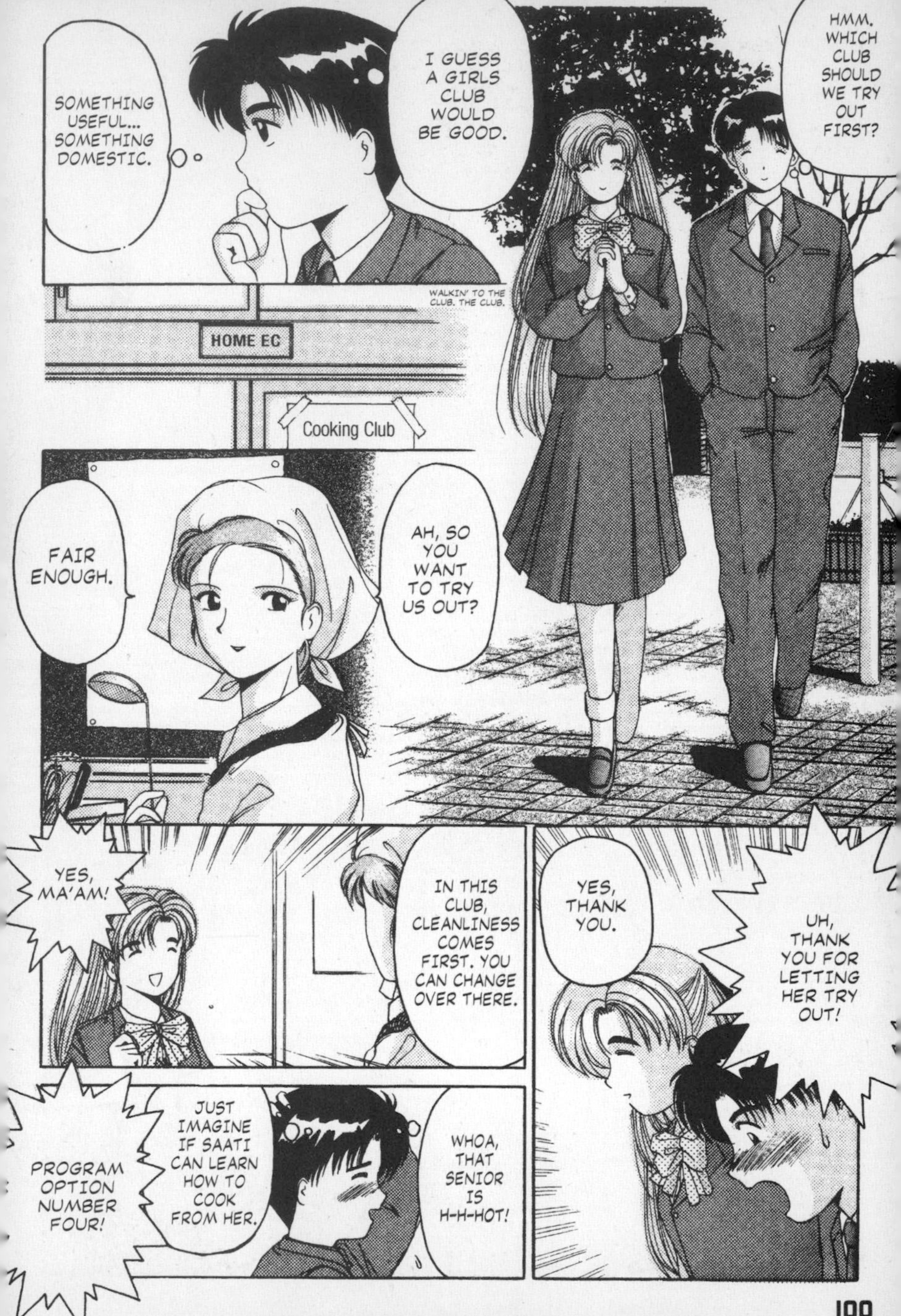
HMM. WHICH CLUB SHOULD WE TRY OUT FIRST?
WALKIN' TO THE CLUB. THE CLUB.
I GUESS A GIRLS CLUB WOULD BE GOOD.
SOMETHING USEFUL... SOMETHING DOMESTIC.
HOME EC
Cooking Club
AH, SO YOU WANT TO TRY US OUT?
FAIR ENOUGH.
UH, THANK YOU FOR LETTING HER TRY OUT!
YES, THANK YOU.
IN THIS CLUB, CLEANLINESS COMES FIRST. YOU CAN CHANGE OVER THERE.
YES, MA'AM!
WHOA, THAT SENIOR IS H-H-HOT!
JUST IMAGINE IF SAATI CAN LEARN HOW TO COOK FROM HER.
PROGRAM OPTION NUMBER FOUR!

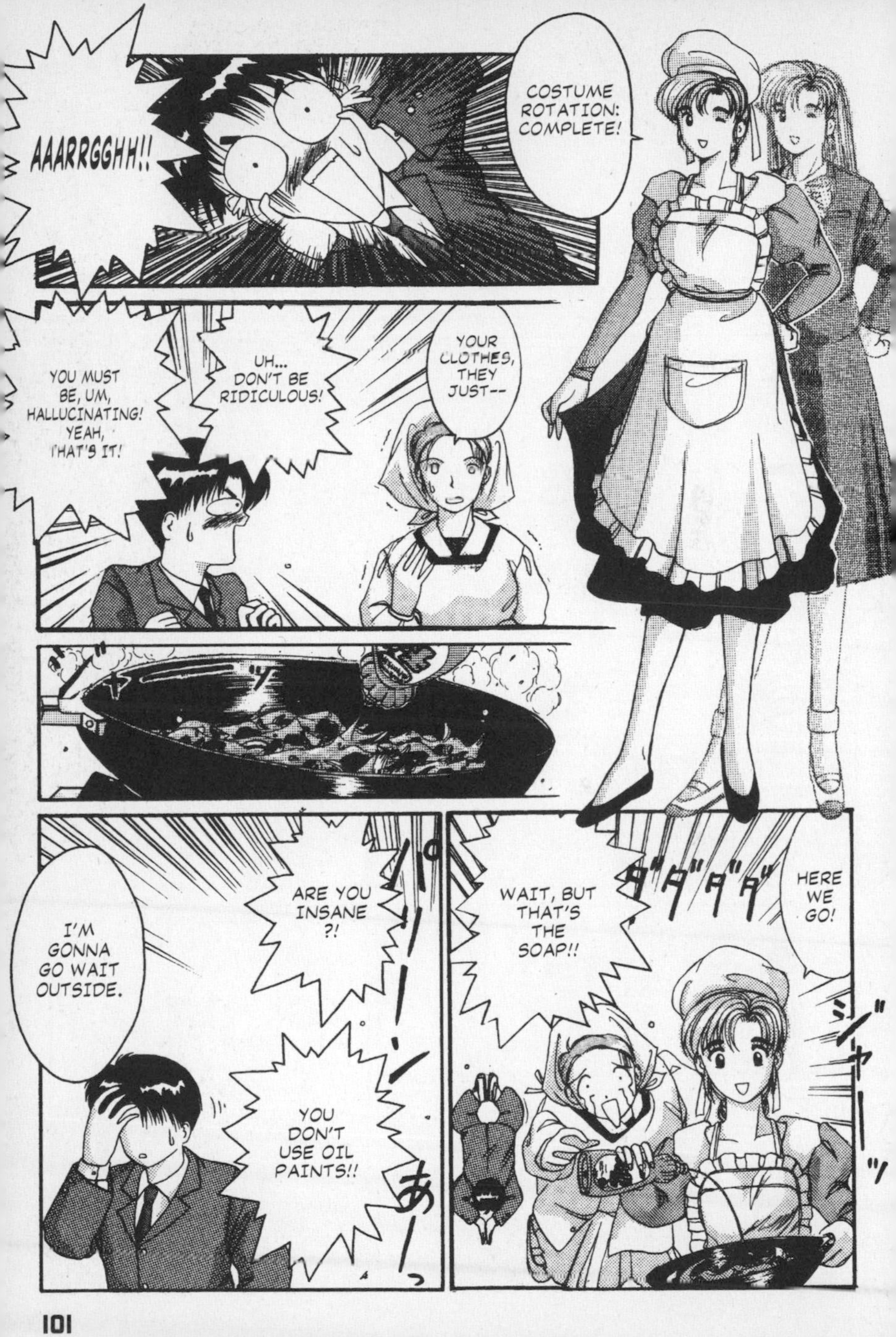
COSTUME ROTATION: COMPLETE!
AAARRGGHH!!
YOUR CLOTHES, THEY JUST--
UH... DON'T BE RIDICULOUS!
YOU MUST BE, UM, HALLUCINATING! YEAH, THAT'S IT!
HERE WE GO!
WAIT, BUT THAT'S THE SOAP!!
ARE YOU INSANE?!
YOU DON'T USE OIL PAINTS!!
I'M GONNA GO WAIT OUTSIDE.

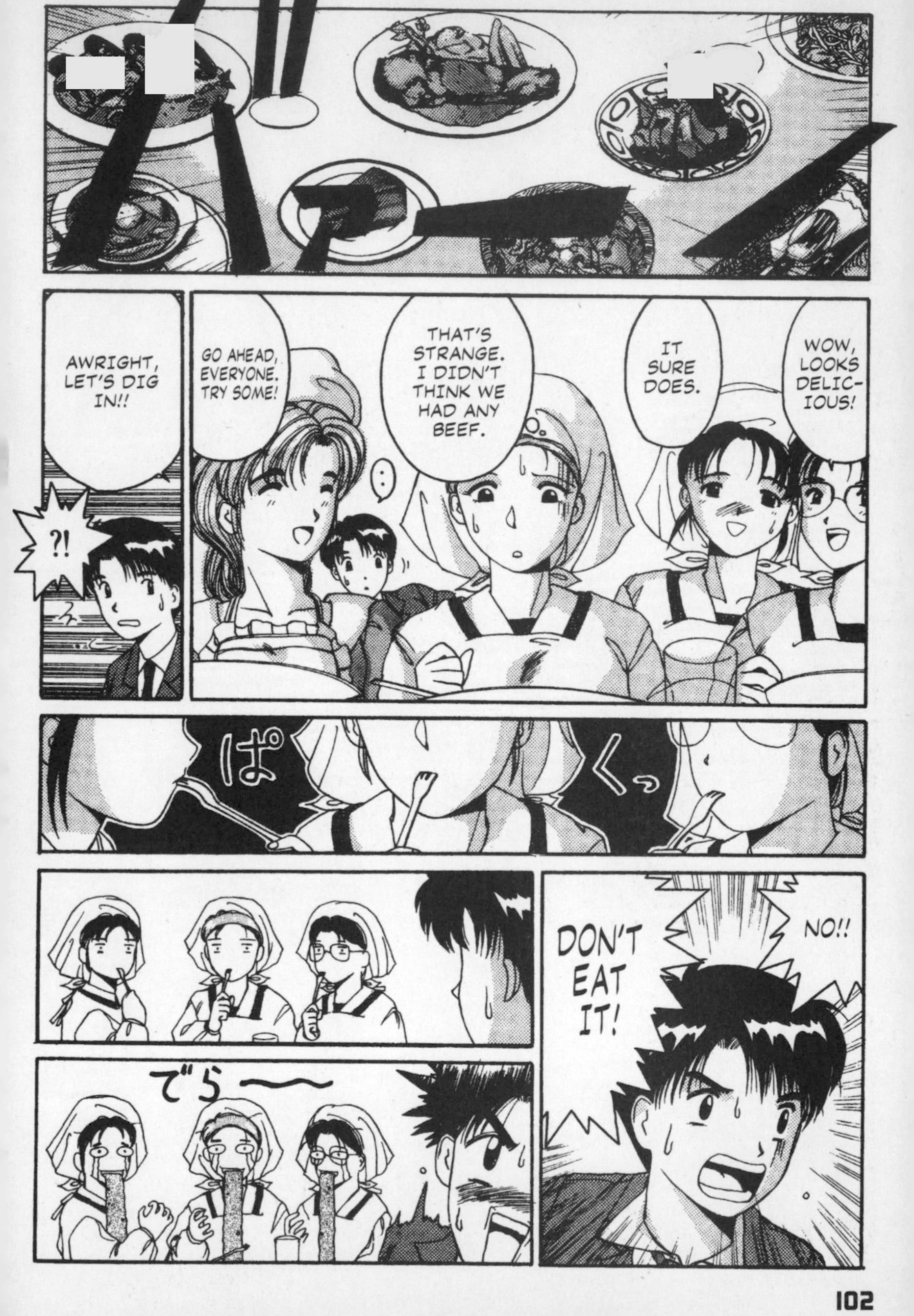
WOW, LOOKS DELICIOUS!
IT SURE DOES.
THAT'S STRANGE. I DIDN'T THINK WE HAD ANY BEEF.
GO AHEAD, EVERYONE. TRY SOME!
AWRIGHT, LET'S DIG IN!!
?!
ぱ
くっ
NO!!
DON'T EAT IT!
でら～～

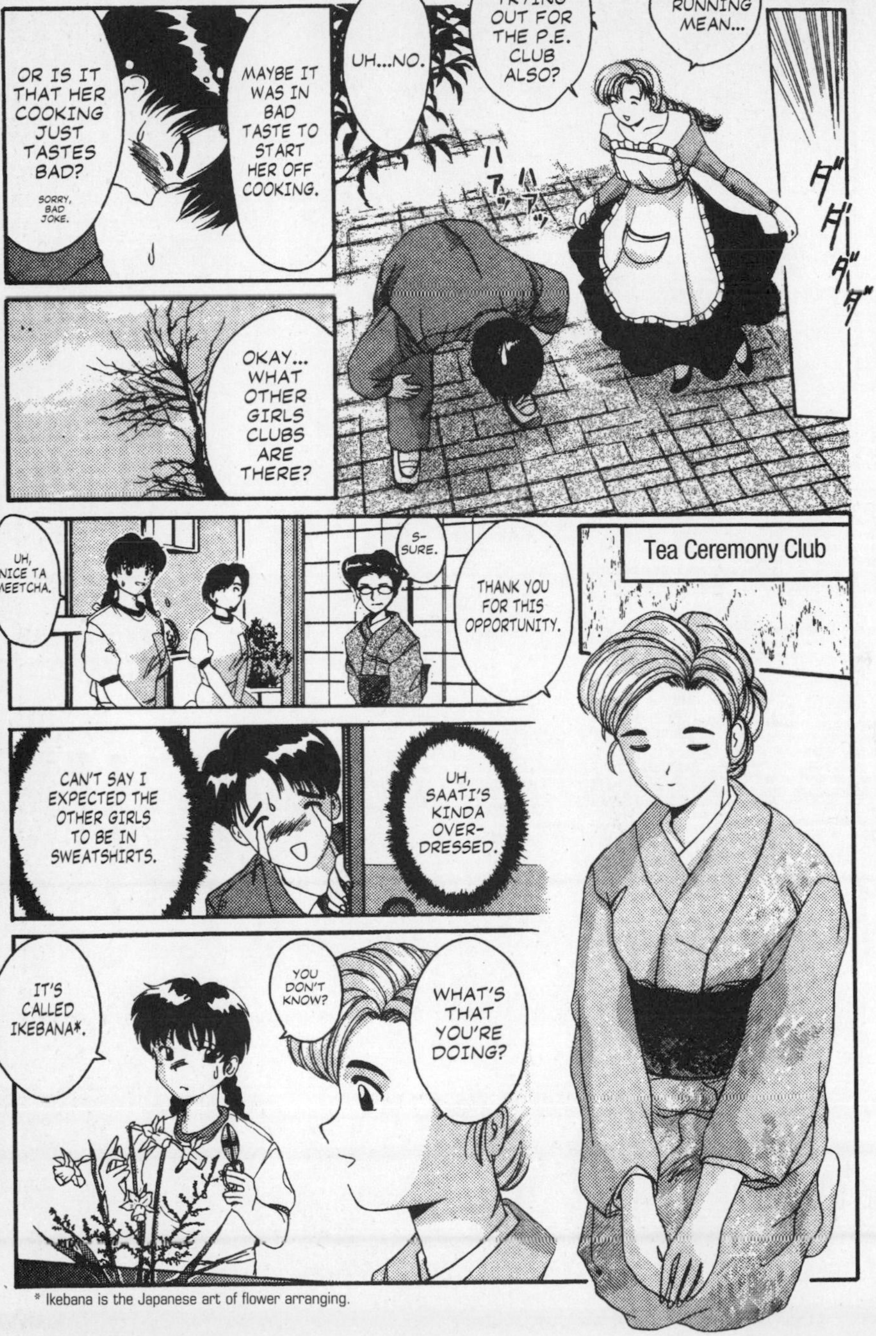
DOES ALL THIS RUNNING MEAN...
...WE'RE TRYING OUT FOR THE P.E. CLUB ALSO?
UH...NO.
ハァッ ハァッ
ダダダダ
MAYBE IT WAS IN BAD TASTE TO START HER OFF COOKING.
OR IS IT THAT HER COOKING JUST TASTES BAD?
SORRY, BAD JOKE.
OKAY... WHAT OTHER GIRLS CLUBS ARE THERE?
Tea Ceremony Club
THANK YOU FOR THIS OPPORTUNITY.
S-SURE.
UH, NICE TA MEETCHA.
UH, SAATI'S KINDA OVER-DRESSED.
CAN'T SAY I EXPECTED THE OTHER GIRLS TO BE IN SWEATSHIRTS.
WHAT'S THAT YOU'RE DOING?
YOU DON'T KNOW?
IT'S CALLED IKEBANA*.

* Ikebana is the Japanese art of flower arranging.

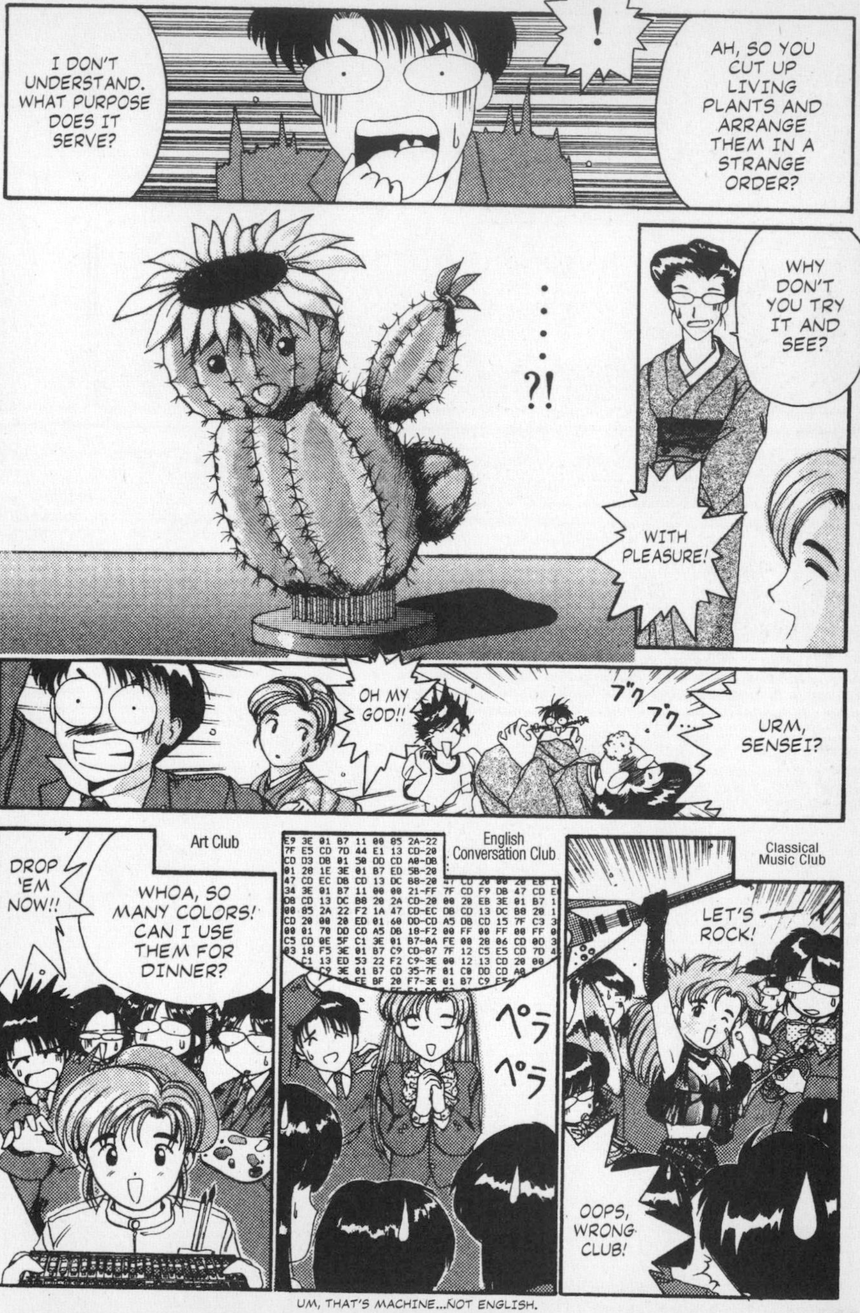
!
AH, SO YOU CUT UP LIVING PLANTS AND ARRANGE THEM IN A STRANGE ORDER?
I DON'T UNDERSTAND. WHAT PURPOSE DOES IT SERVE?
WHY DON'T YOU TRY IT AND SEE?
WITH PLEASURE!
. . . .
?!
URM, SENSEI?
ブク ブク…
OH MY GOD!!
Classical Music Club
LET'S ROCK!
OOPS, WRONG CLUB!
English Conversation Club
ペラ ペラ
Art Club
WHOA, SO MANY COLORS! CAN I USE THEM FOR DINNER?
DROP 'EM NOW!!

UM, THAT'S MACHINE...NOT ENGLISH.

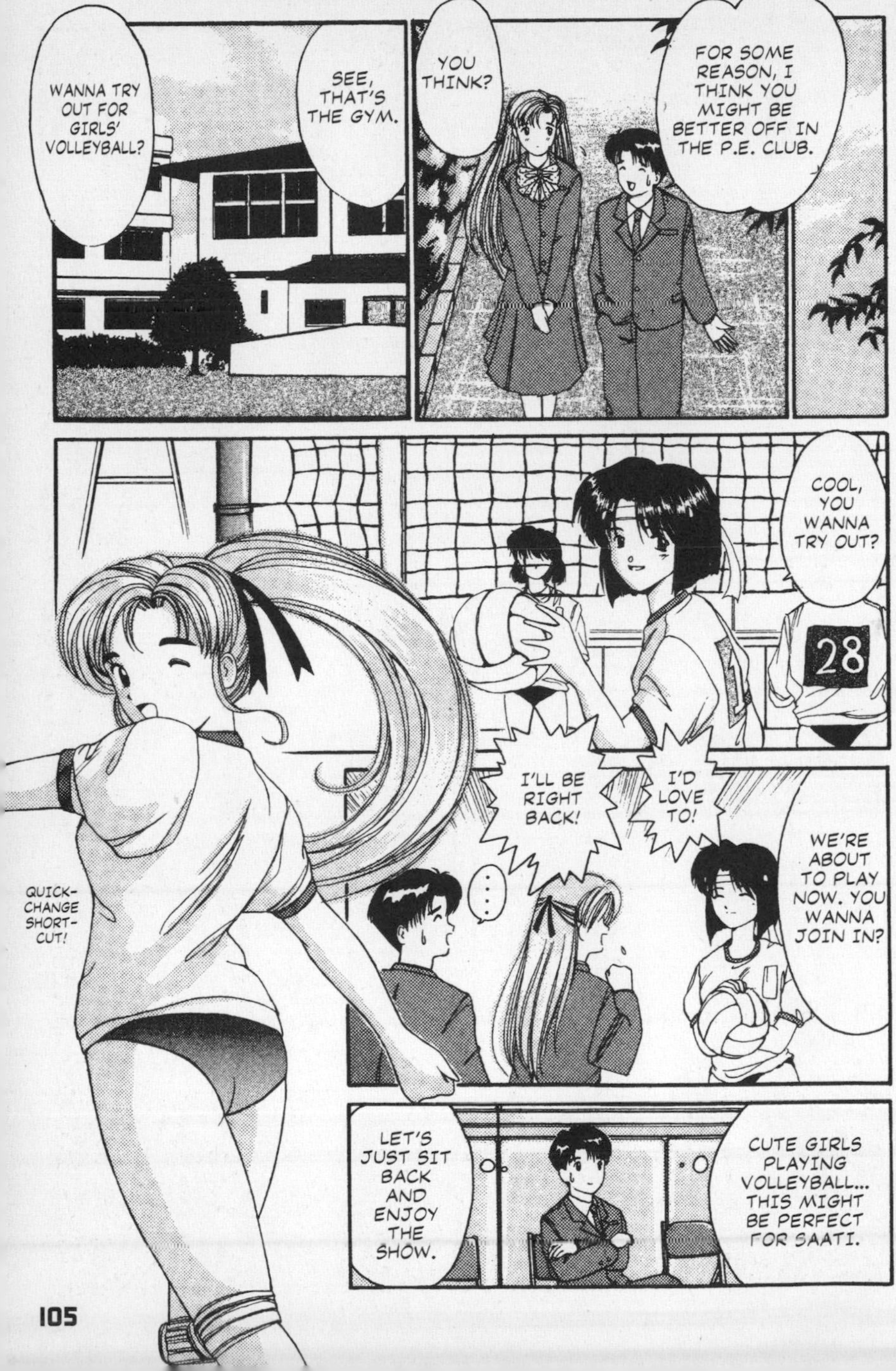
FOR SOME REASON, I THINK YOU MIGHT BE BETTER OFF IN THE P.E. CLUB.
YOU THINK?
SEE, THAT'S THE GYM.
WANNA TRY OUT FOR GIRLS' VOLLEYBALL?
COOL, YOU WANNA TRY OUT?
WE'RE ABOUT TO PLAY NOW. YOU WANNA JOIN IN?
I'D LOVE TO!
I'LL BE RIGHT BACK!
...
QUICK-CHANGE SHORT-CUT!
CUTE GIRLS PLAYING VOLLEYBALL... THIS MIGHT BE PERFECT FOR SAATI.
LET'S JUST SIT BACK AND ENJOY THE SHOW.

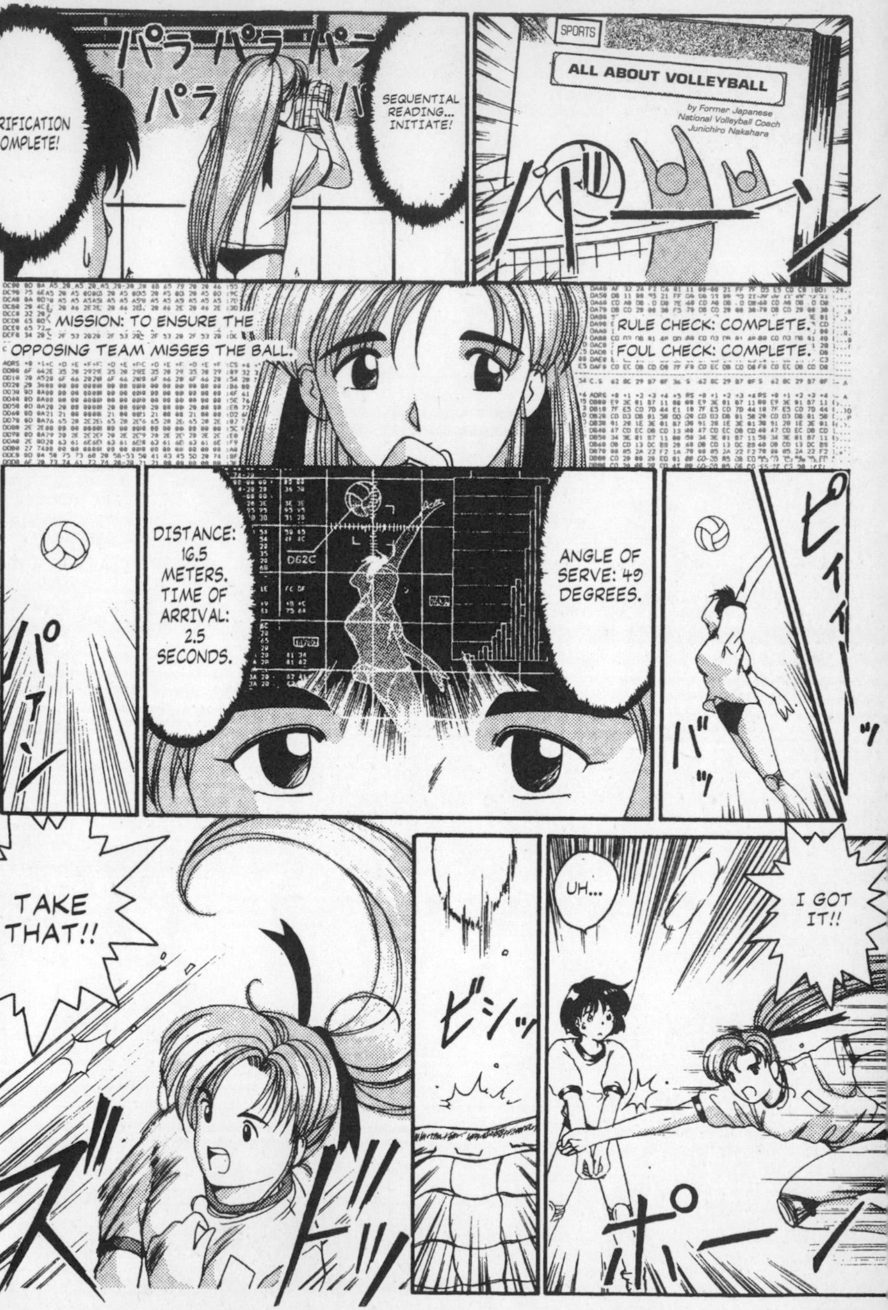
SPORTS
ALL ABOUT VOLLEYBALL
by Former Japanese National Volleyball Coach Junichiro Nakahara
パラ パラ パラ パラ パ
SEQUENTIAL READING... INITIATE!
VERIFICATION COMPLETE!
RULE CHECK: COMPLETE. FOUL CHECK: COMPLETE.
MISSION: TO ENSURE THE OPPOSING TEAM MISSES THE BALL.
ピィィーッ
バッ
ANGLE OF SERVE: 49 DEGREES.
DISTANCE: 16.5 METERS. TIME OF ARRIVAL: 2.5 SECONDS.
D62C
パァーン
I GOT IT!!
UH...
ポーン
ビシッ
TAKE THAT!!
ズドッ

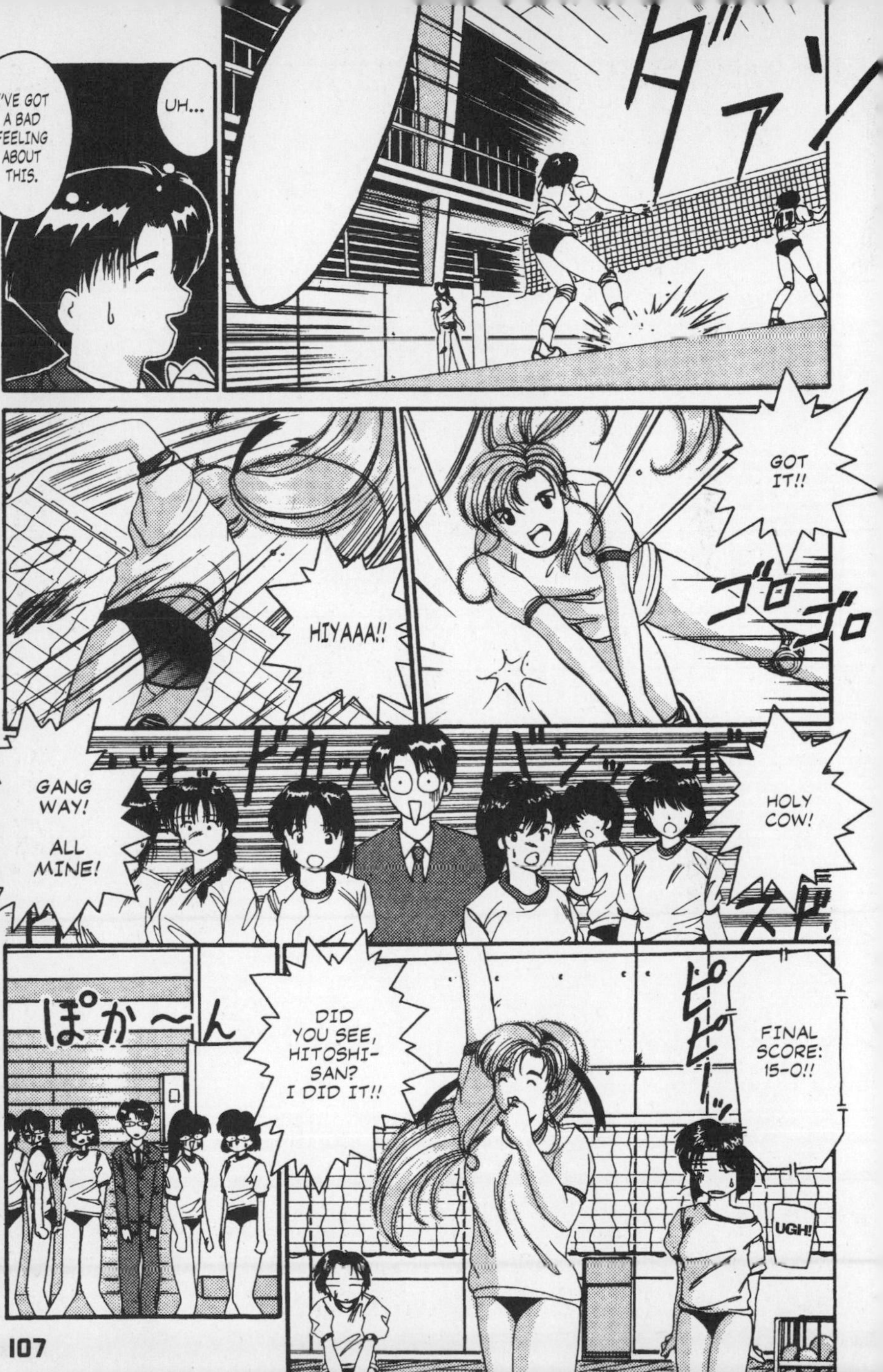

ダァン
UH...
I'VE GOT A BAD FEELING ABOUT THIS.
GOT IT!!
ゴロゴロ
HIYAAA!!
HOLY COW!
GANG WAY!
ALL MINE!
FINAL SCORE: 15-0!!
ピピーッ
UGH!
DID YOU SEE, HITOSHI-SAN? I DID IT!!
ぽか〜ん

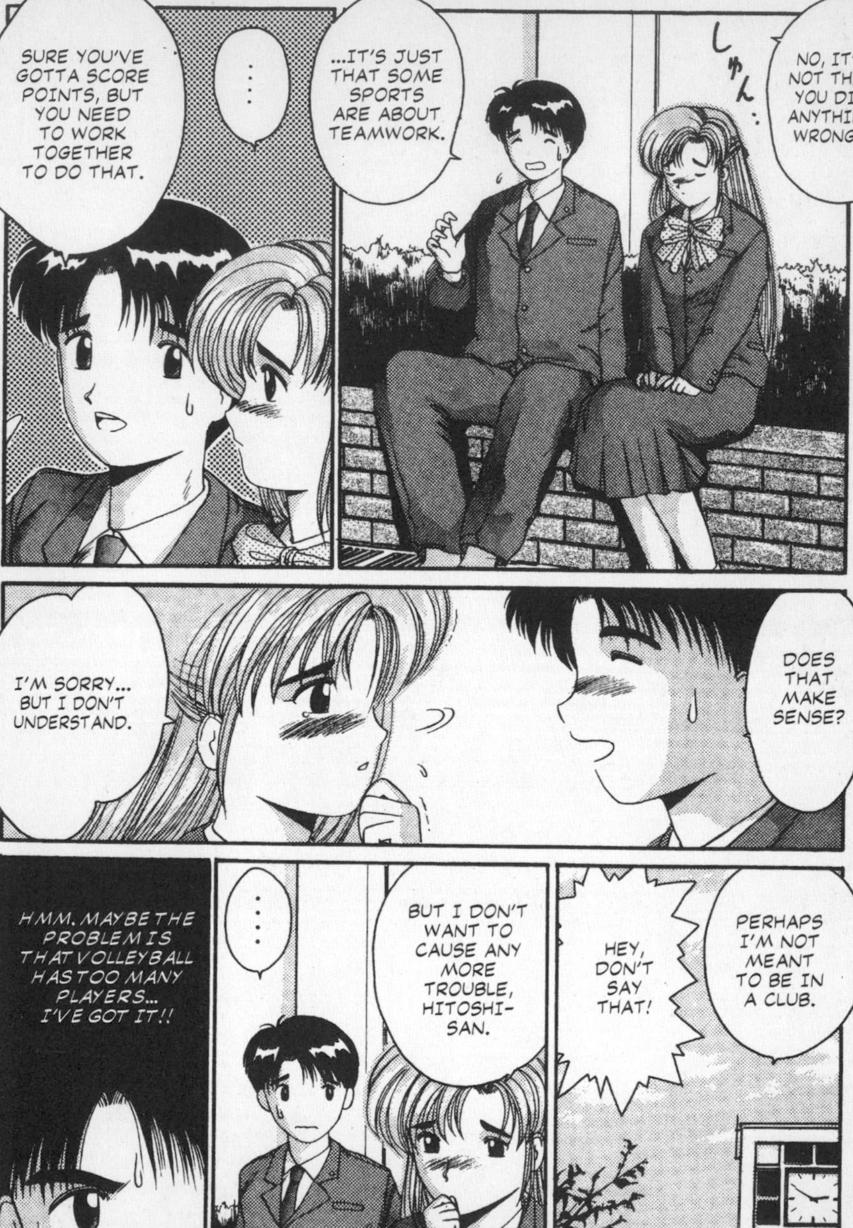
しゅん
NO, IT'S NOT THAT YOU DID ANYTHING WRONG...
...IT'S JUST THAT SOME SPORTS ARE ABOUT TEAMWORK.
....
SURE YOU'VE GOTTA SCORE POINTS, BUT YOU NEED TO WORK TOGETHER TO DO THAT.
DOES THAT MAKE SENSE?
I'M SORRY... BUT I DON'T UNDERSTAND.
PERHAPS I'M NOT MEANT TO BE IN A CLUB.
HEY, DON'T SAY THAT!
BUT I DON'T WANT TO CAUSE ANY MORE TROUBLE, HITOSHI-SAN.
....
HMM. MAYBE THE PROBLEM IS THAT VOLLEYBALL HAS TOO MANY PLAYERS... I'VE GOT IT!!

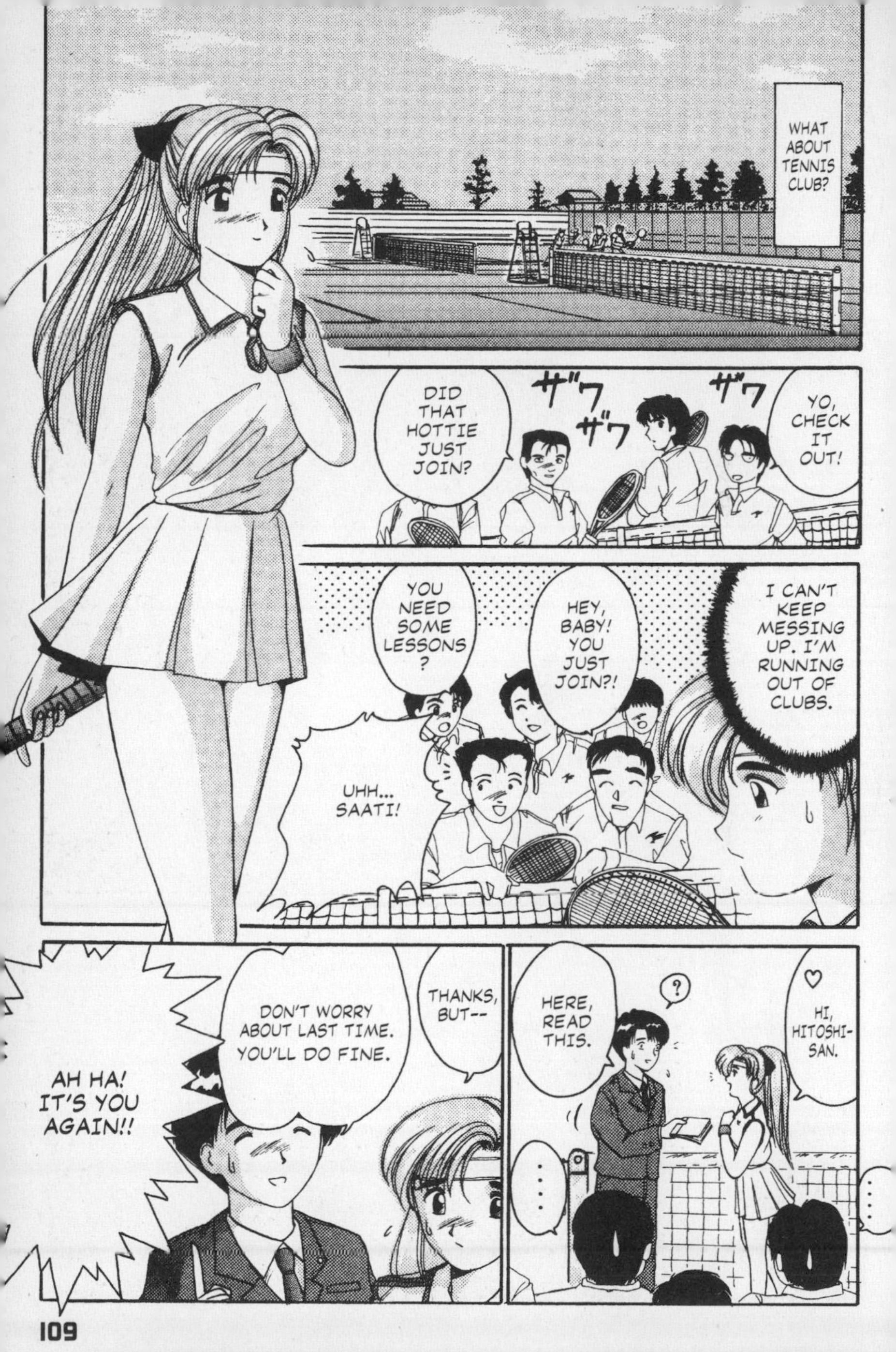
WHAT ABOUT TENNIS CLUB?
YO, CHECK IT OUT!
ザワ
ザワ
ザワ
DID THAT HOTTIE JUST JOIN?
I CAN'T KEEP MESSING UP. I'M RUNNING OUT OF CLUBS.
HEY, BABY! YOU JUST JOIN?!
YOU NEED SOME LESSONS?
UHH... SAATI!
♡
HI, HITOSHI-SAN.
?
HERE, READ THIS.
....
....
THANKS, BUT--
DON'T WORRY ABOUT LAST TIME. YOU'LL DO FINE.
AH HA! IT'S YOU AGAIN!!

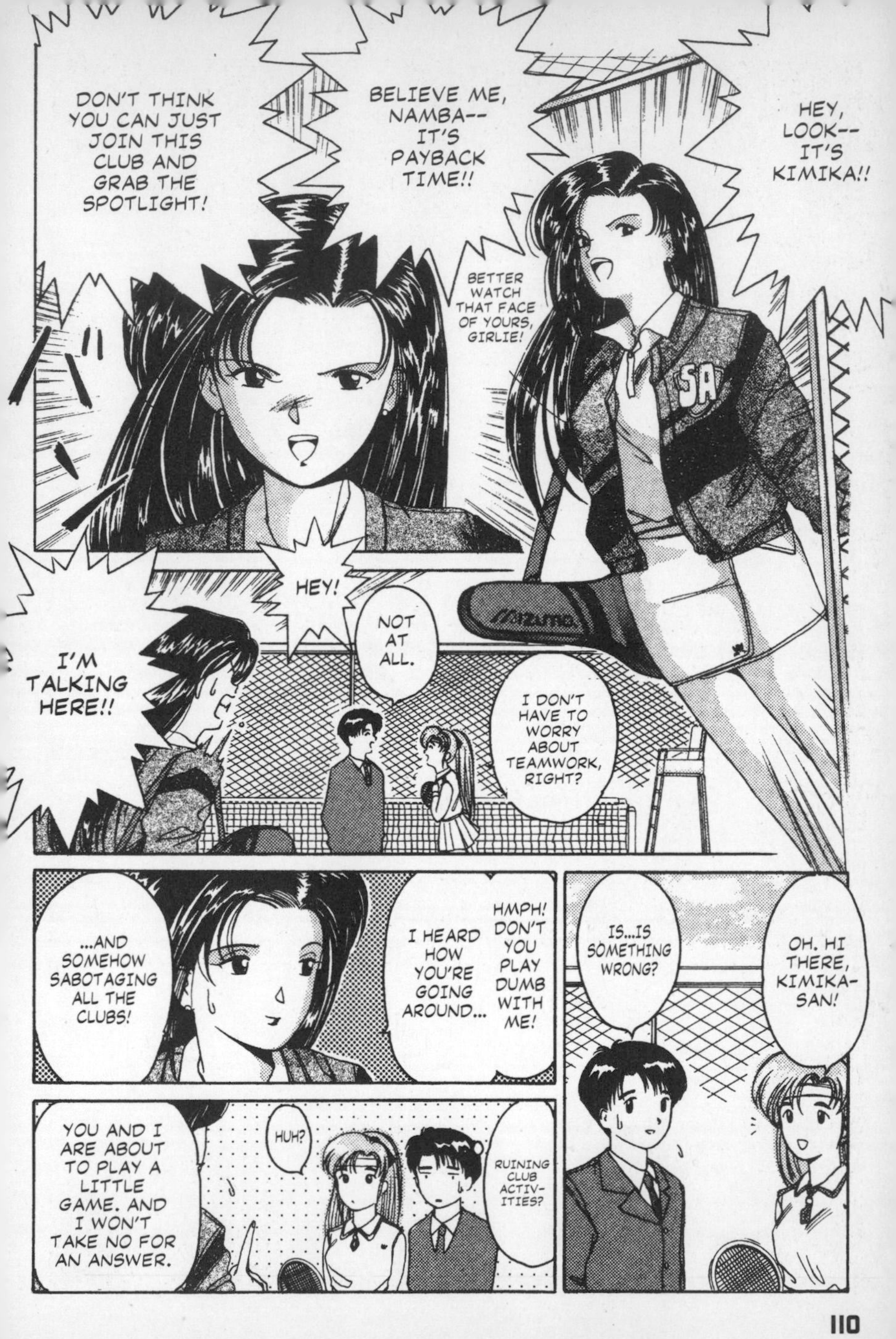
HEY, LOOK-- IT'S KIMIKA!!
BELIEVE ME, NAMBA-- IT'S PAYBACK TIME!!
BETTER WATCH THAT FACE OF YOURS, GIRLIE!
DON'T THINK YOU CAN JUST JOIN THIS CLUB AND GRAB THE SPOTLIGHT!
I DON'T HAVE TO WORRY ABOUT TEAMWORK, RIGHT?
NOT AT ALL.
HEY!
I'M TALKING HERE!!
OH. HI THERE, KIMIKA-SAN!
IS...IS SOMETHING WRONG?
HMPH! DON'T YOU PLAY DUMB WITH ME!
I HEARD HOW YOU'RE GOING AROUND...
...AND SOMEHOW SABOTAGING ALL THE CLUBS!
RUINING CLUB ACTIVITIES?
HUH?
YOU AND I ARE ABOUT TO PLAY A LITTLE GAME. AND I WON'T TAKE NO FOR AN ANSWER.

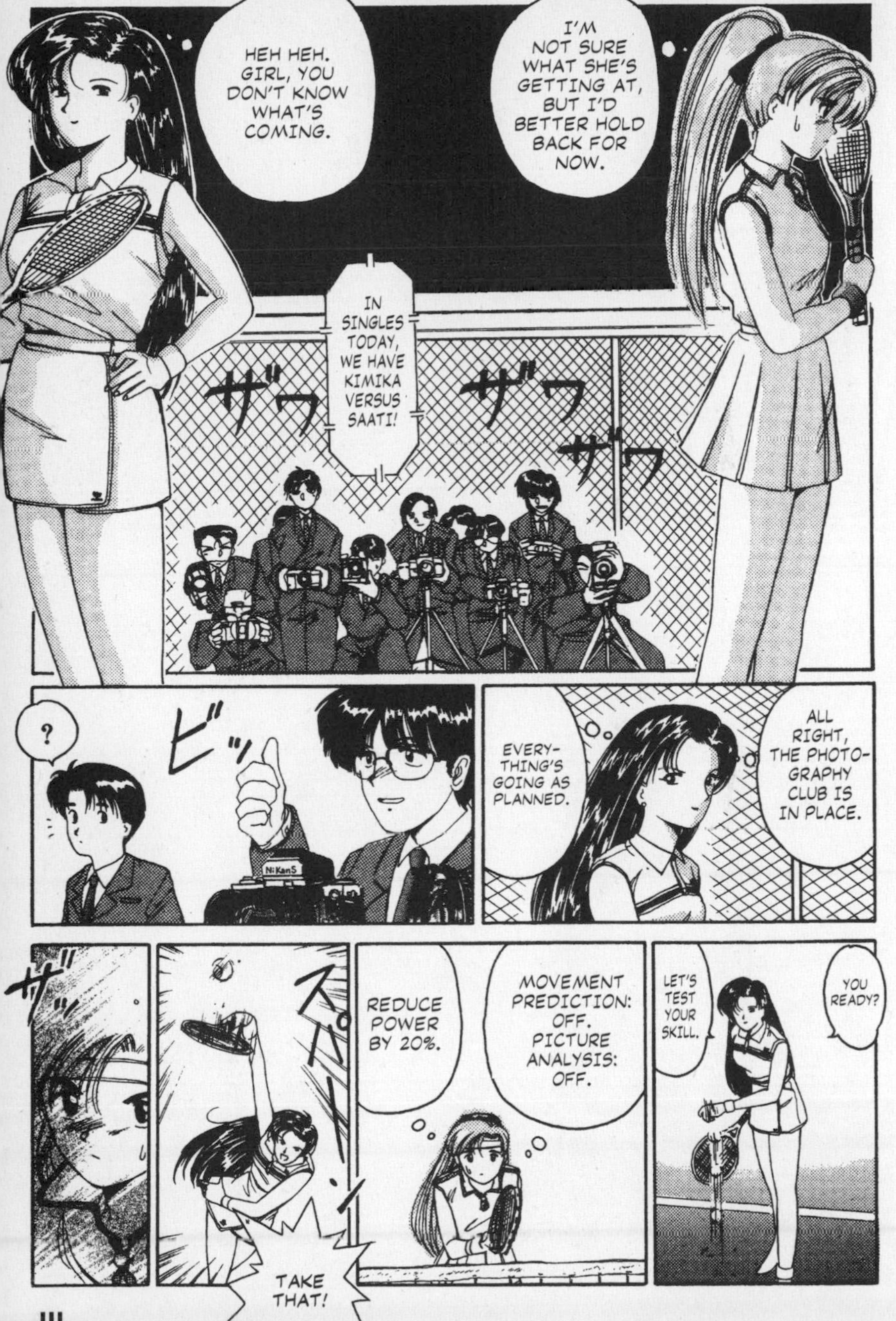
I'M NOT SURE WHAT SHE'S GETTING AT, BUT I'D BETTER HOLD BACK FOR NOW.
HEH HEH. GIRL, YOU DON'T KNOW WHAT'S COMING.
IN SINGLES TODAY, WE HAVE KIMIKA VERSUS SAATI!
ザワ
ザワ
ザワ
ALL RIGHT, THE PHOTOGRAPHY CLUB IS IN PLACE.
EVERYTHING'S GOING AS PLANNED.
ビッ
?
YOU READY?
LET'S TEST YOUR SKILL.
MOVEMENT PREDICTION: OFF. PICTURE ANALYSIS: OFF.
REDUCE POWER BY 20%.
TAKE THAT!
ザッ

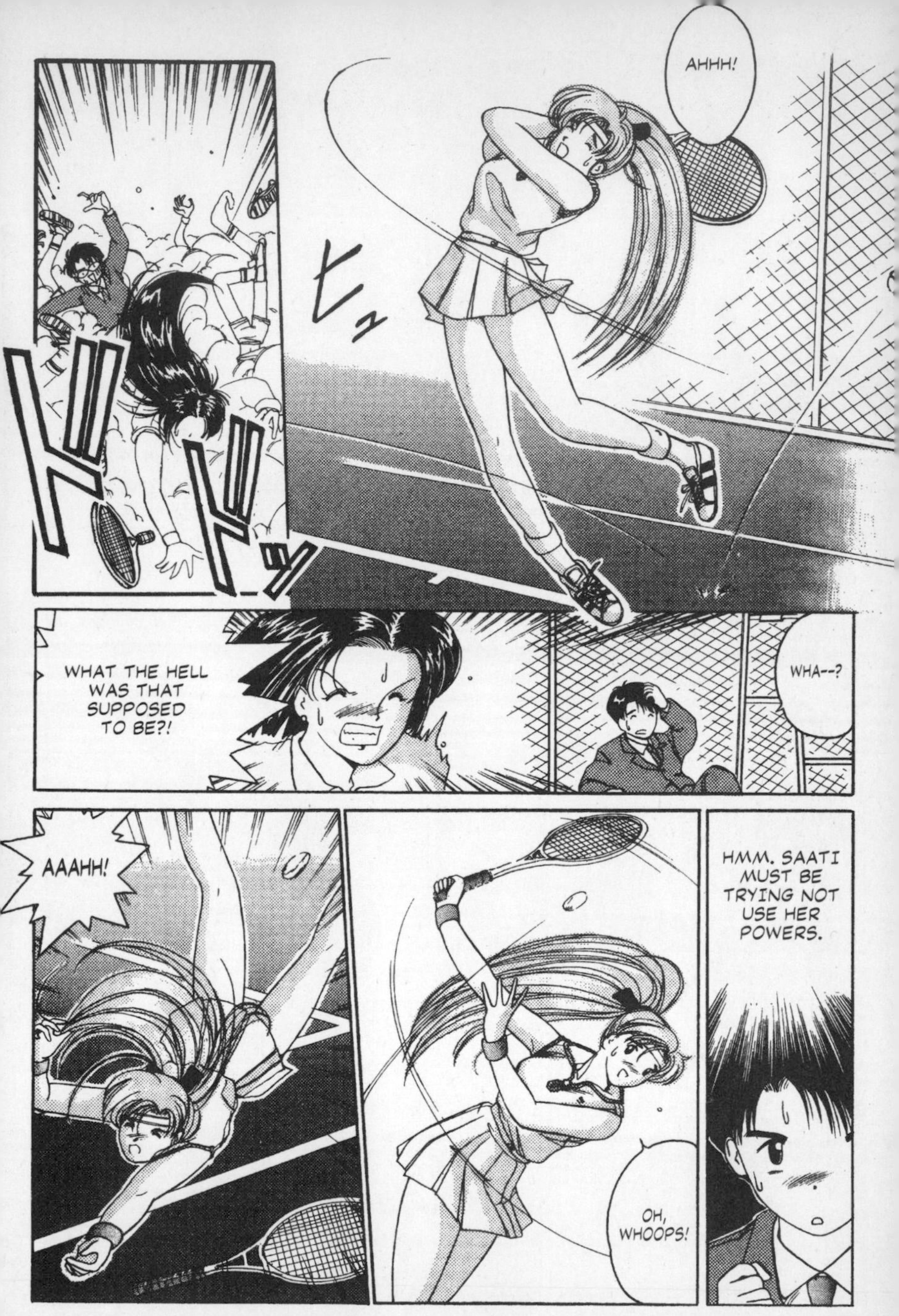
AHHH!
ヒュ
WHA--?
WHAT THE HELL WAS THAT SUPPOSED TO BE?!
HMM. SAATI MUST BE TRYING NOT USE HER POWERS.
OH, WHOOPS!
AAAHH!

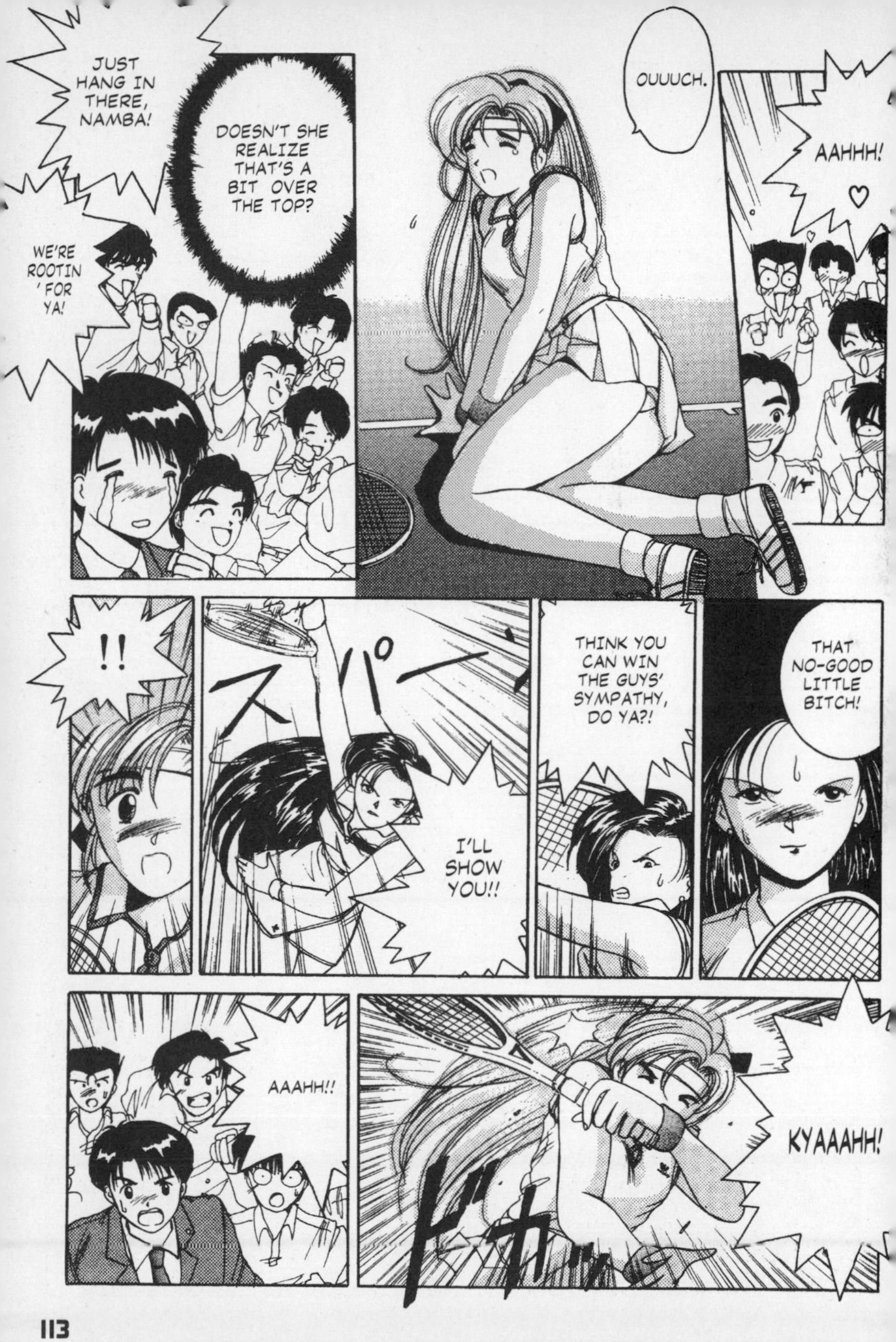
AAHHH! ♡
OUUUCH.
JUST HANG IN THERE, NAMBA!
DOESN'T SHE REALIZE THAT'S A BIT OVER THE TOP?
WE'RE ROOTIN' FOR YA!
THAT NO-GOOD LITTLE BITCH!
THINK YOU CAN WIN THE GUYS' SYMPATHY, DO YA?!
スパー
I'LL SHOW YOU!!
!!
KYAAAHH!
ドカ
AAAHH!!

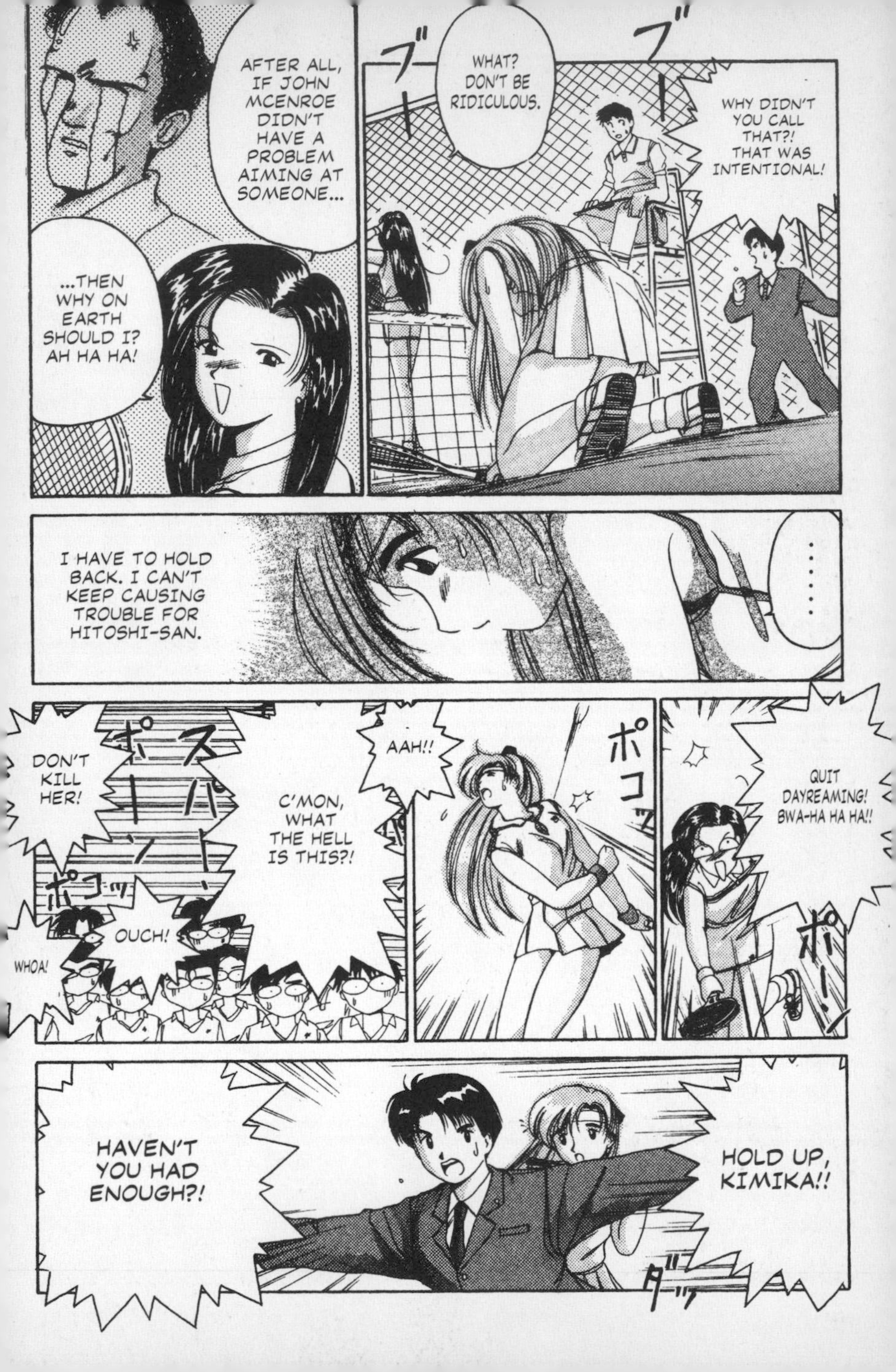
ブー
ブー
WHY DIDN'T YOU CALL THAT?! THAT WAS INTENTIONAL!
WHAT? DON'T BE RIDICULOUS.
AFTER ALL, IF JOHN MCENROE DIDN'T HAVE A PROBLEM AIMING AT SOMEONE...
...THEN WHY ON EARTH SHOULD I? AH HA HA!
......
I HAVE TO HOLD BACK. I CAN'T KEEP CAUSING TROUBLE FOR HITOSHI-SAN.
QUIT DAYREAMING! BWA-HA HA HA!!
ポーン
ポコッ
AAH!!
C'MON, WHAT THE HELL IS THIS?!
スパーン
ポーン
DON'T KILL HER!
ポコッ
OUCH!
WHOA!
HOLD UP, KIMIKA!!
HAVEN'T YOU HAD ENOUGH?!
ダッ

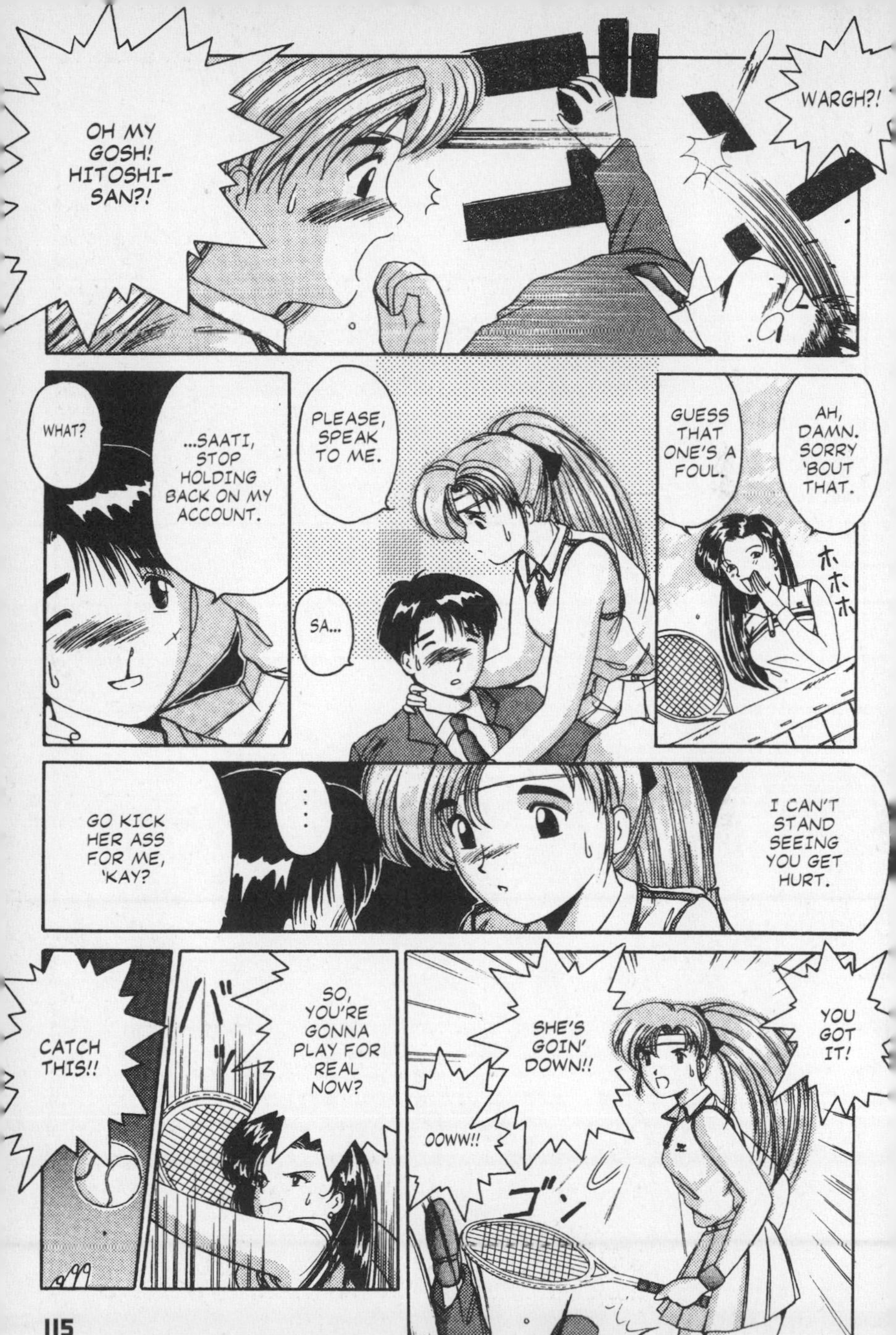

WARGH?!
OH MY GOSH! HITOSHI-SAN?!
AH, DAMN. SORRY 'BOUT THAT.
GUESS THAT ONE'S A FOUL.
ホホホ
PLEASE, SPEAK TO ME.
SA...
...SAATI, STOP HOLDING BACK ON MY ACCOUNT.
WHAT?
I CAN'T STAND SEEING YOU GET HURT.
....
GO KICK HER ASS FOR ME, 'KAY?
YOU GOT IT!
SHE'S GOIN' DOWN!!
OOWW!!
ゴン
SO, YOU'RE GONNA PLAY FOR REAL NOW?
CATCH THIS!!

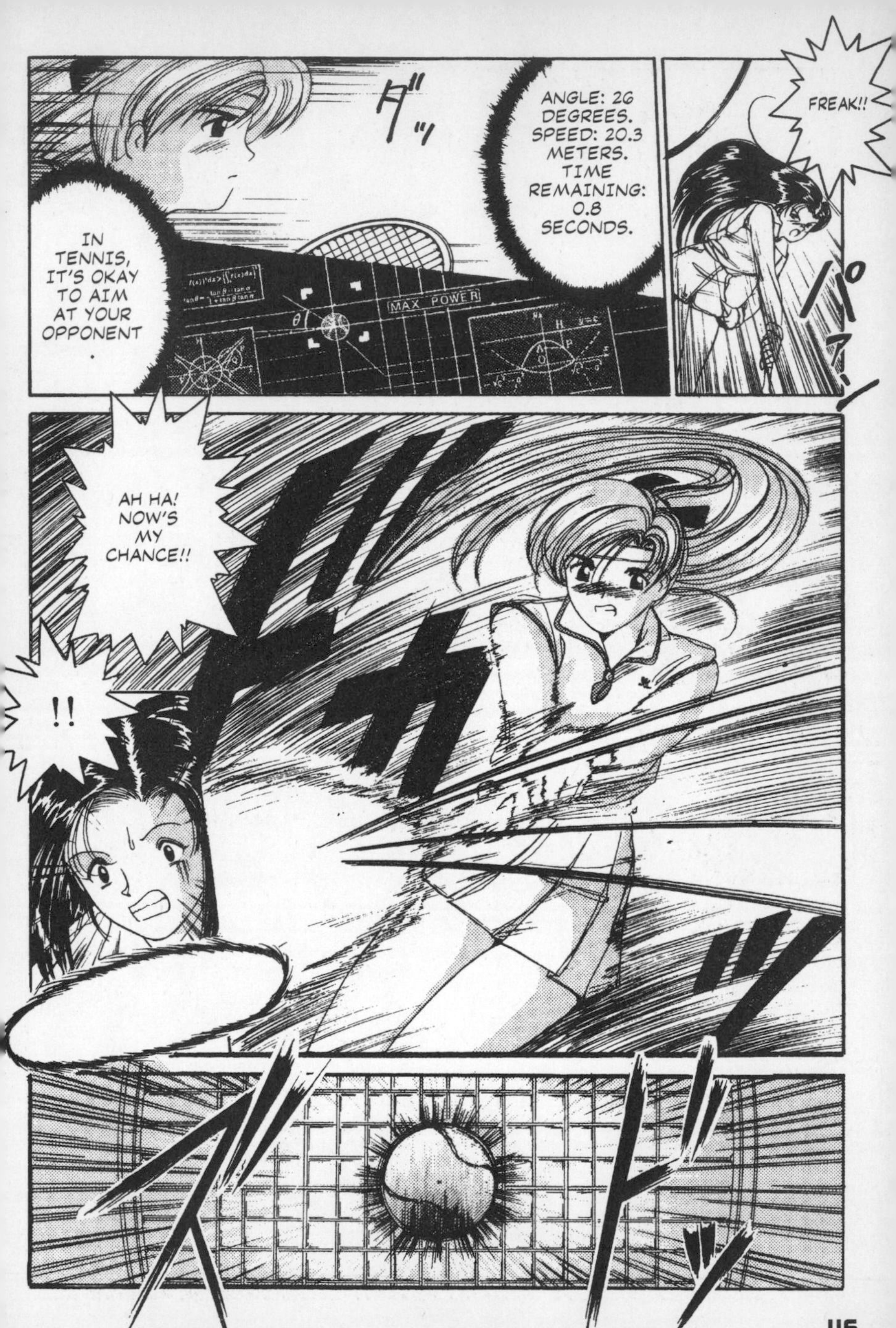
FREAK!!
ANGLE: 26 DEGREES. SPEED: 20.3 METERS. TIME REMAINING: 0.8 SECONDS.
IN TENNIS, IT'S OKAY TO AIM AT YOUR OPPONENT.
MAX POWER
AH HA! NOW'S MY CHANCE!!
!!

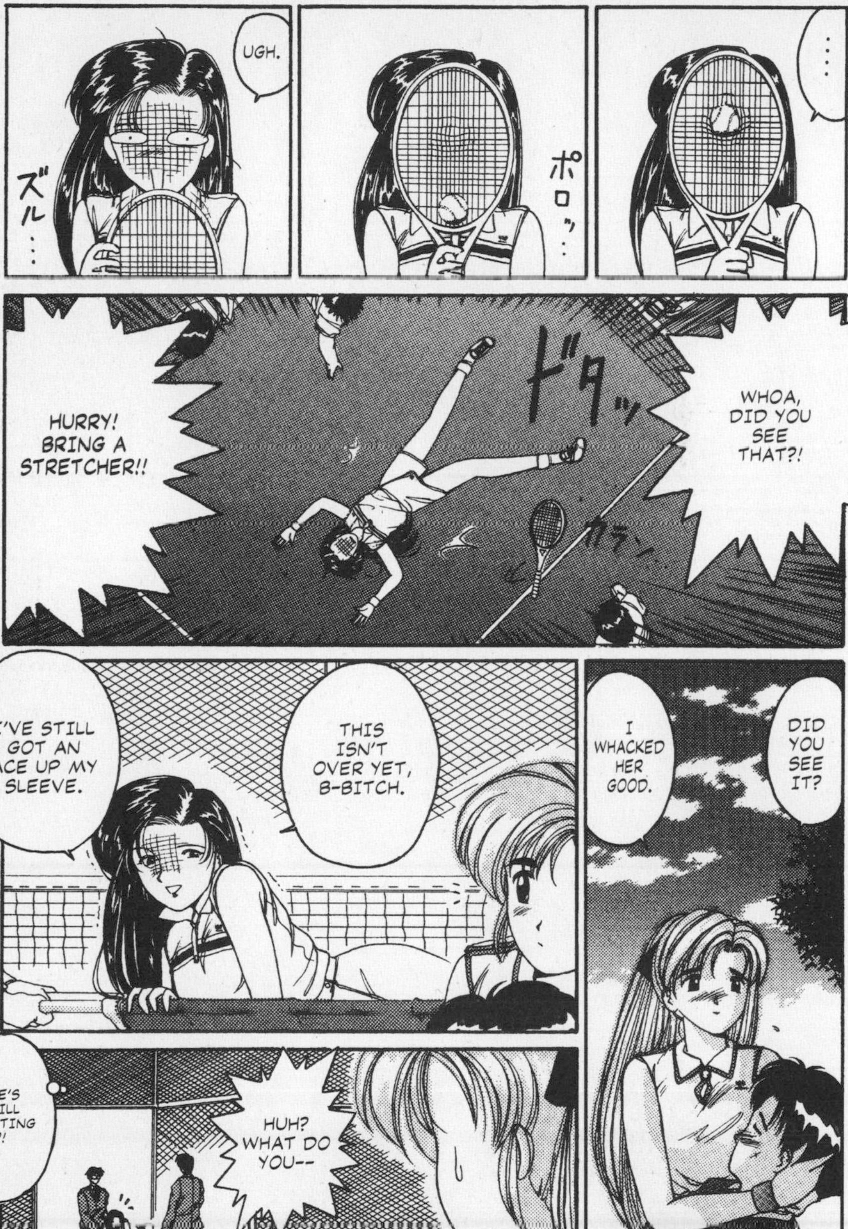
...
ポロッ...
UGH.
ズル...
WHOA, DID YOU SEE THAT?!
ドタッ
カラン
HURRY! BRING A STRETCHER!!
DID YOU SEE IT?
I WHACKED HER GOOD.
THIS ISN'T OVER YET, B-BITCH.
I'VE STILL GOT AN ACE UP MY SLEEVE.
HUH? WHAT DO YOU--
SHE'S STILL FIGHTING ?!

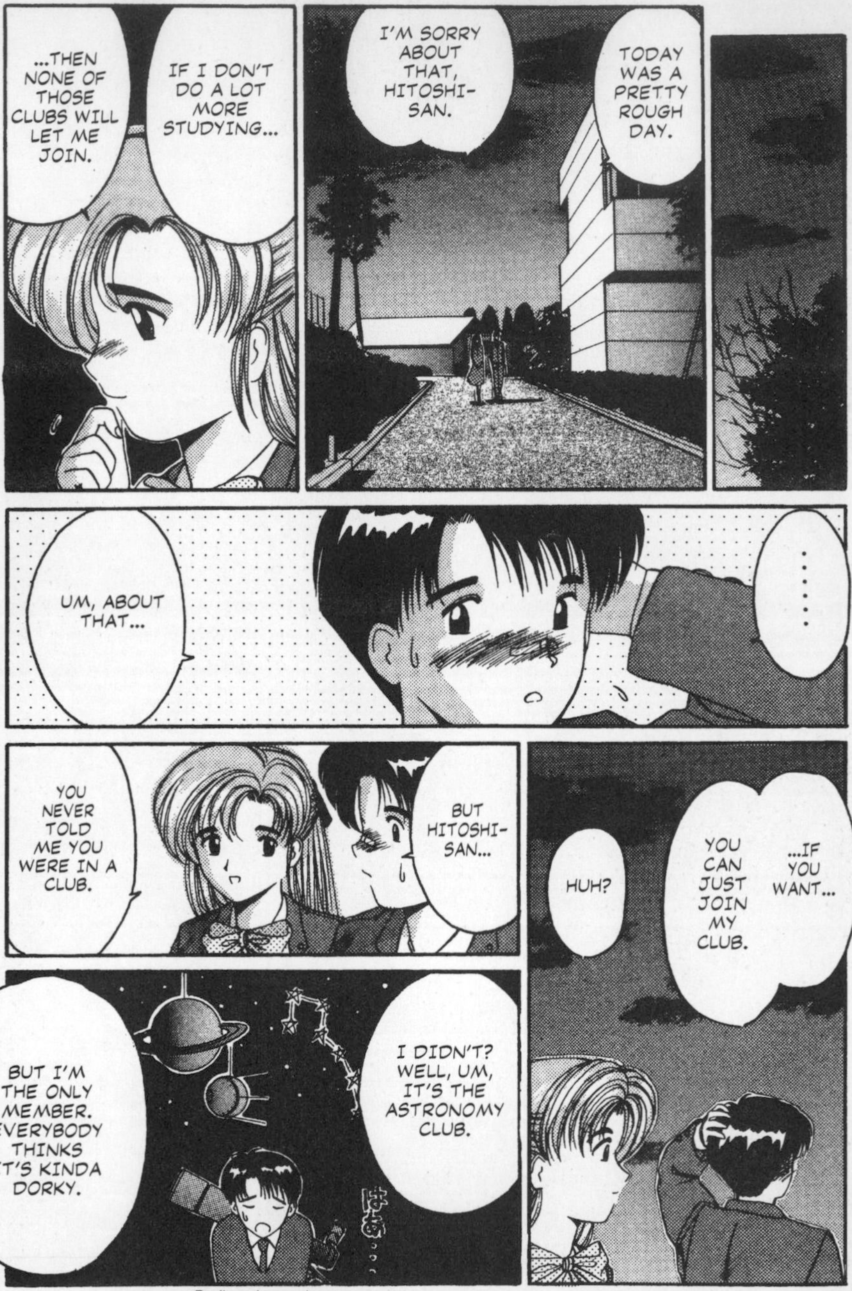
TODAY WAS A PRETTY ROUGH DAY.
I'M SORRY ABOUT THAT, HITOSHI-SAN.
IF I DON'T DO A LOT MORE STUDYING...
...THEN NONE OF THOSE CLUBS WILL LET ME JOIN.
......
UM, ABOUT THAT...
...IF YOU WANT...
YOU CAN JUST JOIN MY CLUB.
HUH?
BUT HITOSHI-SAN...
YOU NEVER TOLD ME YOU WERE IN A CLUB.
I DIDN'T? WELL, UM, IT'S THE ASTRONOMY CLUB.
BUT I'M THE ONLY MEMBER. EVERYBODY THINKS IT'S KINDA DORKY.
はぁ・・・

Really embarrassing.

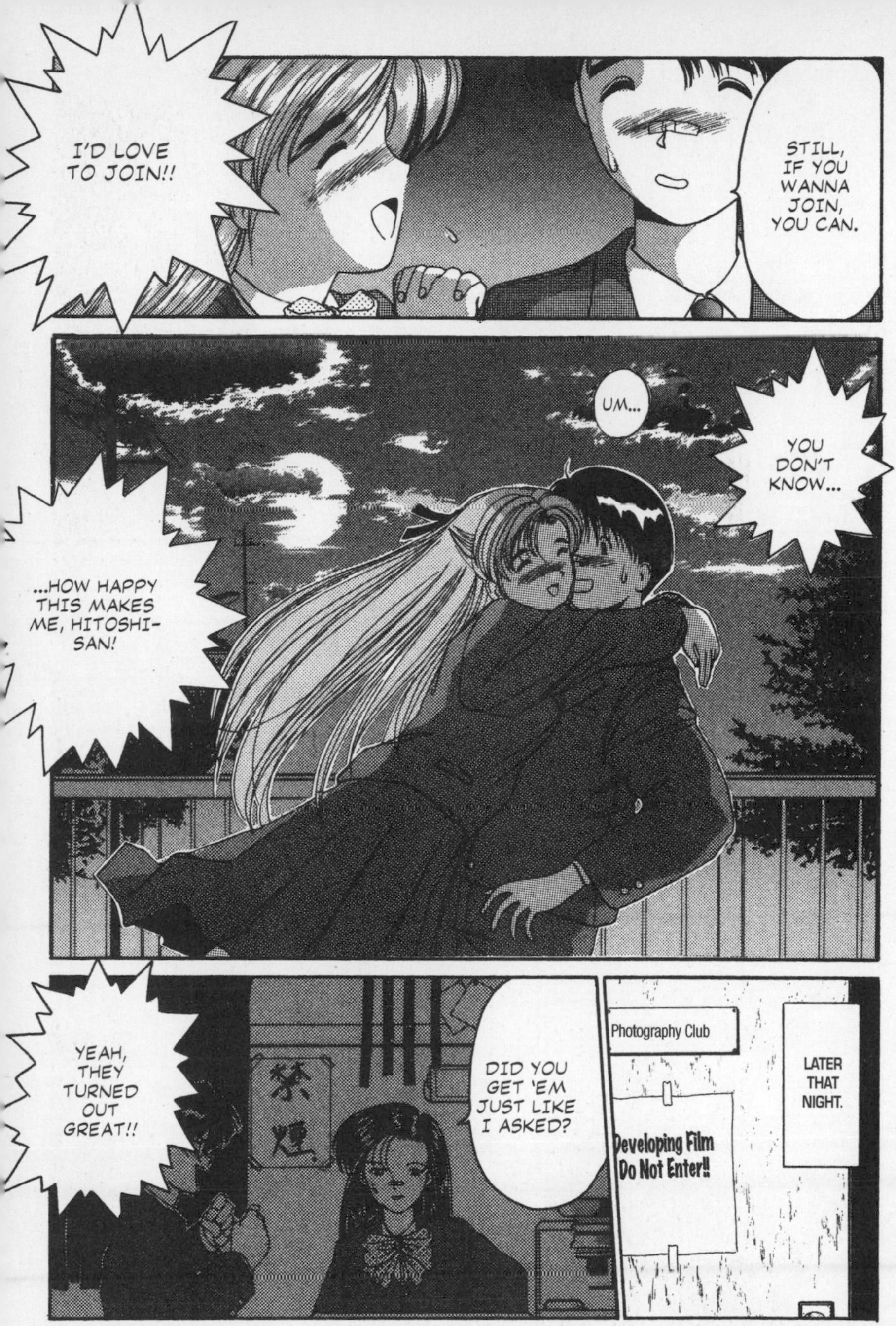
STILL, IF YOU WANNA JOIN, YOU CAN.
I'D LOVE TO JOIN!!
UM...
YOU DON'T KNOW...
...HOW HAPPY THIS MAKES ME, HITOSHI-SAN!
LATER THAT NIGHT.
Photography Club
Developing Film Do Not Enter!!
DID YOU GET 'EM JUST LIKE I ASKED?
YEAH, THEY TURNED OUT GREAT!!

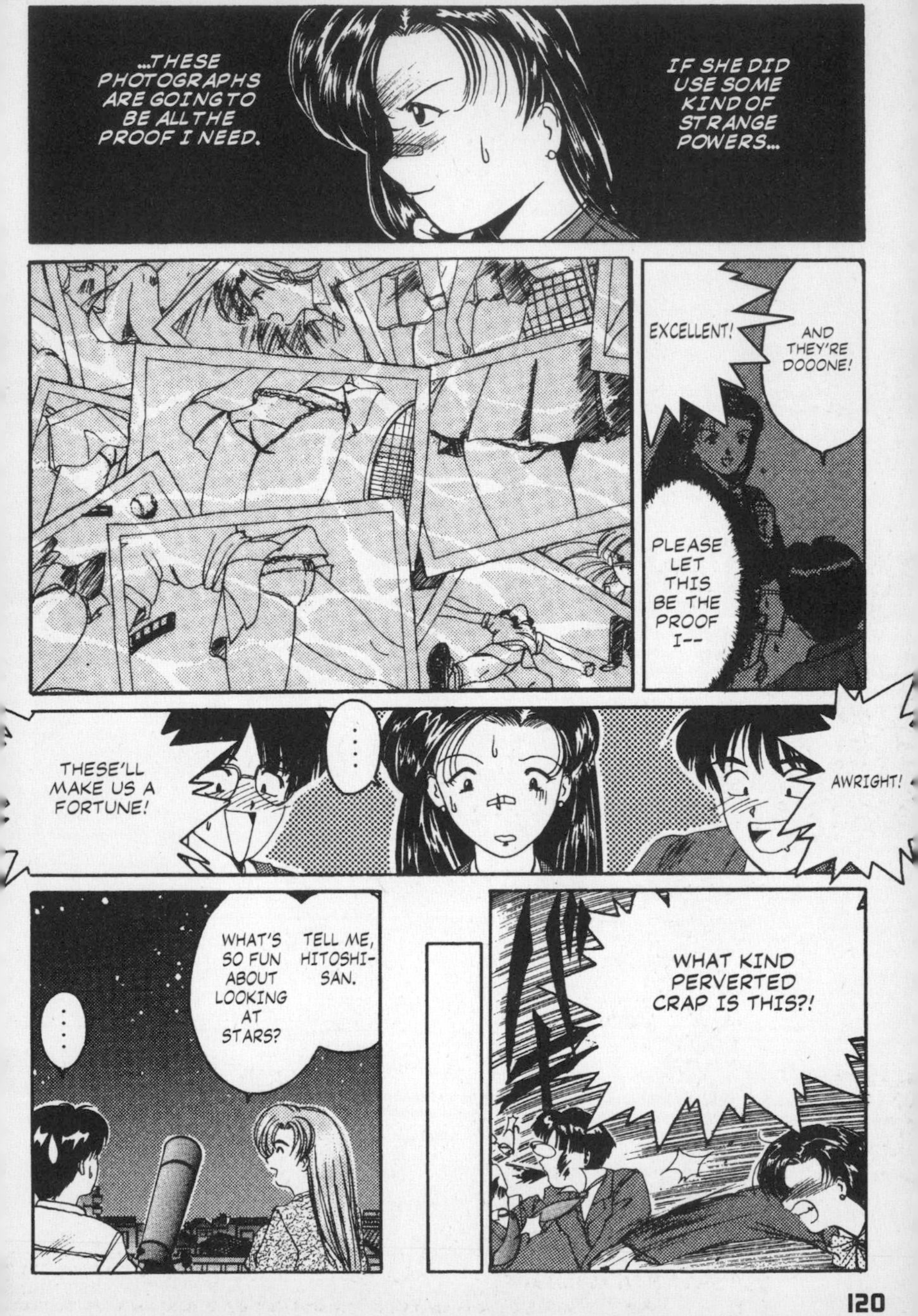
IF SHE DID USE SOME KIND OF STRANGE POWERS...
...THESE PHOTOGRAPHS ARE GOING TO BE ALL THE PROOF I NEED.
AND THEY'RE DOOONE!
EXCELLENT!
PLEASE LET THIS BE THE PROOF I--
AWRIGHT!
....
THESE'LL MAKE US A FORTUNE!
WHAT KIND PERVERTED CRAP IS THIS?!
TELL ME, HITOSHI-SAN.
WHAT'S SO FUN ABOUT LOOKING AT STARS?
....

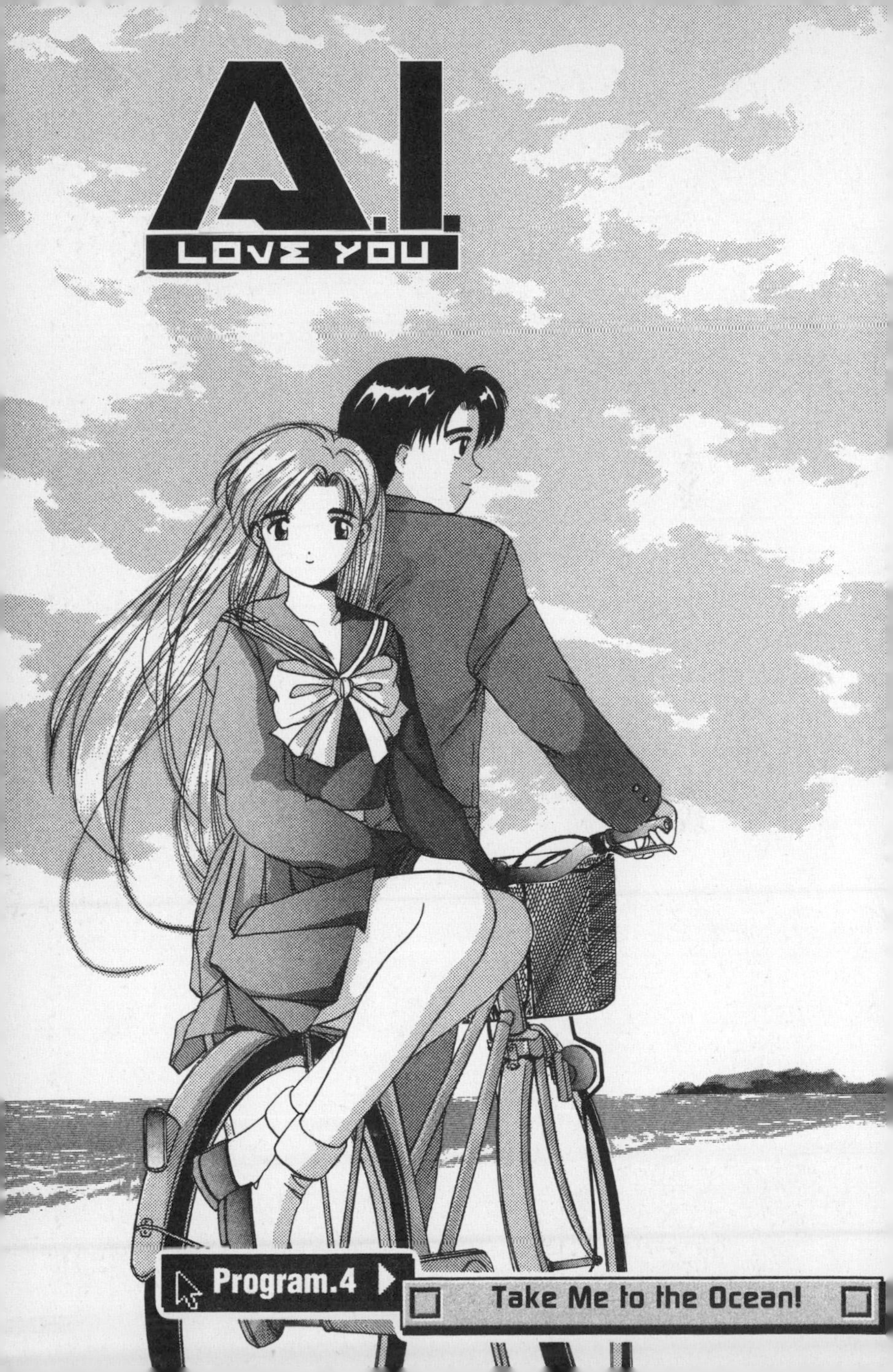
A.I.
LOVE YOU
Program.4
Take Me to the Ocean!

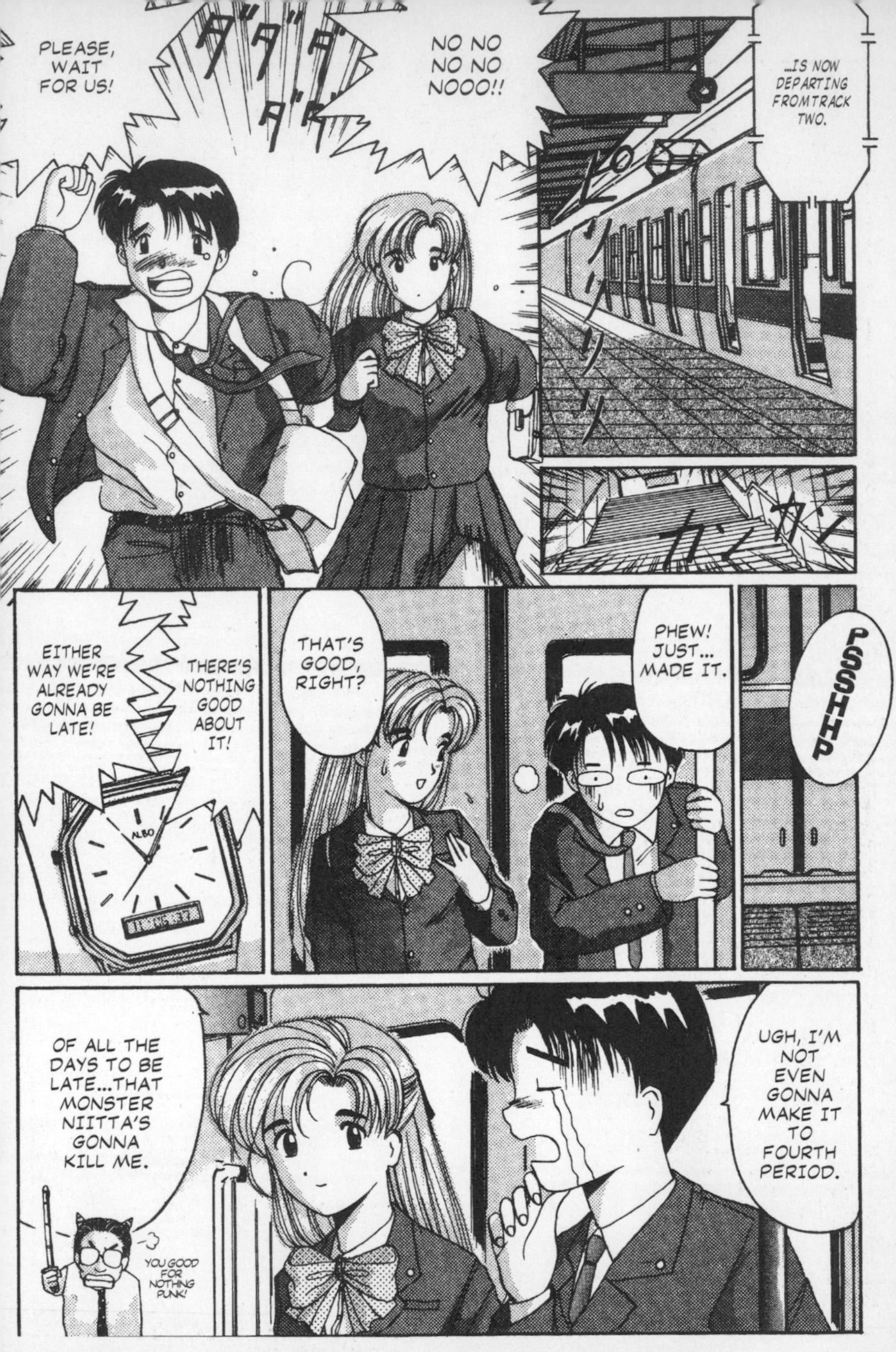
...IS NOW DEPARTING FROMTRACK TWO.
NO NO NO NO NOOO!!
PLEASE, WAIT FOR US!
PSSHHP
PHEW! JUST... MADE IT.
THAT'S GOOD, RIGHT?
THERE'S NOTHING GOOD ABOUT IT!
EITHER WAY WE'RE ALREADY GONNA BE LATE!
ALBO
UGH, I'M NOT EVEN GONNA MAKE IT TO FOURTH PERIOD.
OF ALL THE DAYS TO BE LATE...THAT MONSTER NIITTA'S GONNA KILL ME.
YOU GOOD FOR NOTHING PUNK!

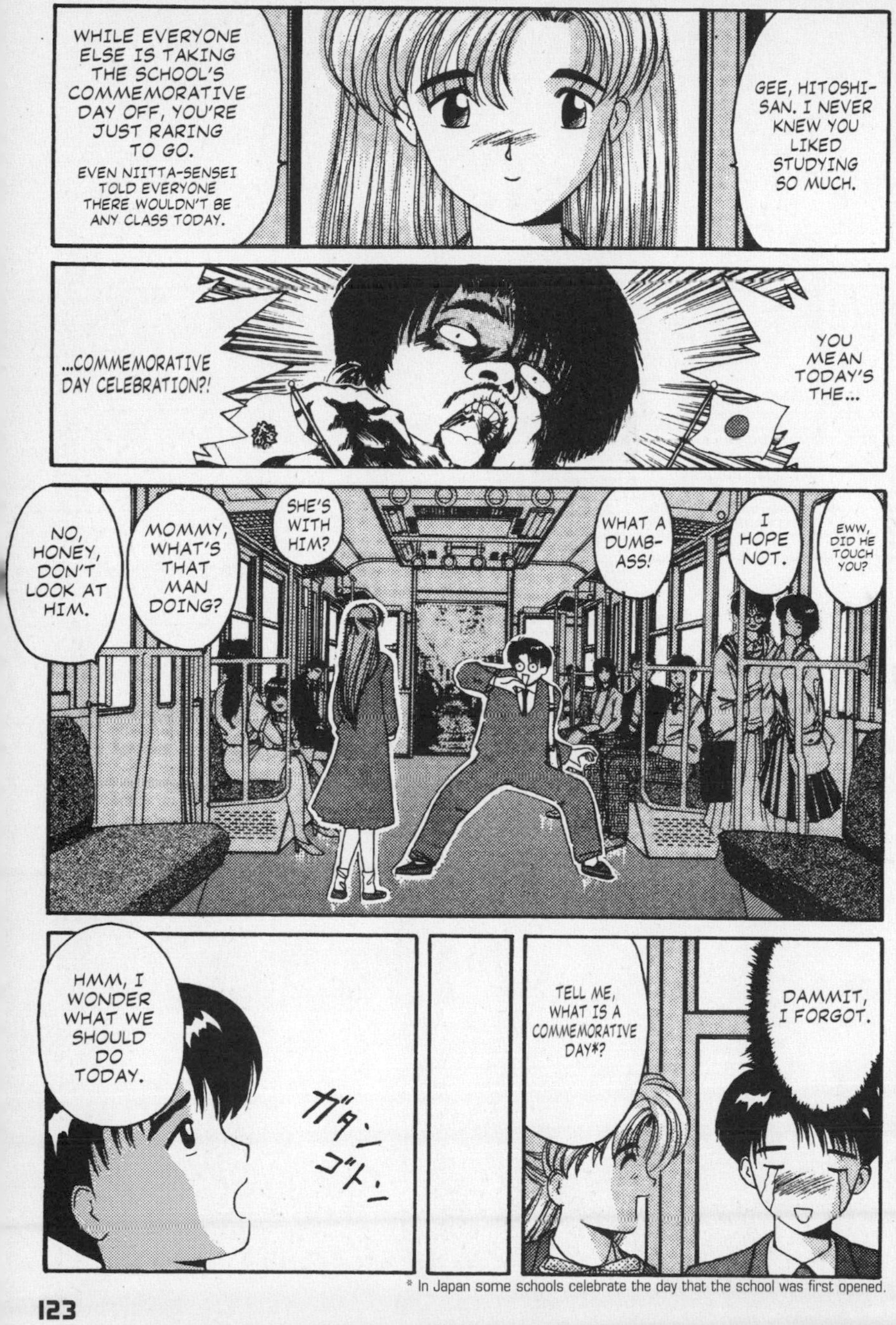

GEE, HITOSHI-SAN. I NEVER KNEW YOU LIKED STUDYING SO MUCH.
WHILE EVERYONE ELSE IS TAKING THE SCHOOL'S COMMEMORATIVE DAY OFF, YOU'RE JUST RARING TO GO.
EVEN NIITTA-SENSEI TOLD EVERYONE THERE WOULDN'T BE ANY CLASS TODAY.
YOU MEAN TODAY'S THE...
...COMMEMORATIVE DAY CELEBRATION?!
EWW, DID HE TOUCH YOU?
I HOPE NOT.
WHAT A DUMB-ASS!
SHE'S WITH HIM?
MOMMY, WHAT'S THAT MAN DOING?
NO, HONEY, DON'T LOOK AT HIM.
DAMMIT, I FORGOT.
TELL ME, WHAT IS A COMMEMORATIVE DAY*?
ガタン
ゴトン
HMM, I WONDER WHAT WE SHOULD DO TODAY.

* In Japan some schools celebrate the day that the school was first opened.

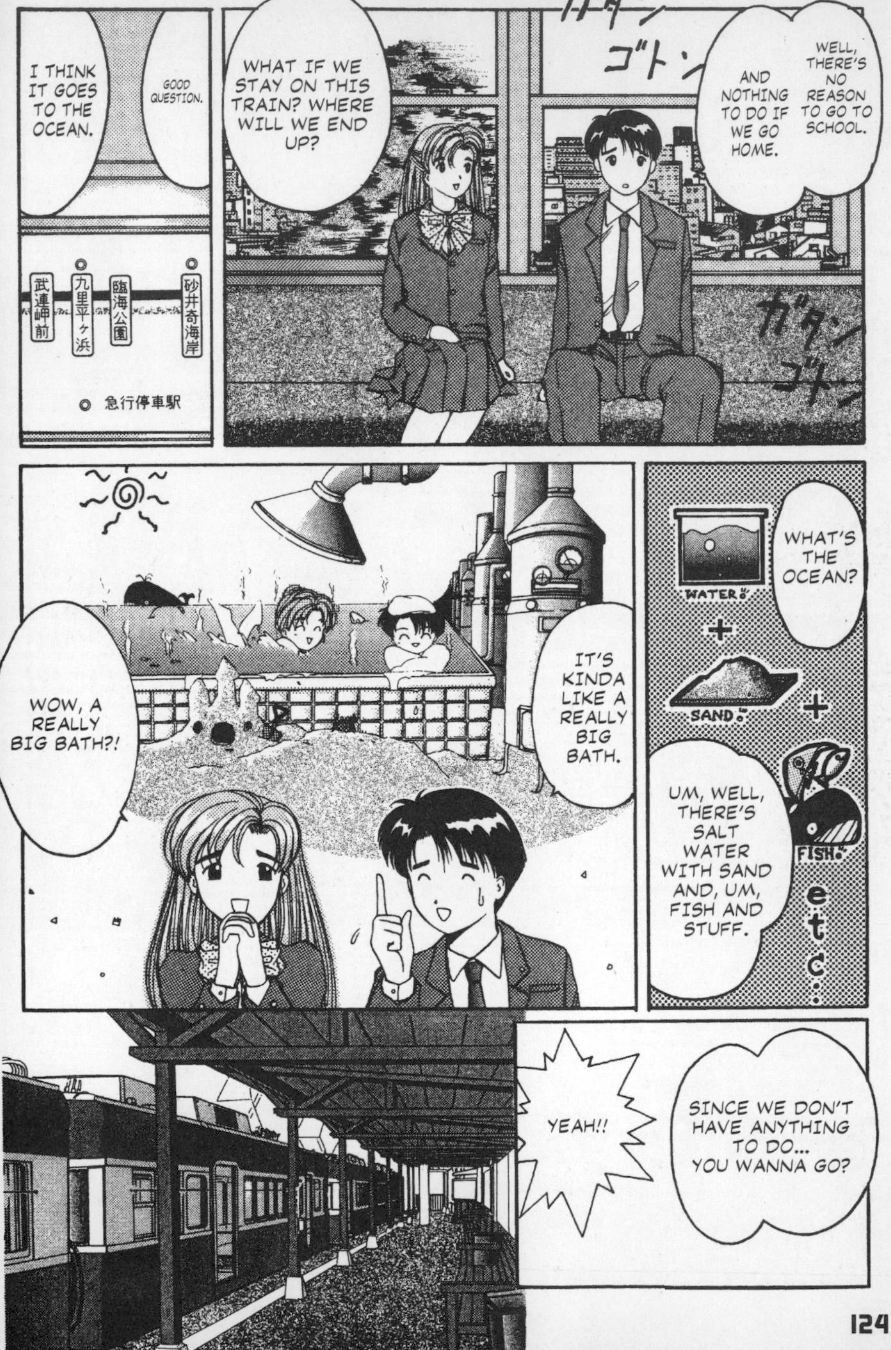
ガタン
ゴトン
WELL, THERE'S NO REASON TO GO TO SCHOOL.
AND NOTHING TO DO IF WE GO HOME.
ガタン
ゴトン
WHAT IF WE STAY ON THIS TRAIN? WHERE WILL WE END UP?
GOOD QUESTION.
I THINK IT GOES TO THE OCEAN.
砂井奇海岸
臨海公園
九里平ヶ浜
武連岬前
◎ 急行停車駅
WHAT'S THE OCEAN?
WATER
+
SAND
+
FISH
etc...
UM, WELL, THERE'S SALT WATER WITH SAND AND, UM, FISH AND STUFF.
IT'S KINDA LIKE A REALLY BIG BATH.
WOW, A REALLY BIG BATH?!
SINCE WE DON'T HAVE ANYTHING TO DO... YOU WANNA GO?
YEAH!!

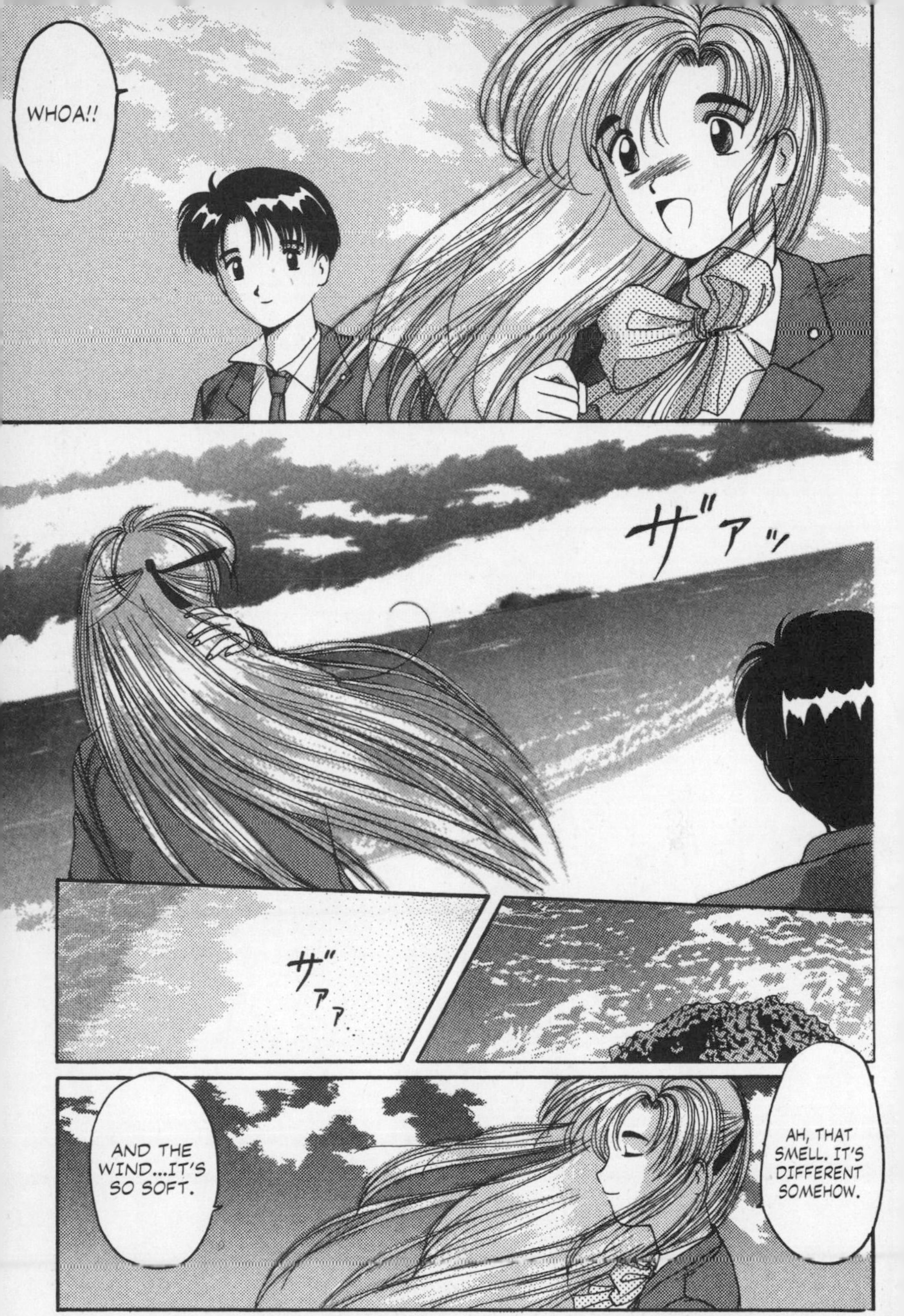
WHOA!!
ザアッ
ザァァ
AH, THAT SMELL. IT'S DIFFERENT SOMEHOW.
AND THE WIND...IT'S SO SOFT.

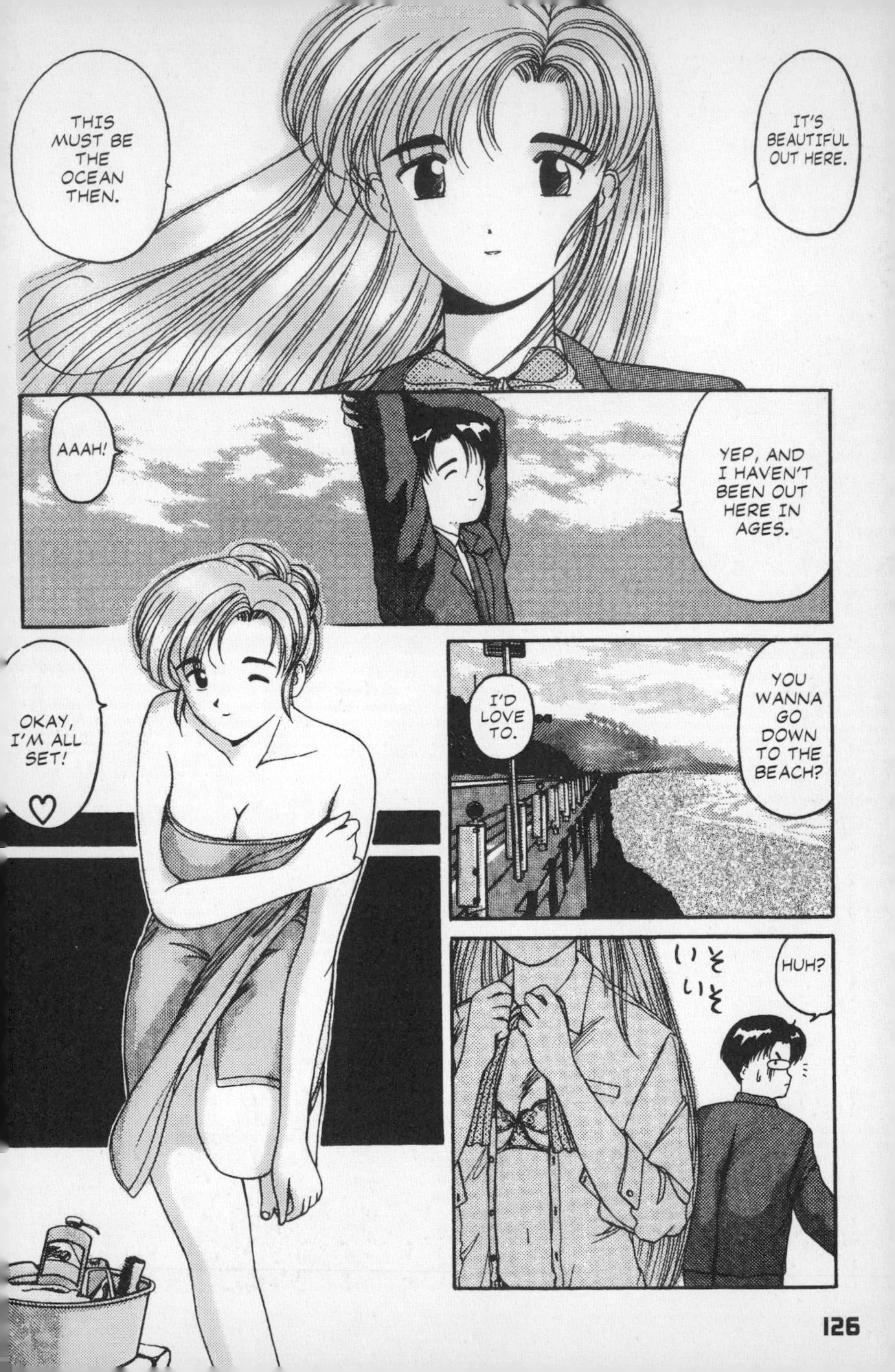
IT'S BEAUTIFUL OUT HERE.
THIS MUST BE THE OCEAN THEN.
YEP, AND I HAVEN'T BEEN OUT HERE IN AGES.
AAAH!
YOU WANNA GO DOWN TO THE BEACH?
I'D LOVE TO.
HUH?
いそ いそ
OKAY, I'M ALL SET! ♡

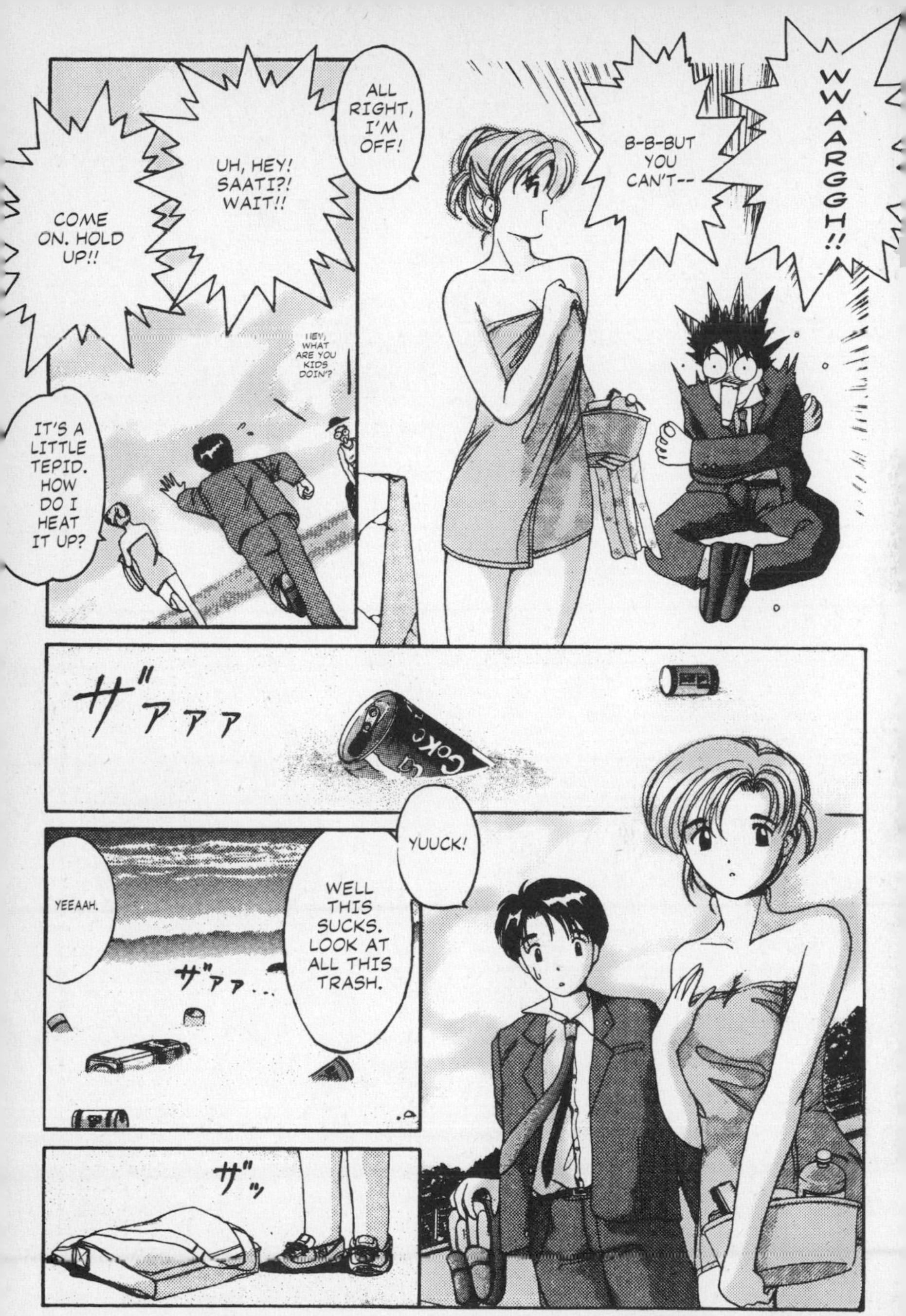

WWAARGH!!
B-B-BUT YOU CAN'T--
ALL RIGHT, I'M OFF!
UH, HEY! SAATI?! WAIT!!
COME ON. HOLD UP!!
HEY, WHAT ARE YOU KIDS DOIN'?
IT'S A LITTLE TEPID. HOW DO I HEAT IT UP?
ザァァァ
YUUCK!
WELL THIS SUCKS. LOOK AT ALL THIS TRASH.
YEEAAH.
ザァァ...
ザッ

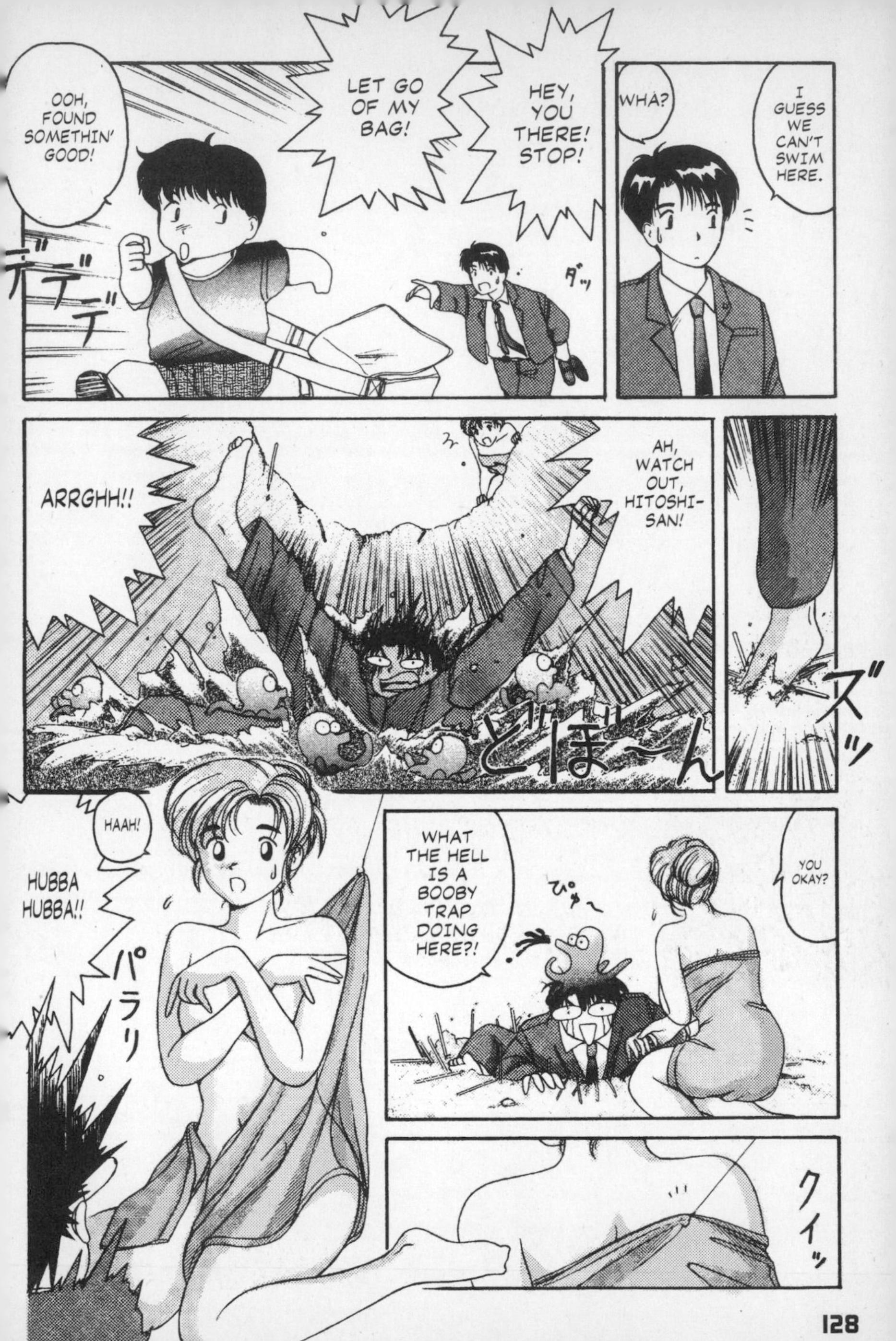
I GUESS WE CAN'T SWIM HERE.
WHA?
HEY, YOU THERE! STOP!
LET GO OF MY BAG!
ダッ
OOH, FOUND SOMETHIN' GOOD!
デデデ
ズッ
AH, WATCH OUT, HITOSHI-SAN!
ARRGHH!!
どぼ〜ん
YOU OKAY?
WHAT THE HELL IS A BOOBY TRAP DOING HERE?!
ぴゅ〜
クイッ
HAAH!
HUBBA HUBBA!!
パラリ

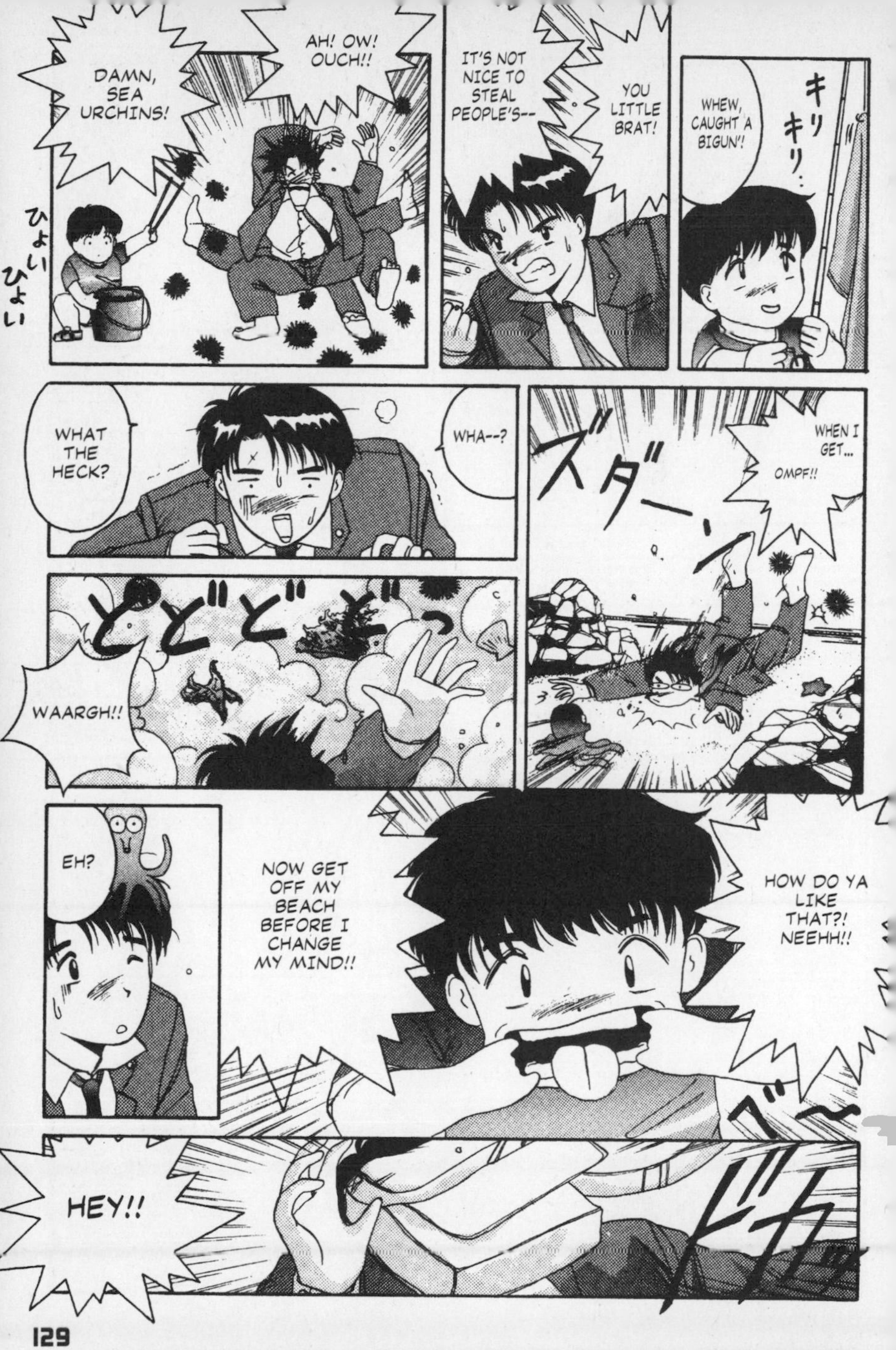
キリキリ
WHEW, CAUGHT A BIGUN'!
YOU LITTLE BRAT!
IT'S NOT NICE TO STEAL PEOPLE'S--
AH! OW! OUCH!!
DAMN, SEA URCHINS!
ひょいひょいひょい
ズダー
WHEN I GET...
OMPF!!
WHA--?
WHAT THE HECK?
どどどどっ
WAARGH!!
HOW DO YA LIKE THAT?! NEEHH!!
NOW GET OFF MY BEACH BEFORE I CHANGE MY MIND!!
べ～
EH?
ドカッ
HEY!!

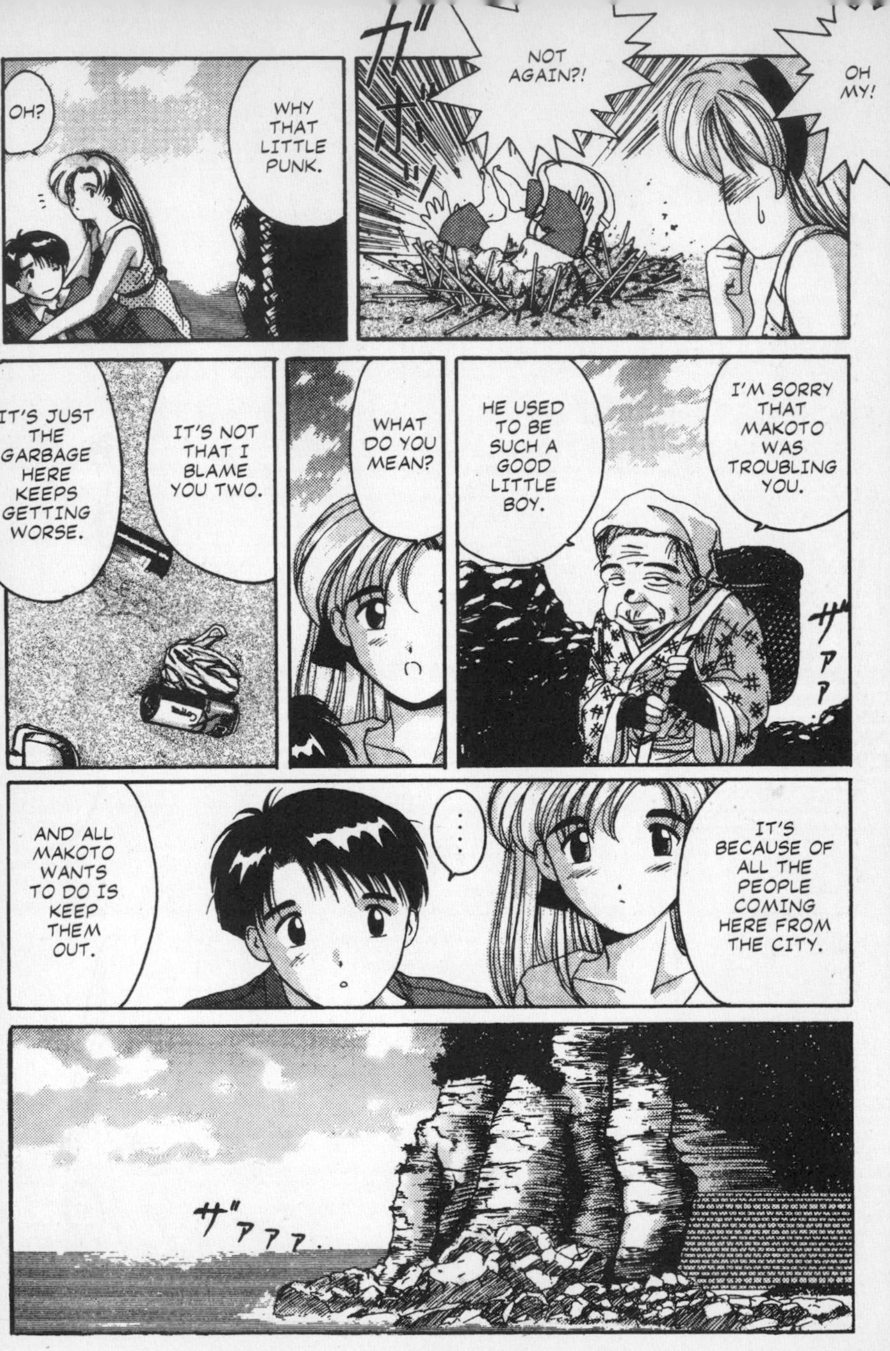
OH MY!
NOT AGAIN?!
WHY THAT LITTLE PUNK.
OH?
I'M SORRY THAT MAKOTO WAS TROUBLING YOU.
HE USED TO BE SUCH A GOOD LITTLE BOY.
ザァァ
WHAT DO YOU MEAN?
IT'S NOT THAT I BLAME YOU TWO.
IT'S JUST THE GARBAGE HERE KEEPS GETTING WORSE.
IT'S BECAUSE OF ALL THE PEOPLE COMING HERE FROM THE CITY.
......
AND ALL MAKOTO WANTS TO DO IS KEEP THEM OUT.
ザァァァ

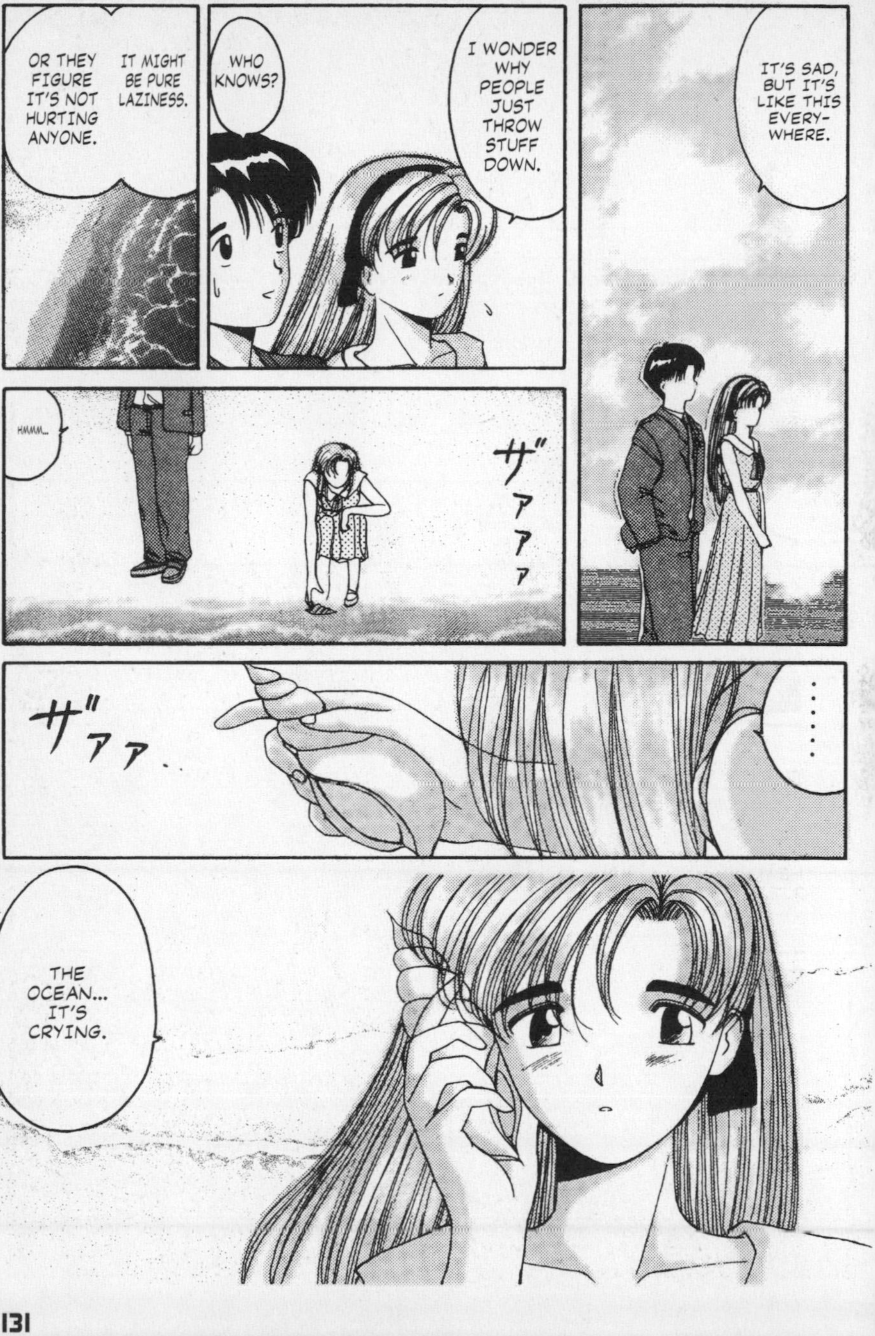
IT'S SAD, BUT IT'S LIKE THIS EVERYWHERE.
I WONDER WHY PEOPLE JUST THROW STUFF DOWN.
WHO KNOWS?
IT MIGHT BE PURE LAZINESS.
OR THEY FIGURE IT'S NOT HURTING ANYONE.
ザァァァ
HMMM...
......
ザァァ
THE OCEAN... IT'S CRYING.

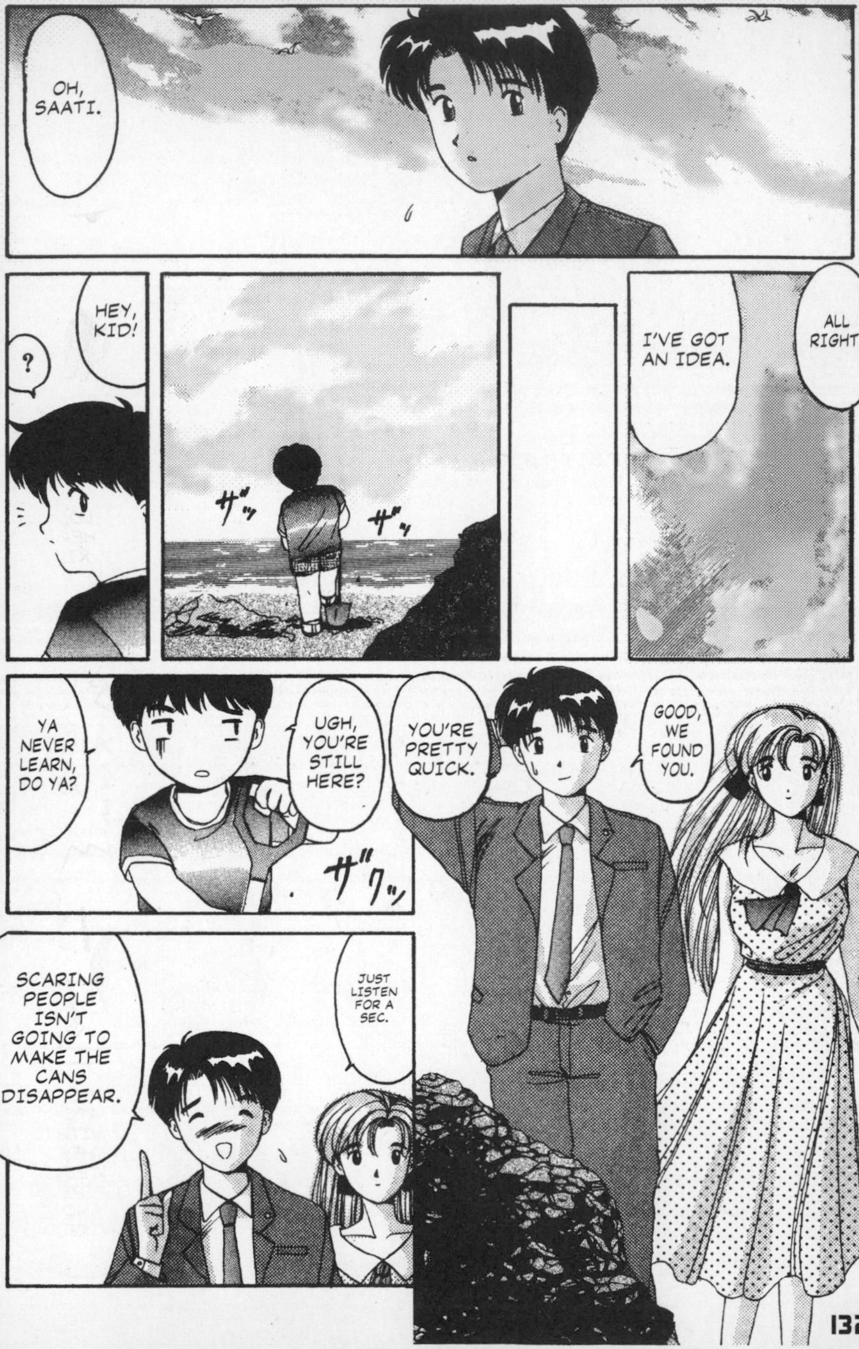
OH, SAATI.
ALL RIGHT.
I'VE GOT AN IDEA.
ザッ
ザッ
HEY, KID!
?
GOOD, WE FOUND YOU.
YOU'RE PRETTY QUICK.
UGH, YOU'RE STILL HERE?
YA NEVER LEARN, DO YA?
ザクッ
JUST LISTEN FOR A SEC.
SCARING PEOPLE ISN'T GOING TO MAKE THE CANS DISAPPEAR.

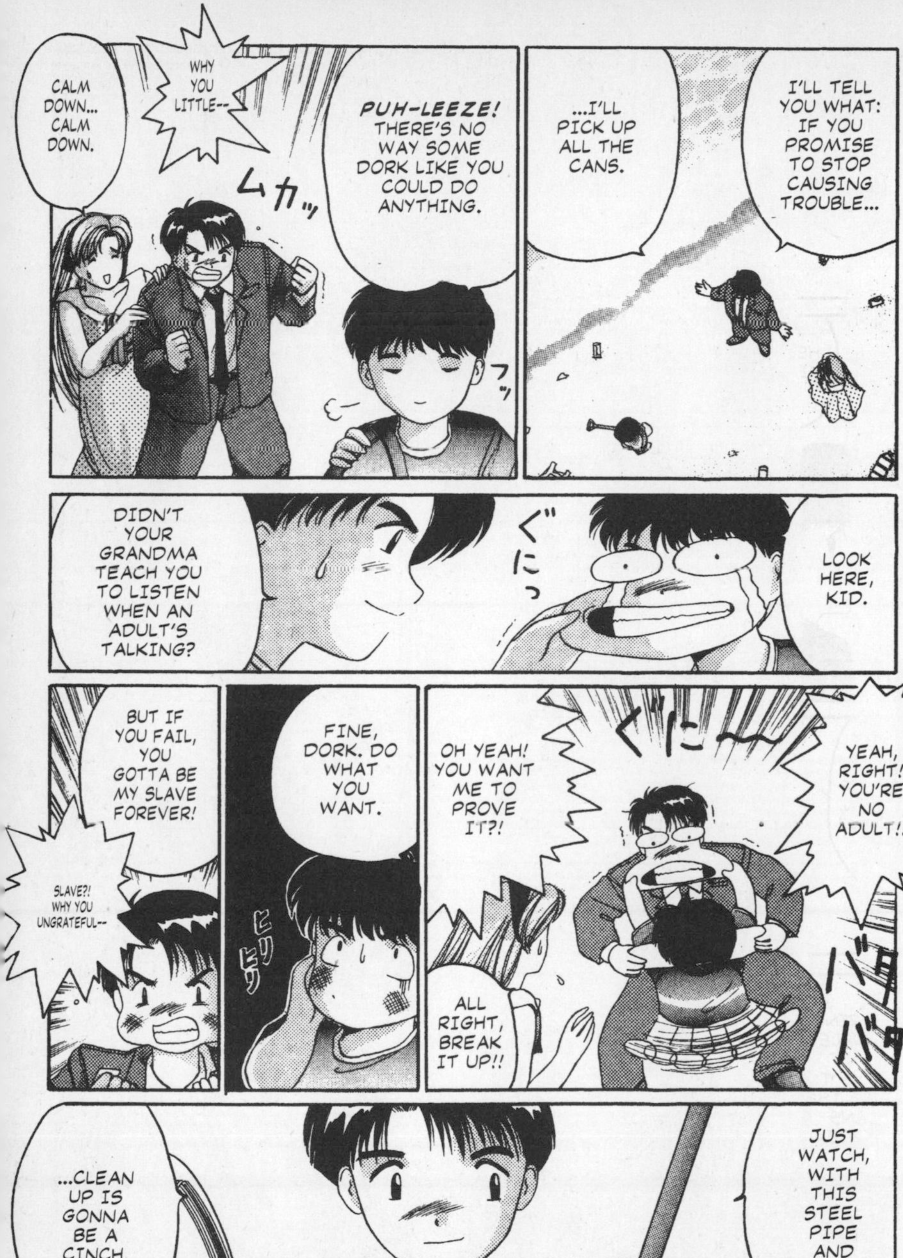
I'LL TELL YOU WHAT: IF YOU PROMISE TO STOP CAUSING TROUBLE...
...I'LL PICK UP ALL THE CANS.
PUH-LEEZE! THERE'S NO WAY SOME DORK LIKE YOU COULD DO ANYTHING.
フッ
WHY YOU LITTLE--
ムカッ
CALM DOWN... CALM DOWN.
LOOK HERE, KID.
ぐにっ
DIDN'T YOUR GRANDMA TEACH YOU TO LISTEN WHEN AN ADULT'S TALKING?
YEAH, RIGHT! YOU'RE NO ADULT!!
ぐに〜〜
OH YEAH! YOU WANT ME TO PROVE IT?!
バタバタ
ALL RIGHT, BREAK IT UP!!
FINE, DORK. DO WHAT YOU WANT.
ヒリヒリ
BUT IF YOU FAIL, YOU GOTTA BE MY SLAVE FOREVER!
SLAVE?! WHY YOU UNGRATEFUL--
JUST WATCH, WITH THIS STEEL PIPE AND WIRE...
...CLEAN UP IS GONNA BE A CINCH.

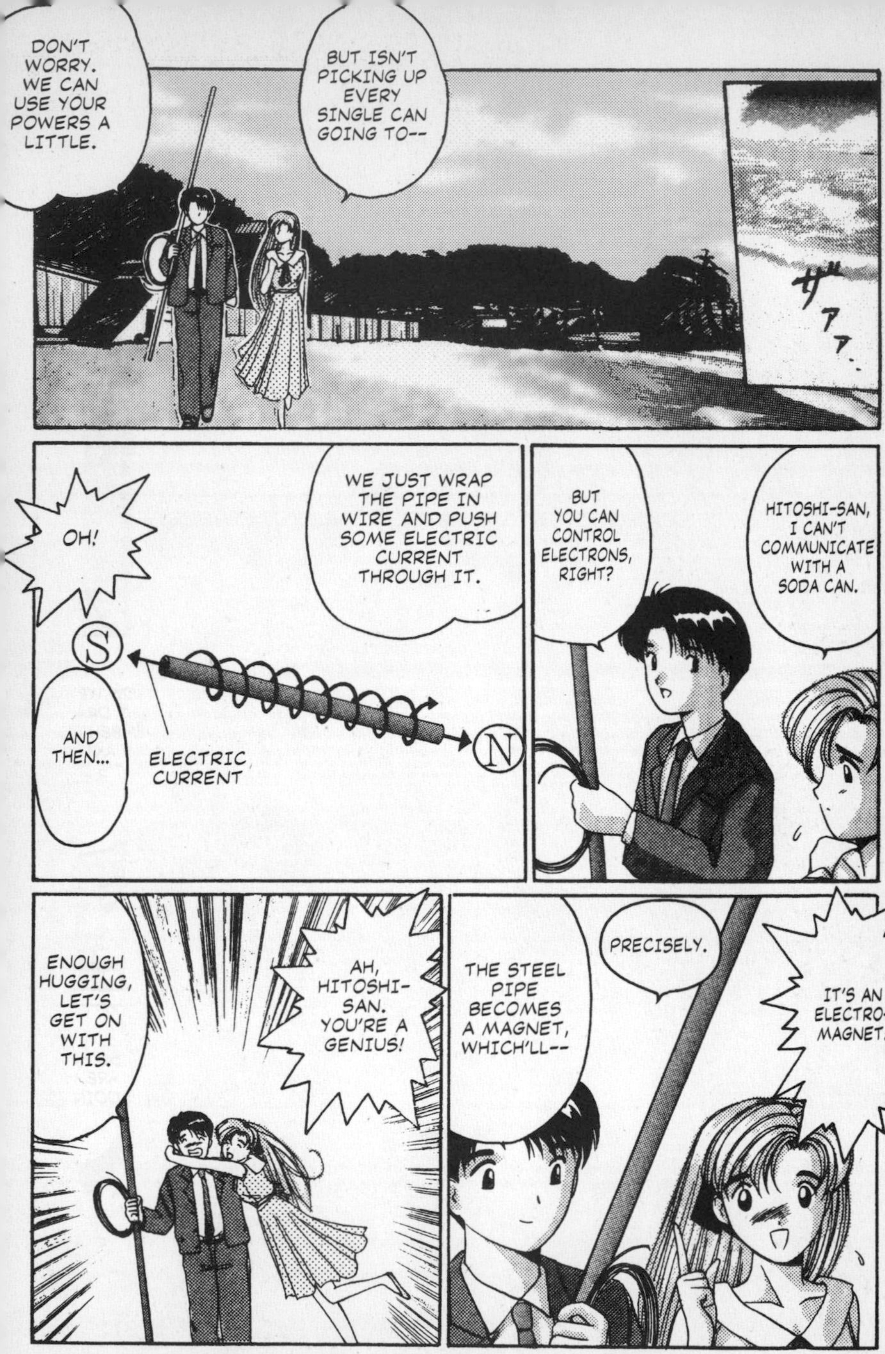
ザァァ..
BUT ISN'T PICKING UP EVERY SINGLE CAN GOING TO--
DON'T WORRY. WE CAN USE YOUR POWERS A LITTLE.
HITOSHI-SAN, I CAN'T COMMUNICATE WITH A SODA CAN.
BUT YOU CAN CONTROL ELECTRONS, RIGHT?
WE JUST WRAP THE PIPE IN WIRE AND PUSH SOME ELECTRIC CURRENT THROUGH IT.
OH!
S
N
AND THEN...
ELECTRIC CURRENT
IT'S AN ELECTRO-MAGNET!
PRECISELY.
THE STEEL PIPE BECOMES A MAGNET, WHICH'LL--
AH, HITOSHI-SAN. YOU'RE A GENIUS!
ENOUGH HUGGING, LET'S GET ON WITH THIS.

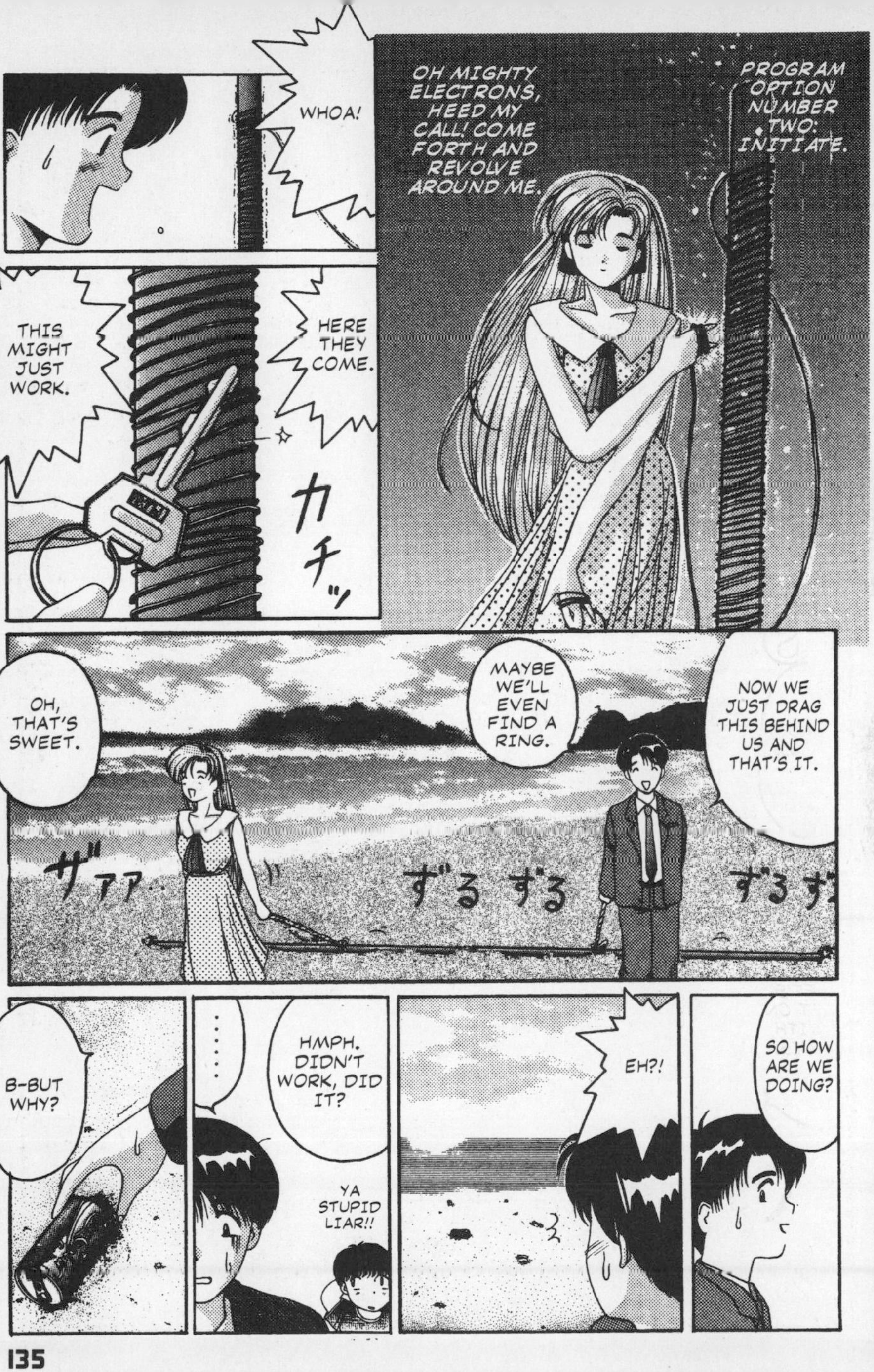

PROGRAM OPTION NUMBER TWO: INITIATE.
OH MIGHTY ELECTRONS, HEED MY CALL! COME FORTH AND REVOLVE AROUND ME.
WHOA!
HERE THEY COME.
THIS MIGHT JUST WORK.
カチッ
NOW WE JUST DRAG THIS BEHIND US AND THAT'S IT.
MAYBE WE'LL EVEN FIND A RING.
OH, THAT'S SWEET.
ずるず
ずる ずる
ザァア
SO HOW ARE WE DOING?
EH?!
HMPH. DIDN'T WORK, DID IT?
YA STUPID LIAR!!
......
B-BUT WHY?

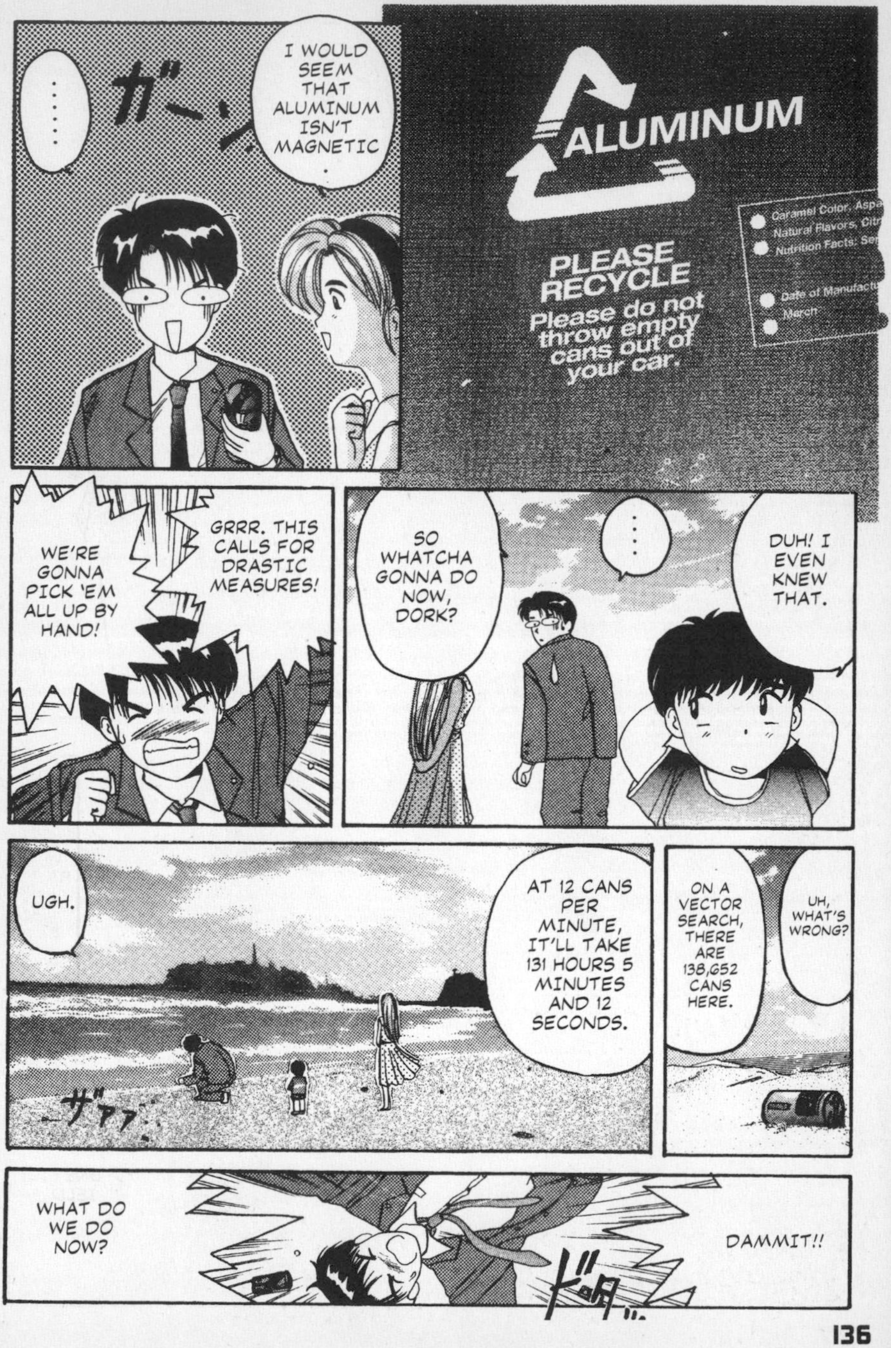
ALUMINUM
PLEASE RECYCLE
Please do not throw empty cans out of your car.
Caramel Color,
Natural Flavors,
Nutrition Facts:
March
I WOULD SEEM THAT ALUMINUM ISN'T MAGNETIC.
ガーン
......
DUH! I EVEN KNEW THAT.
....
SO WHATCHA GONNA DO NOW, DORK?
GRRR. THIS CALLS FOR DRASTIC MEASURES!
WE'RE GONNA PICK 'EM ALL UP BY HAND!
UH, WHAT'S WRONG?
ON A VECTOR SEARCH, THERE ARE 138,652 CANS HERE.
AT 12 CANS PER MINUTE, IT'LL TAKE 131 HOURS 5 MINUTES AND 12 SECONDS.
UGH.
ザァァ
DAMMIT!!
WHAT DO WE DO NOW?

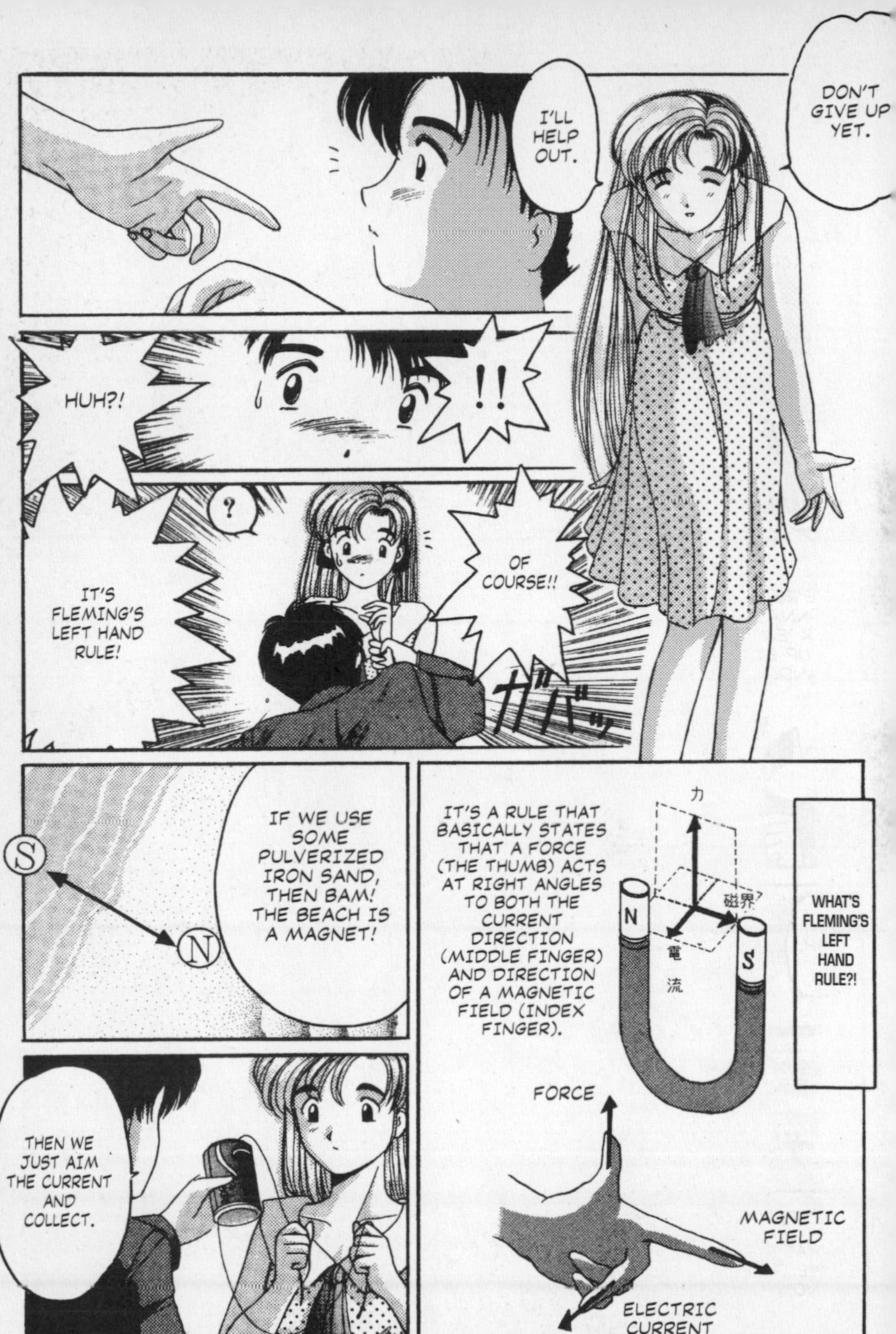

DON'T GIVE UP YET.
I'LL HELP OUT.
!!
HUH?!
OF COURSE!!
?
IT'S FLEMING'S LEFT HAND RULE!
ガバッ
WHAT'S FLEMING'S LEFT HAND RULE?!
IT'S A RULE THAT BASICALLY STATES THAT A FORCE (THE THUMB) ACTS AT RIGHT ANGLES TO BOTH THE CURRENT DIRECTION (MIDDLE FINGER) AND DIRECTION OF A MAGNETIC FIELD (INDEX FINGER).
力
磁界
電流
N
S
FORCE
MAGNETIC FIELD
ELECTRIC CURRENT
IF WE USE SOME PULVERIZED IRON SAND, THEN BAM! THE BEACH IS A MAGNET!
S
N
THEN WE JUST AIM THE CURRENT AND COLLECT.

Sir John Ambrose Fleming (1849-1945) - An English electrical engineer whose vacuum tube helped jump-start modern electronics.

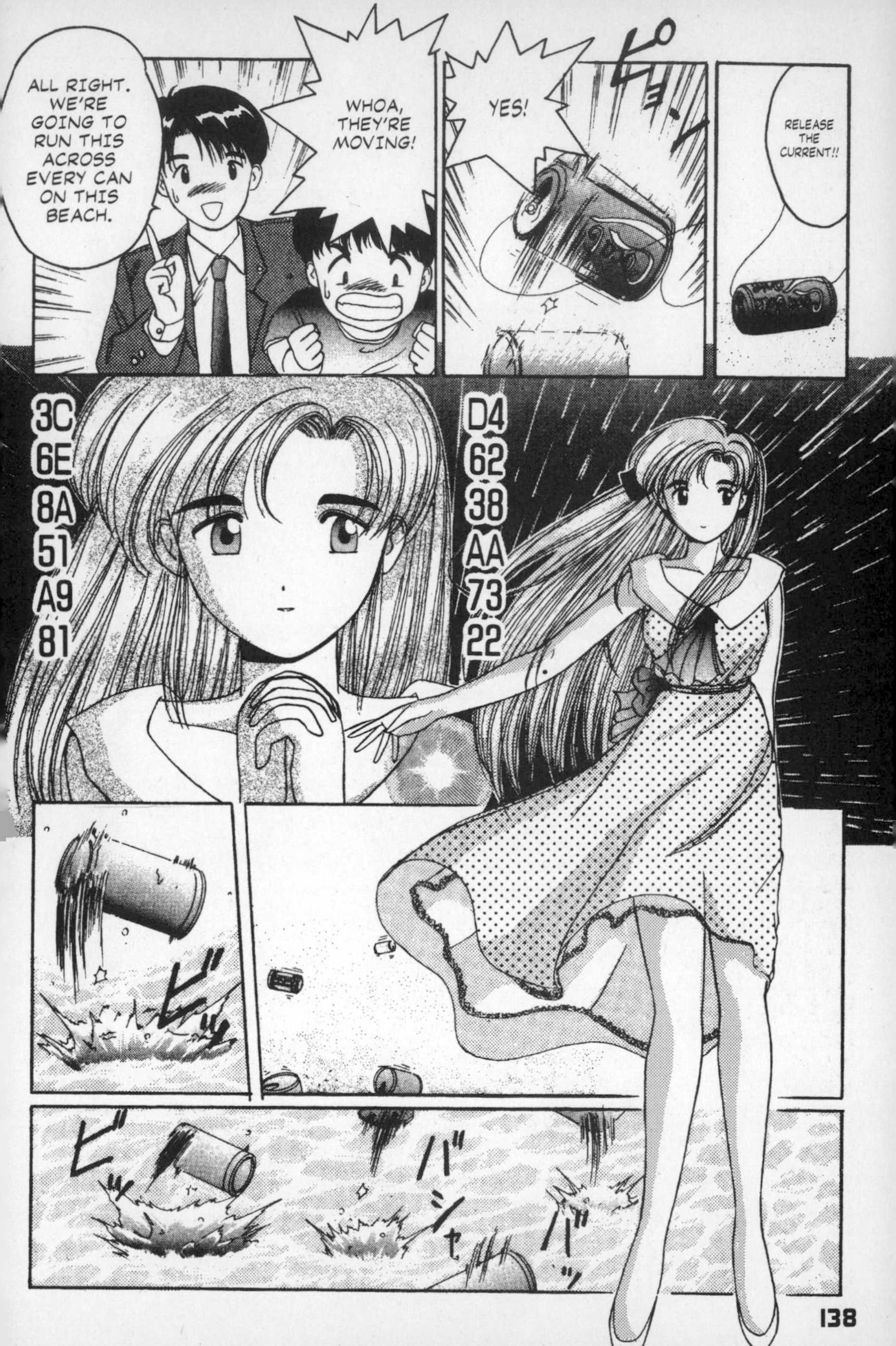
RELEASE THE CURRENT!!
YES!
WHOA, THEY'RE MOVING!
ALL RIGHT. WE'RE GOING TO RUN THIS ACROSS EVERY CAN ON THIS BEACH.
D4 62 38 AA 73 22
3C 6E 8A 51 A9 81

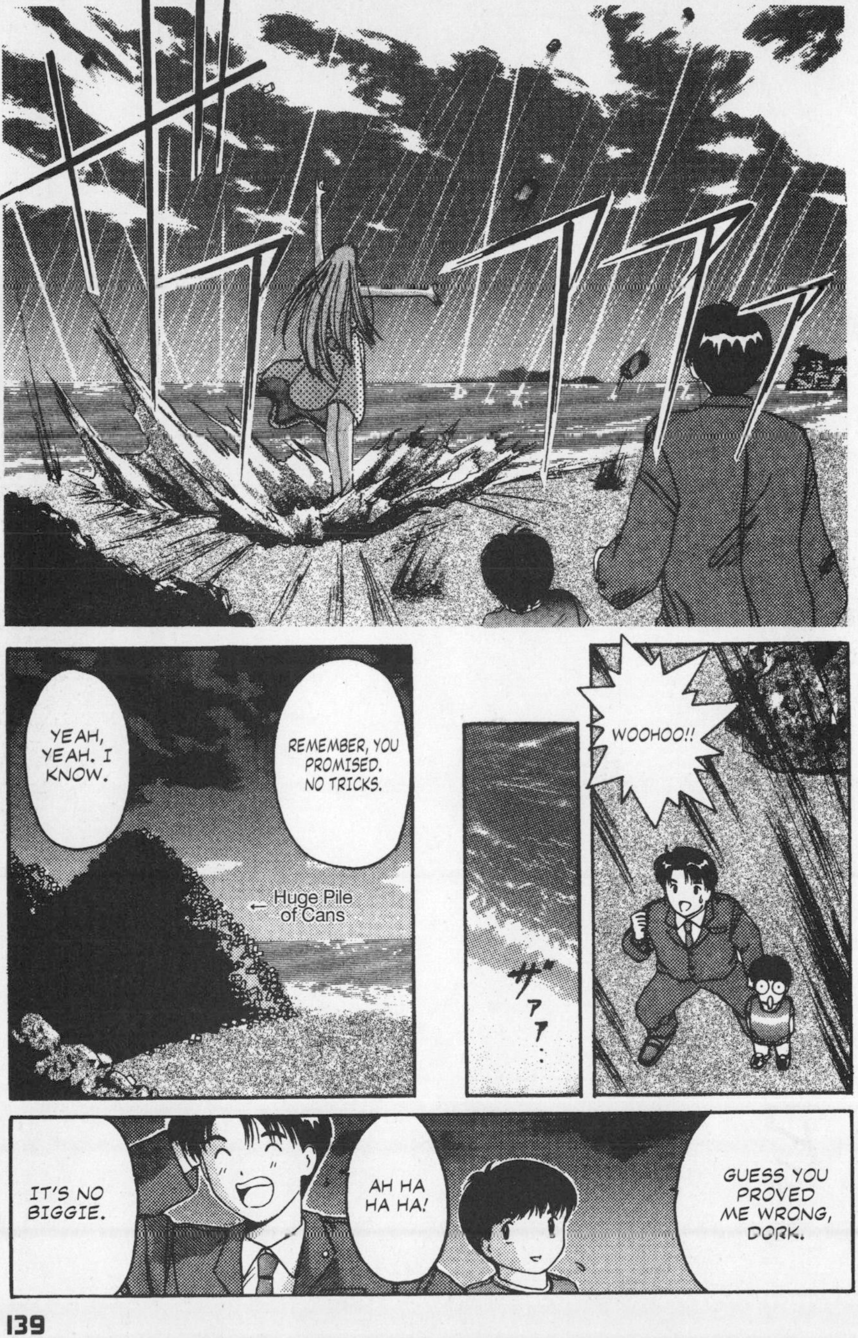
WOOHOO!!
ザァァ…
REMEMBER, YOU PROMISED. NO TRICKS.
YEAH, YEAH. I KNOW.
← Huge Pile of Cans
GUESS YOU PROVED ME WRONG, DORK.
AH HA HA HA!
IT'S NO BIGGIE.

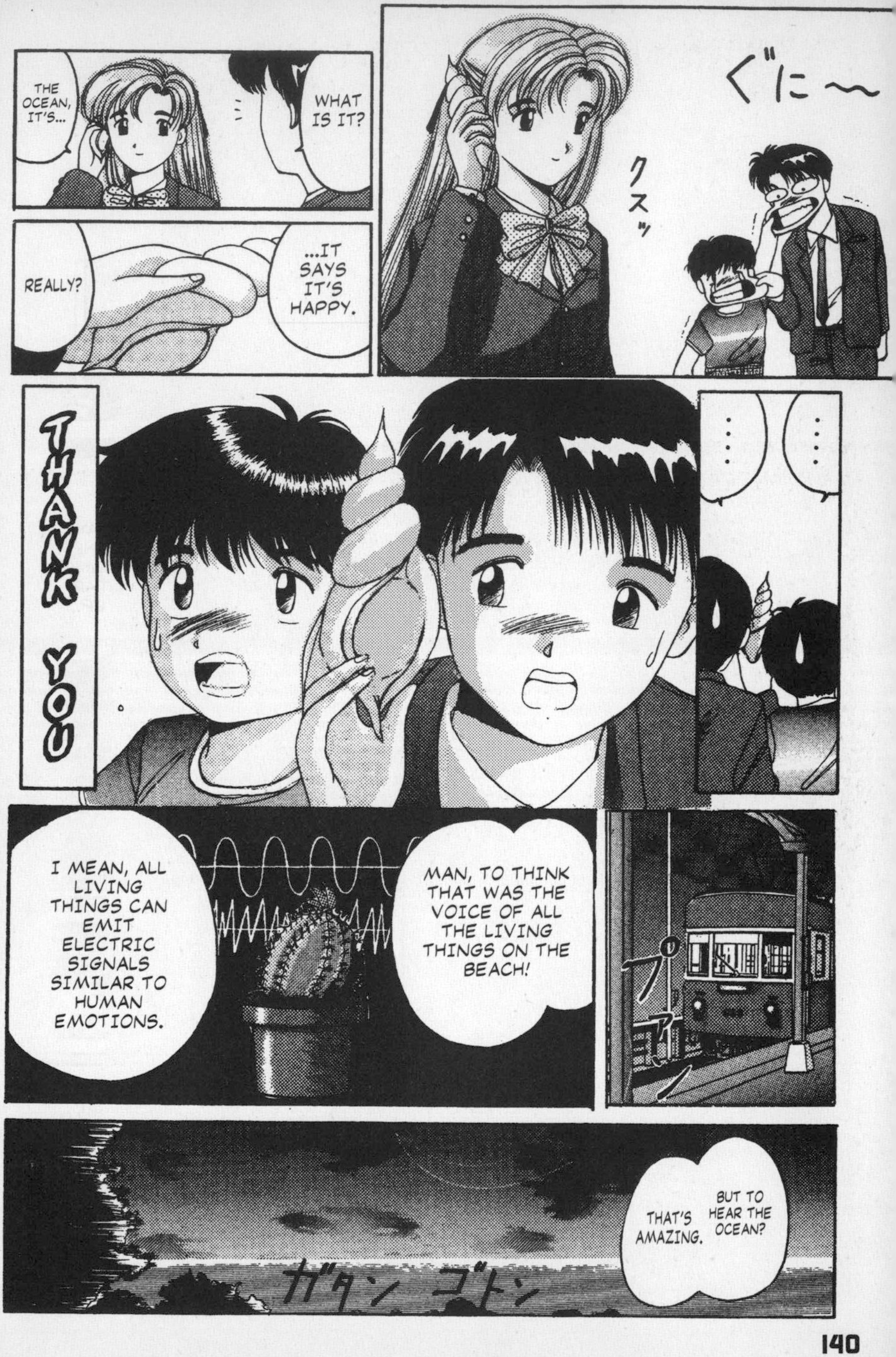
ぐに〜〜
クスッ
WHAT IS IT?
THE OCEAN, IT'S...
...IT SAYS IT'S HAPPY.
REALLY?
....
....
THANK YOU
プァーン
MAN, TO THINK THAT WAS THE VOICE OF ALL THE LIVING THINGS ON THE BEACH!
I MEAN, ALL LIVING THINGS CAN EMIT ELECTRIC SIGNALS SIMILAR TO HUMAN EMOTIONS.
BUT TO HEAR THE OCEAN?
THAT'S AMAZING.
ガタン ゴトン

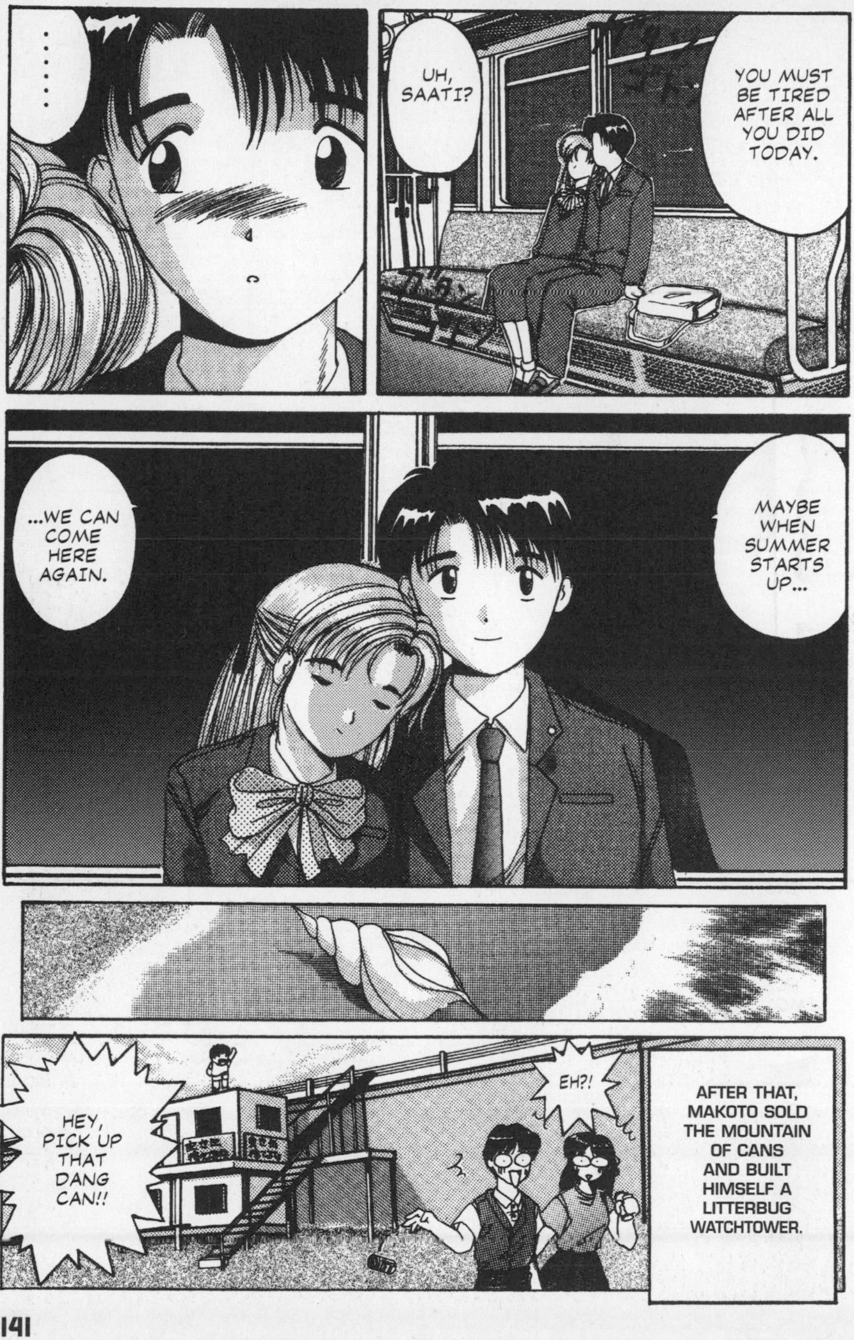
YOU MUST BE TIRED AFTER ALL YOU DID TODAY.
UH, SAATI?
......
MAYBE WHEN SUMMER STARTS UP...
...WE CAN COME HERE AGAIN.
AFTER THAT, MAKOTO SOLD THE MOUNTAIN OF CANS AND BUILT HIMSELF A LITTERBUG WATCHTOWER.
EH?!
HEY, PICK UP THAT DANG CAN!!

THE WORLD OF A.I. LOVE YOU

LOVE TALK!

KEN AKAMATSU TELLS ALL

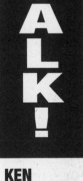

Musings from Ken Akamatsu about his favorite stories from volume one and how it felt to draw Saati years later.

KEN AKAMATSU Special talk

Did you base the main character, Hitoshi, on yourself?

Akamatsu: Yes, I did. I'm not sure why, but even though my taste in women changes, my male characters, be it Hitoshi or Keitaro, always seem to stay the same. It's probably a sign that I'm not maturing at all. (laughs)

What is your favorite story from volume one?

Akamatsu: I'd have to say the one about the Peter Virus [from Program.5]. For that one I altered the name of an actual virus that was spreading at the time and I wanted to realistically convey what a virus could do. Like, deleting files or hiding information. Of course, a clown doesn't jump out at you in real life (laughs). I took some artistic liberties, which resulted a very harsh and cruel character, or rather, program. Still, not many people had personal computers when I did that story. Guess I'm guilty of spreading false information then. (laughs)

I'm guilty of spreading false information

It's been 5 years since you finished A.I. Love You, how does it feel to be drawing Saati again?

Akamatsu: I'm sure you've noticed by the cover, but my style is quite different now. Still, the basic foundations I built the characters on are still there. A.I. Love You was my first project and I'd like for people to think of it as a piece that set the tone for my later work. And I hope that after people read this volume, they'll be looking forward to the next one.

A piece that set the tone for my later work

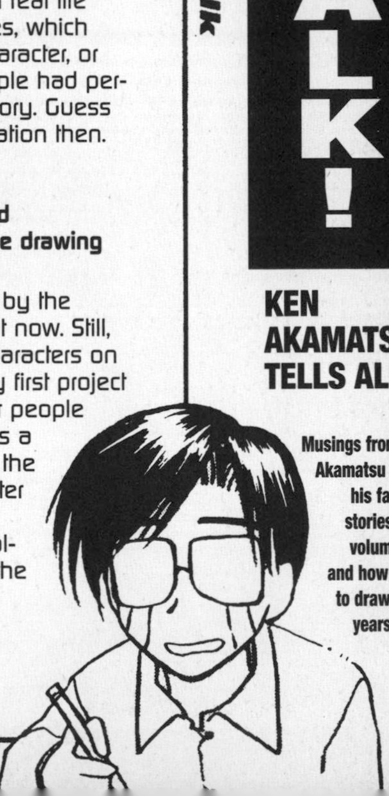

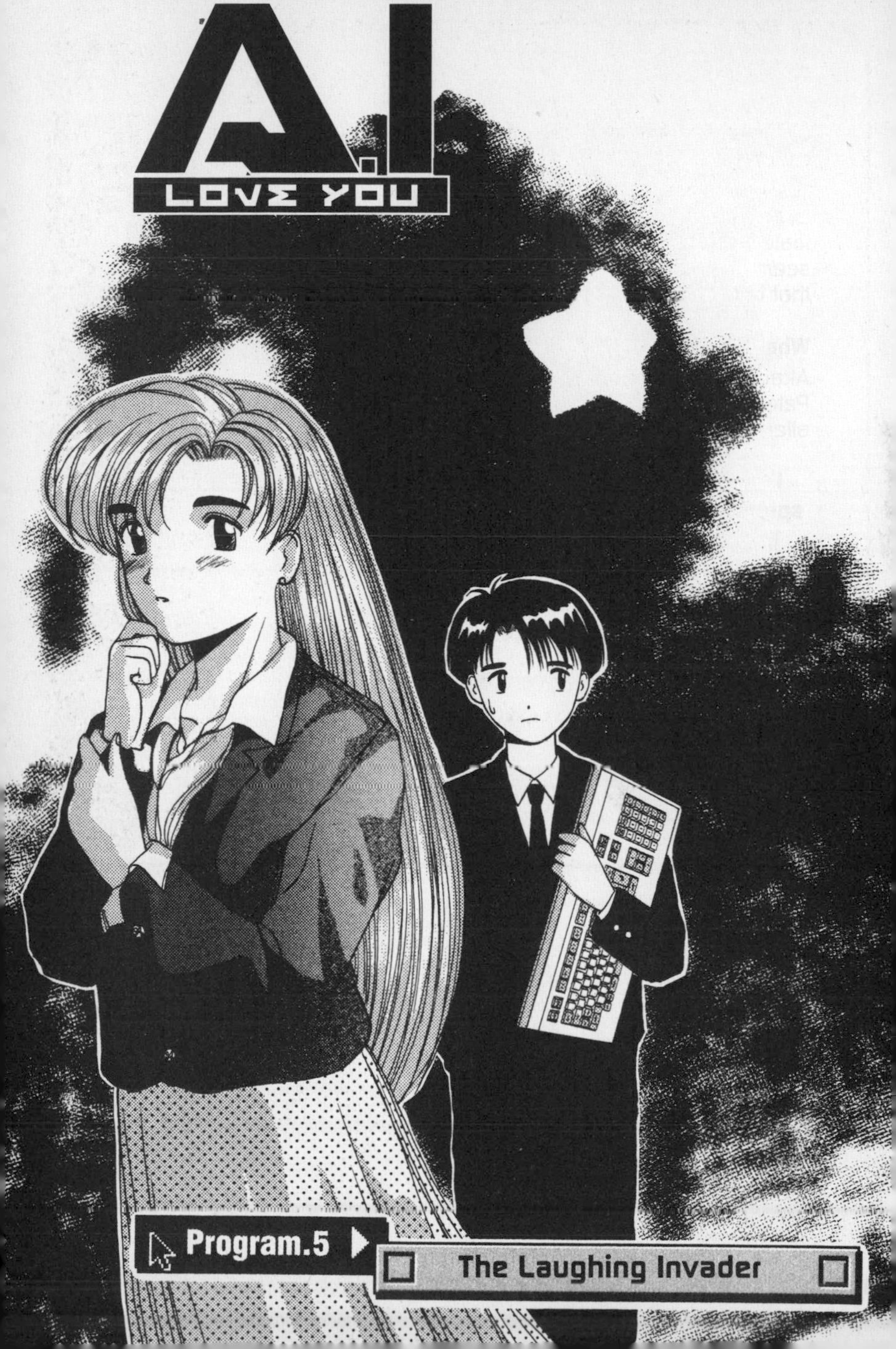
A.I LOVE YOU
Program.5
The Laughing Invader

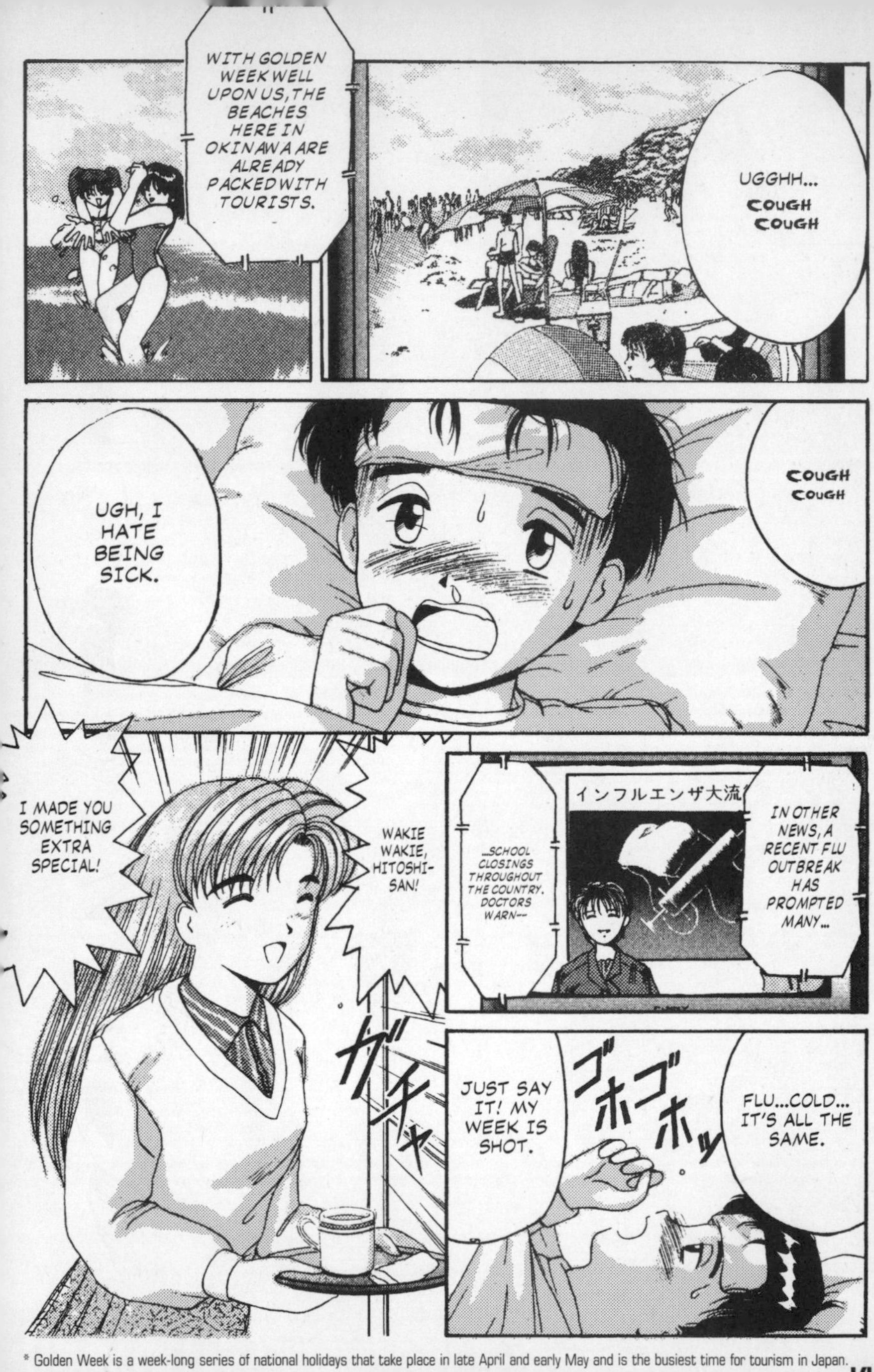

WITH GOLDEN WEEK WELL UPON US, THE BEACHES HERE IN OKINAWA ARE ALREADY PACKED WITH TOURISTS.
UGGHH... COUGH COUGH
COUGH COUGH
UGH, I HATE BEING SICK.
インフルエンザ大流
IN OTHER NEWS, A RECENT FLU OUTBREAK HAS PROMPTED MANY...
...SCHOOL CLOSINGS THROUGHOUT THE COUNTRY. DOCTORS WARN--
ゴホゴホッ
FLU...COLD... IT'S ALL THE SAME.
JUST SAY IT! MY WEEK IS SHOT.
ガチャ
WAKIE WAKIE, HITOSHI-SAN!
I MADE YOU SOMETHING EXTRA SPECIAL!

* Golden Week is a week-long series of national holidays that take place in late April and early May and is the busiest time for tourism in Japan.

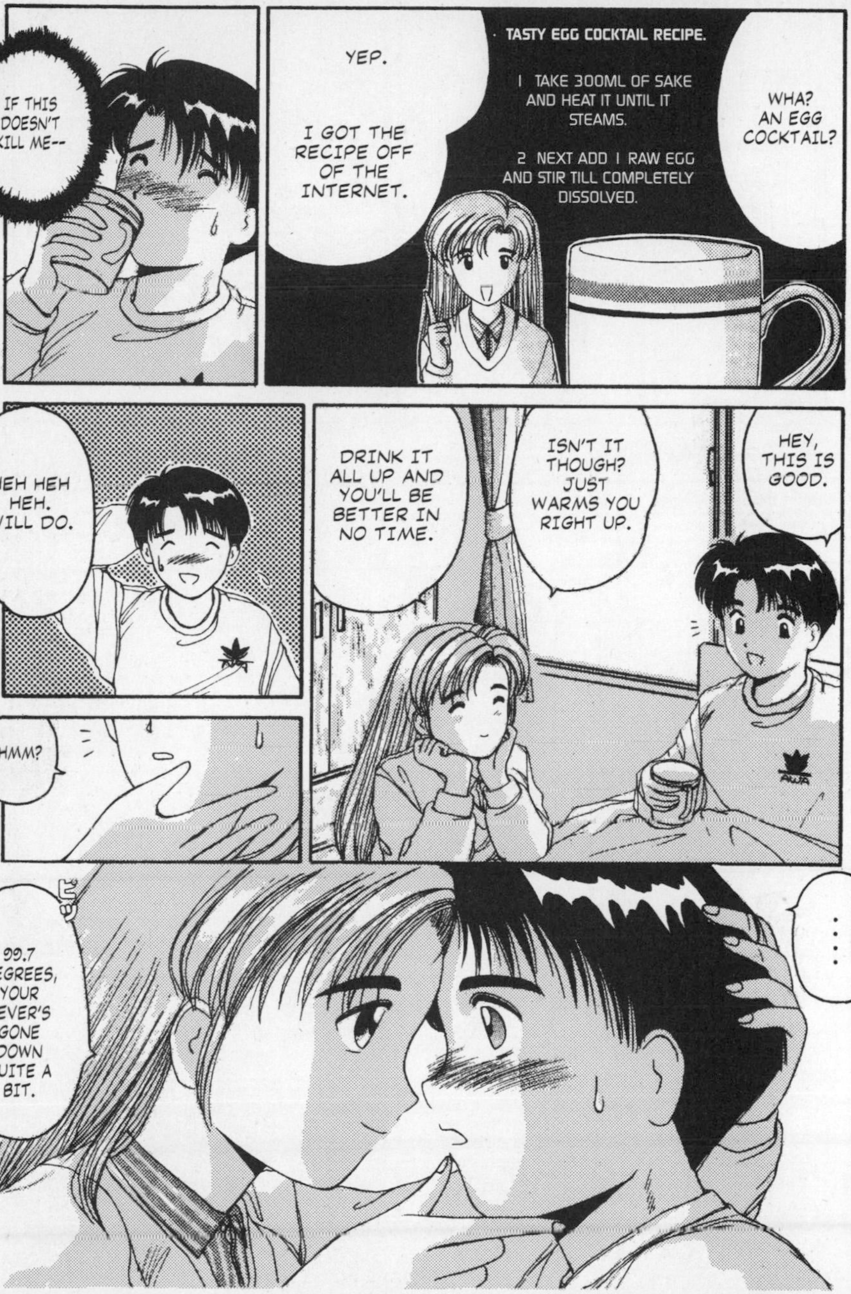
WHA? AN EGG COCKTAIL?
TASTY EGG COCKTAIL RECIPE.
1 TAKE 300ML OF SAKE AND HEAT IT UNTIL IT STEAMS.
2 NEXT ADD 1 RAW EGG AND STIR TILL COMPLETELY DISSOLVED.
YEP.
I GOT THE RECIPE OFF OF THE INTERNET.
IF THIS DOESN'T KILL ME--
HEY, THIS IS GOOD.
ISN'T IT THOUGH? JUST WARMS YOU RIGHT UP.
DRINK IT ALL UP AND YOU'LL BE BETTER IN NO TIME.
HEH HEH HEH. WILL DO.
HMM?
.....
ピッ
99.7 DEGREES, YOUR FEVER'S GONE DOWN QUITE A BIT.

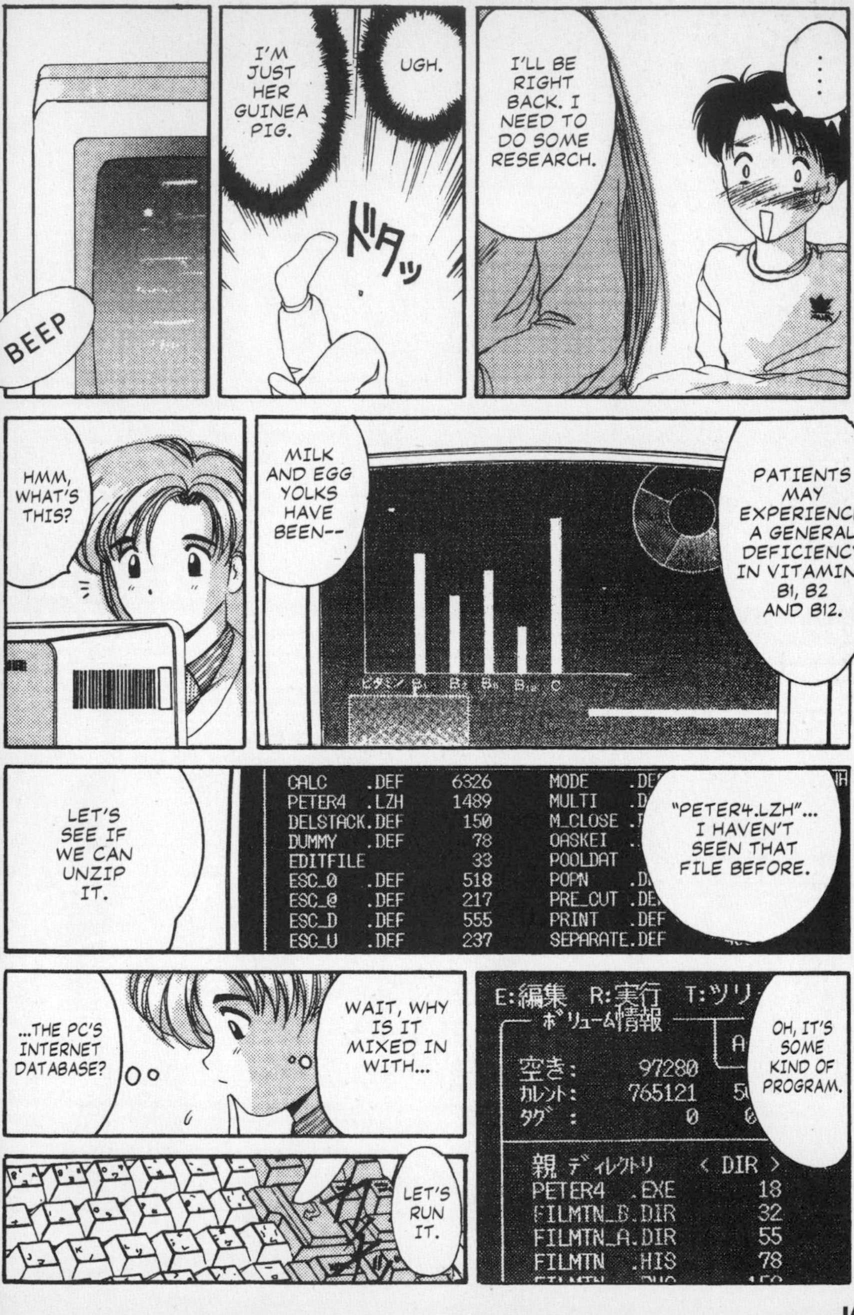
....
I'LL BE RIGHT BACK. I NEED TO DO SOME RESEARCH.
UGH.
I'M JUST HER GUINEA PIG.
ドタッ
BEEP
PATIENTS MAY EXPERIENCE A GENERAL DEFICIENCY IN VITAMINS B1, B2 AND B12.
MILK AND EGG YOLKS HAVE BEEN--
ビタミン B1 B2 B6 B12 C
HMM, WHAT'S THIS?
"PETER4.LZH"... I HAVEN'T SEEN THAT FILE BEFORE.
CALC .DEF 6326
PETER4 .LZH 1489
DELSTACK.DEF 150
DUMMY .DEF 78
EDITFILE 33
ESC_0 .DEF 518
ESC_@ .DEF 217
ESC_D .DEF 555
ESC_U .DEF 237
MODE
MULTI
M_CLOSE
OASKEI
POOLDAT
POPN
PRE_CUT
PRINT .DEF
SEPARATE.DEF
LET'S SEE IF WE CAN UNZIP IT.
OH, IT'S SOME KIND OF PROGRAM.
E:編集 R:実行 T:ツリ
ボリューム情報
空き: 97280
カレント: 765121
タグ : 0
親 ディレクトリ < DIR >
PETER4 .EXE 18
FILMTN_B.DIR 32
FILMTN_A.DIR 55
FILMTN .HIS 78
WAIT, WHY IS IT MIXED IN WITH...
...THE PC'S INTERNET DATABASE?
LET'S RUN IT.

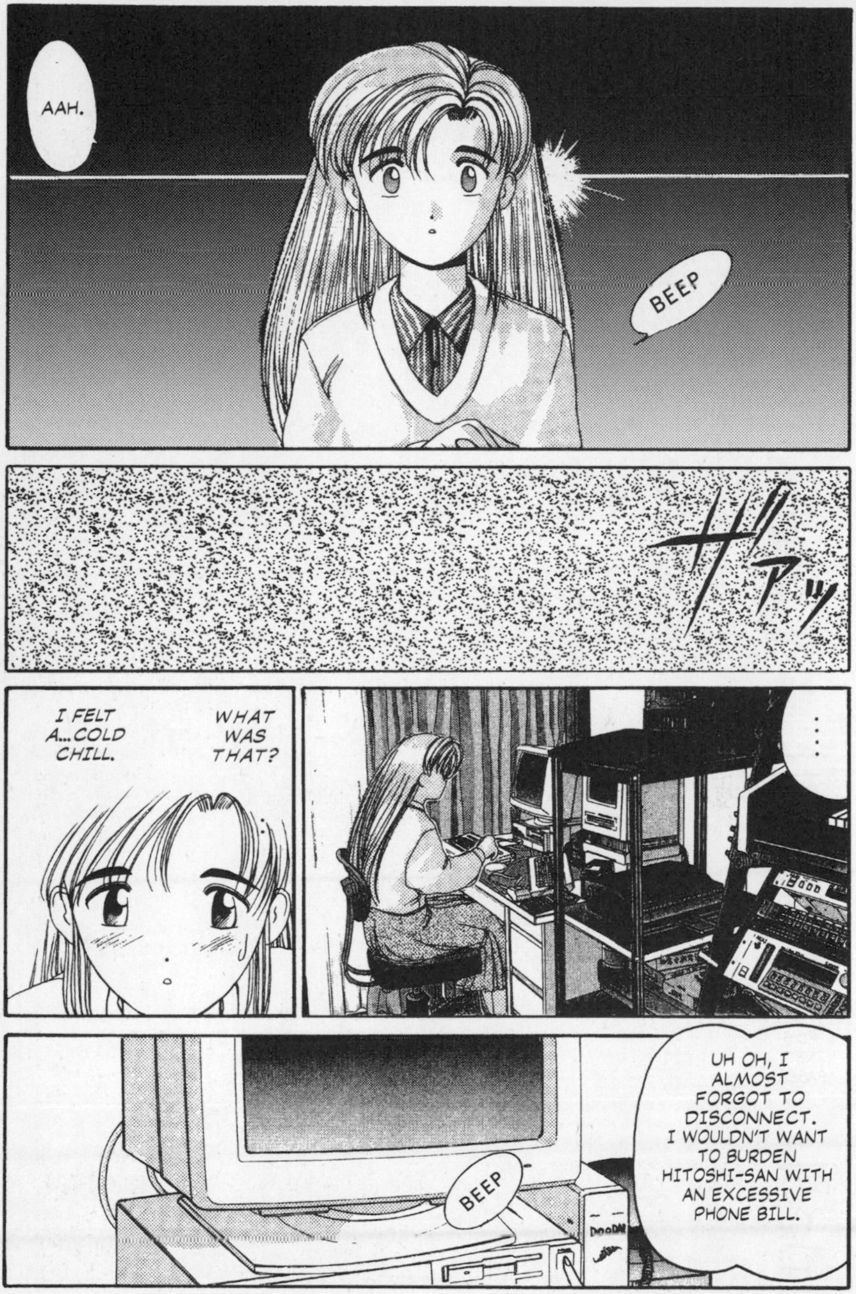
AAH.
BEEP
ザアッ
....
WHAT WAS THAT?
I FELT A...COLD CHILL.
UH OH, I ALMOST FORGOT TO DISCONNECT. I WOULDN'T WANT TO BURDEN HITOSHI-SAN WITH AN EXCESSIVE PHONE BILL.
BEEP

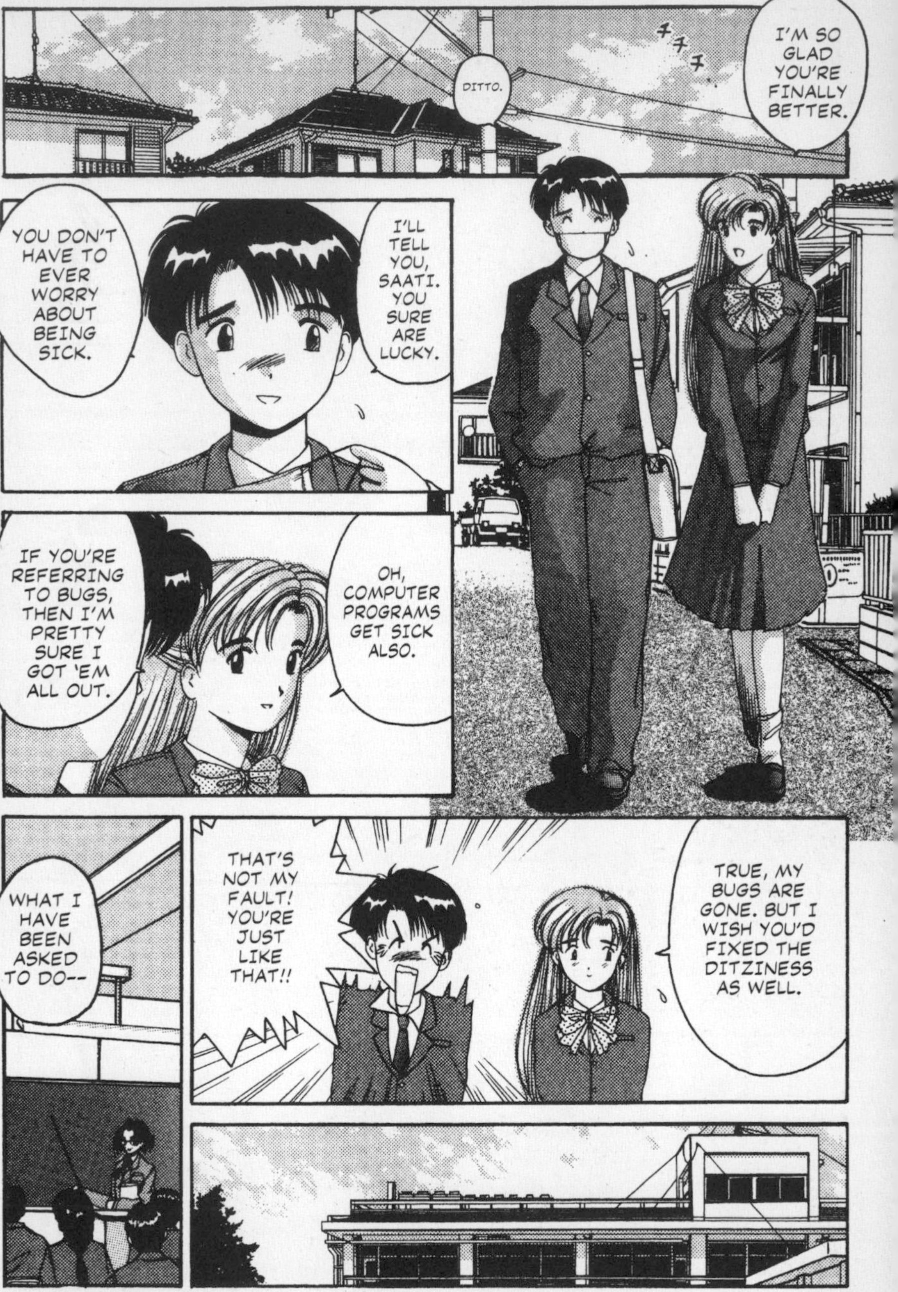
I'M SO GLAD YOU'RE FINALLY BETTER.
チチチ
DITTO.
I'LL TELL YOU, SAATI. YOU SURE ARE LUCKY.
YOU DON'T HAVE TO EVER WORRY ABOUT BEING SICK.
OH, COMPUTER PROGRAMS GET SICK ALSO.
IF YOU'RE REFERRING TO BUGS, THEN I'M PRETTY SURE I GOT 'EM ALL OUT.
TRUE, MY BUGS ARE GONE. BUT I WISH YOU'D FIXED THE DITZINESS AS WELL.
THAT'S NOT MY FAULT! YOU'RE JUST LIKE THAT!!
WHAT I HAVE BEEN ASKED TO DO--

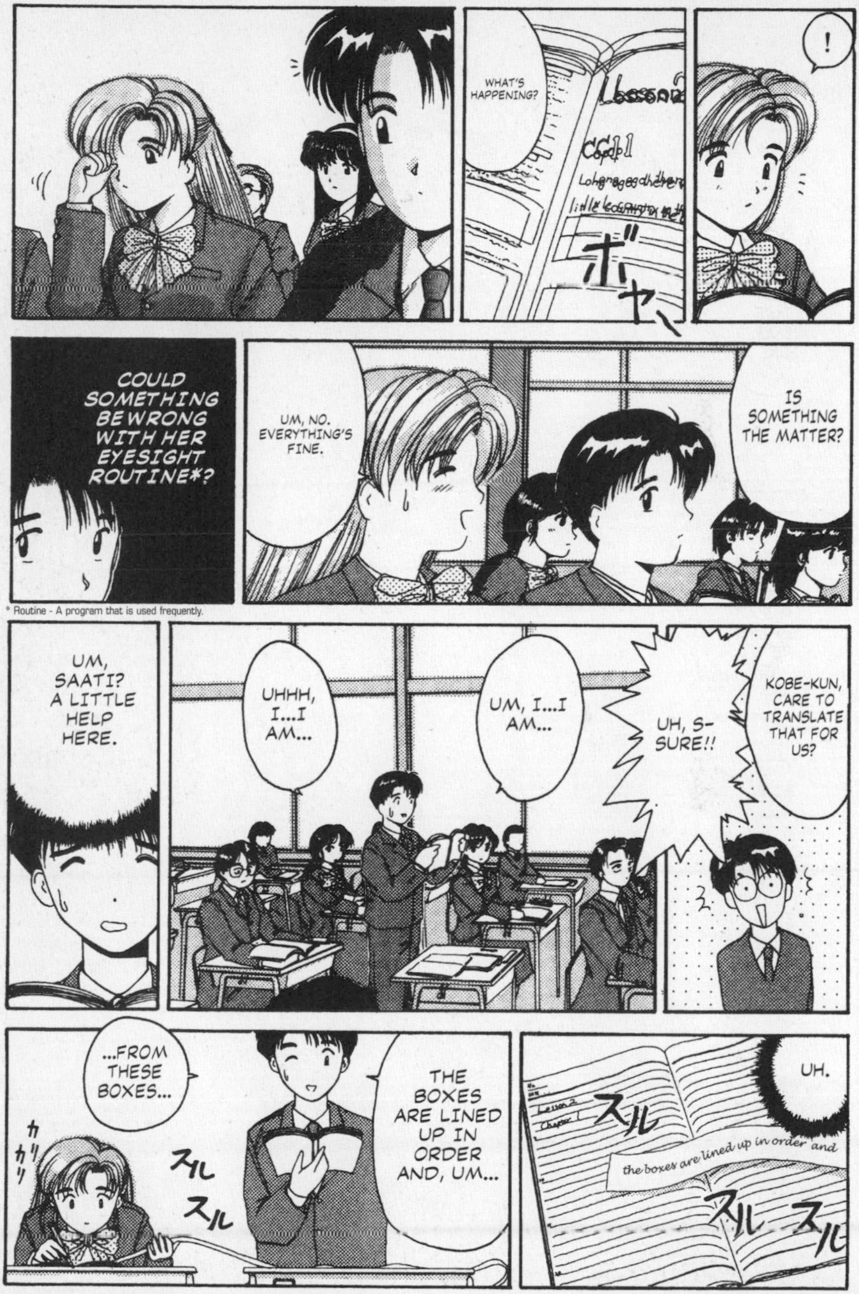
!
WHAT'S HAPPENING?
ボヤ
IS SOMETHING THE MATTER?
UM, NO. EVERYTHING'S FINE.
COULD SOMETHING BE WRONG WITH HER EYESIGHT ROUTINE*?
KOBE-KUN, CARE TO TRANSLATE THAT FOR US?
UH, S-SURE!!
UM, I...I AM...
UHHH, I...I AM...
UM, SAATI? A LITTLE HELP HERE.
UH.
スル
the boxes are lined up in order and
スル スル
THE BOXES ARE LINED UP IN ORDER AND, UM...
...FROM THESE BOXES...
カリカリ
スル スル

* Routine - A program that is used frequently.

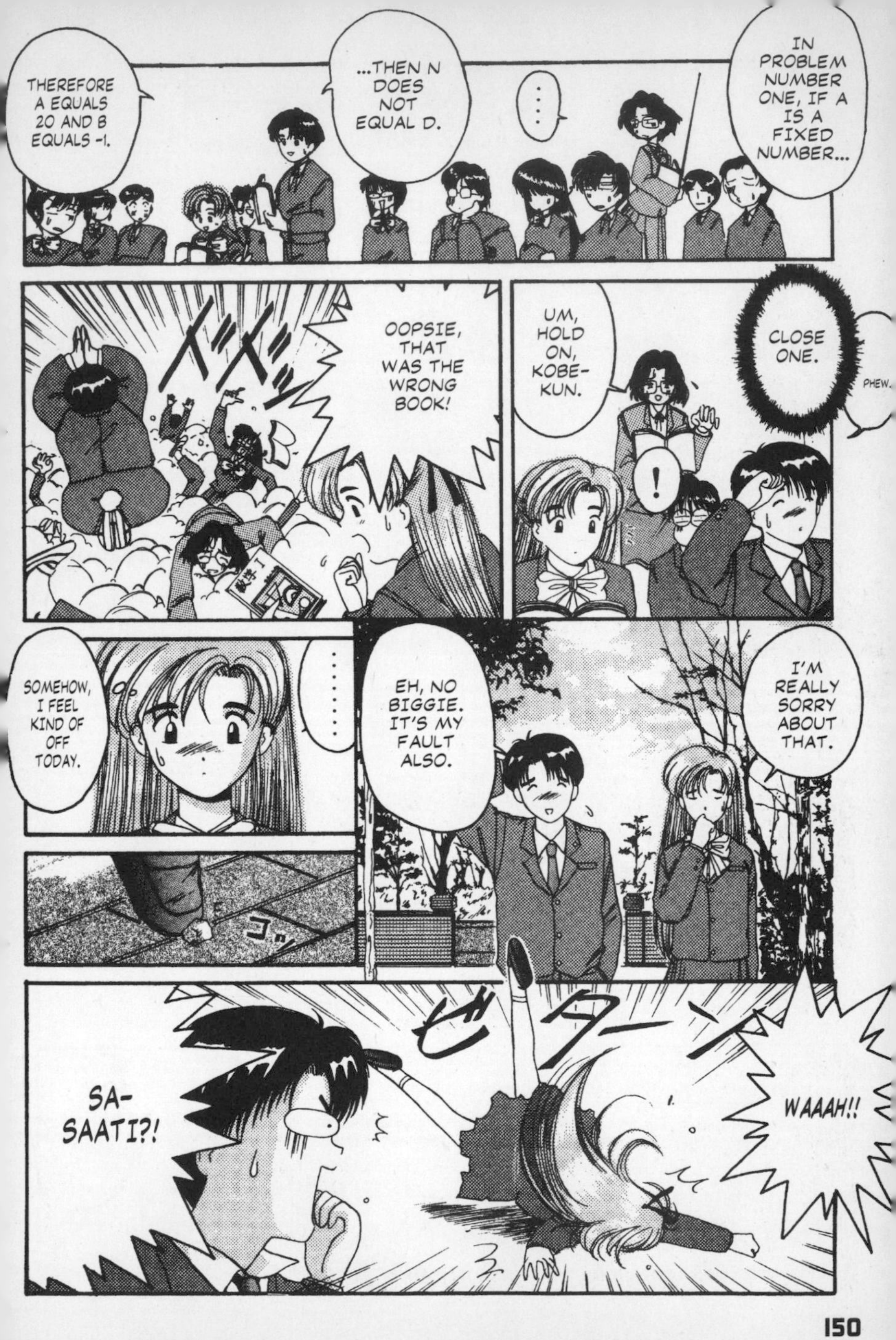
IN PROBLEM NUMBER ONE, IF A IS A FIXED NUMBER...
....
...THEN N DOES NOT EQUAL D.
THEREFORE A EQUALS 20 AND B EQUALS -1.
CLOSE ONE.
PHEW.
UM, HOLD ON, KOBE-KUN.
!
OOPSIE, THAT WAS THE WRONG BOOK!
I'M REALLY SORRY ABOUT THAT.
EH, NO BIGGIE. IT'S MY FAULT ALSO.
......
SOMEHOW, I FEEL KIND OF OFF TODAY.
WAAAH!!
SA-SAATI?!

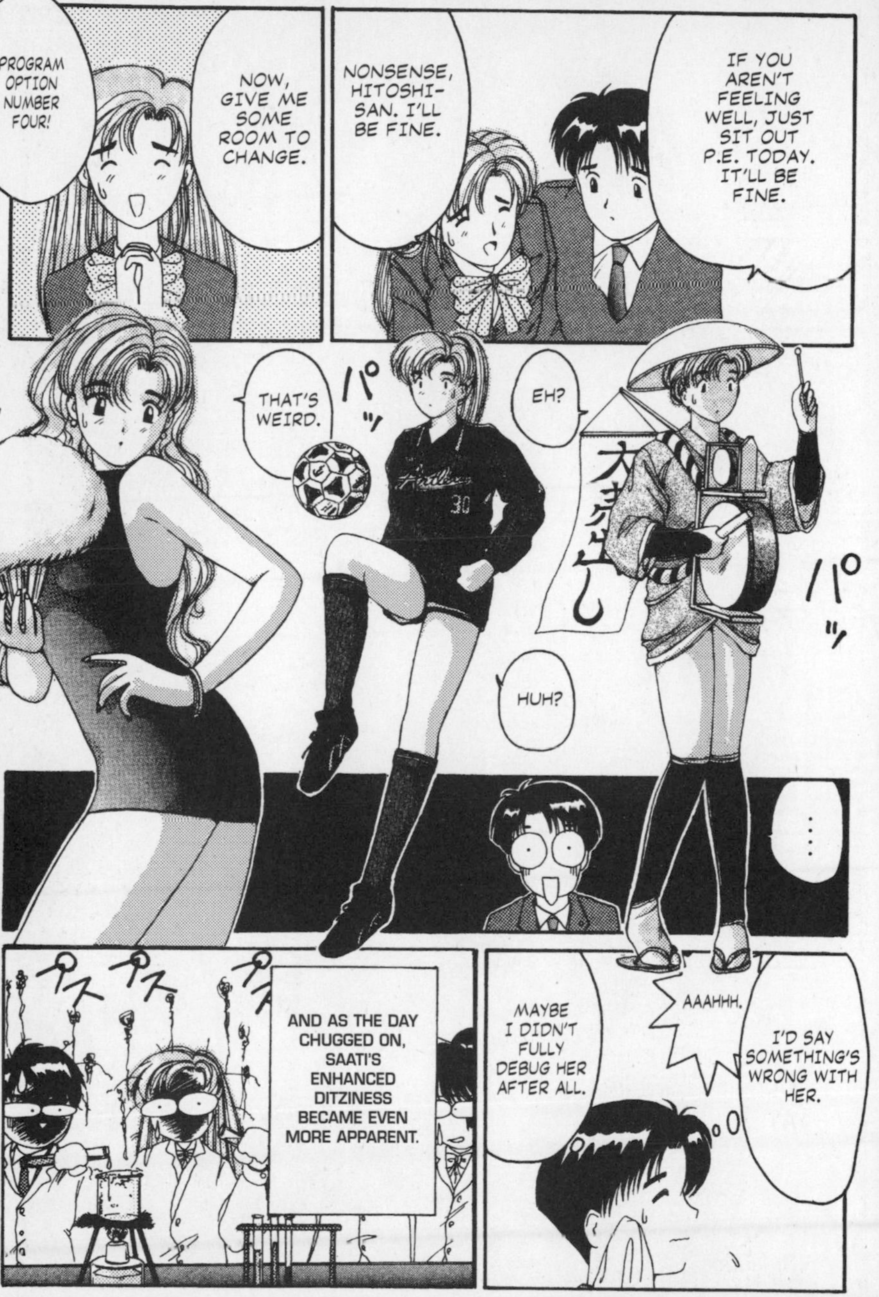
IF YOU AREN'T FEELING WELL, JUST SIT OUT P.E. TODAY. IT'LL BE FINE.
NONSENSE, HITOSHI-SAN. I'LL BE FINE.
NOW, GIVE ME SOME ROOM TO CHANGE.
PROGRAM OPTION NUMBER FOUR!
パッ
EH?
大売出し
HUH?
....
パッ
THAT'S WEIRD.
パッ
I'D SAY SOMETHING'S WRONG WITH HER.
AAAHHH.
MAYBE I DIDN'T FULLY DEBUG HER AFTER ALL.
AND AS THE DAY CHUGGED ON, SAATI'S ENHANCED DITZINESS BECAME EVEN MORE APPARENT.
プス
プス
プス

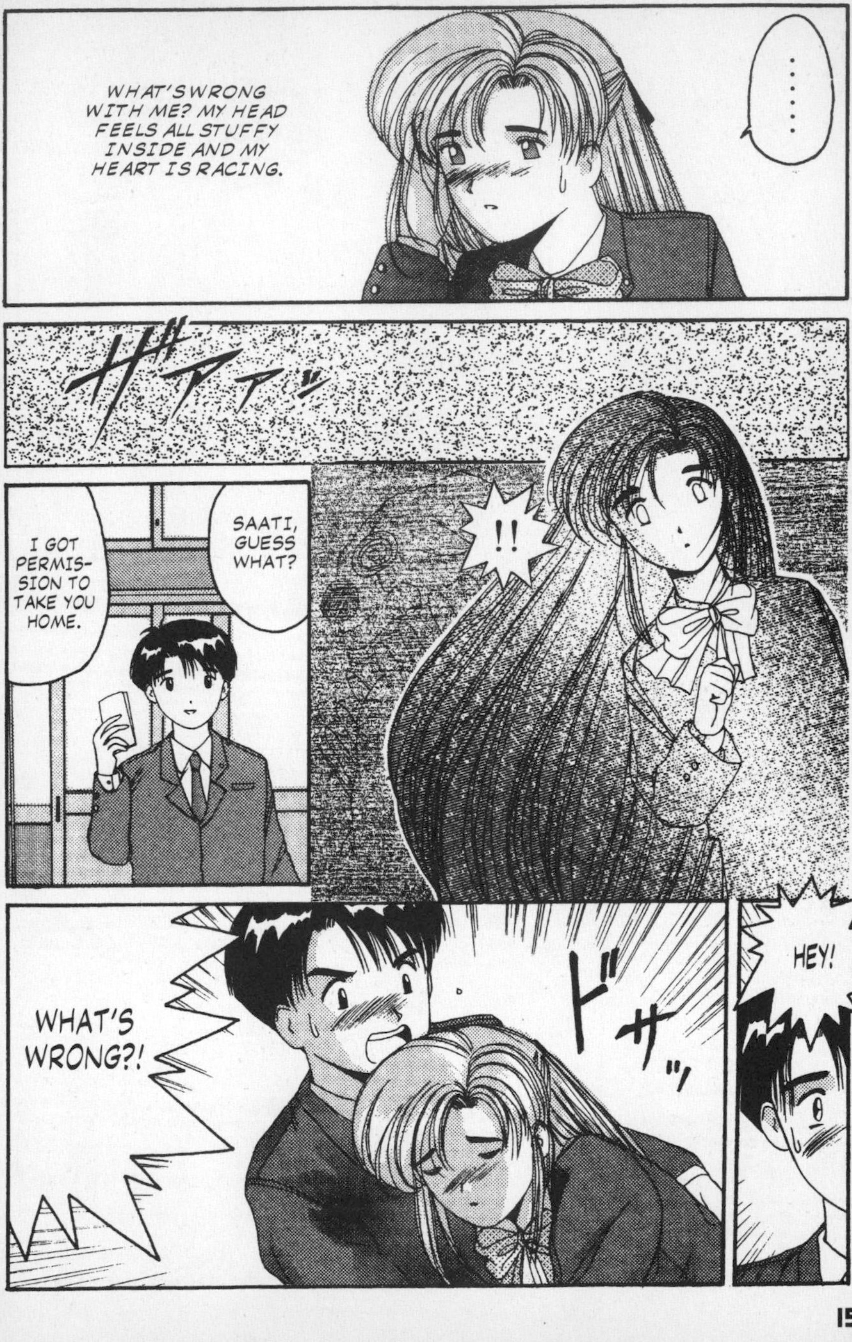
......
WHAT'S WRONG WITH ME? MY HEAD FEELS ALL STUFFY INSIDE AND MY HEART IS RACING.
ザアアッ
!!
SAATI, GUESS WHAT?
I GOT PERMISSION TO TAKE YOU HOME.
HEY!
ドサッ
WHAT'S WRONG?!

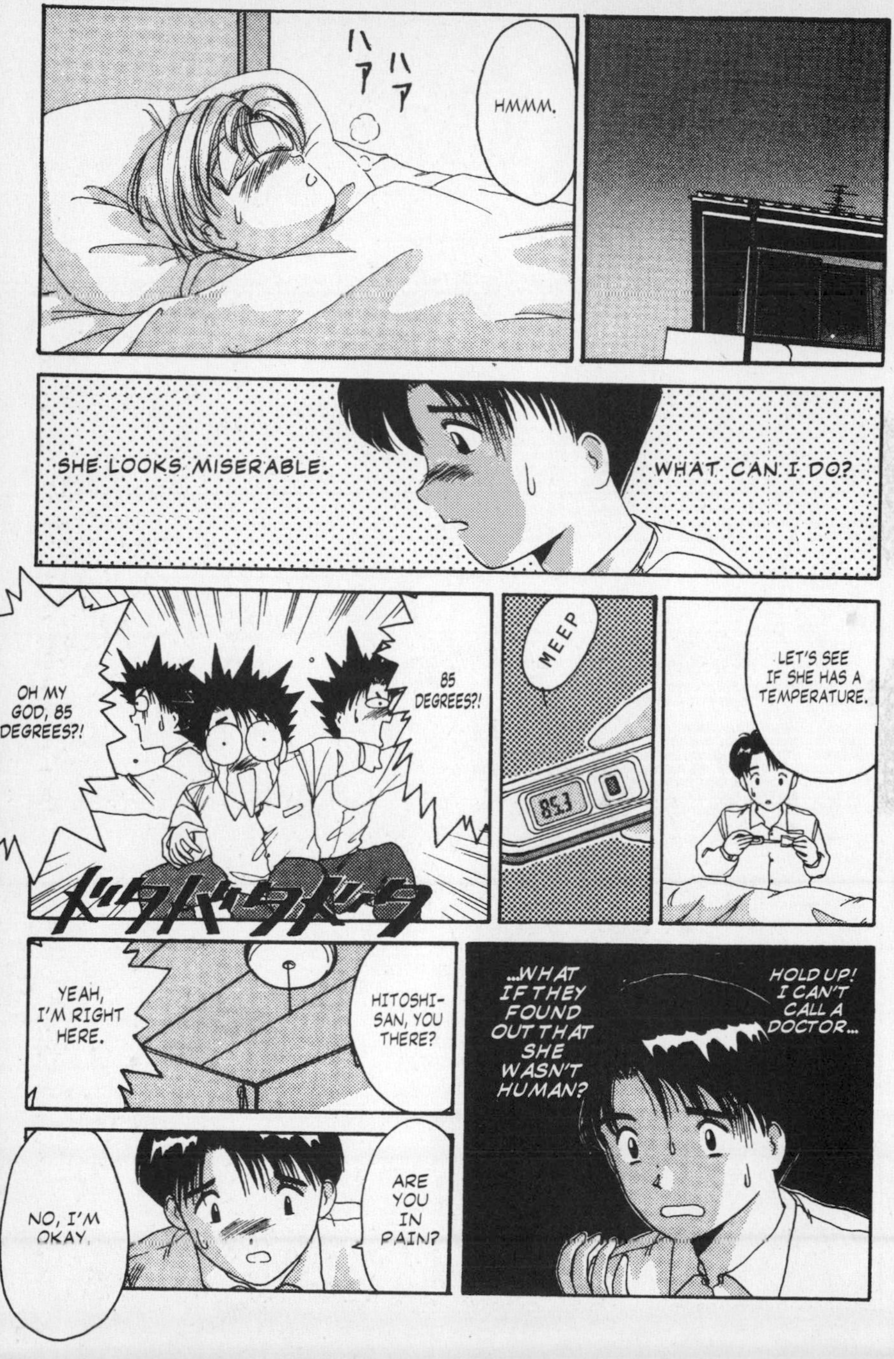
HMMM.
ハア ハア
SHE LOOKS MISERABLE.
WHAT CAN I DO?
LET'S SEE IF SHE HAS A TEMPERATURE.
MEEP
85 DEGREES?!
OH MY GOD, 85 DEGREES?!
HOLD UP! I CAN'T CALL A DOCTOR...
...WHAT IF THEY FOUND OUT THAT SHE WASN'T HUMAN?
HITOSHI-SAN, YOU THERE?
YEAH, I'M RIGHT HERE.
ARE YOU IN PAIN?
NO, I'M OKAY.

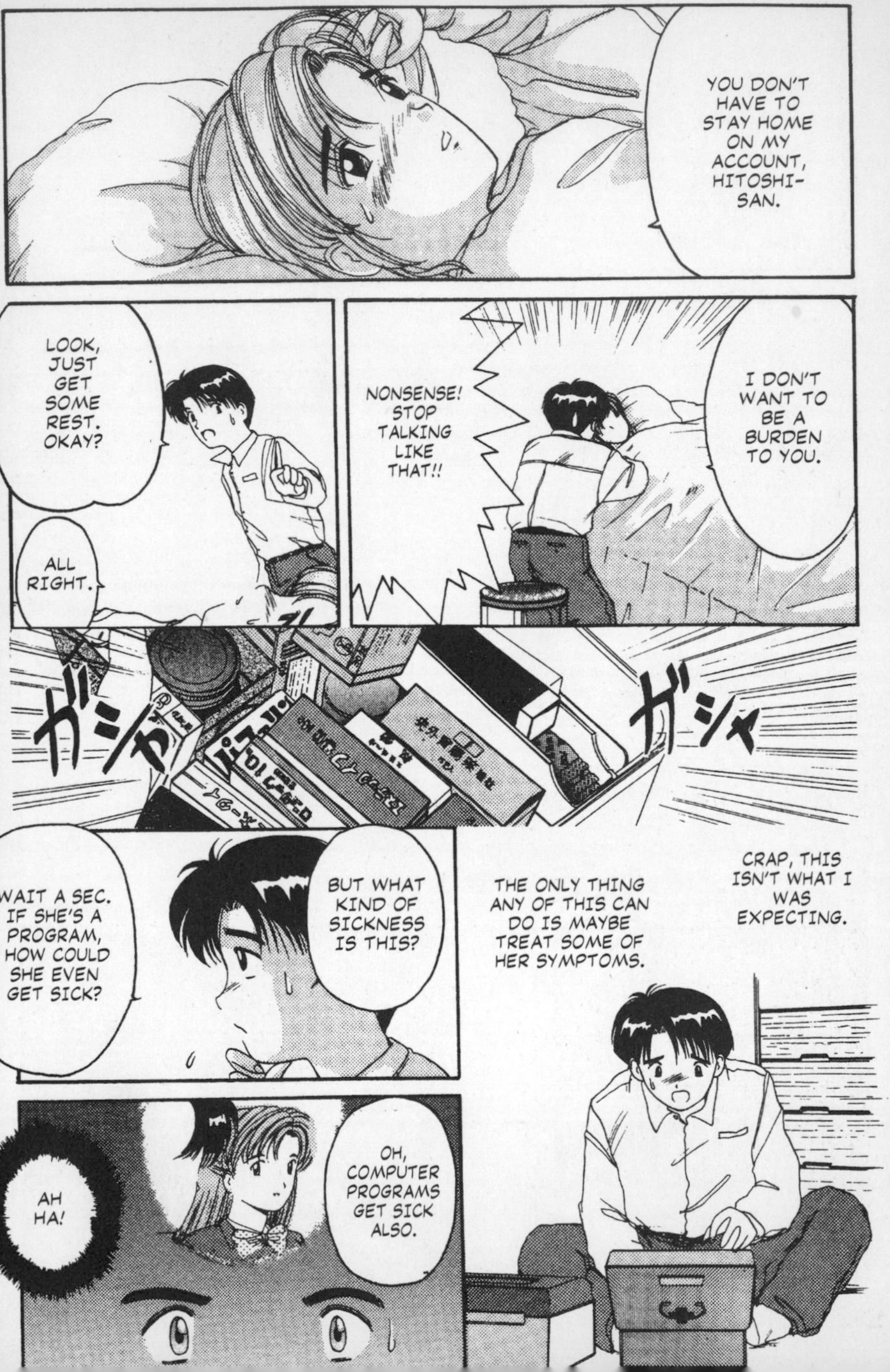

YOU DON'T HAVE TO STAY HOME ON MY ACCOUNT, HITOSHI-SAN.
I DON'T WANT TO BE A BURDEN TO YOU.
NONSENSE! STOP TALKING LIKE THAT!!
LOOK, JUST GET SOME REST. OKAY?
ALL RIGHT.
ガシャ
CRAP, THIS ISN'T WHAT I WAS EXPECTING.
THE ONLY THING ANY OF THIS CAN DO IS MAYBE TREAT SOME OF HER SYMPTOMS.
BUT WHAT KIND OF SICKNESS IS THIS?
WAIT A SEC. IF SHE'S A PROGRAM, HOW COULD SHE EVEN GET SICK?
OH, COMPUTER PROGRAMS GET SICK ALSO.
AH HA!

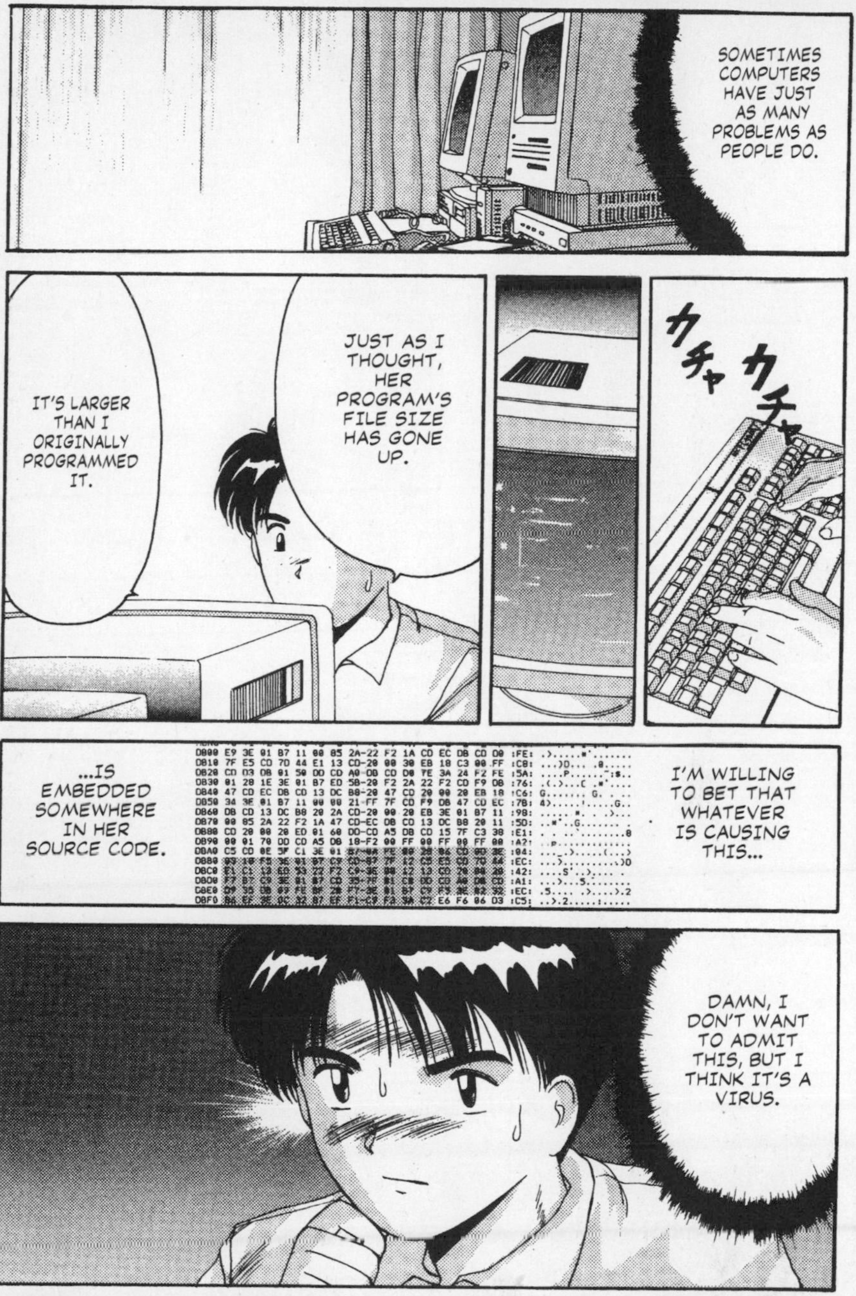
SOMETIMES COMPUTERS HAVE JUST AS MANY PROBLEMS AS PEOPLE DO.
カチャ
カチャ
JUST AS I THOUGHT, HER PROGRAM'S FILE SIZE HAS GONE UP.
IT'S LARGER THAN I ORIGINALLY PROGRAMMED IT.
I'M WILLING TO BET THAT WHATEVER IS CAUSING THIS...
...IS EMBEDDED SOMEWHERE IN HER SOURCE CODE.
DAMN, I DON'T WANT TO ADMIT THIS, BUT I THINK IT'S A VIRUS.

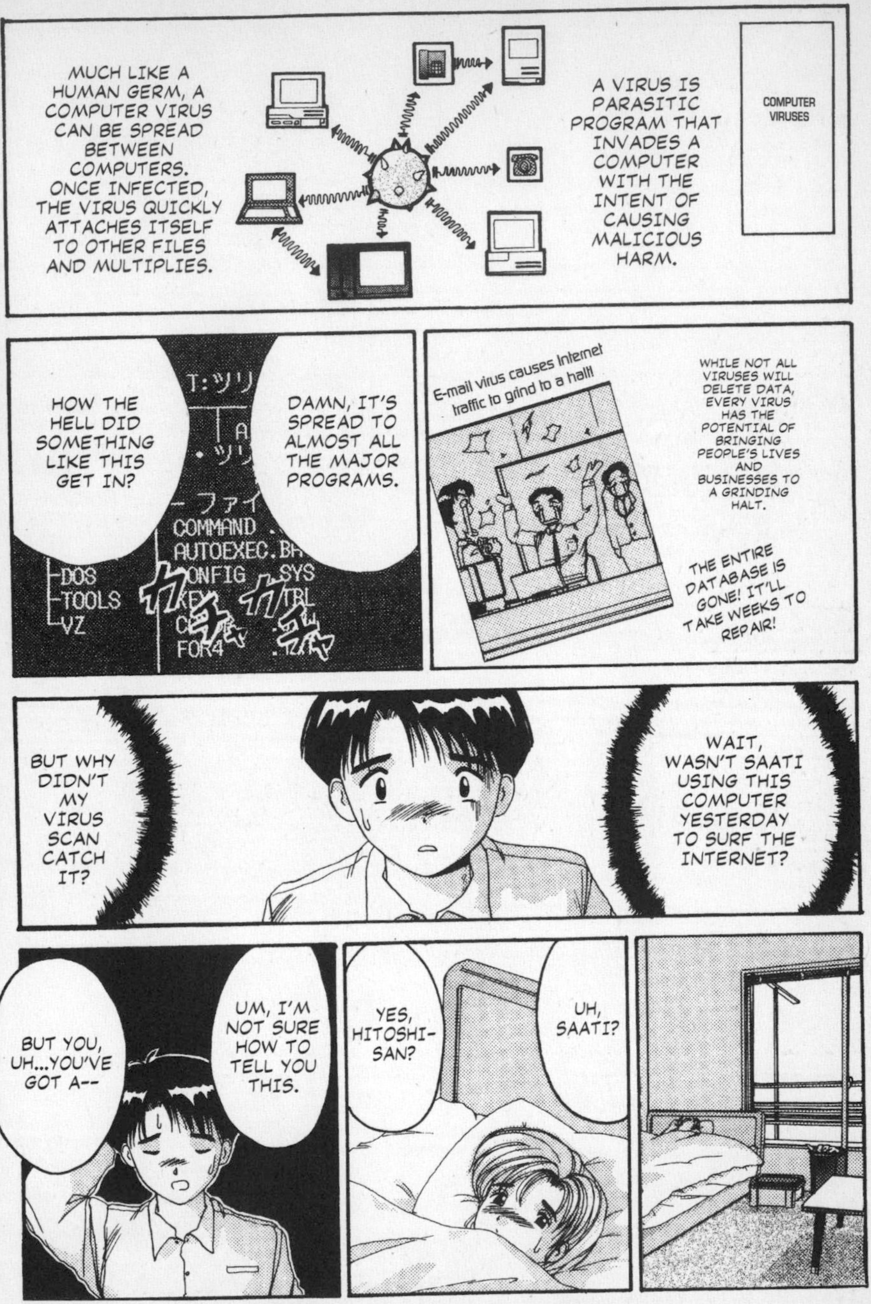

COMPUTER VIRUSES
A VIRUS IS PARASITIC PROGRAM THAT INVADES A COMPUTER WITH THE INTENT OF CAUSING MALICIOUS HARM.
MUCH LIKE A HUMAN GERM, A COMPUTER VIRUS CAN BE SPREAD BETWEEN COMPUTERS. ONCE INFECTED, THE VIRUS QUICKLY ATTACHES ITSELF TO OTHER FILES AND MULTIPLIES.
WHILE NOT ALL VIRUSES WILL DELETE DATA, EVERY VIRUS HAS THE POTENTIAL OF BRINGING PEOPLE'S LIVES AND BUSINESSES TO A GRINDING HALT.
E-mail virus causes Internet traffic to grind to a halt!
THE ENTIRE DATABASE IS GONE! IT'LL TAKE WEEKS TO REPAIR!
DAMN, IT'S SPREAD TO ALMOST ALL THE MAJOR PROGRAMS.
HOW THE HELL DID SOMETHING LIKE THIS GET IN?
T:ツリ
COMMAND
AUTOEXEC.BA
CONFIG SYS
DOS
TOOLS
VZ
FOR4
カチャ カチャ
WAIT, WASN'T SAATI USING THIS COMPUTER YESTERDAY TO SURF THE INTERNET?
BUT WHY DIDN'T MY VIRUS SCAN CATCH IT?
UH, SAATI?
YES, HITOSHI-SAN?
UM, I'M NOT SURE HOW TO TELL YOU THIS.
BUT YOU, UH...YOU'VE GOT A--

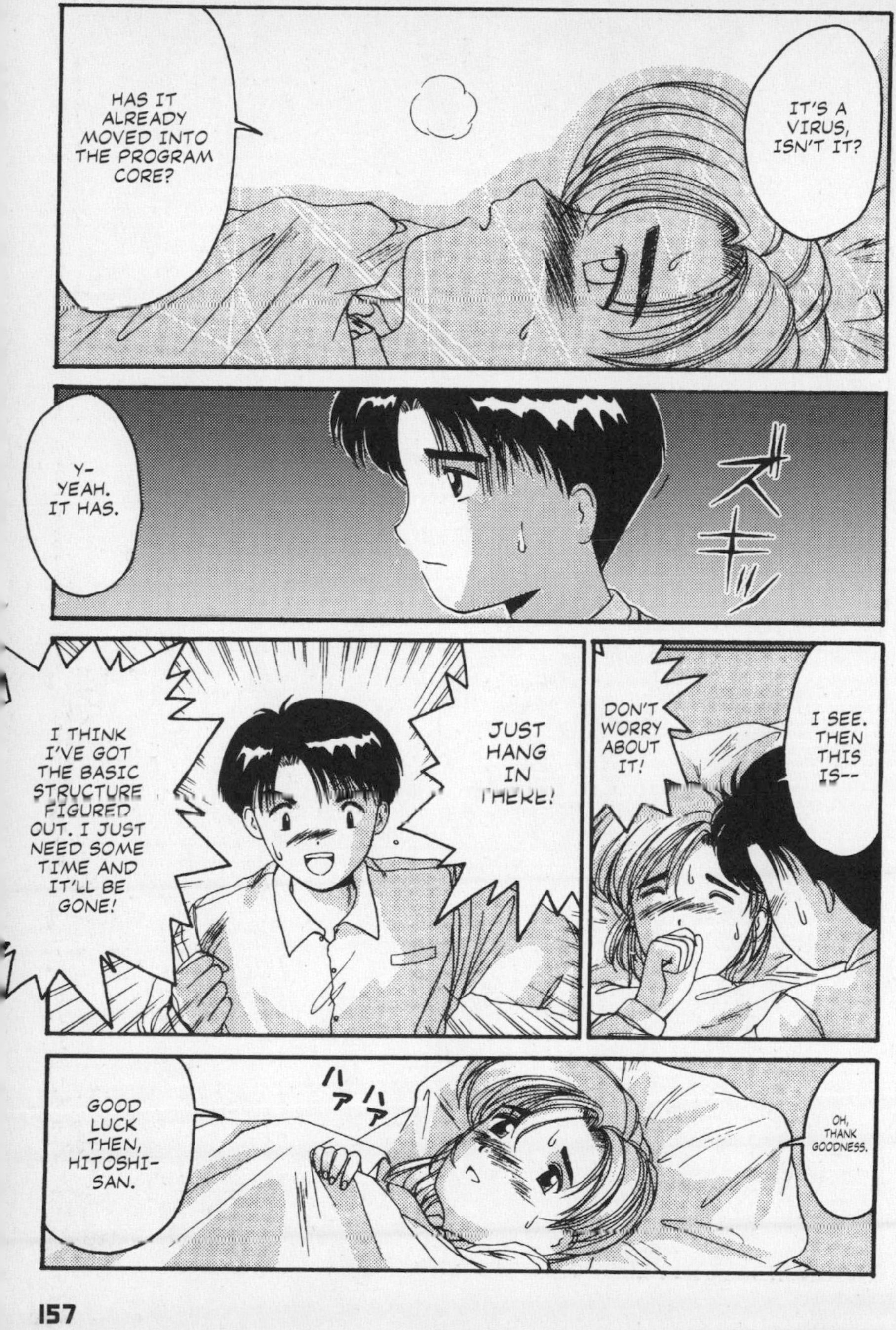
IT'S A VIRUS, ISN'T IT?
HAS IT ALREADY MOVED INTO THE PROGRAM CORE?
ズキッ
Y-YEAH. IT HAS.
I SEE. THEN THIS IS--
DON'T WORRY ABOUT IT!
JUST HANG IN THERE!
I THINK I'VE GOT THE BASIC STRUCTURE FIGURED OUT. I JUST NEED SOME TIME AND IT'LL BE GONE!
OH, THANK GOODNESS.
ハァ ハァ
GOOD LUCK THEN, HITOSHI-SAN.

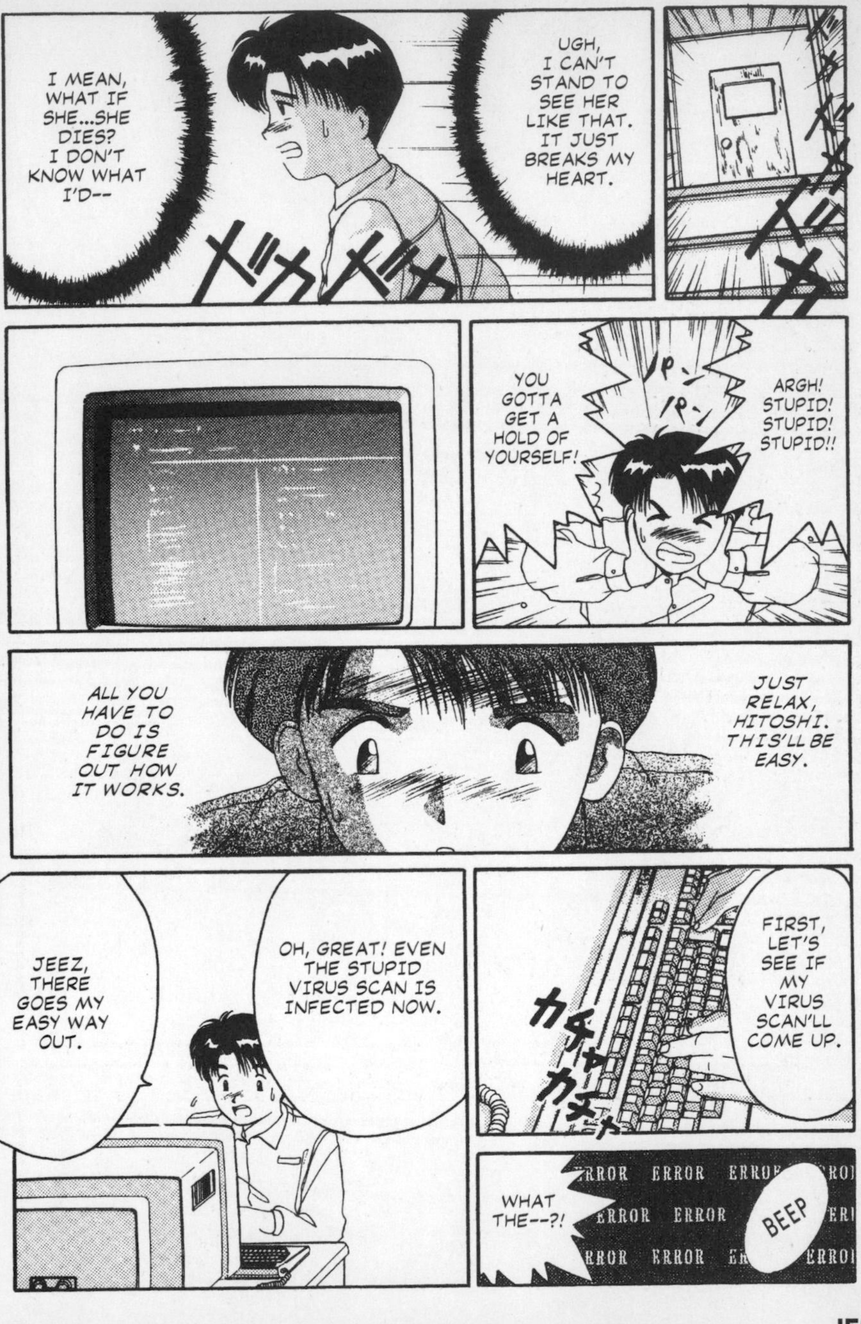
UGH, I CAN'T STAND TO SEE HER LIKE THAT. IT JUST BREAKS MY HEART.
I MEAN, WHAT IF SHE...SHE DIES? I DON'T KNOW WHAT I'D--
ARGH! STUPID! STUPID! STUPID!!
パン
パン
YOU GOTTA GET A HOLD OF YOURSELF!
JUST RELAX, HITOSHI. THIS'LL BE EASY.
ALL YOU HAVE TO DO IS FIGURE OUT HOW IT WORKS.
FIRST, LET'S SEE IF MY VIRUS SCAN'LL COME UP.
BEEP
WHAT THE--?!
OH, GREAT! EVEN THE STUPID VIRUS SCAN IS INFECTED NOW.
JEEZ, THERE GOES MY EASY WAY OUT.

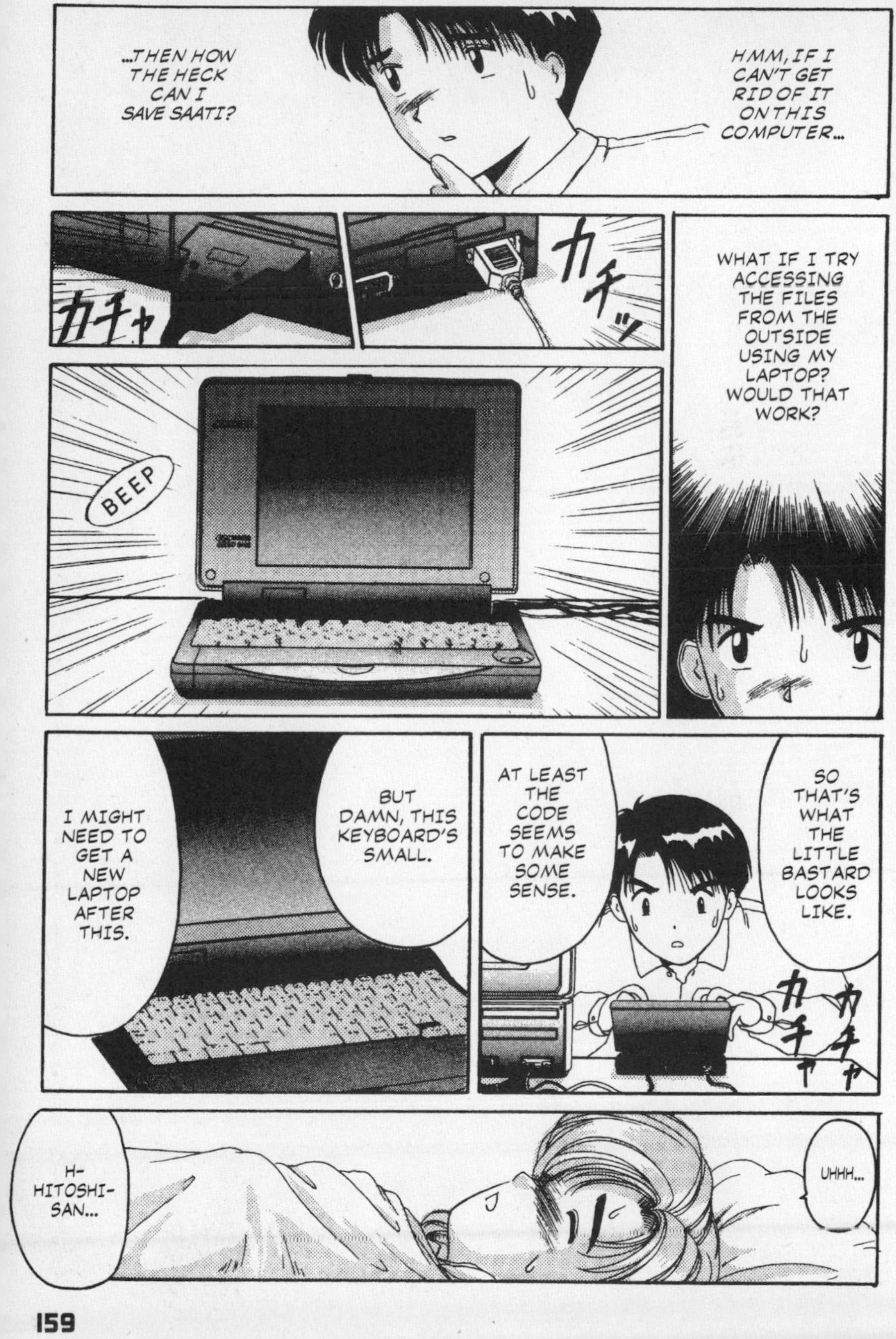
HMM, IF I CAN'T GET RID OF IT ON THIS COMPUTER...
...THEN HOW THE HECK CAN I SAVE SAATI?
WHAT IF I TRY ACCESSING THE FILES FROM THE OUTSIDE USING MY LAPTOP? WOULD THAT WORK?
カチッ
カチャ
BEEP
SO THAT'S WHAT THE LITTLE BASTARD LOOKS LIKE.
AT LEAST THE CODE SEEMS TO MAKE SOME SENSE.
カチャ
カチャ
BUT DAMN, THIS KEYBOARD'S SMALL.
I MIGHT NEED TO GET A NEW LAPTOP AFTER THIS.
UHHH...
H-HITOSHI-SAN...

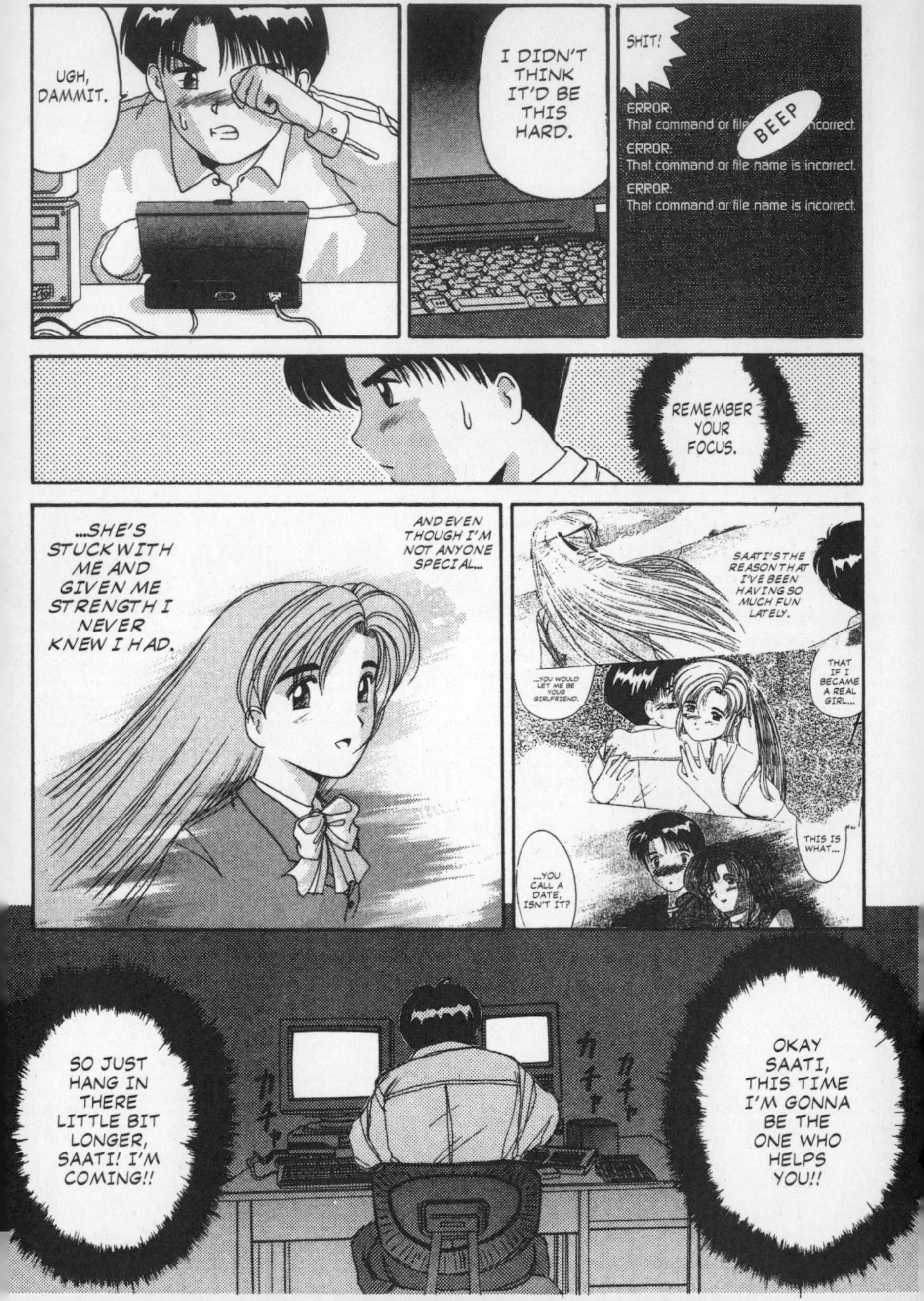
SHIT!
ERROR:
That command or file
incorrect.
BEEP
ERROR:
That command or file name is incorrect.
ERROR:
That command or file name is incorrect.
I DIDN'T THINK IT'D BE THIS HARD.
UGH, DAMMIT.
REMEMBER YOUR FOCUS.
SAATI'S THE REASON THAT I'VE BEEN HAVING SO MUCH FUN LATELY.
THAT IF I BECAME A REAL GIRL...
...YOU WOULD LET ME BE YOUR GIRLFRIEND.
THIS IS WHAT...
...YOU CALL A DATE, ISN'T IT?
AND EVEN THOUGH I'M NOT ANYONE SPECIAL...
...SHE'S STUCK WITH ME AND GIVEN ME STRENGTH I NEVER KNEW I HAD.
OKAY SAATI, THIS TIME I'M GONNA BE THE ONE WHO HELPS YOU!!
カチャ
カチャ
SO JUST HANG IN THERE LITTLE BIT LONGER, SAATI! I'M COMING!!

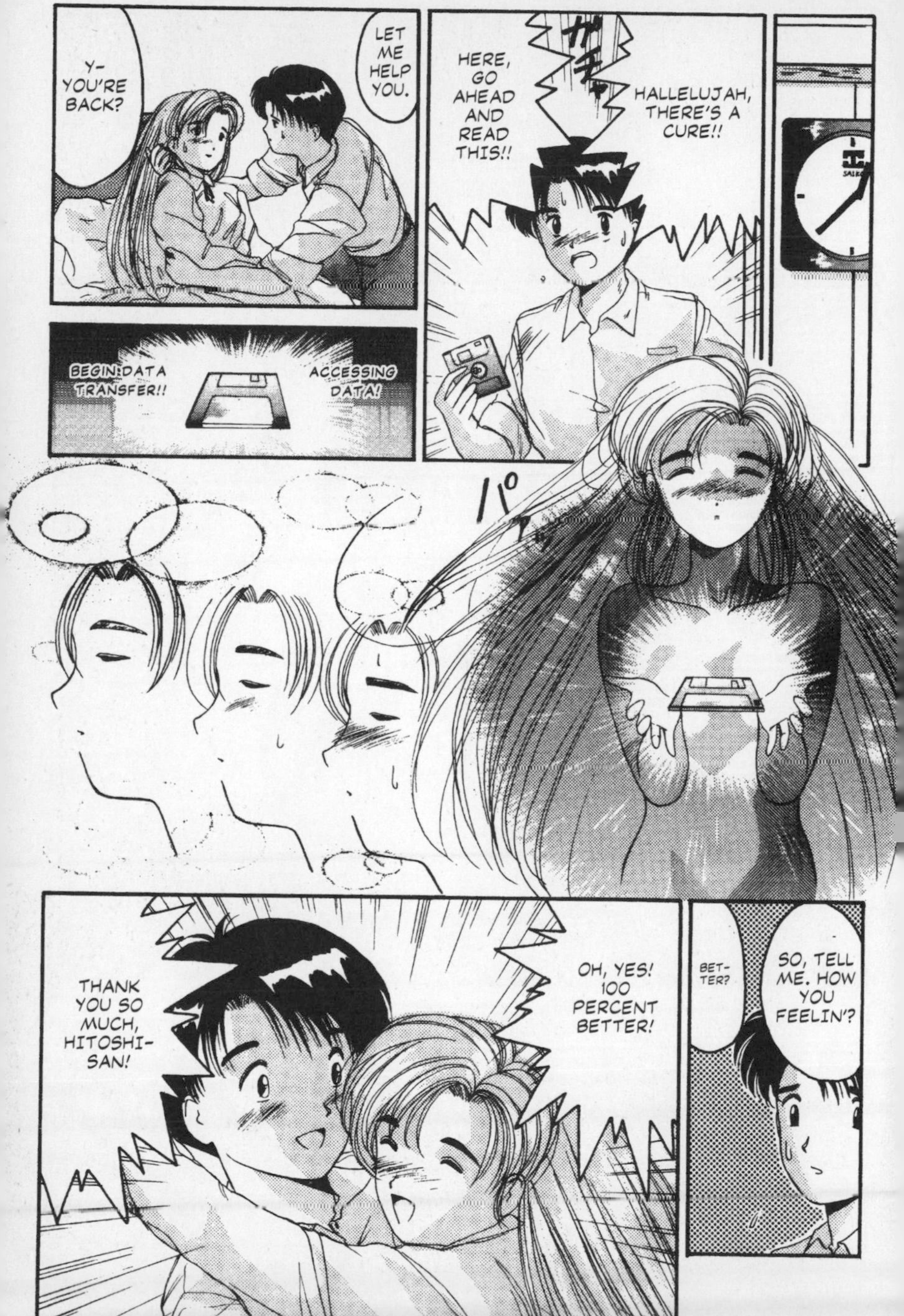
ガチャ
HALLELUJAH, THERE'S A CURE!!
HERE, GO AHEAD AND READ THIS!!
LET ME HELP YOU.
Y-YOU'RE BACK?
ACCESSING DATA!
BEGIN: DATA TRANSFER!!
パ
SO, TELL ME. HOW YOU FEELIN'?
BET-TER?
OH, YES! 100 PERCENT BETTER!
THANK YOU SO MUCH, HITOSHI-SAN!

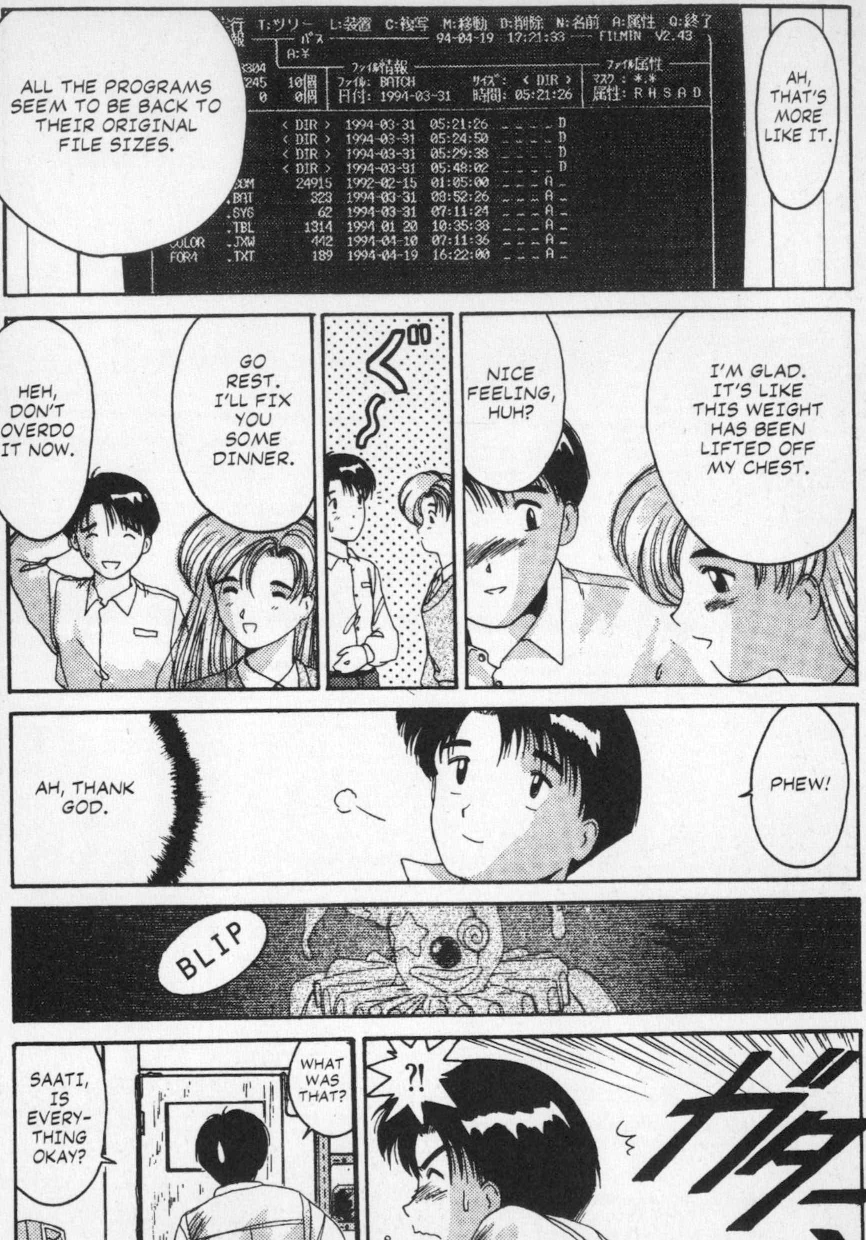
AH, THAT'S MORE LIKE IT.
ALL THE PROGRAMS SEEM TO BE BACK TO THEIR ORIGINAL FILE SIZES.
I'M GLAD. IT'S LIKE THIS WEIGHT HAS BEEN LIFTED OFF MY CHEST.
NICE FEELING, HUH?
GO REST. I'LL FIX YOU SOME DINNER.
HEH, DON'T OVERDO IT NOW.
PHEW!
AH, THANK GOD.
BLIP
?!
WHAT WAS THAT?
SAATI, IS EVERY-THING OKAY?

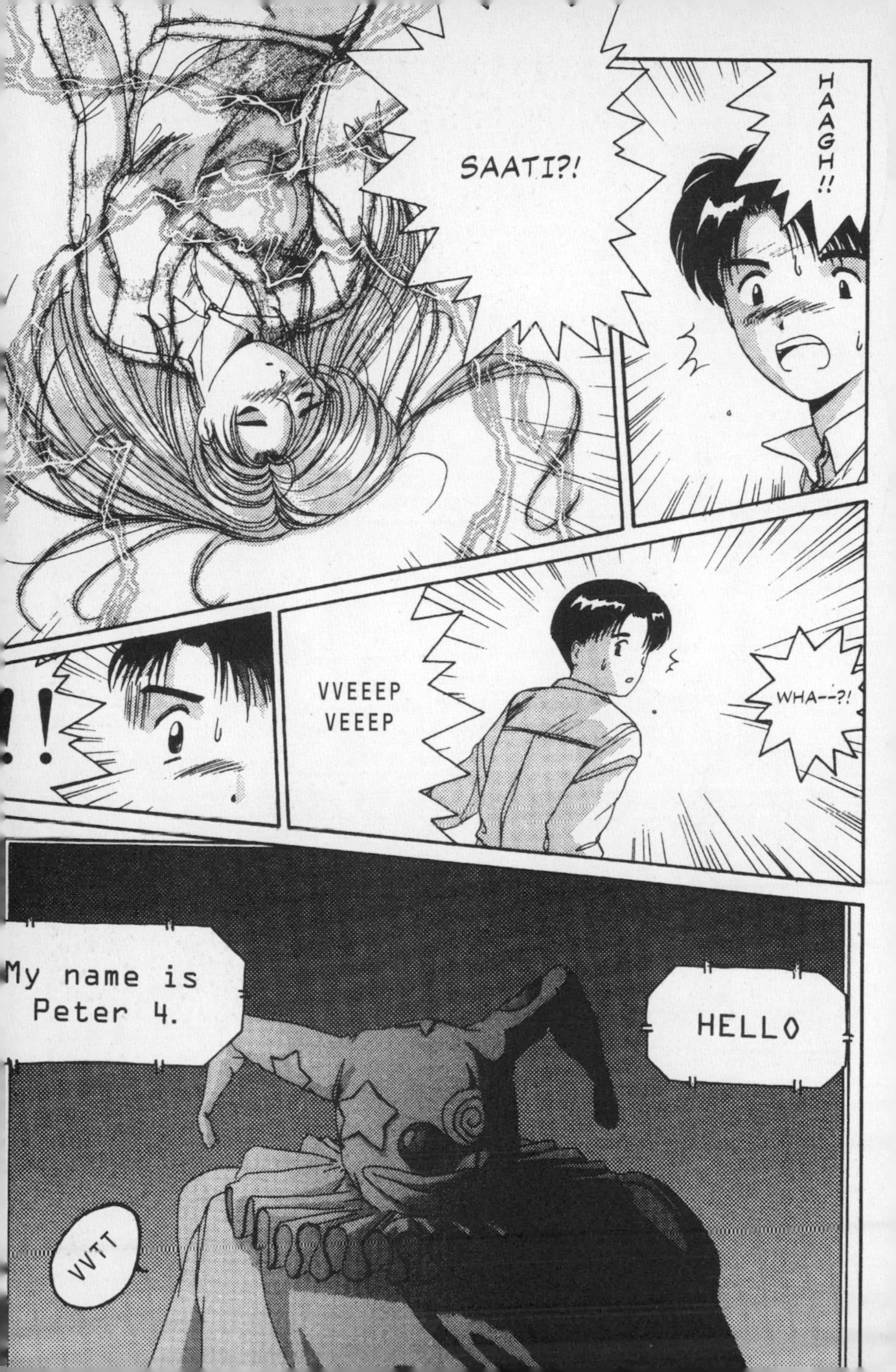

HAAGH!!
SAATI?!
WHA--?!
VVEEEP VEEEP
!!
HELLO
My name is Peter 4.
VVTT

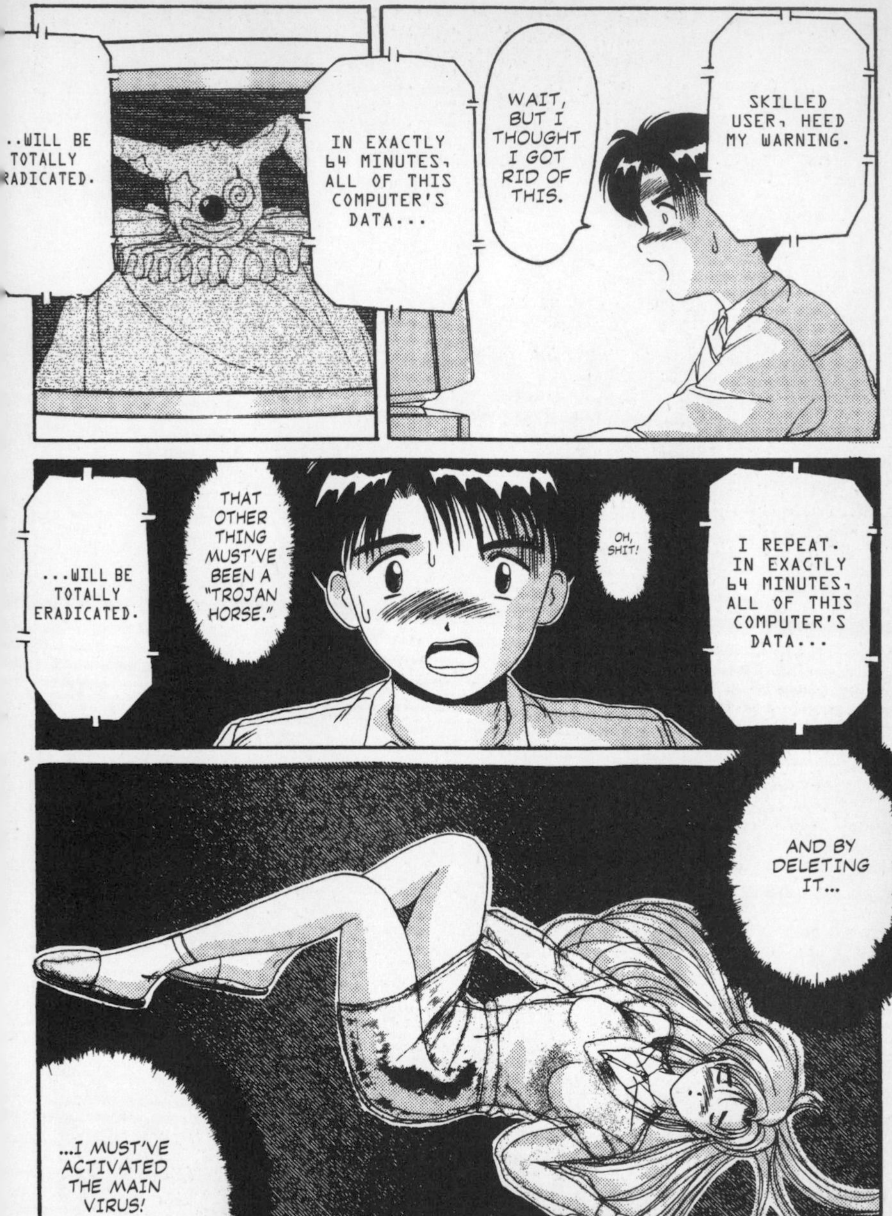
SKILLED USER, HEED MY WARNING.
WAIT, BUT I THOUGHT I GOT RID OF THIS.
IN EXACTLY 64 MINUTES, ALL OF THIS COMPUTER'S DATA...
..WILL BE TOTALLY RADICATED.
I REPEAT. IN EXACTLY 64 MINUTES, ALL OF THIS COMPUTER'S DATA...
OH, SHIT!
THAT OTHER THING MUST'VE BEEN A "TROJAN HORSE."
...WILL BE TOTALLY ERADICATED.
AND BY DELETING IT...
...I MUST'VE ACTIVATED THE MAIN VIRUS!

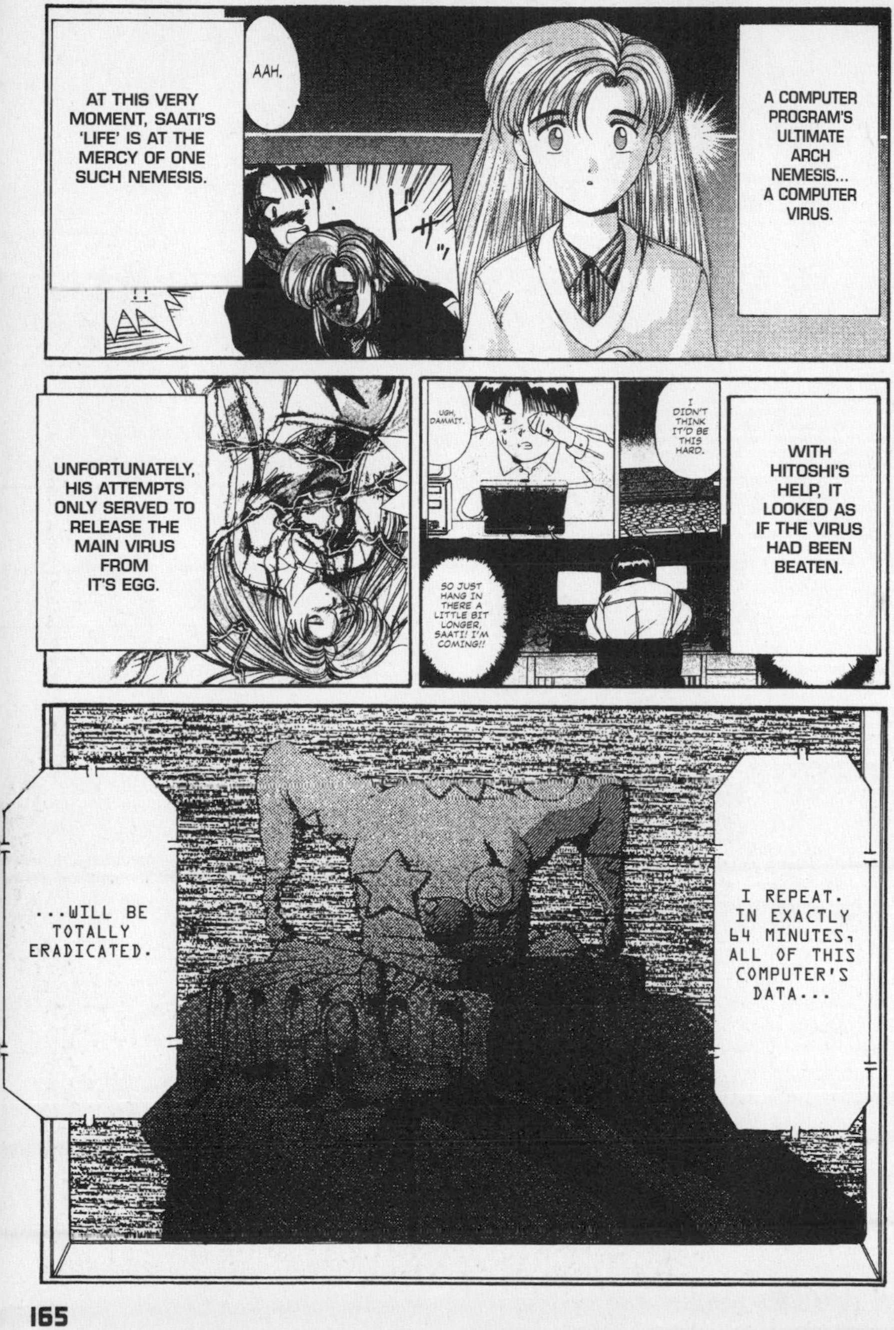

A COMPUTER PROGRAM'S ULTIMATE ARCH NEMESIS... A COMPUTER VIRUS.
AAH.
AT THIS VERY MOMENT, SAATI'S 'LIFE' IS AT THE MERCY OF ONE SUCH NEMESIS.
WITH HITOSHI'S HELP, IT LOOKED AS IF THE VIRUS HAD BEEN BEATEN.
I DIDN'T THINK IT'D BE THIS HARD.
UGH, DAMMIT.
SO JUST HANG IN THERE A LITTLE BIT LONGER, SAATI! I'M COMING!!
UNFORTUNATELY, HIS ATTEMPTS ONLY SERVED TO RELEASE THE MAIN VIRUS FROM IT'S EGG.
I REPEAT. IN EXACTLY 64 MINUTES, ALL OF THIS COMPUTER'S DATA...
...WILL BE TOTALLY ERADICATED.

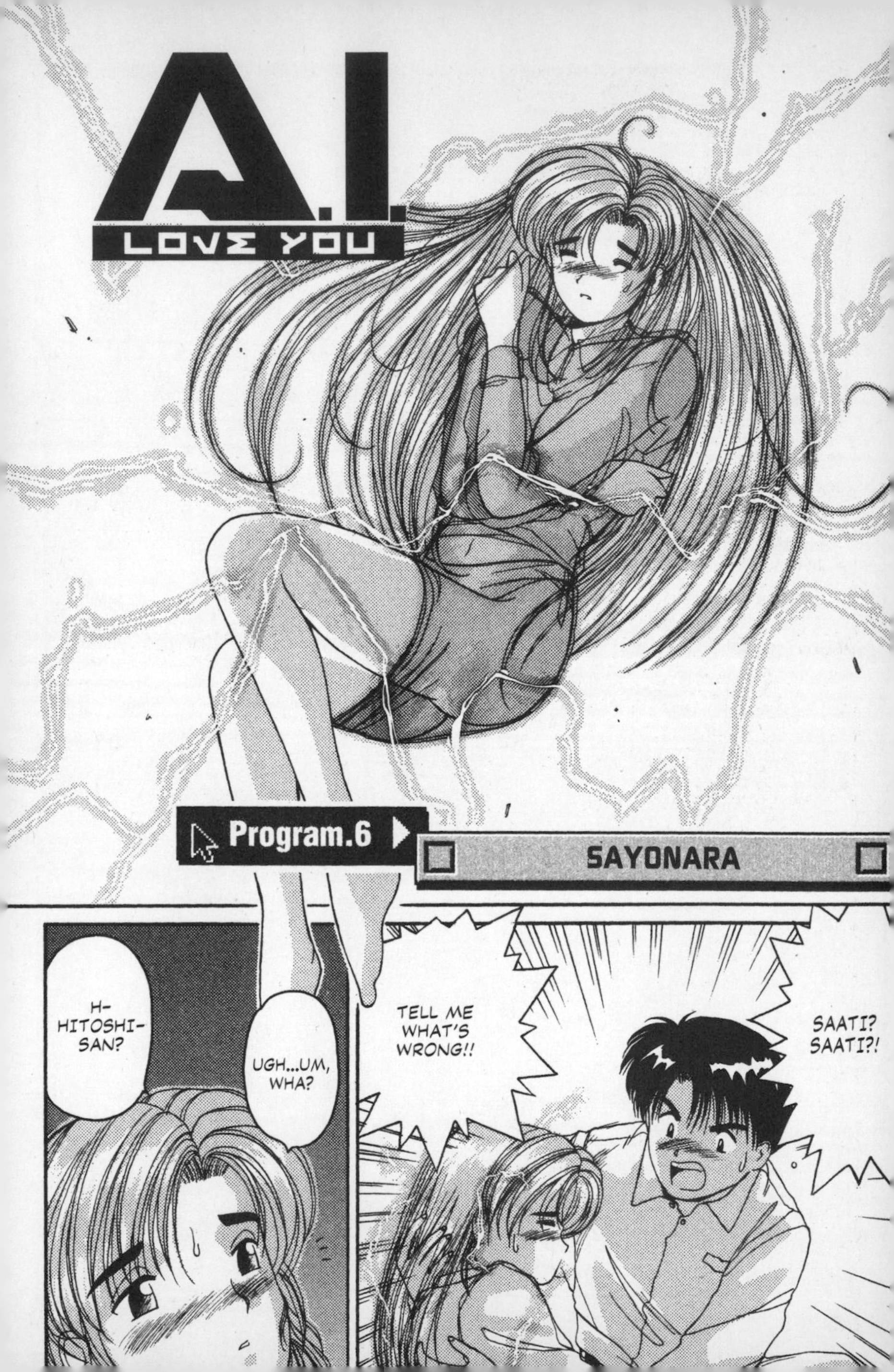
A.I. LOVE YOU
Program.6
SAYONARA
SAATI? SAATI?!
TELL ME WHAT'S WRONG!!
UGH...UM, WHA?
H-HITOSHI-SAN?

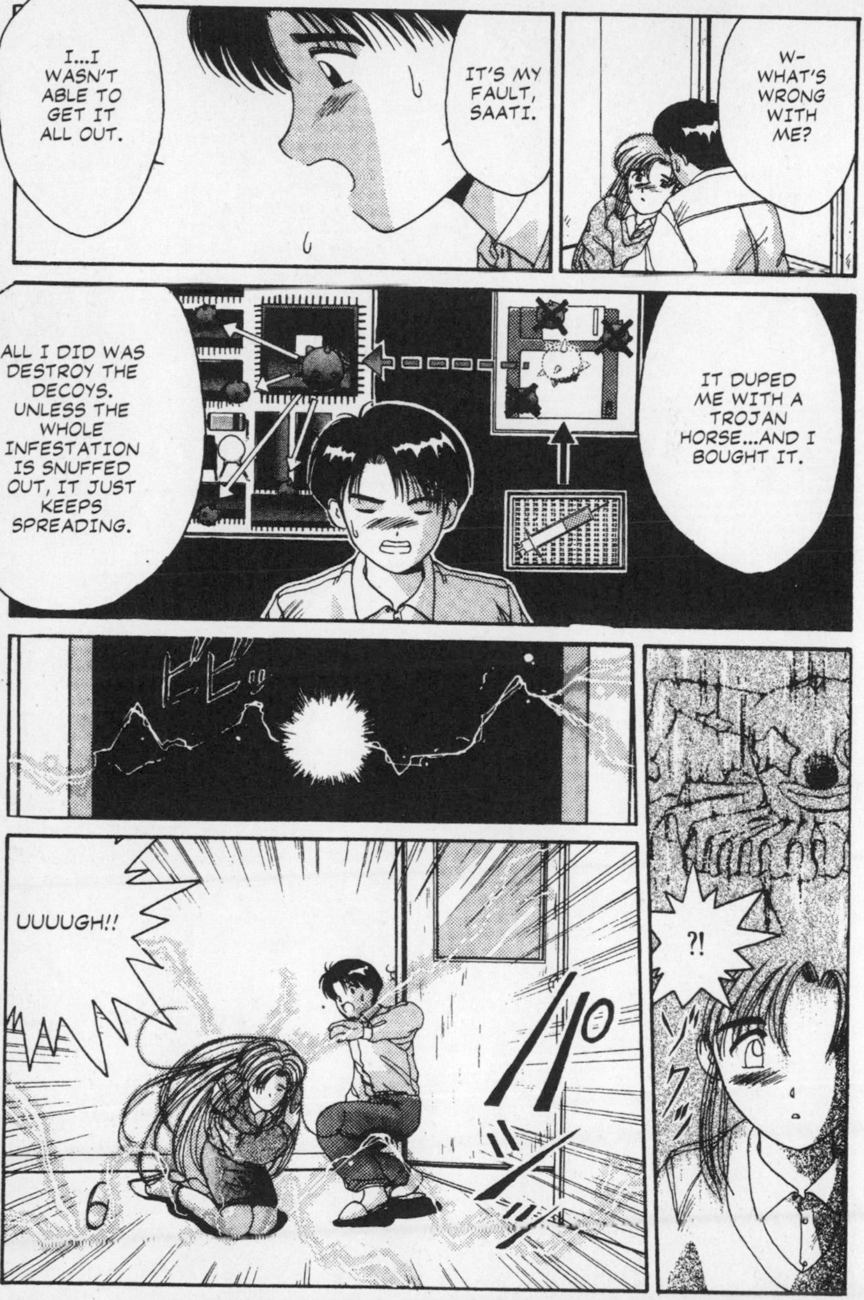
W-WHAT'S WRONG WITH ME?
IT'S MY FAULT, SAATI.
I...I WASN'T ABLE TO GET IT ALL OUT.
IT DUPED ME WITH A TROJAN HORSE...AND I BOUGHT IT.
ALL I DID WAS DESTROY THE DECOYS. UNLESS THE WHOLE INFESTATION IS SNUFFED OUT, IT JUST KEEPS SPREADING.
?!
UUUUGH!!

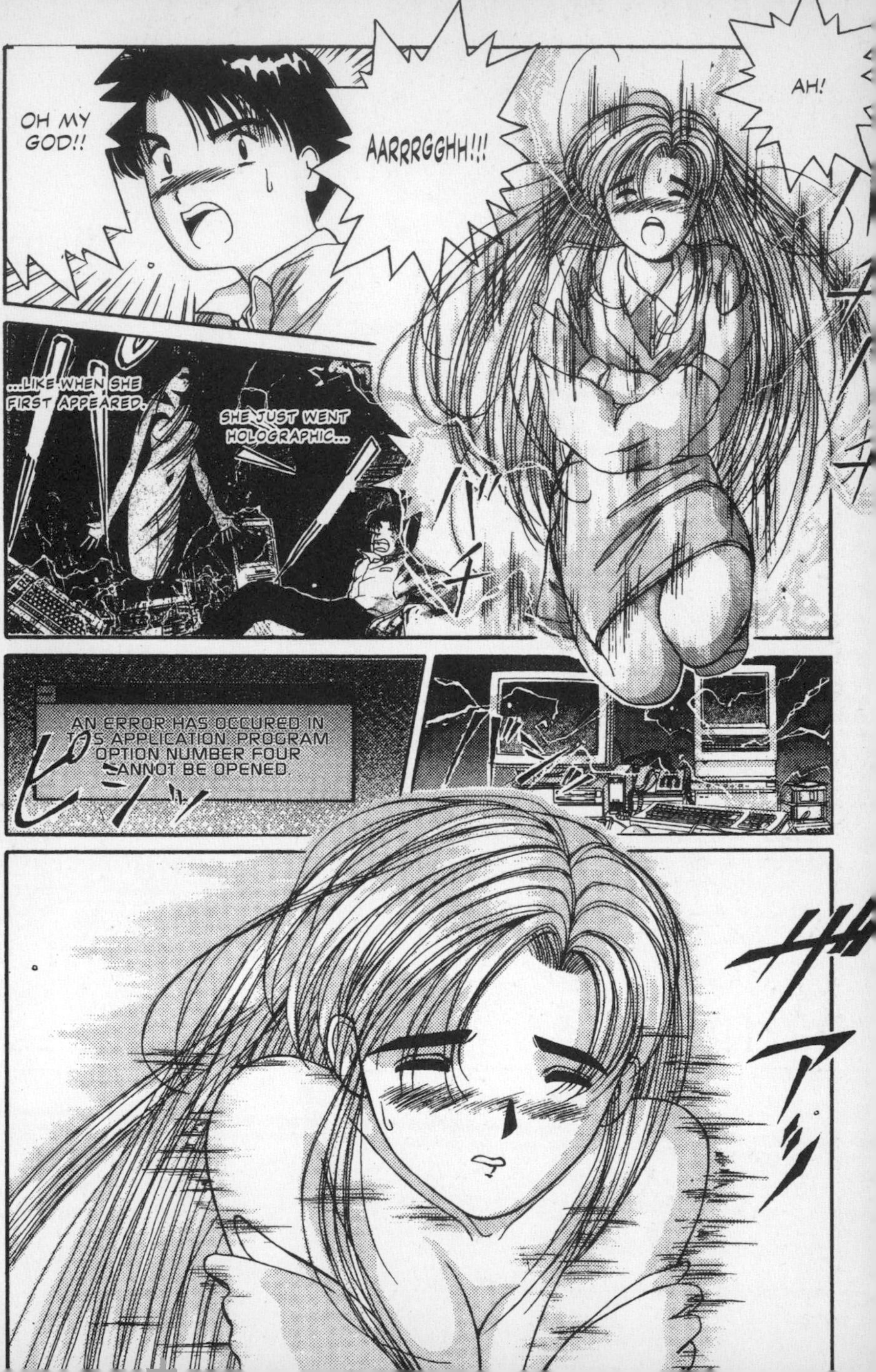
AH!
AARRRGGHH!!!
OH MY GOD!!
SHE JUST WENT HOLOGRAPHIC...
...LIKE WHEN SHE FIRST APPEARED.
AN ERROR HAS OCCURED IN THIS APPLICATION PROGRAM OPTION NUMBER FOUR CANNOT BE OPENED.

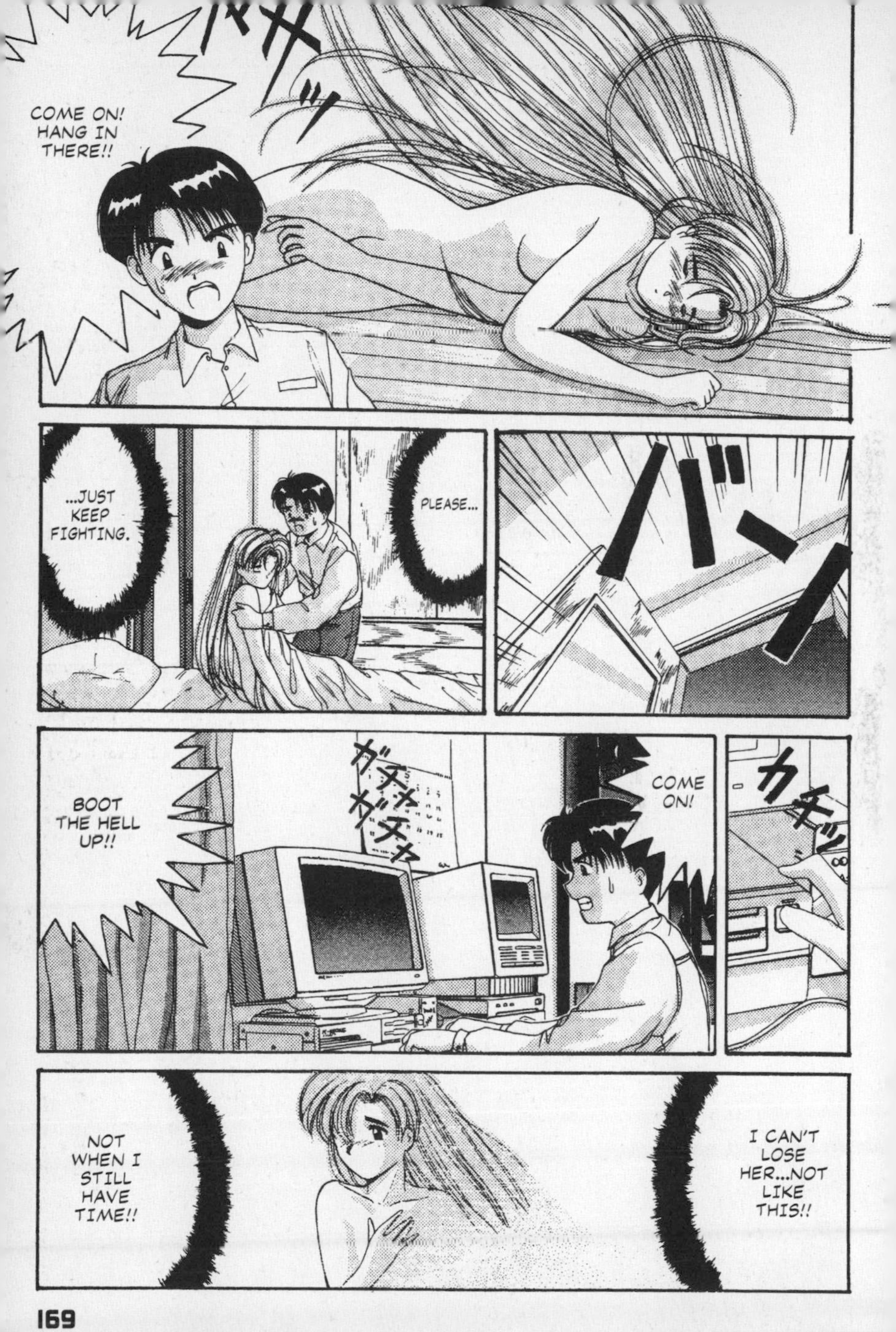

バサッ
COME ON! HANG IN THERE!!
バン
PLEASE...
...JUST KEEP FIGHTING.
カチッ
COME ON!
ガタガタ
BOOT THE HELL UP!!
I CAN'T LOSE HER...NOT LIKE THIS!!
NOT WHEN I STILL HAVE TIME!!

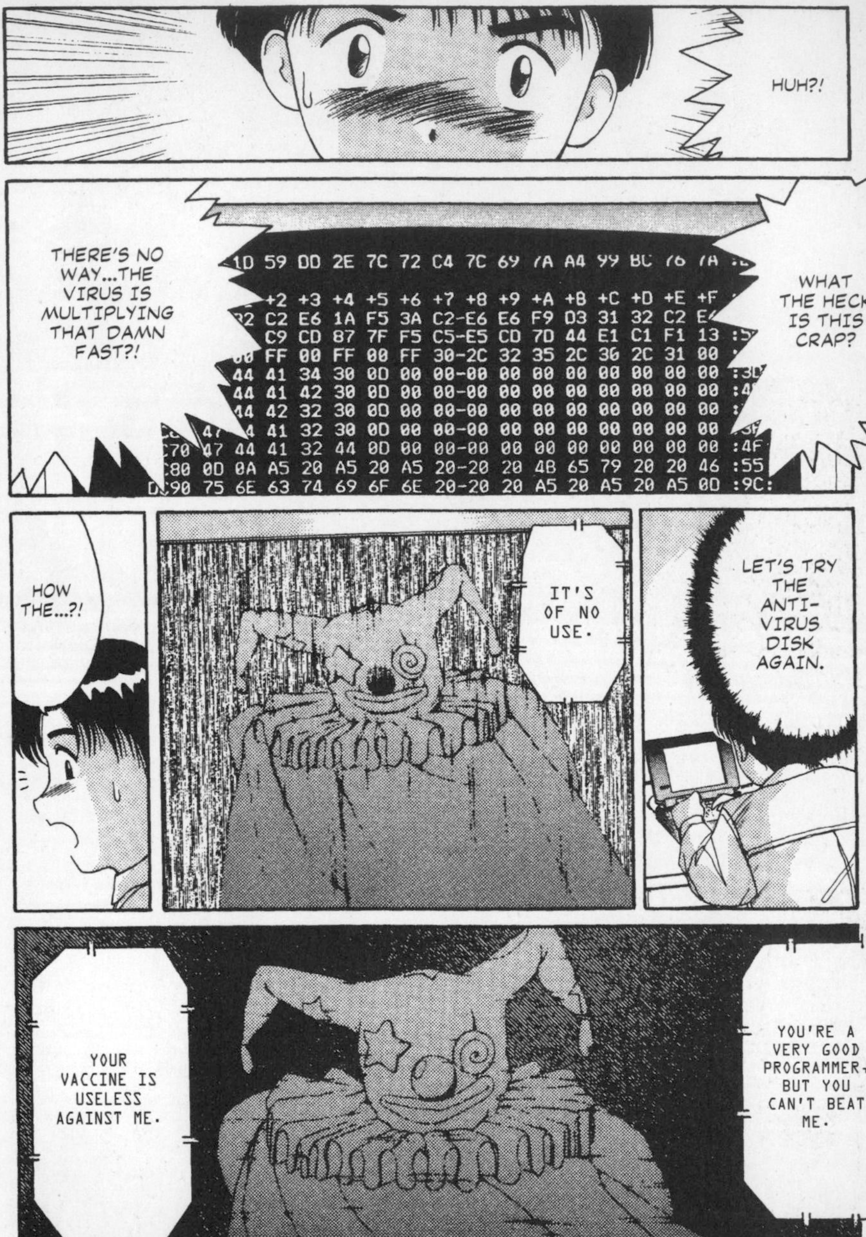
HUH?!
WHAT THE HECK IS THIS CRAP?
THERE'S NO WAY...THE VIRUS IS MULTIPLYING THAT DAMN FAST?!
1D 59 0D 2E 7C 72 C4 7C 69 7A A4 99 BC 76 7A
+2 +3 +4 +5 +6 +7 +8 +9 +A +B +C +D +E +F
C2 E6 1A F5 3A C2-E6 E6 F9 D3 31 32 C2
C9 CD 87 7F F5 C5-E5 CD 7D 44 E1 C1 F1 13
FF 00 FF 00 FF 30-2C 32 35 2C 36 2C 31 00
44 41 34 30 0D 00 00-00 00 00 00 00 00 00 00
44 41 42 30 0D 00 00-00 00 00 00 00 00 00 00
44 42 32 30 0D 00 00-00 00 00 00 00 00 00 00
41 32 30 0D 00 00-00 00 00 00 00 00 00 00
C70 47 44 41 32 44 0D 00 00-00 00 00 00 00 00 00 00 :4F
C80 0D 0A A5 20 A5 20 A5 20-20 20 4B 65 79 20 20 46 :55
C90 75 6E 63 74 69 6F 6E 20-20 20 A5 20 A5 20 A5 0D :9C:
LET'S TRY THE ANTI-VIRUS DISK AGAIN.
IT'S OF NO USE.
HOW THE...?!
YOU'RE A VERY GOOD PROGRAMMER, BUT YOU CAN'T BEAT ME.
YOUR VACCINE IS USELESS AGAINST ME.

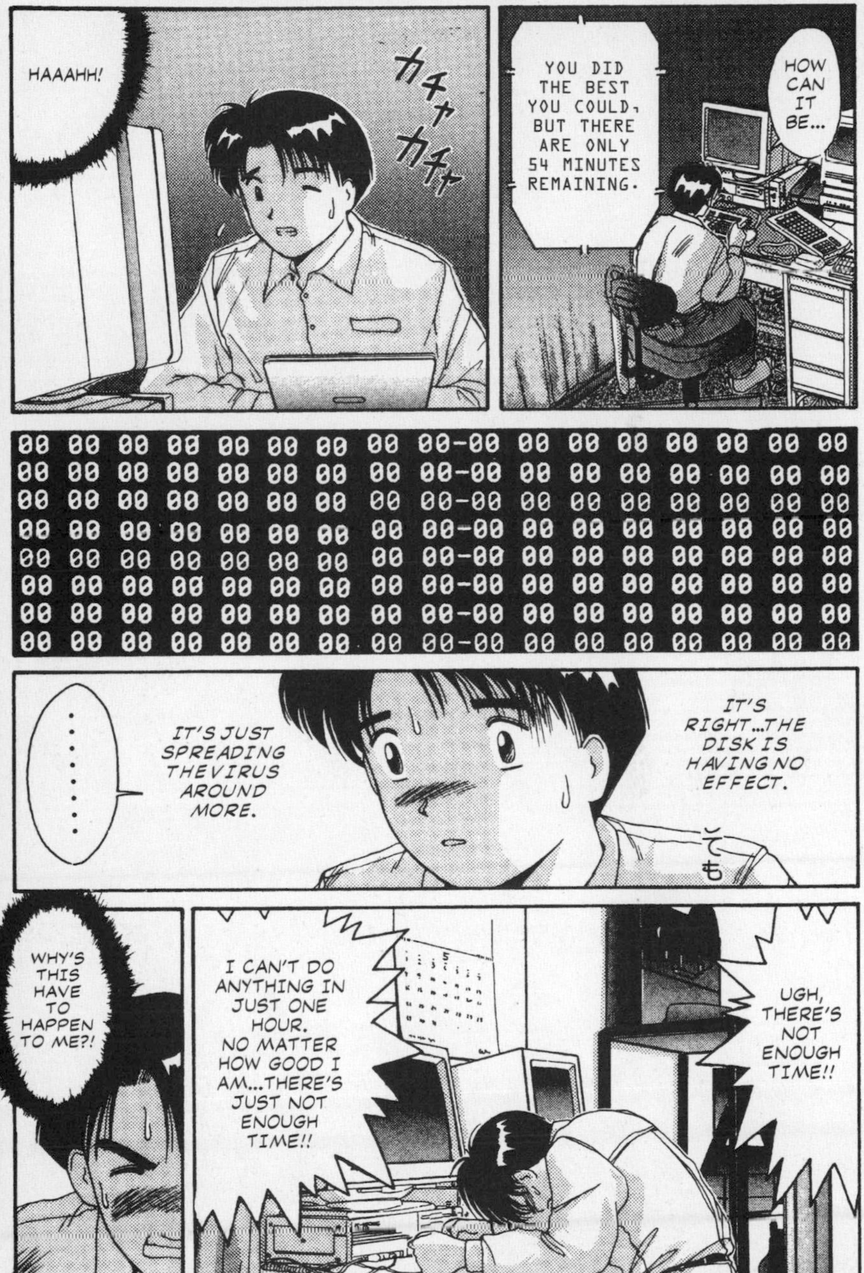
HOW CAN IT BE...
YOU DID THE BEST YOU COULD, BUT THERE ARE ONLY 54 MINUTES REMAINING.
カチャカチャ
HAAAHH!
00 00 00 00 00 00 00 00 00-00 00 00 00 00 00 00 00
00 00 00 00 00 00 00 00 00-00 00 00 00 00 00 00 00
00 00 00 00 00 00 00 00 00-00 00 00 00 00 00 00 00
00 00 00 00 00 00 00 00 00-00 00 00 00 00 00 00 00
00 00 00 00 00 00 00 00 00-00 00 00 00 00 00 00 00
00 00 00 00 00 00 00 00 00-00 00 00 00 00 00 00 00
00 00 00 00 00 00 00 00 00-00 00 00 00 00 00 00 00
00 00 00 00 00 00 00 00 00-00 00 00 00 00 00 00 00
IT'S RIGHT...THE DISK IS HAVING NO EFFECT.
でも
IT'S JUST SPREADING THE VIRUS AROUND MORE.
....
UGH, THERE'S NOT ENOUGH TIME!!
I CAN'T DO ANYTHING IN JUST ONE HOUR. NO MATTER HOW GOOD I AM...THERE'S JUST NOT ENOUGH TIME!!
WHY'S THIS HAVE TO HAPPEN TO ME?!

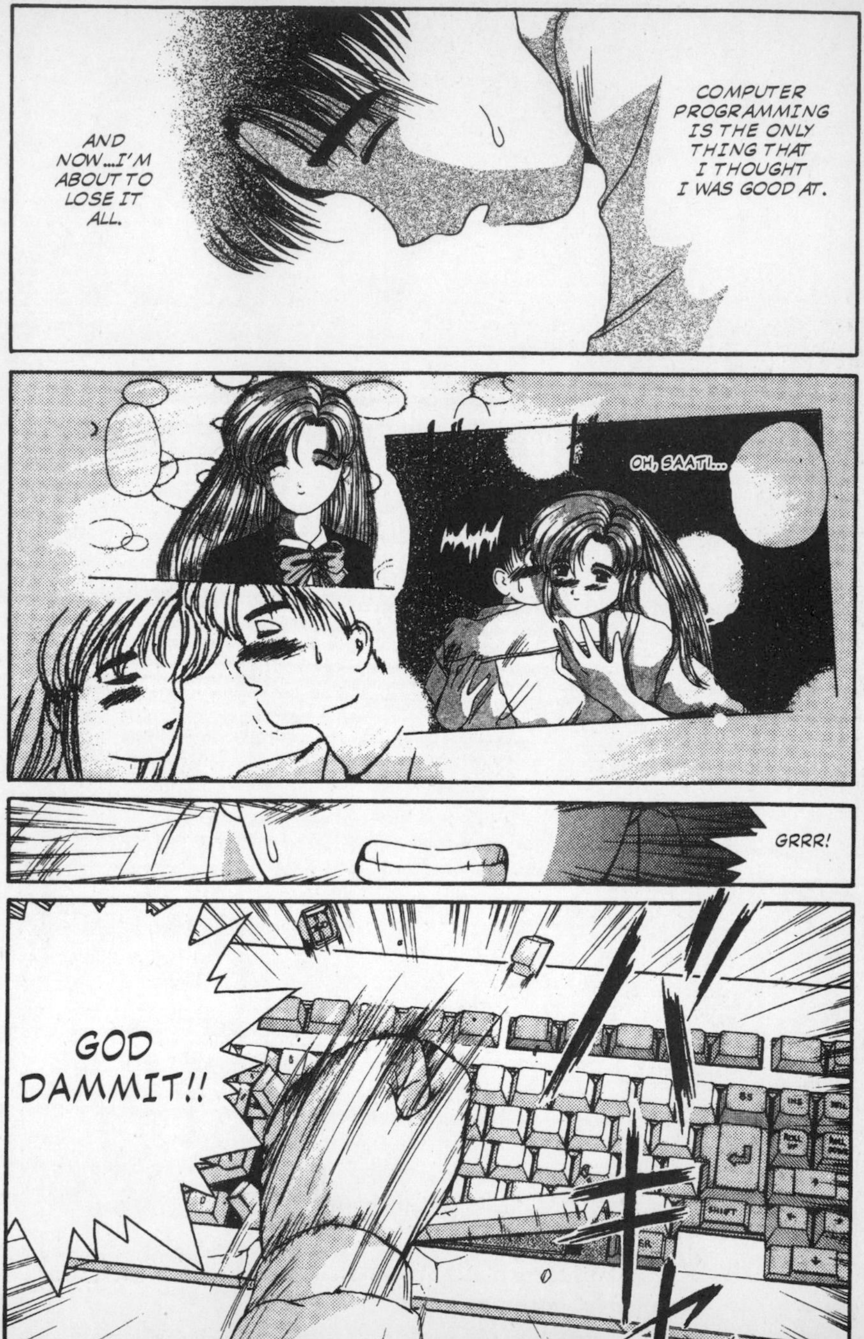
COMPUTER PROGRAMMING IS THE ONLY THING THAT I THOUGHT I WAS GOOD AT.
AND NOW...I'M ABOUT TO LOSE IT ALL.
OH, SAATI...
GRRR!
GOD DAMMIT!!

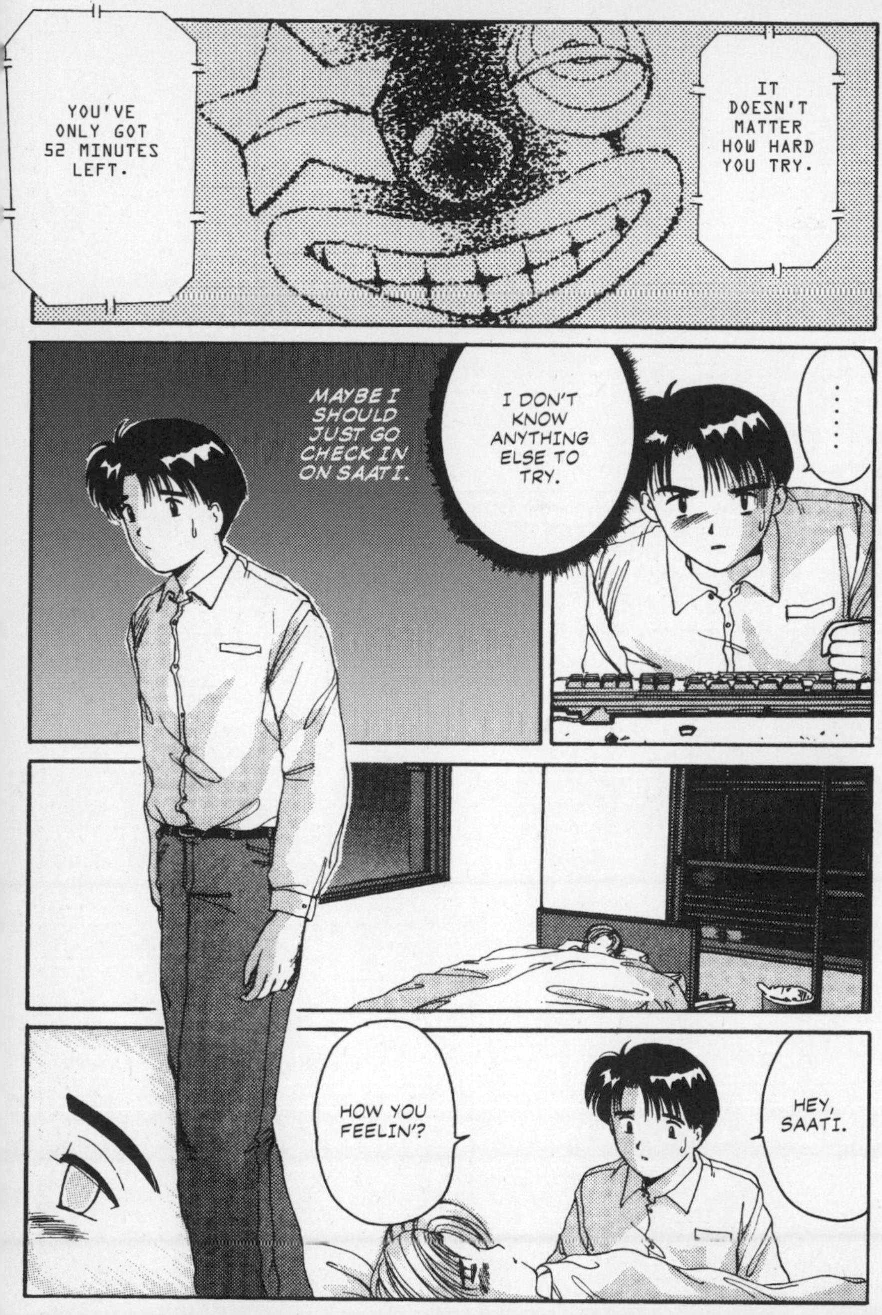
IT DOESN'T MATTER HOW HARD YOU TRY.
YOU'VE ONLY GOT 52 MINUTES LEFT.
......
I DON'T KNOW ANYTHING ELSE TO TRY.
MAYBE I SHOULD JUST GO CHECK IN ON SAATI.
HEY, SAATI.
HOW YOU FEELIN'?

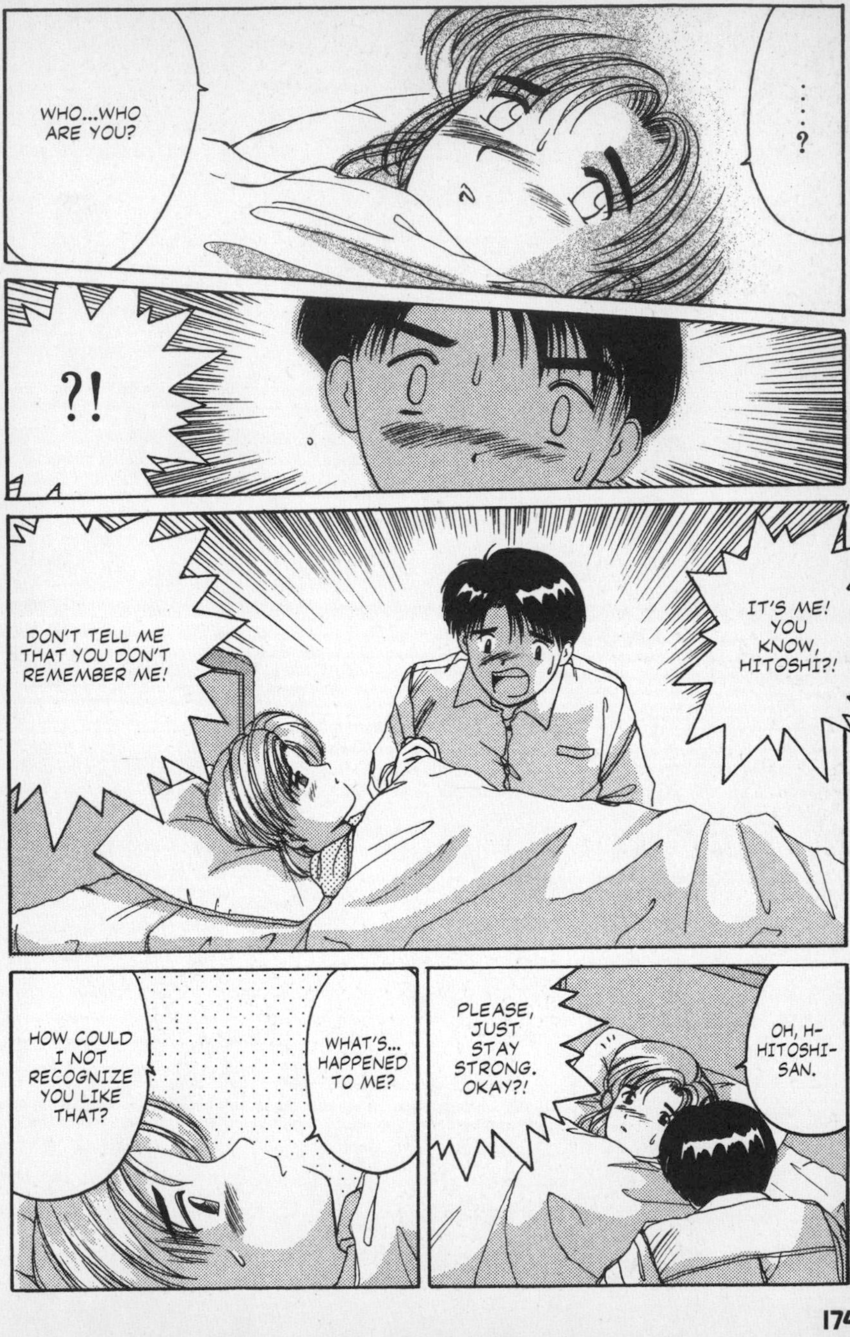
...?
WHO...WHO ARE YOU?
?!
IT'S ME! YOU KNOW, HITOSHI?!
DON'T TELL ME THAT YOU DON'T REMEMBER ME!
OH, H-HITOSHI-SAN.
PLEASE, JUST STAY STRONG. OKAY?!
WHAT'S... HAPPENED TO ME?
HOW COULD I NOT RECOGNIZE YOU LIKE THAT?

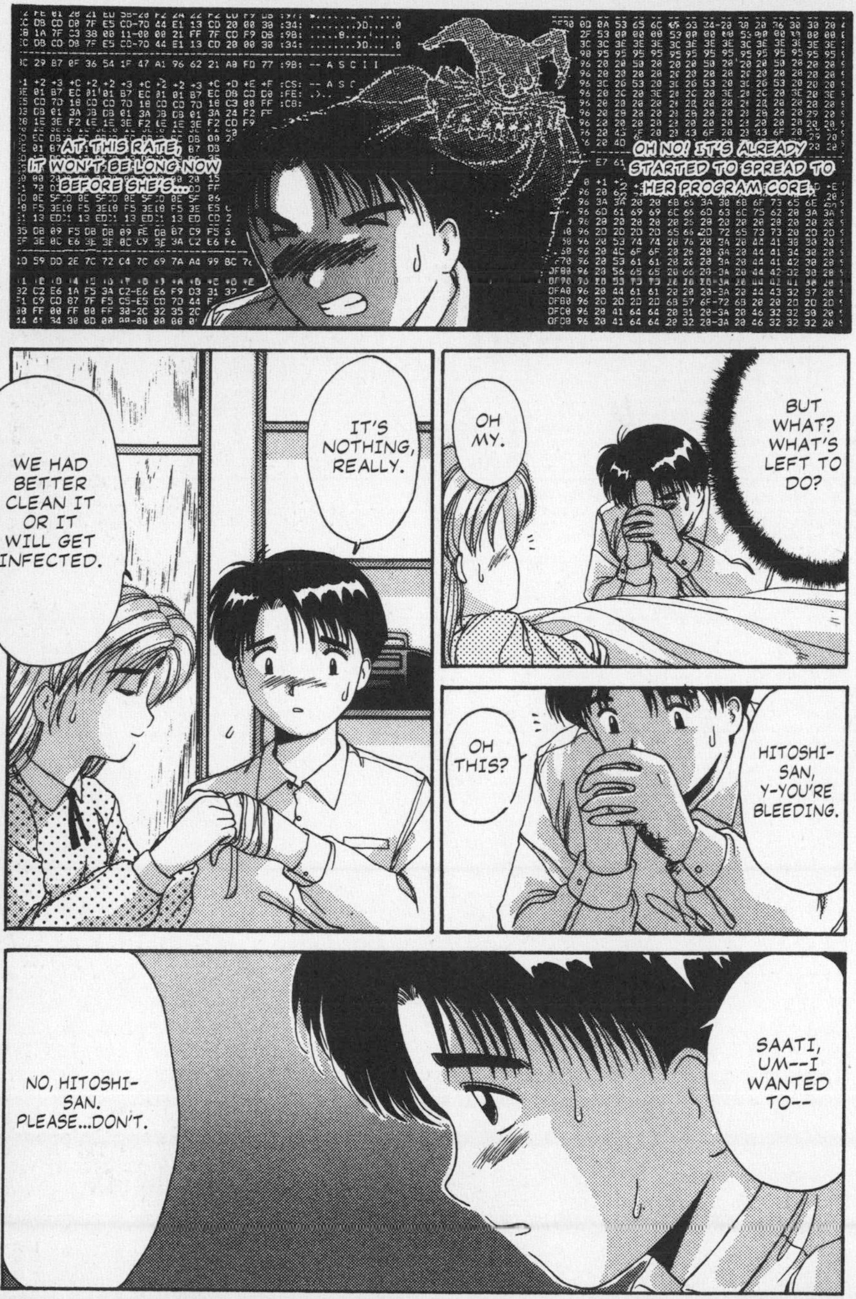
OH NO! IT'S ALREADY STARTED TO SPREAD TO HER PROGRAM CORE.
AT THIS RATE, IT WON'T BE LONG NOW BEFORE SHE'S...
BUT WHAT? WHAT'S LEFT TO DO?
OH MY.
HITOSHI-SAN, Y-YOU'RE BLEEDING.
OH THIS?
IT'S NOTHING, REALLY.
WE HAD BETTER CLEAN IT OR IT WILL GET INFECTED.
SAATI, UM--I WANTED TO--
NO, HITOSHI-SAN. PLEASE...DON'T.

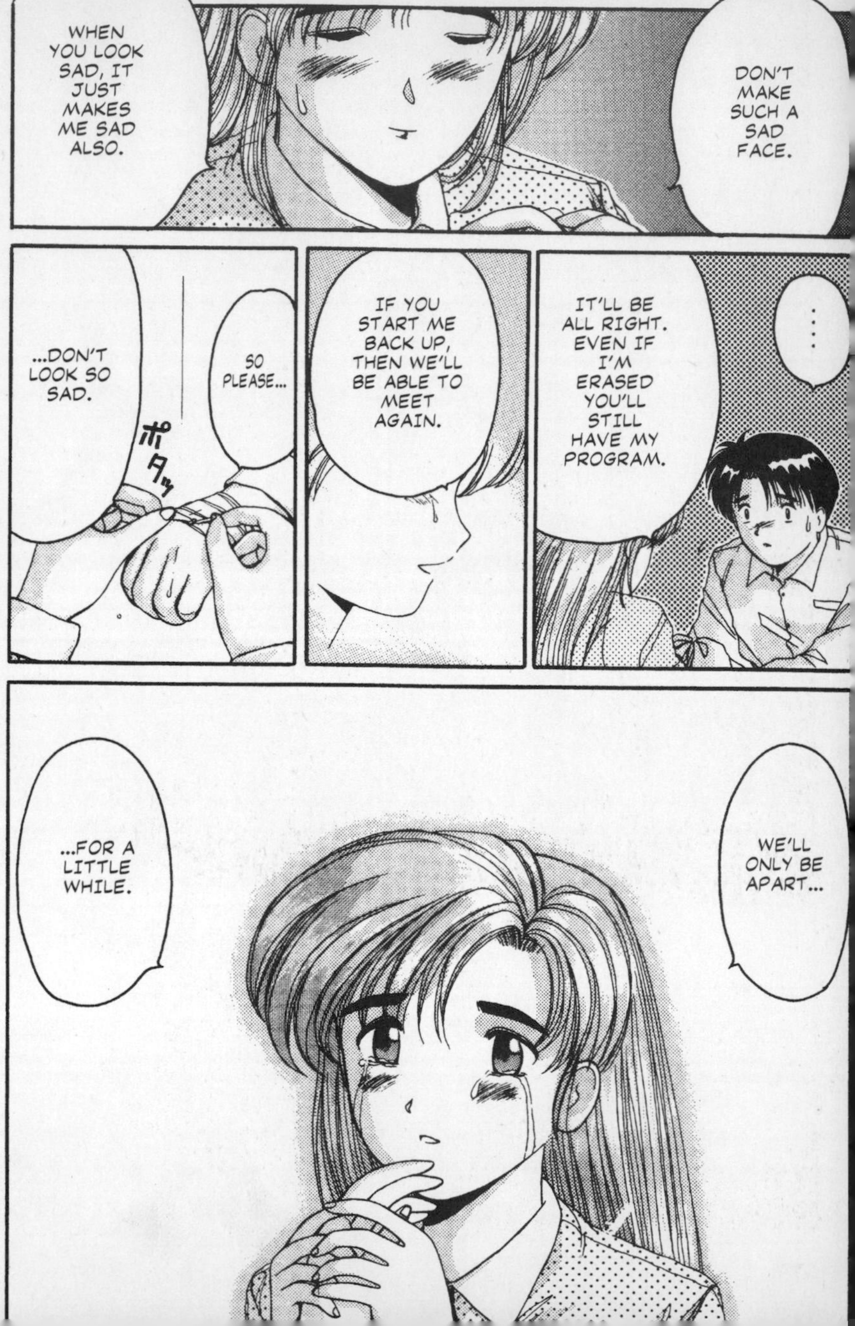
DON'T MAKE SUCH A SAD FACE.
WHEN YOU LOOK SAD, IT JUST MAKES ME SAD ALSO.
...
IT'LL BE ALL RIGHT. EVEN IF I'M ERASED YOU'LL STILL HAVE MY PROGRAM.
IF YOU START ME BACK UP, THEN WE'LL BE ABLE TO MEET AGAIN.
SO PLEASE...
ポタッ
...DON'T LOOK SO SAD.
WE'LL ONLY BE APART...
...FOR A LITTLE WHILE.

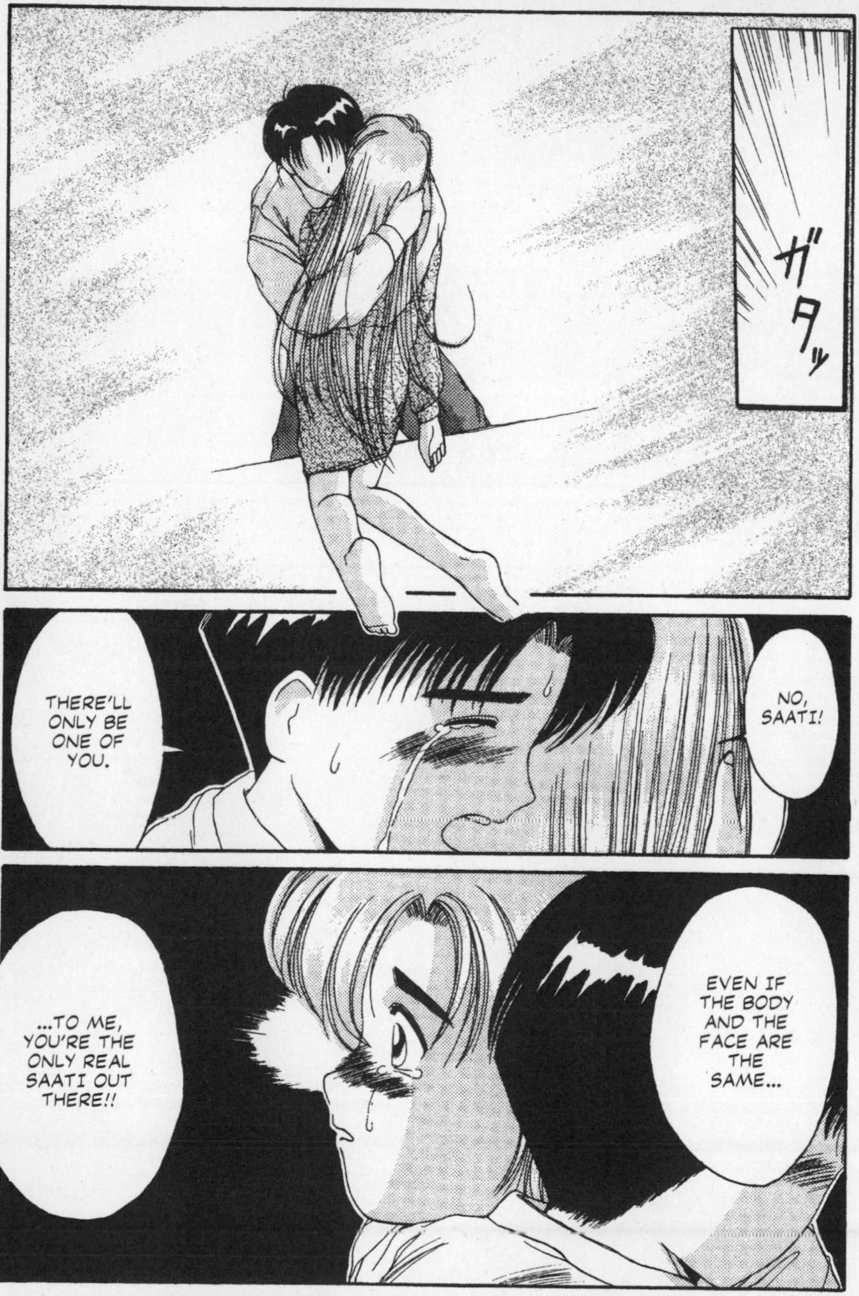
ガタッ
NO, SAATI!
THERE'LL ONLY BE ONE OF YOU.
EVEN IF THE BODY AND THE FACE ARE THE SAME...
...TO ME, YOU'RE THE ONLY REAL SAATI OUT THERE!!

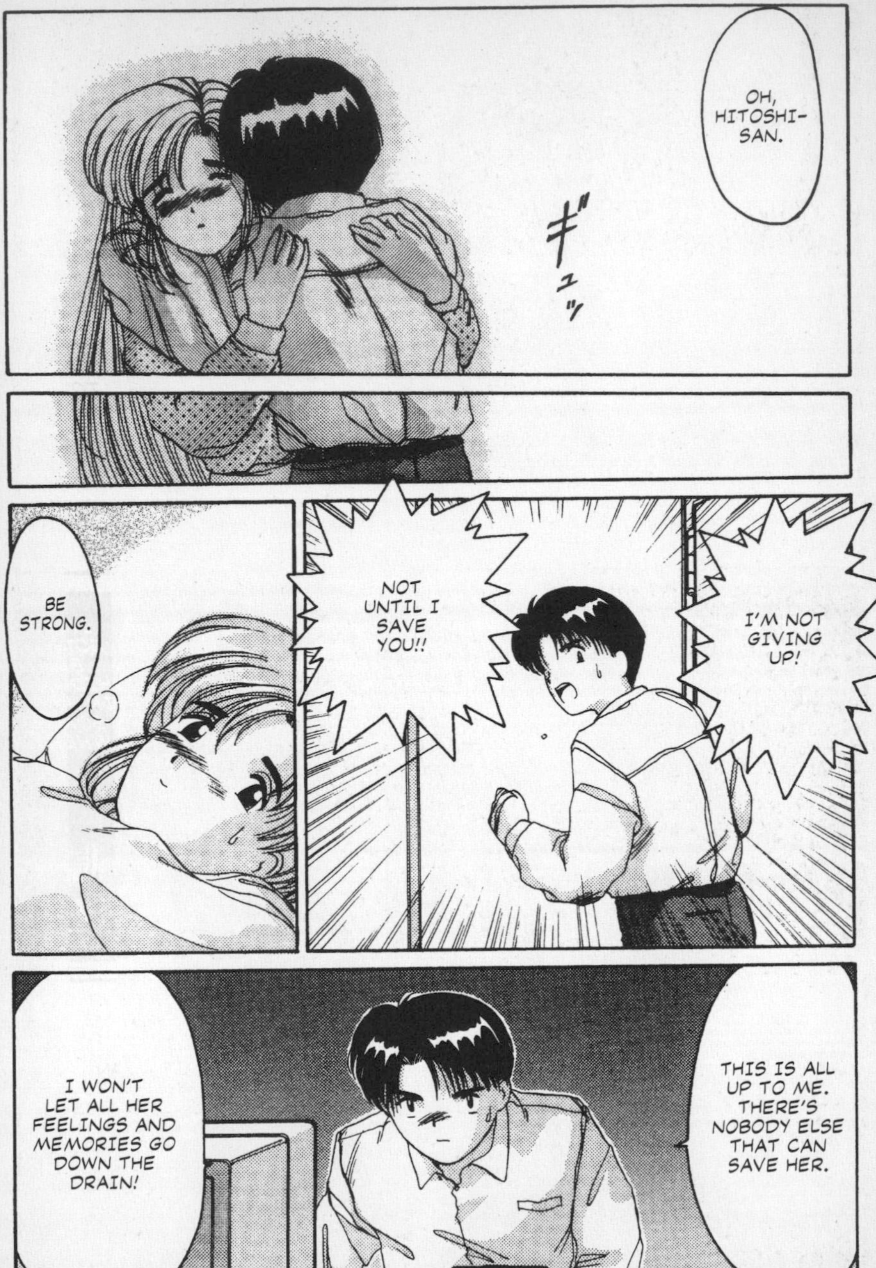
OH, HITOSHI-SAN.
ギュッ
I'M NOT GIVING UP!
NOT UNTIL I SAVE YOU!!
BE STRONG.
THIS IS ALL UP TO ME. THERE'S NOBODY ELSE THAT CAN SAVE HER.
I WON'T LET ALL HER FEELINGS AND MEMORIES GO DOWN THE DRAIN!

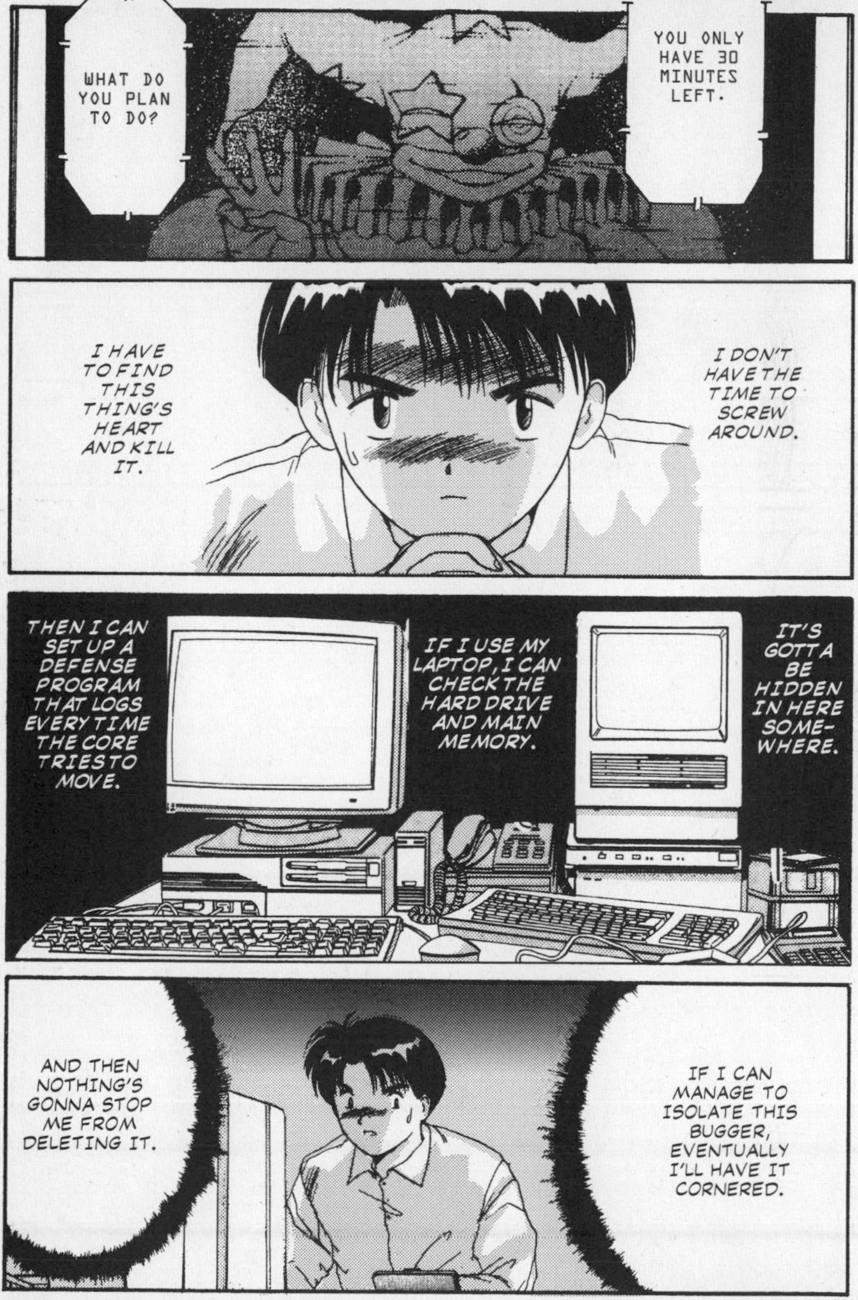
YOU ONLY HAVE 30 MINUTES LEFT.
WHAT DO YOU PLAN TO DO?
I DON'T HAVE THE TIME TO SCREW AROUND.
I HAVE TO FIND THIS THING'S HEART AND KILL IT.
IT'S GOTTA BE HIDDEN IN HERE SOME-WHERE.
IF I USE MY LAPTOP, I CAN CHECK THE HARD DRIVE AND MAIN MEMORY.
THEN I CAN SET UP A DEFENSE PROGRAM THAT LOGS EVERY TIME THE CORE TRIES TO MOVE.
IF I CAN MANAGE TO ISOLATE THIS BUGGER, EVENTUALLY I'LL HAVE IT CORNERED.
AND THEN NOTHING'S GONNA STOP ME FROM DELETING IT.

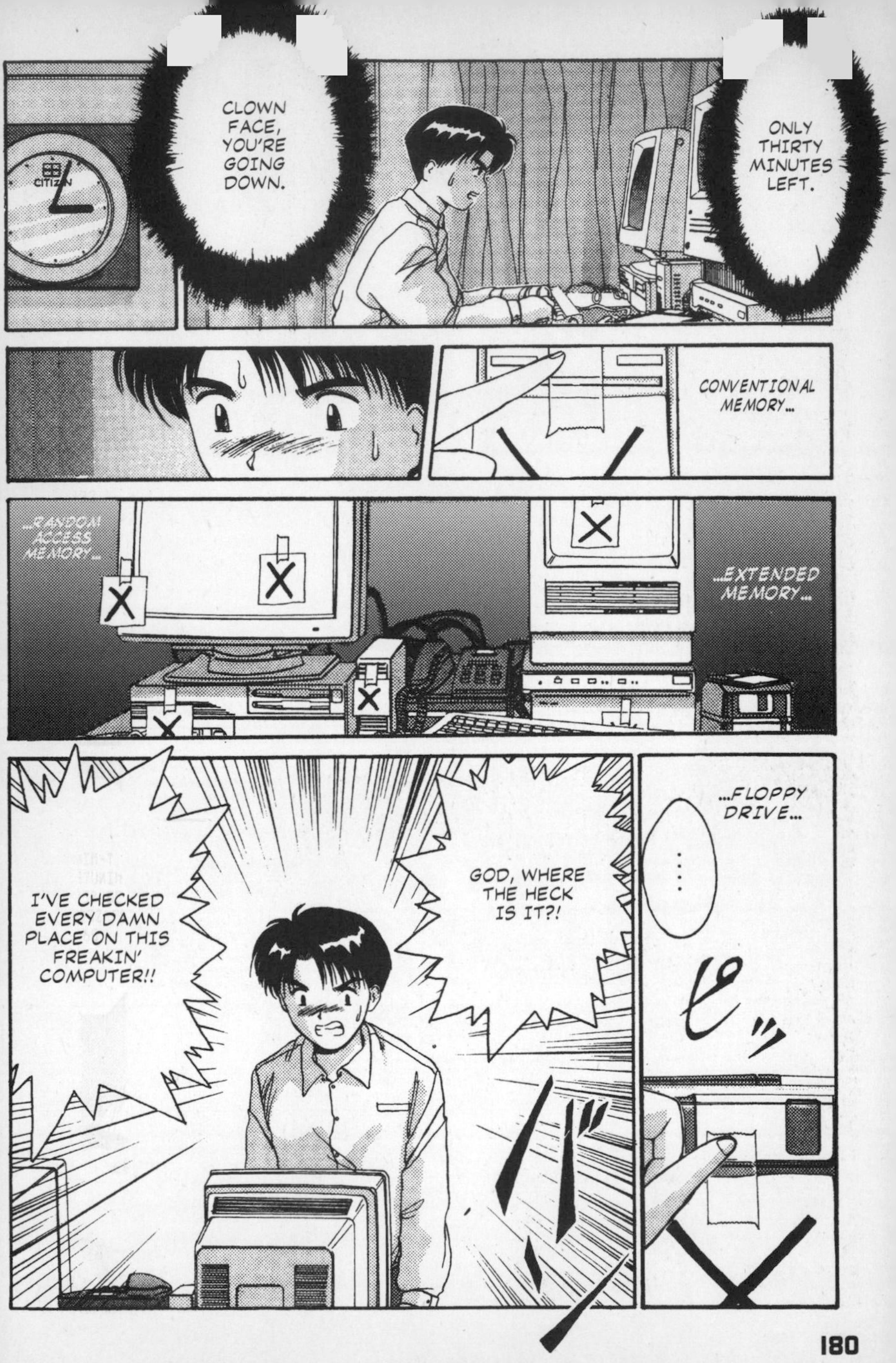
ONLY THIRTY MINUTES LEFT.
CLOWN FACE, YOU'RE GOING DOWN.
CITIZEN
CONVENTIONAL MEMORY...
...EXTENDED MEMORY...
...RANDOM ACCESS MEMORY...
...FLOPPY DRIVE...
....
ピッ
GOD, WHERE THE HECK IS IT?!
I'VE CHECKED EVERY DAMN PLACE ON THIS FREAKIN' COMPUTER!!
バ

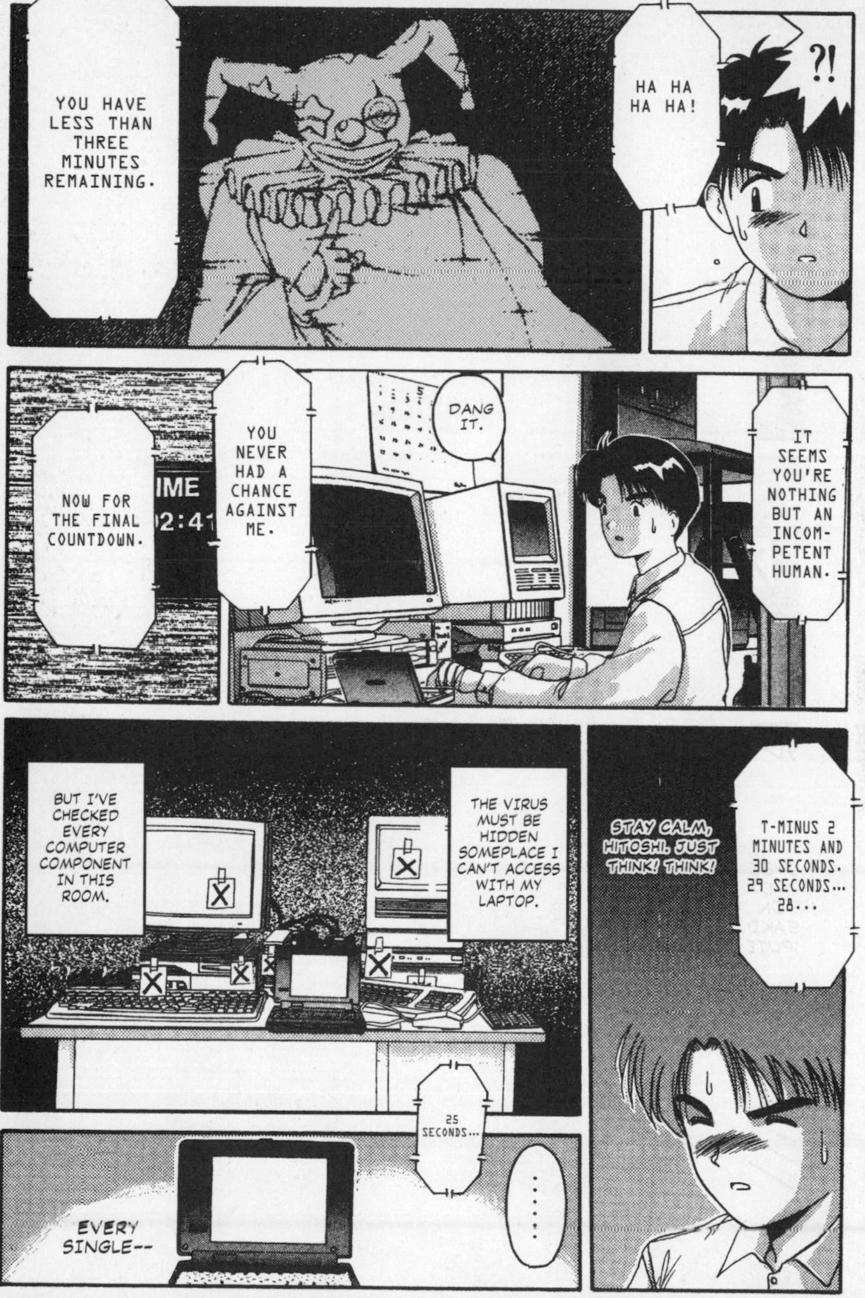

HA HA HA HA!
?!
YOU HAVE LESS THAN THREE MINUTES REMAINING.
IT SEEMS YOU'RE NOTHING BUT AN INCOMPETENT HUMAN.
DANG IT.
YOU NEVER HAD A CHANCE AGAINST ME.
NOW FOR THE FINAL COUNTDOWN.
T-MINUS 2 MINUTES AND 30 SECONDS. 29 SECONDS... 28...
STAY CALM, HITOSHI, JUST THINK! THINK!
THE VIRUS MUST BE HIDDEN SOMEPLACE I CAN'T ACCESS WITH MY LAPTOP.
BUT I'VE CHECKED EVERY COMPUTER COMPONENT IN THIS ROOM.
25 SECONDS...
......
EVERY SINGLE--

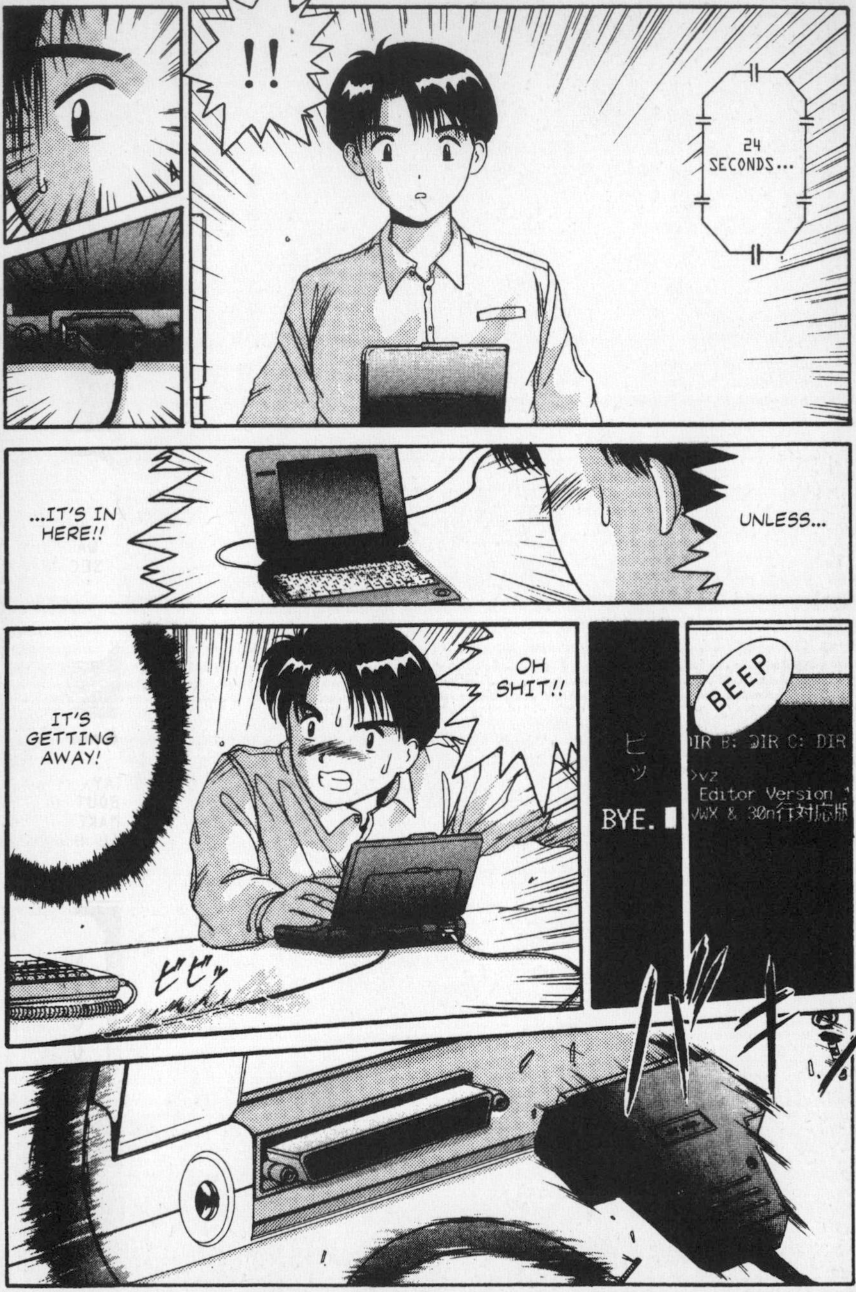
24 SECONDS...
!!
UNLESS...
...IT'S IN HERE!!
BEEP
DIR B: DIR C: DIR
>vz
Editor Version
VWX & 30n行対応版
ピッ
BYE.
OH SHIT!!
IT'S GETTING AWAY!
ビビッ

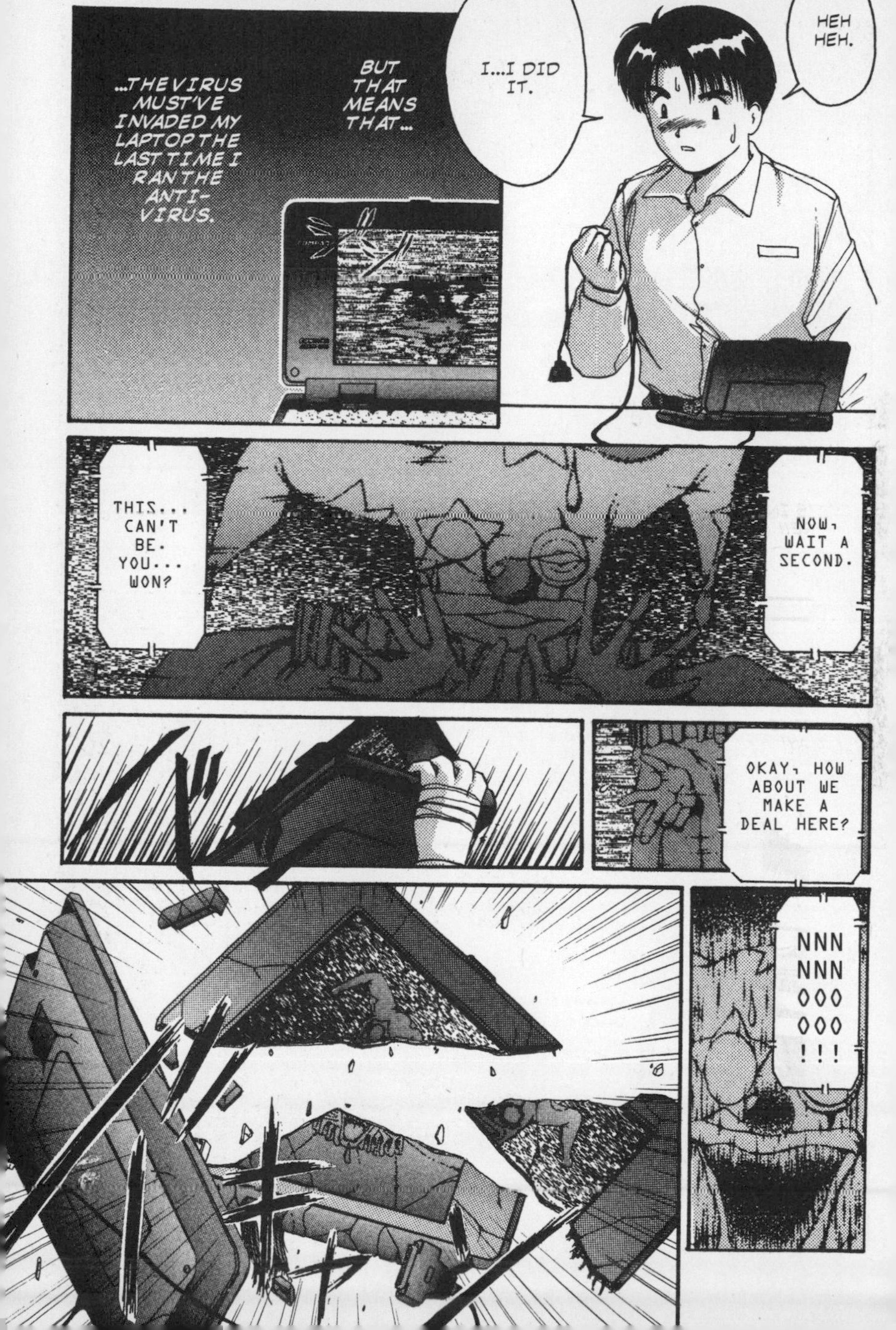
HEH HEH.
I...I DID IT.
BUT THAT MEANS THAT...
...THE VIRUS MUST'VE INVADED MY LAPTOP THE LAST TIME I RAN THE ANTI-VIRUS.
NOW, WAIT A SECOND.
THIS... CAN'T BE. YOU... WON?
OKAY, HOW ABOUT WE MAKE A DEAL HERE?
NNN NNN OOO OOO !!!

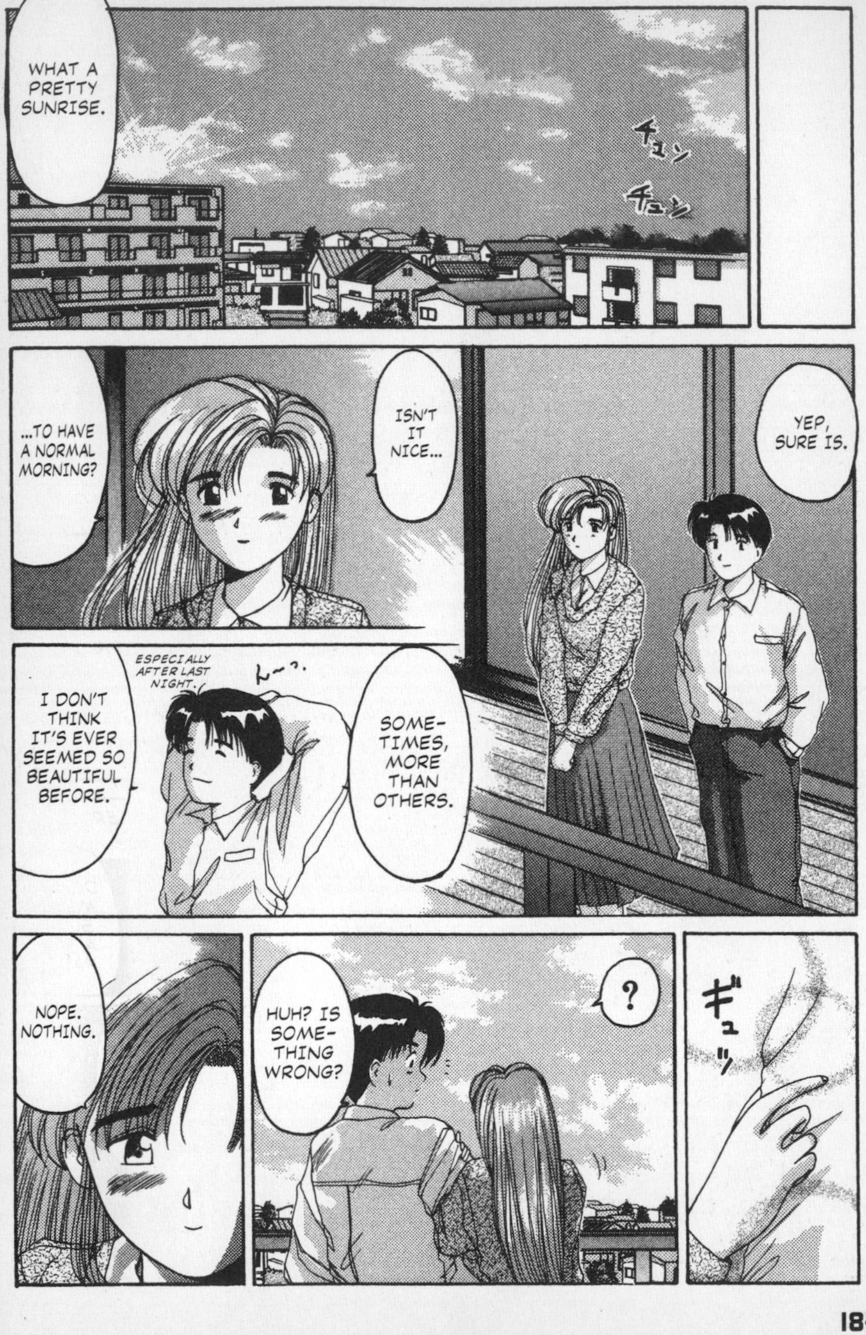
WHAT A PRETTY SUNRISE.
チュン
チュン
YEP, SURE IS.
ISN'T IT NICE...
...TO HAVE A NORMAL MORNING?
ん~っ.
SOME-TIMES, MORE THAN OTHERS.
ESPECIALLY AFTER LAST NIGHT.
I DON'T THINK IT'S EVER SEEMED SO BEAUTIFUL BEFORE.
ギュッ
?
HUH? IS SOME-THING WRONG?
NOPE. NOTHING.

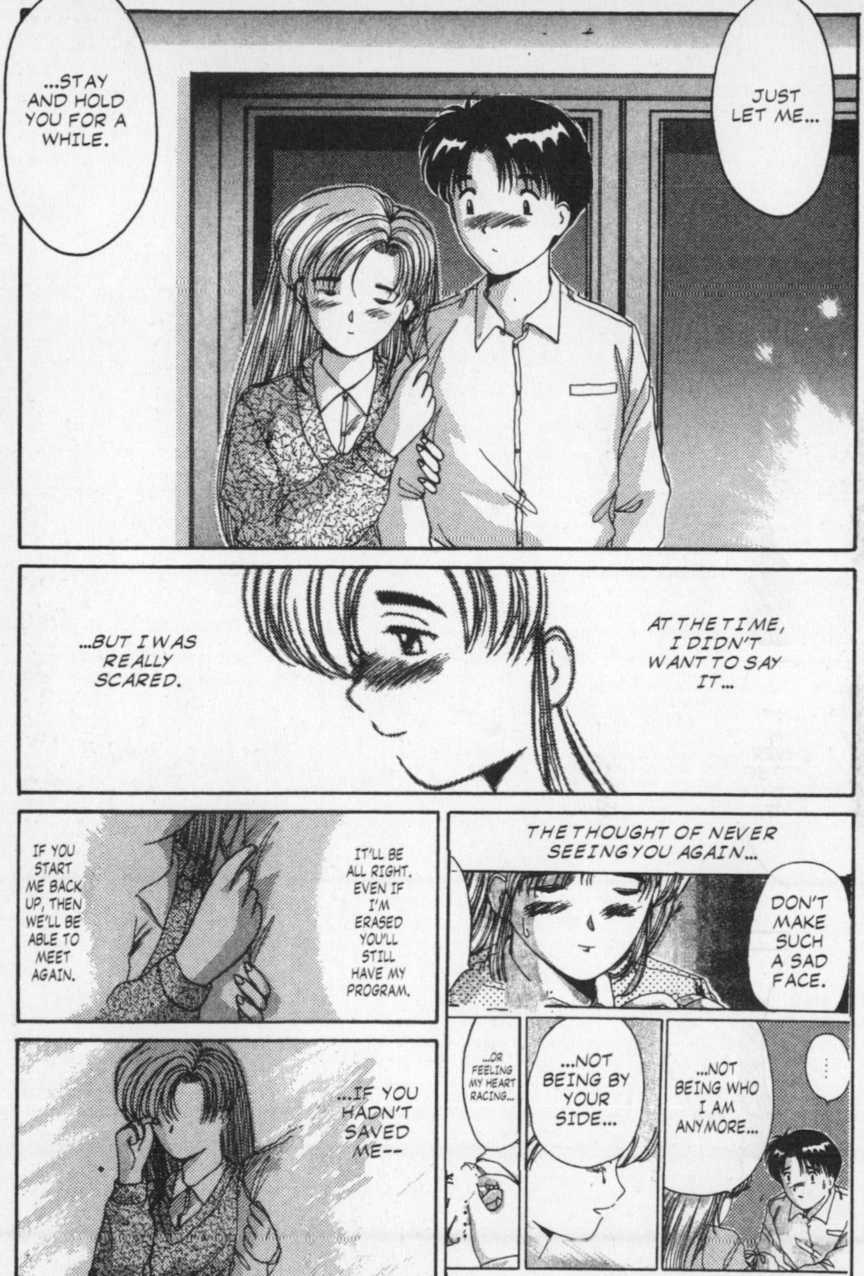
JUST LET ME...
...STAY AND HOLD YOU FOR A WHILE.
AT THE TIME, I DIDN'T WANT TO SAY IT...
...BUT I WAS REALLY SCARED.
THE THOUGHT OF NEVER SEEING YOU AGAIN...
DON'T MAKE SUCH A SAD FACE.
...
...NOT BEING WHO I AM ANYMORE...
...NOT BEING BY YOUR SIDE...
...OR FEELING MY HEART RACING...
IT'LL BE ALL RIGHT. EVEN IF I'M ERASED YOU'LL STILL HAVE MY PROGRAM.
IF YOU START ME BACK UP, THEN WE'LL BE ABLE TO MEET AGAIN.
...IF YOU HADN'T SAVED ME--

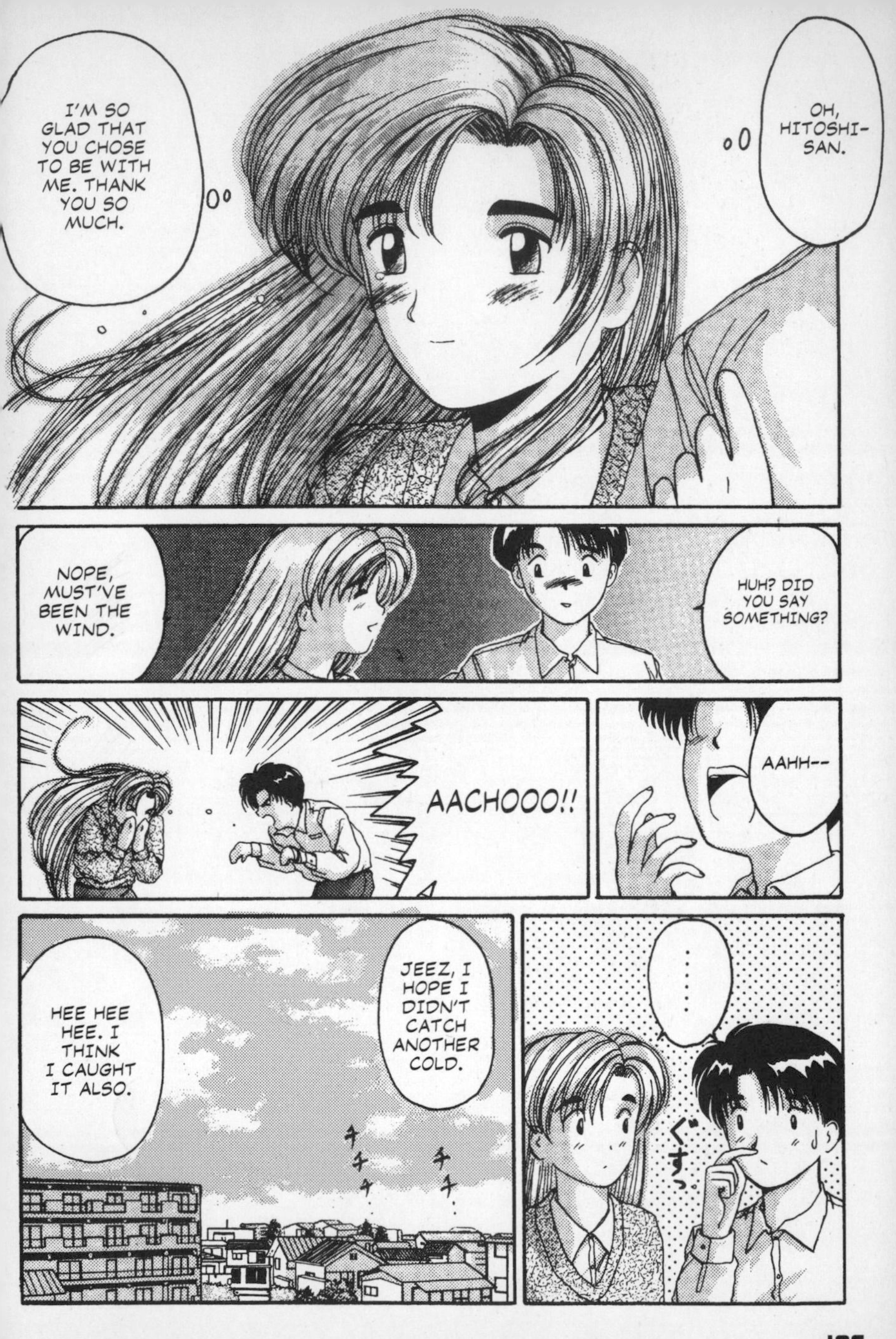
OH, HITOSHI-SAN.
I'M SO GLAD THAT YOU CHOSE TO BE WITH ME. THANK YOU SO MUCH.
HUH? DID YOU SAY SOMETHING?
NOPE, MUST'VE BEEN THE WIND.
AAHH--
AACHOOO!!
.....
ぐすっ
JEEZ, I HOPE I DIDN'T CATCH ANOTHER COLD.
HEE HEE HEE. I THINK I CAUGHT IT ALSO.
チチチ...
チチ...

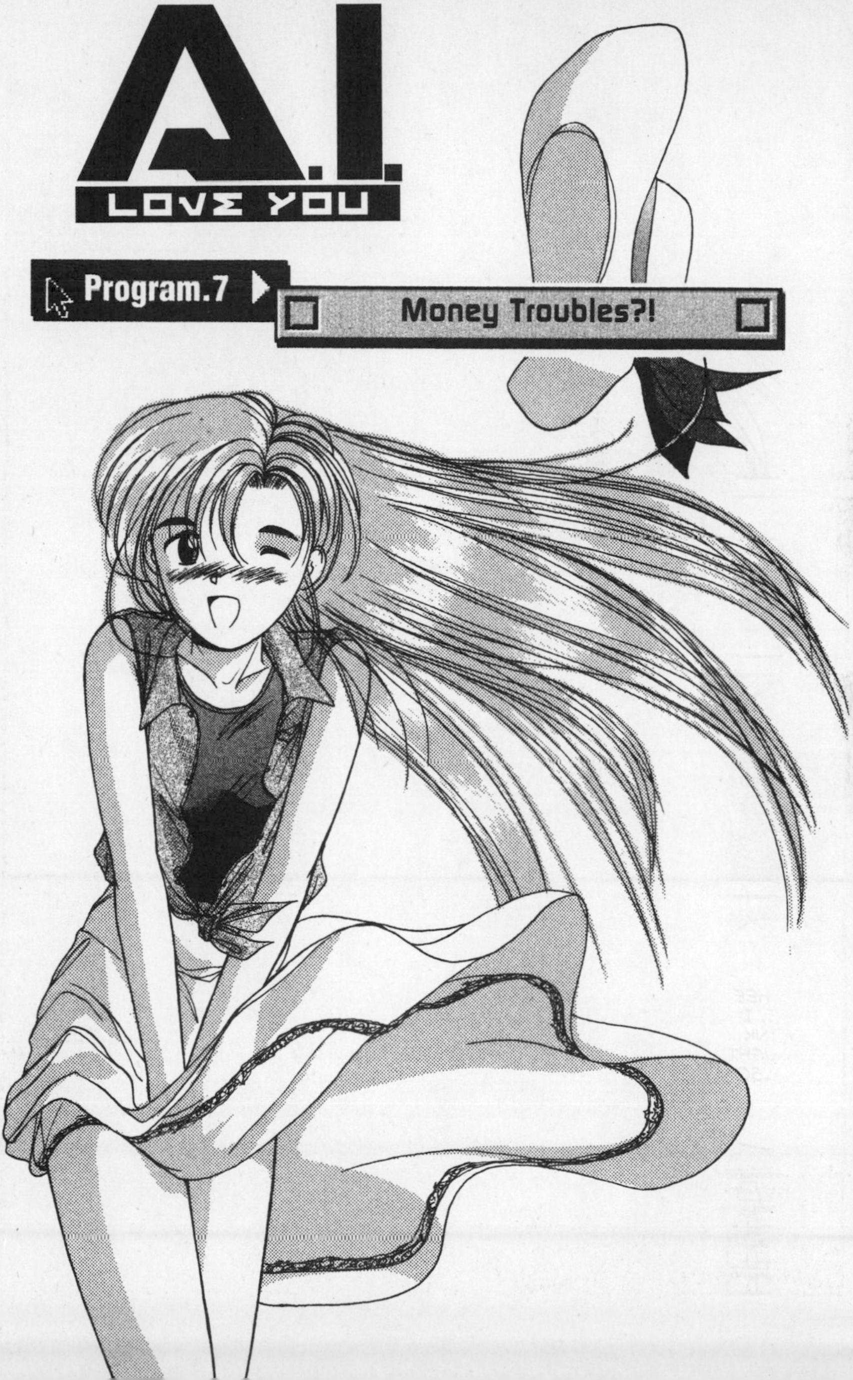
A.I.
LOVE YOU
Program.7
Money Troubles?!

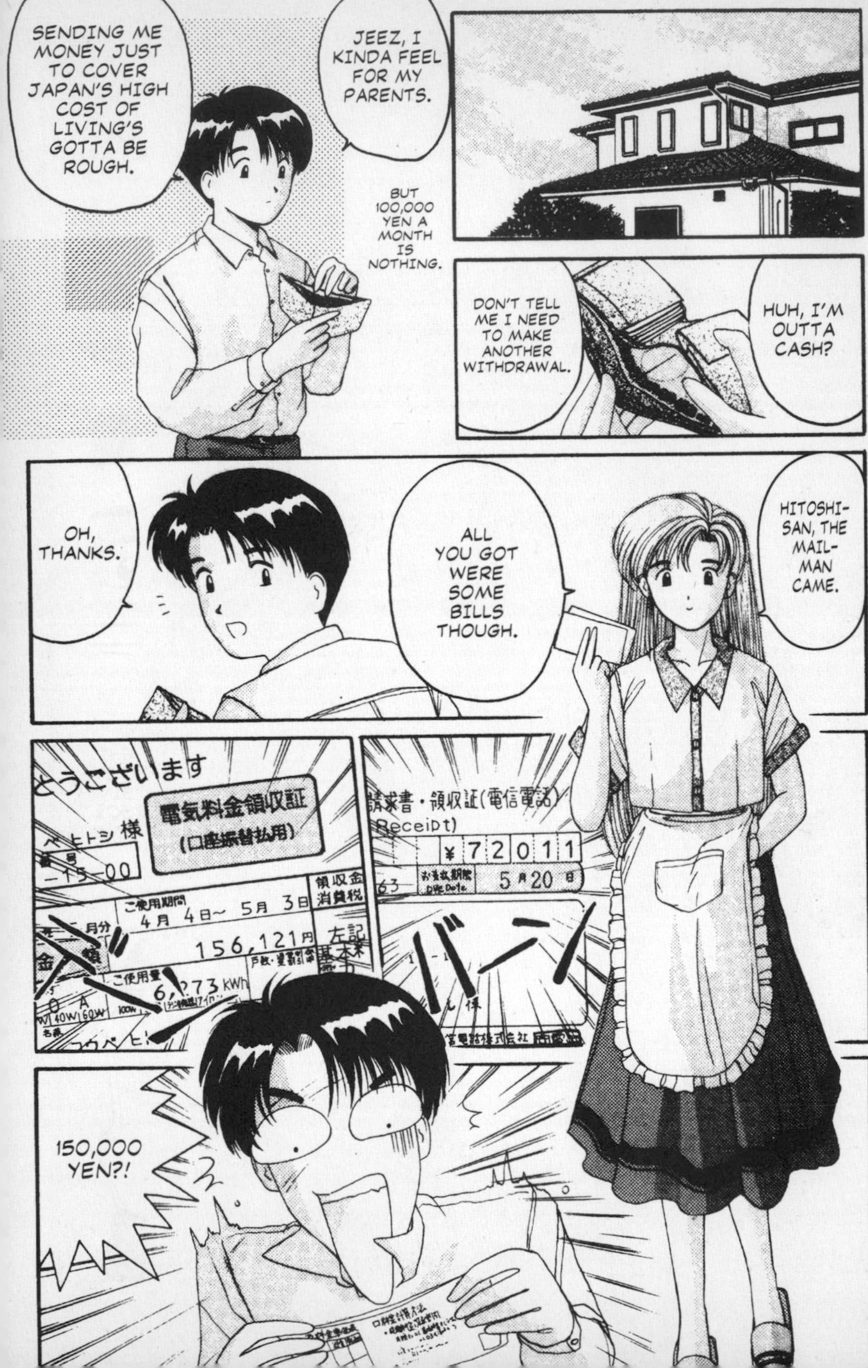
HUH, I'M OUTTA CASH?
DON'T TELL ME I NEED TO MAKE ANOTHER WITHDRAWAL.
JEEZ, I KINDA FEEL FOR MY PARENTS.
SENDING ME MONEY JUST TO COVER JAPAN'S HIGH COST OF LIVING'S GOTTA BE ROUGH.
BUT 100,000 YEN A MONTH IS NOTHING.
HITOSHI-SAN, THE MAILMAN CAME.
ALL YOU GOT WERE SOME BILLS THOUGH.
OH, THANKS.
請求書・領収証(電信電話)
Receipt)
¥72011
お支払期限 Due Date 5月20日
バーー
とうございます
電気料金領収証
(口座振替払用)
ご使用期間 4月 4日~ 5月 3日
156,121円
150,000 YEN?!

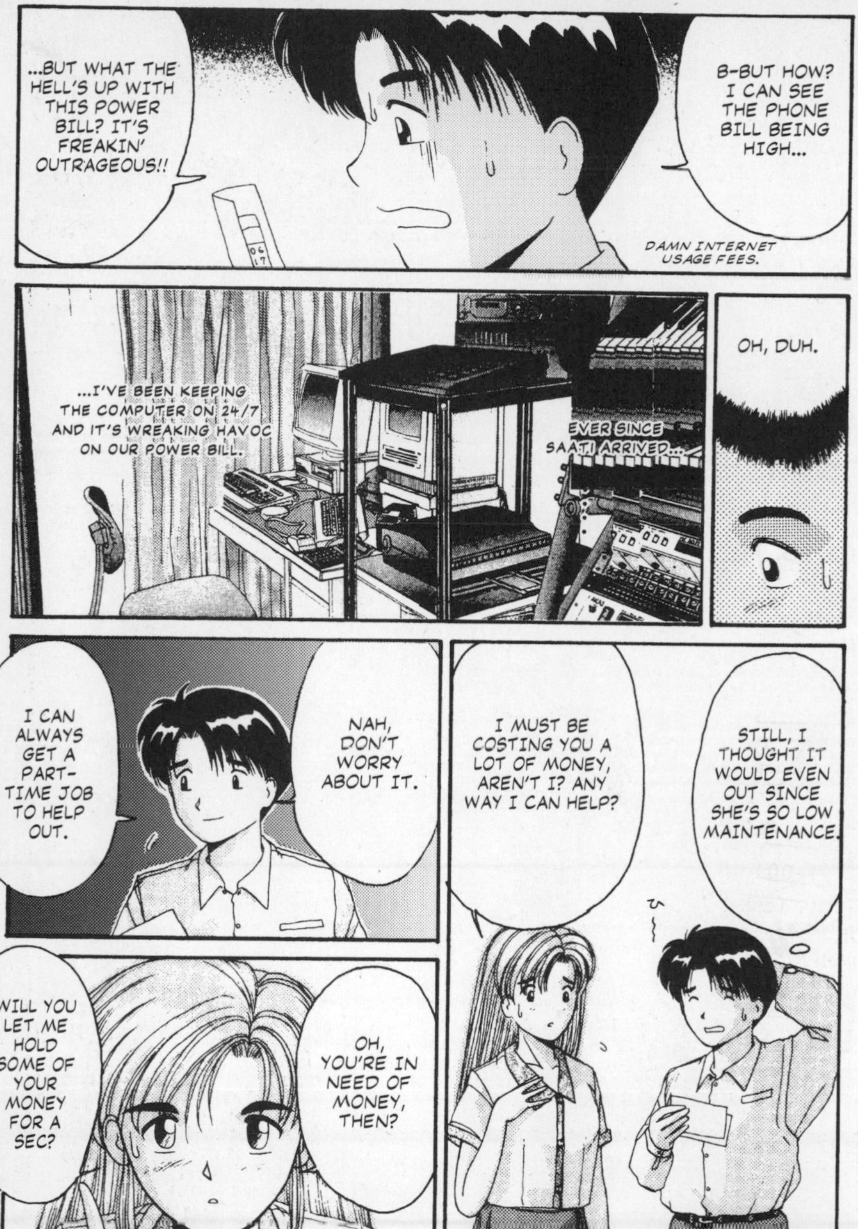
B-BUT HOW? I CAN SEE THE PHONE BILL BEING HIGH...
DAMN INTERNET USAGE FEES.
...BUT WHAT THE HELL'S UP WITH THIS POWER BILL? IT'S FREAKIN' OUTRAGEOUS!!
OH, DUH.
EVER SINCE SAATI ARRIVED...
...I'VE BEEN KEEPING THE COMPUTER ON 24/7 AND IT'S WREAKING HAVOC ON OUR POWER BILL.
STILL, I THOUGHT IT WOULD EVEN OUT SINCE SHE'S SO LOW MAINTENANCE.
I MUST BE COSTING YOU A LOT OF MONEY, AREN'T I? ANY WAY I CAN HELP?
NAH, DON'T WORRY ABOUT IT.
I CAN ALWAYS GET A PART-TIME JOB TO HELP OUT.
OH, YOU'RE IN NEED OF MONEY, THEN?
WILL YOU LET ME HOLD SOME OF YOUR MONEY FOR A SEC?

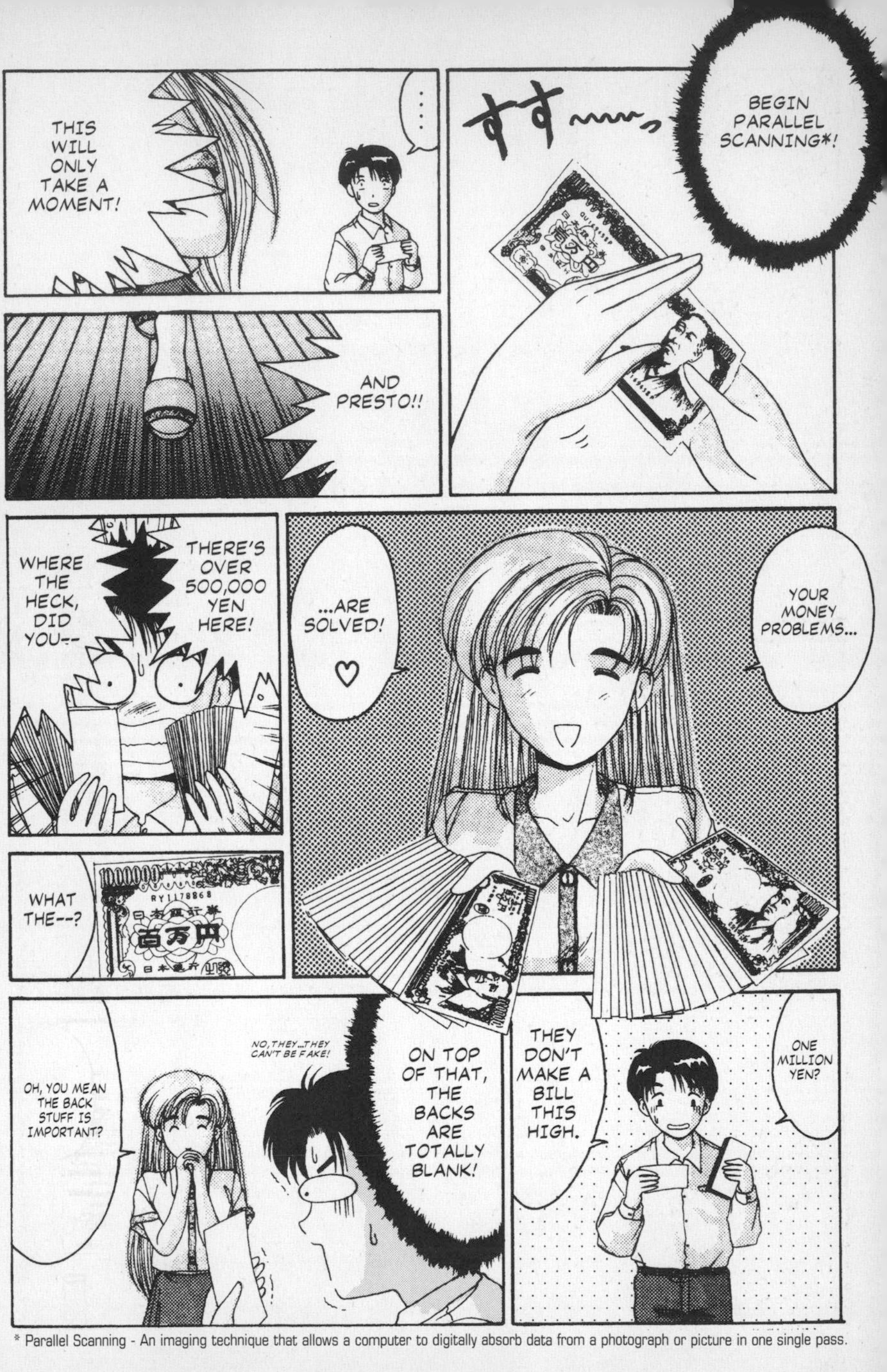
BEGIN PARALLEL SCANNING*!
すす~~~
....
THIS WILL ONLY TAKE A MOMENT!
AND PRESTO!!
YOUR MONEY PROBLEMS...
...ARE SOLVED! ♡
THERE'S OVER 500,000 YEN HERE!
WHERE THE HECK, DID YOU--
1000000
RY1178868
百万円
WHAT THE--?
ONE MILLION YEN?
THEY DON'T MAKE A BILL THIS HIGH.
ON TOP OF THAT, THE BACKS ARE TOTALLY BLANK!
NO, THEY...THEY CAN'T BE FAKE!
OH, YOU MEAN THE BACK STUFF IS IMPORTANT?

* Parallel Scanning - An imaging technique that allows a computer to digitally absorb data from a photograph or picture in one single pass.

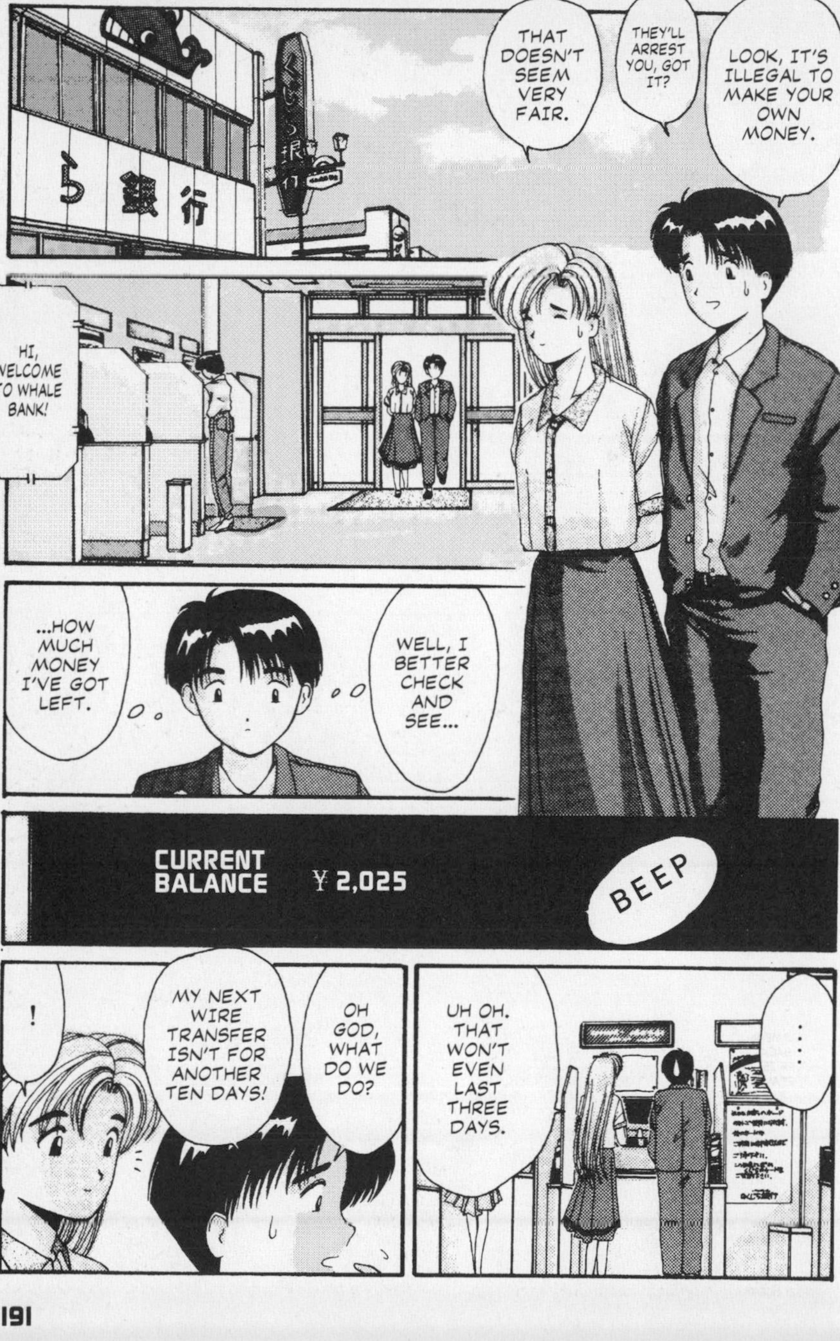

LOOK, IT'S ILLEGAL TO MAKE YOUR OWN MONEY.
THEY'LL ARREST YOU, GOT IT?
THAT DOESN'T SEEM VERY FAIR.
HI, WELCOME TO WHALE BANK!
WELL, I BETTER CHECK AND SEE...
...HOW MUCH MONEY I'VE GOT LEFT.
BEEP
CURRENT BALANCE ¥2,025
....
UH OH. THAT WON'T EVEN LAST THREE DAYS.
OH GOD, WHAT DO WE DO?
MY NEXT WIRE TRANSFER ISN'T FOR ANOTHER TEN DAYS!
!

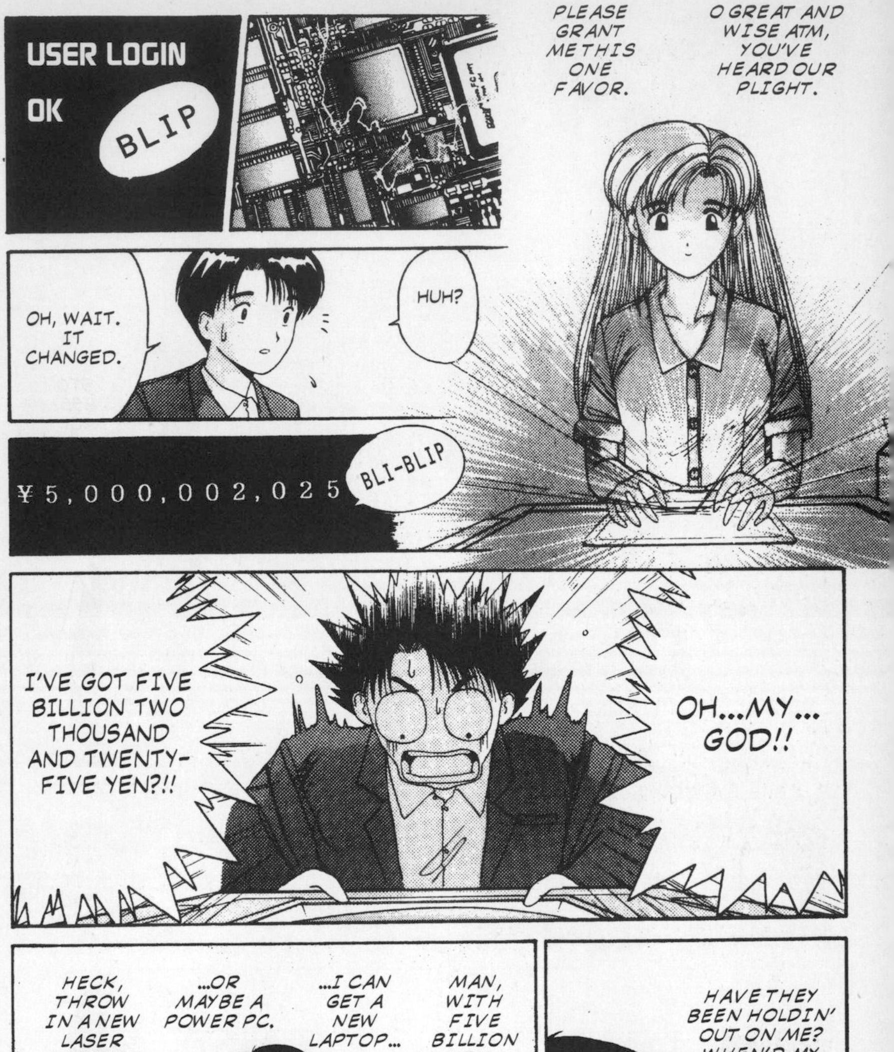
O GREAT AND WISE ATM, YOU'VE HEARD OUR PLIGHT.
PLEASE GRANT ME THIS ONE FAVOR.
USER LOGIN OK
BLIP
HUH?
OH, WAIT. IT CHANGED.
BLI-BLIP
¥5,000,002,025
OH...MY... GOD!!
I'VE GOT FIVE BILLION TWO THOUSAND AND TWENTY-FIVE YEN?!!
HAVE THEY BEEN HOLDIN' OUT ON ME? WHEN'D MY PARENTS GET TO BE THIS LOADED?
MAN, WITH FIVE BILLION YEN...
...I CAN GET A NEW LAPTOP...
...OR MAYBE A POWER PC.
HECK, THROW IN A NEW LASER PRINTER ALSO.

SEE, A LITTLE MONEY CAN BRING A LOT OF JOY. ♡

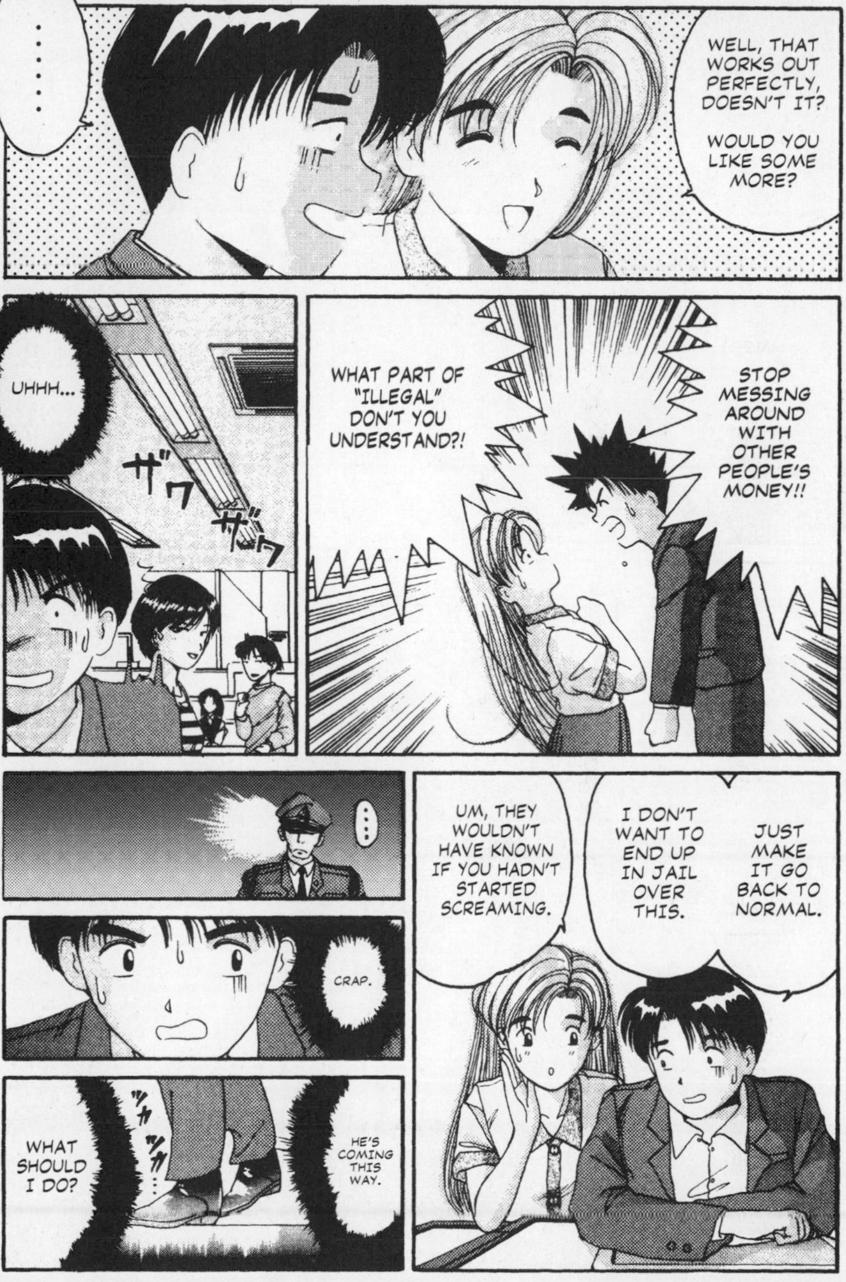
WELL, THAT WORKS OUT PERFECTLY, DOESN'T IT?
WOULD YOU LIKE SOME MORE?
......
STOP MESSING AROUND WITH OTHER PEOPLE'S MONEY!!
WHAT PART OF "ILLEGAL" DON'T YOU UNDERSTAND?!
UHHH...
ザワ
ザワ
JUST MAKE IT GO BACK TO NORMAL.
I DON'T WANT TO END UP IN JAIL OVER THIS.
UM, THEY WOULDN'T HAVE KNOWN IF YOU HADN'T STARTED SCREAMING.
...
CRAP.
HE'S COMING THIS WAY.
ツカ
ツカ
WHAT SHOULD I DO?

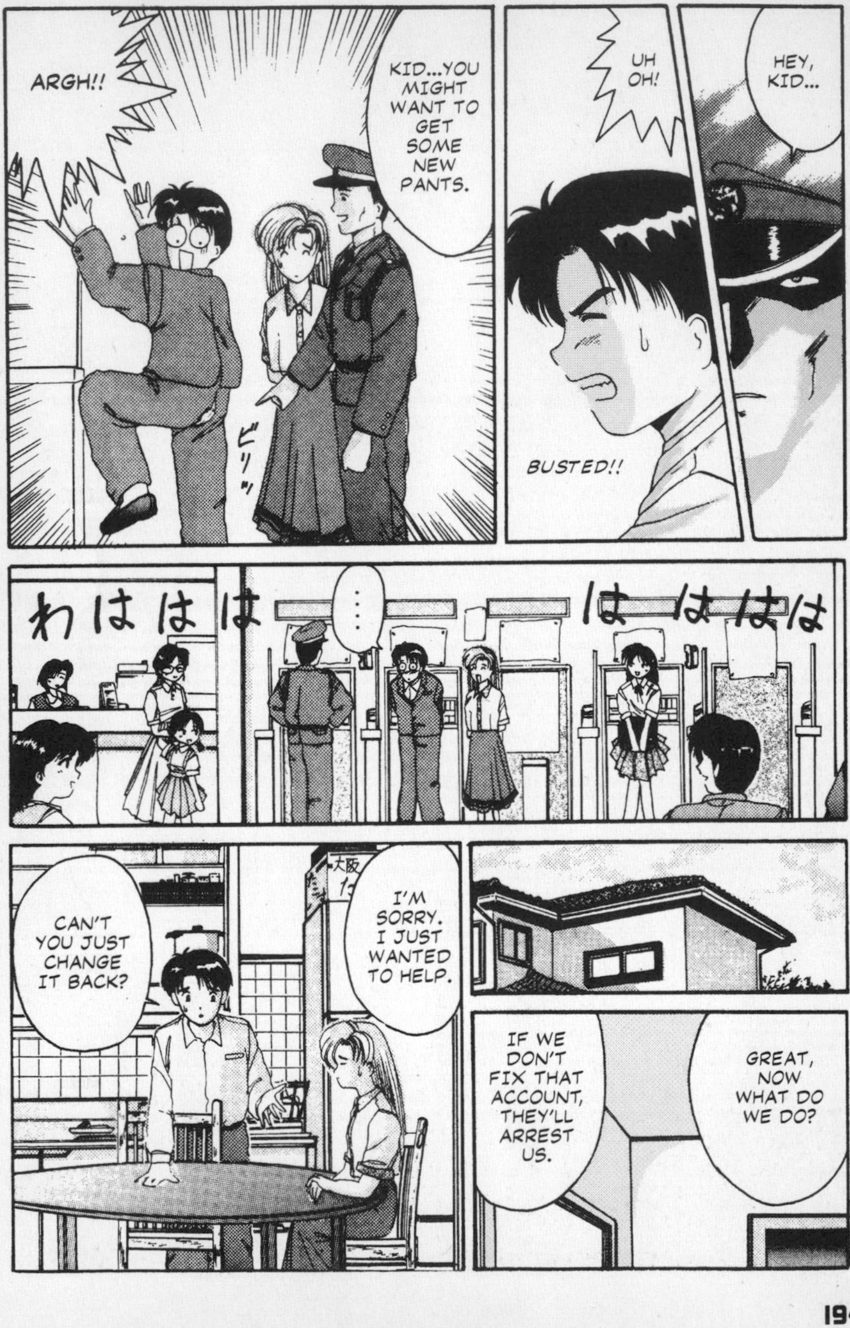
HEY, KID...
UH OH!
BUSTED!!
KID...YOU MIGHT WANT TO GET SOME NEW PANTS.
ARGH!!
ビリッ
わははは はははは
....
GREAT, NOW WHAT DO WE DO?
IF WE DON'T FIX THAT ACCOUNT, THEY'LL ARREST US.
I'M SORRY. I JUST WANTED TO HELP.
CAN'T YOU JUST CHANGE IT BACK?

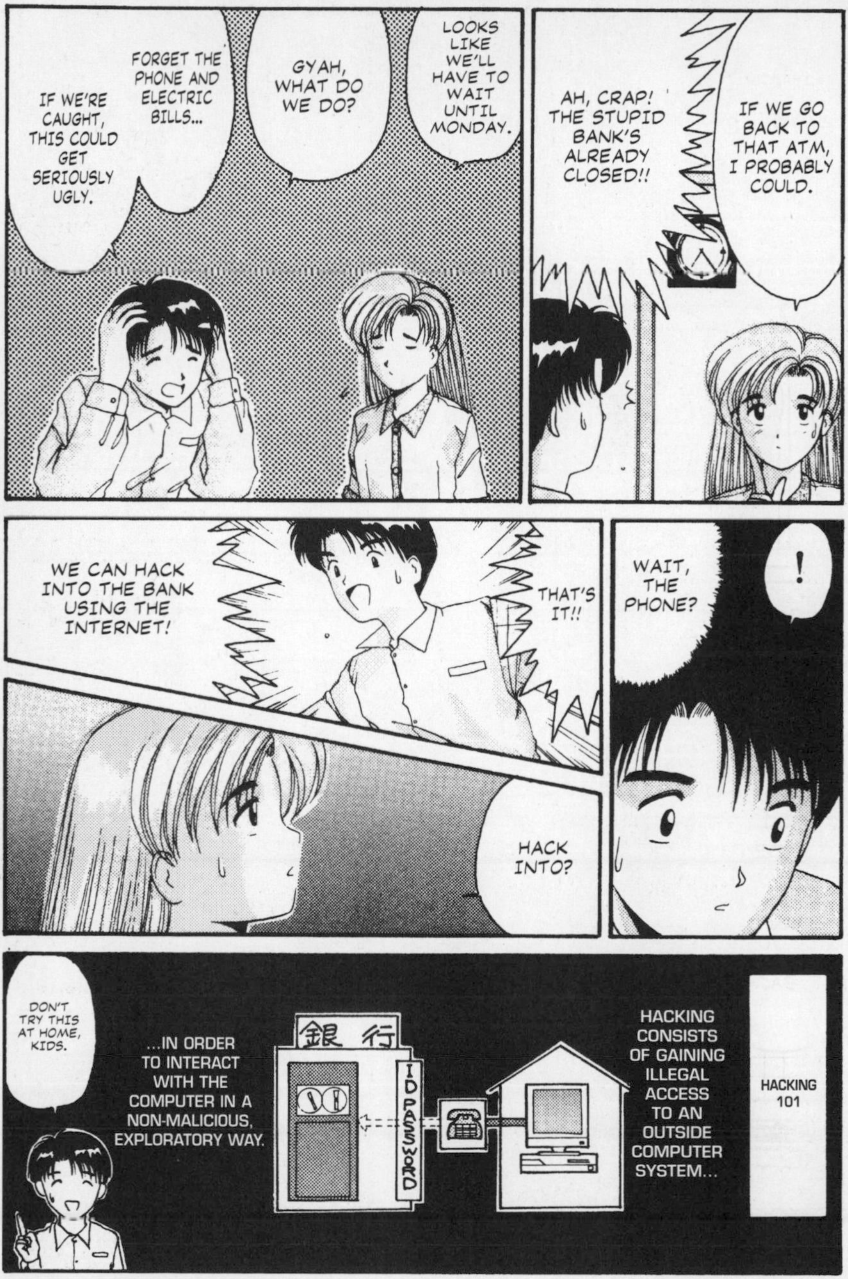

IF WE GO BACK TO THAT ATM, I PROBABLY COULD.
AH, CRAP! THE STUPID BANK'S ALREADY CLOSED!!
LOOKS LIKE WE'LL HAVE TO WAIT UNTIL MONDAY.
GYAH, WHAT DO WE DO?
FORGET THE PHONE AND ELECTRIC BILLS...
IF WE'RE CAUGHT, THIS COULD GET SERIOUSLY UGLY.
!
WAIT, THE PHONE?
THAT'S IT!!
WE CAN HACK INTO THE BANK USING THE INTERNET!
HACK INTO?
HACKING 101
HACKING CONSISTS OF GAINING ILLEGAL ACCESS TO AN OUTSIDE COMPUTER SYSTEM...
銀行
ID PASSWORD
...IN ORDER TO INTERACT WITH THE COMPUTER IN A NON-MALICIOUS, EXPLORATORY WAY.
DON'T TRY THIS AT HOME, KIDS.

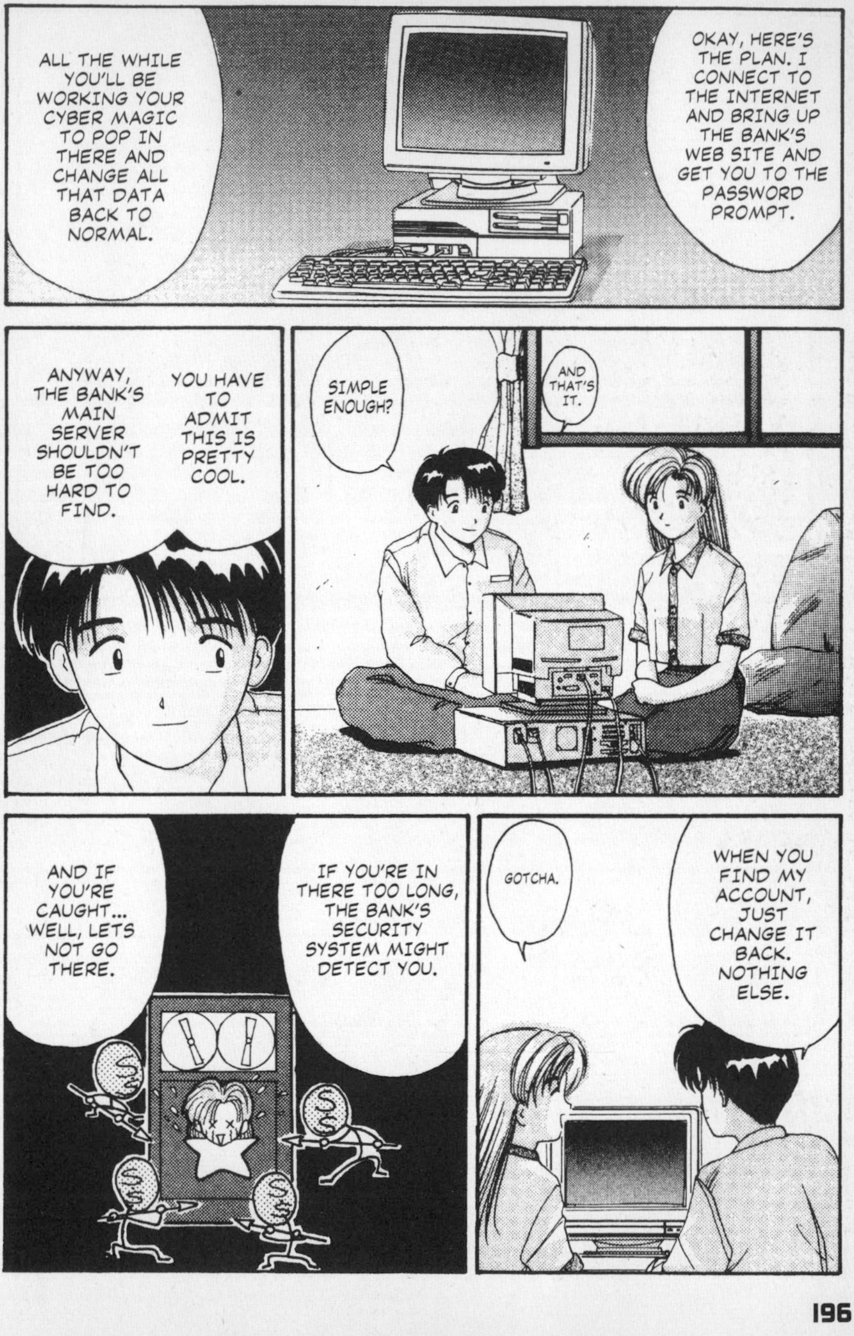
OKAY, HERE'S THE PLAN. I CONNECT TO THE INTERNET AND BRING UP THE BANK'S WEB SITE AND GET YOU TO THE PASSWORD PROMPT.
ALL THE WHILE YOU'LL BE WORKING YOUR CYBER MAGIC TO POP IN THERE AND CHANGE ALL THAT DATA BACK TO NORMAL.
AND THAT'S IT.
SIMPLE ENOUGH?
YOU HAVE TO ADMIT THIS IS PRETTY COOL.
ANYWAY, THE BANK'S MAIN SERVER SHOULDN'T BE TOO HARD TO FIND.
WHEN YOU FIND MY ACCOUNT, JUST CHANGE IT BACK. NOTHING ELSE.
GOTCHA.
IF YOU'RE IN THERE TOO LONG, THE BANK'S SECURITY SYSTEM MIGHT DETECT YOU.
AND IF YOU'RE CAUGHT... WELL, LETS NOT GO THERE.

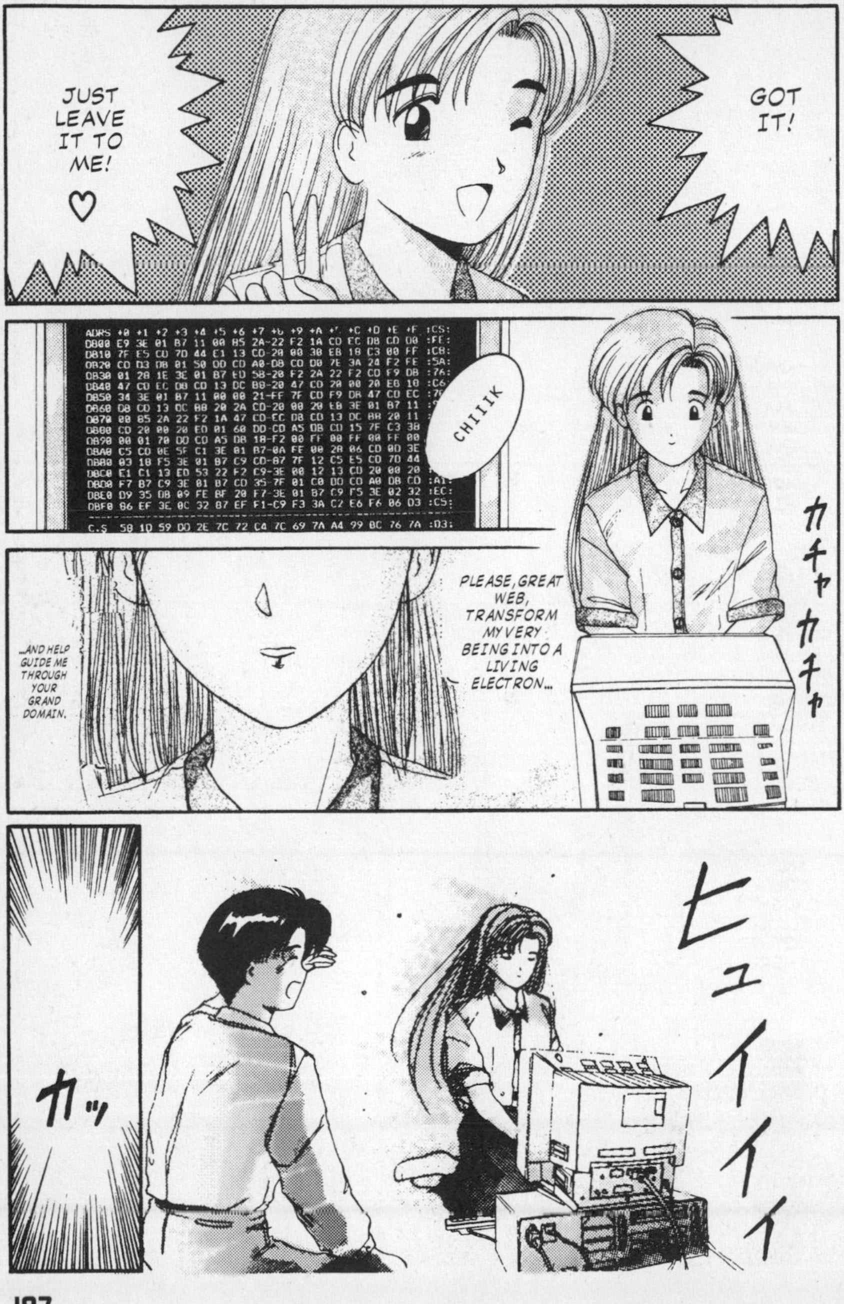
GOT IT!
JUST LEAVE IT TO ME! ♡
カチャカチャ
PLEASE, GREAT WEB, TRANSFORM MY VERY BEING INTO A LIVING ELECTRON...
CHIIIK
...AND HELP GUIDE ME THROUGH YOUR GRAND DOMAIN.
ヒュイイイ
カッ

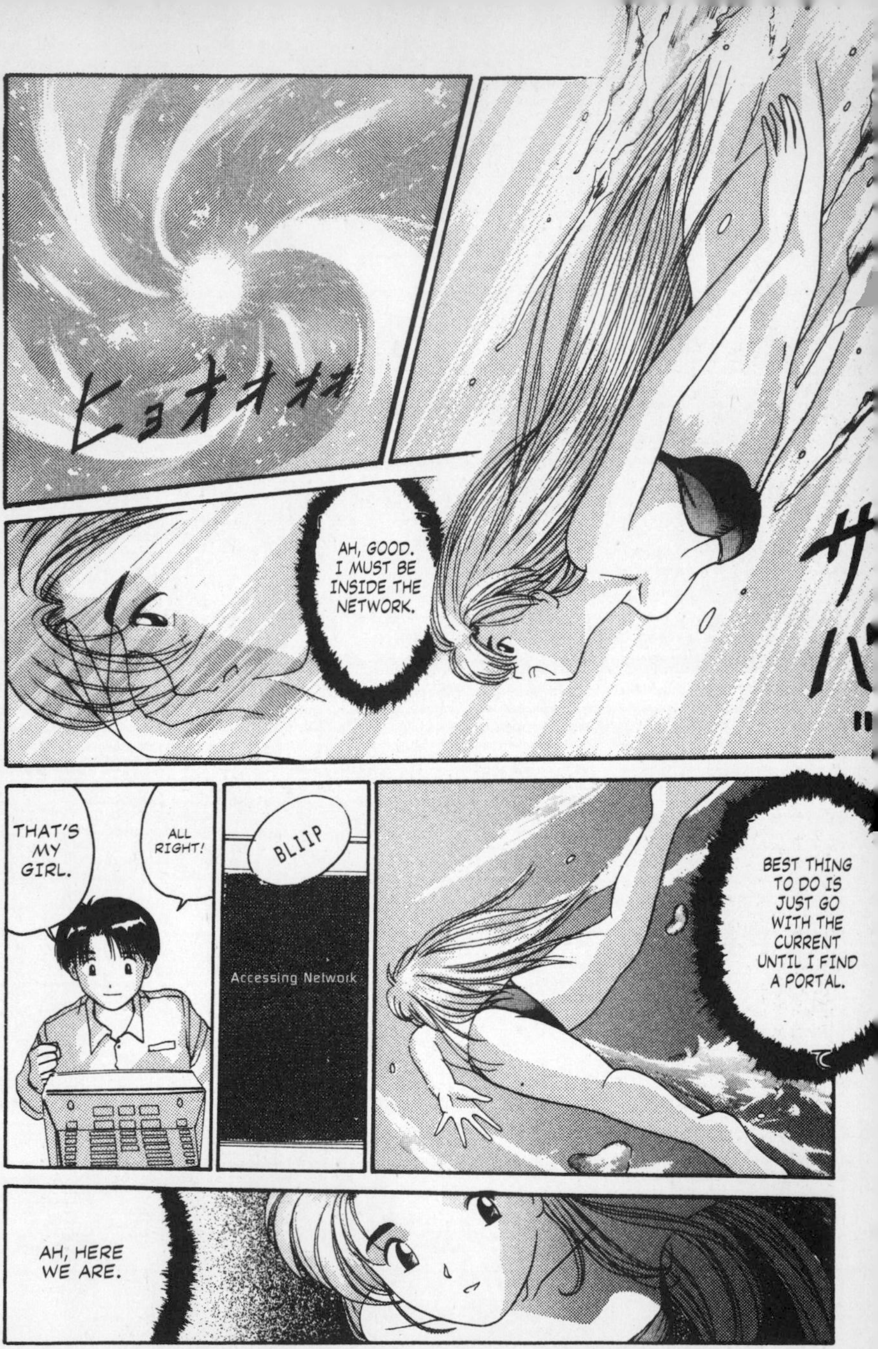
サバッ
ヒョオオオオ
AH, GOOD. I MUST BE INSIDE THE NETWORK.
BEST THING TO DO IS JUST GO WITH THE CURRENT UNTIL I FIND A PORTAL.
BLIIP
Accessing Network
ALL RIGHT!
THAT'S MY GIRL.
AH, HERE WE ARE.

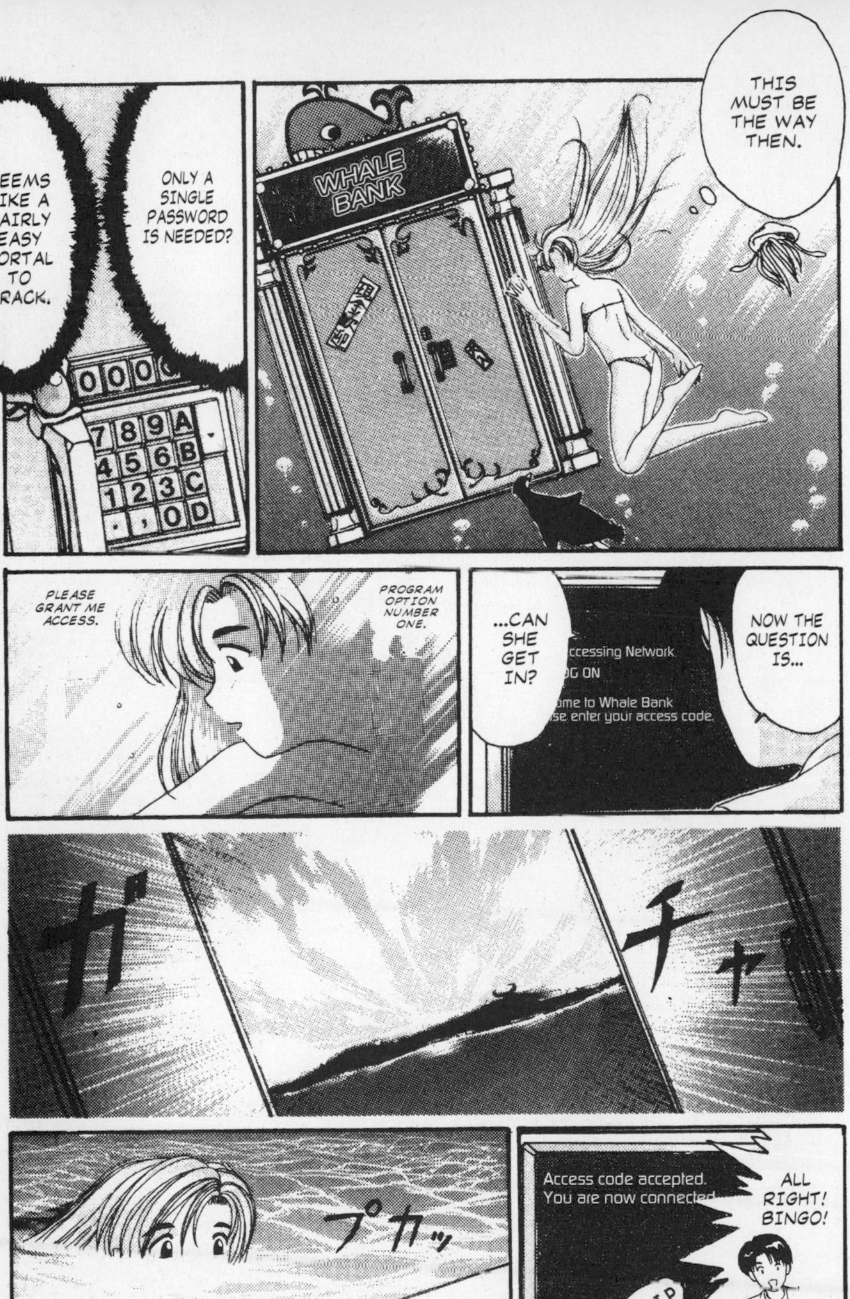
THIS MUST BE THE WAY THEN.
WHALE BANK
ONLY A SINGLE PASSWORD IS NEEDED?
SEEMS LIKE A FAIRLY EASY PORTAL TO CRACK.
NOW THE QUESTION IS...
...CAN SHE GET IN?
ccessing Network
OG ON
ome to Whale Bank
se enter your access code.
PROGRAM OPTION NUMBER ONE.
PLEASE GRANT ME ACCESS.
ガチャ
Access code accepted.
You are now connect
ALL RIGHT! BINGO!
BLIIP
プカッ

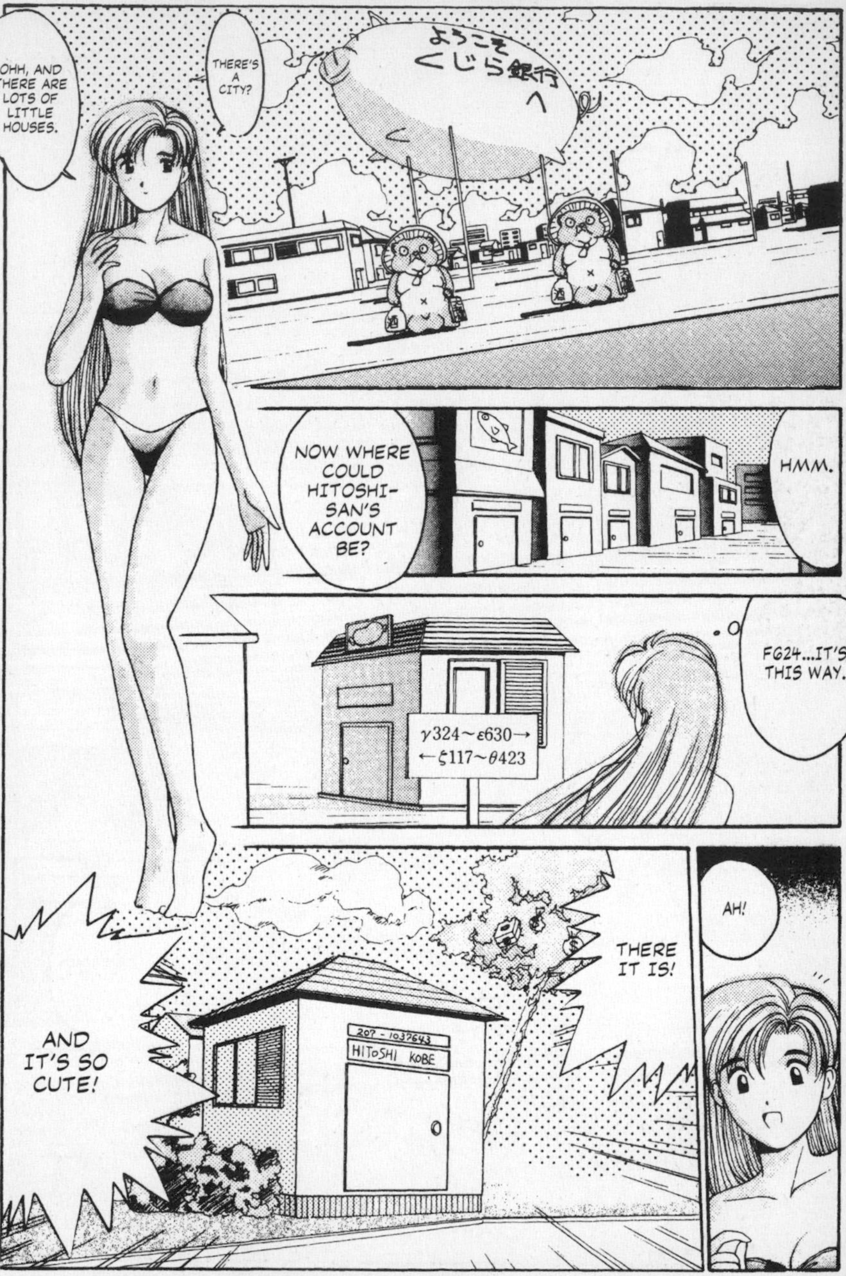

ようこそ
くじら銀行へ
THERE'S A CITY?
OHH, AND THERE ARE LOTS OF LITTLE HOUSES.
HMM.
NOW WHERE COULD HITOSHI-SAN'S ACCOUNT BE?
F624...IT'S THIS WAY.
γ324~ε630→
←ζ117~θ423
AH!
THERE IT IS!
207 - 1037643
HITOSHI KOBE
AND IT'S SO CUTE!

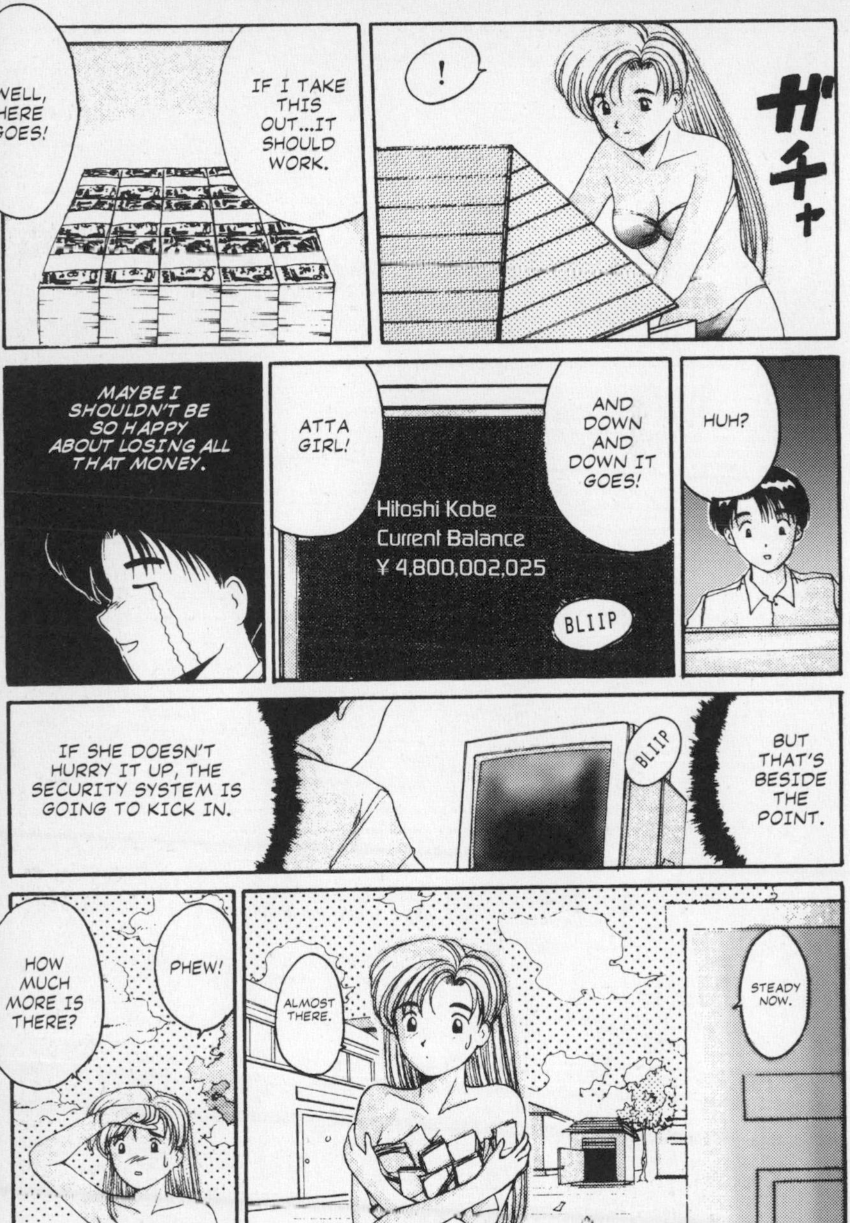
!
ガチャ
IF I TAKE THIS OUT...IT SHOULD WORK.
WELL, HERE GOES!
HUH?
AND DOWN AND DOWN IT GOES!
ATTA GIRL!
Hitoshi Kobe
Current Balance
¥ 4,800,002,025
BLIIP
MAYBE I SHOULDN'T BE SO HAPPY ABOUT LOSING ALL THAT MONEY.
BUT THAT'S BESIDE THE POINT.
BLIIP
IF SHE DOESN'T HURRY IT UP, THE SECURITY SYSTEM IS GOING TO KICK IN.
STEADY NOW.
ALMOST THERE.
PHEW!
HOW MUCH MORE IS THERE?

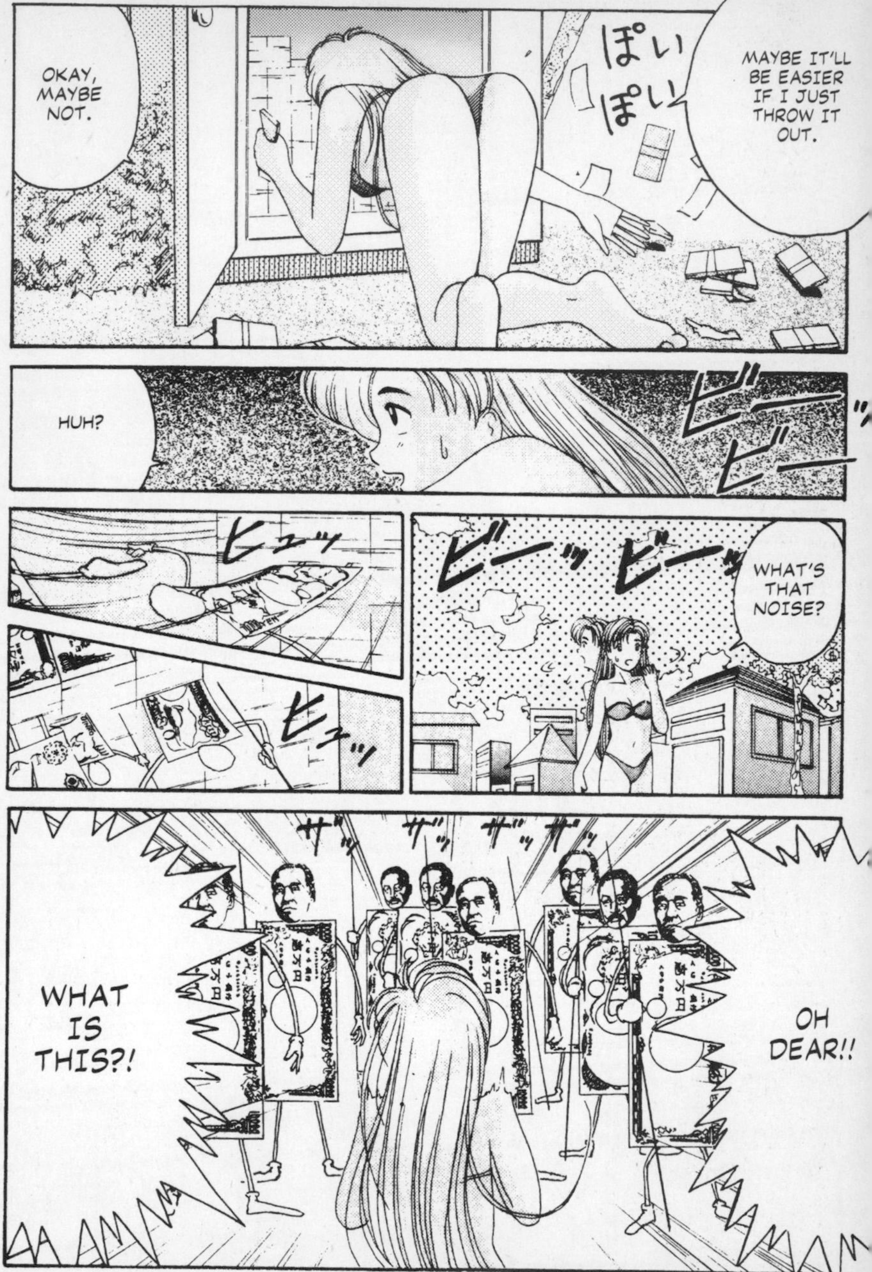
MAYBE IT'LL BE EASIER IF I JUST THROW IT OUT.
ぽい ぽい
OKAY, MAYBE NOT.
ビーッ ビー
HUH?
WHAT'S THAT NOISE?
ビーッ ビーッ
ヒュッ
ヒュッ
OH DEAR!!
ザッ ザッ ザッ ザッ
WHAT IS THIS?!

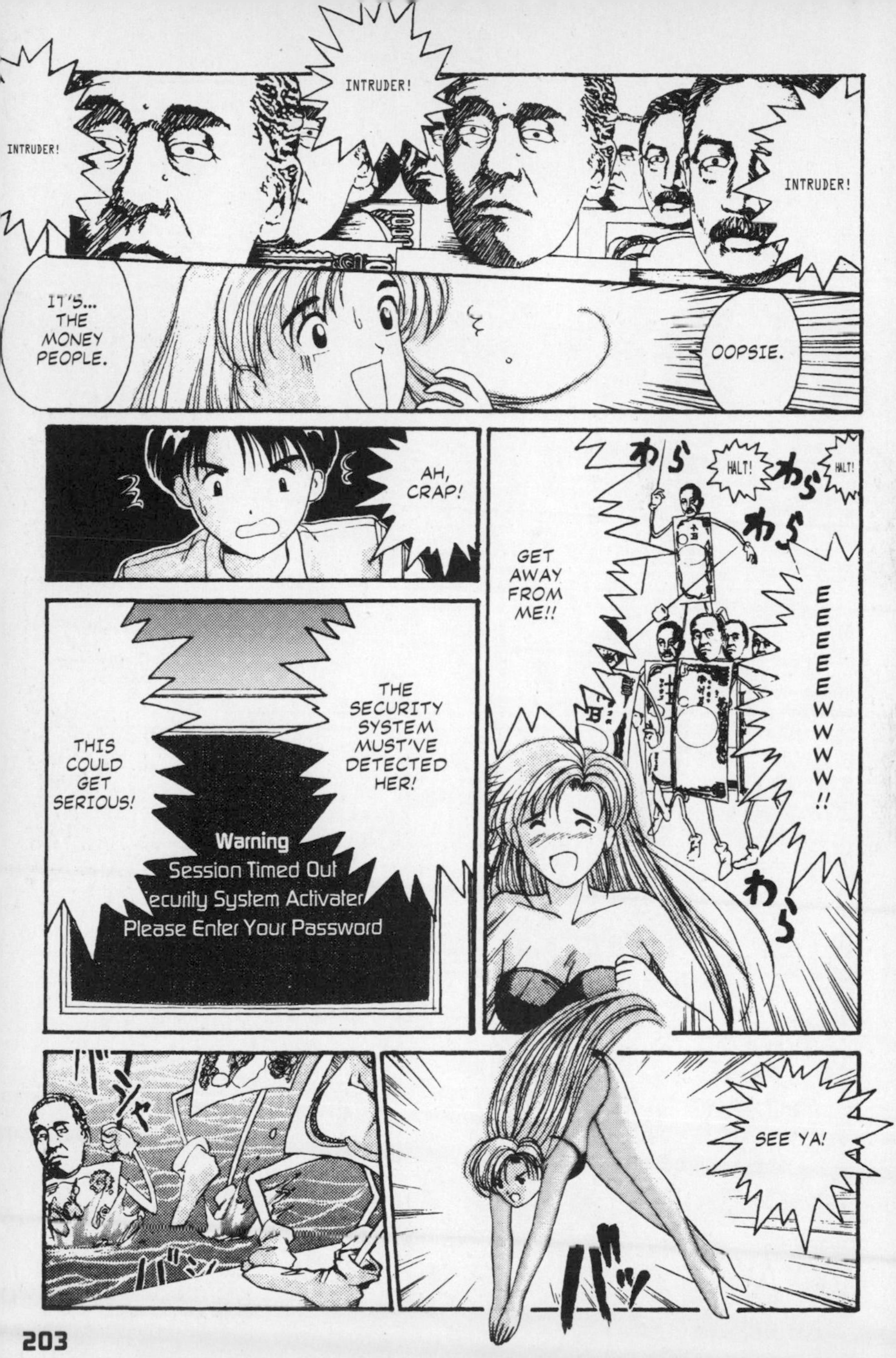

INTRUDER!
INTRUDER!
INTRUDER!
OOPSIE.
IT'S... THE MONEY PEOPLE.
わら
HALT!
わら
HALT!
わら
GET AWAY FROM ME!!
EEEEEWWWW!!
わら
AH, CRAP!
THE SECURITY SYSTEM MUST'VE DETECTED HER!
THIS COULD GET SERIOUS!
Warning
Session Timed Out
ecurity System Activater
Please Enter Your Password
SEE YA!
バッ

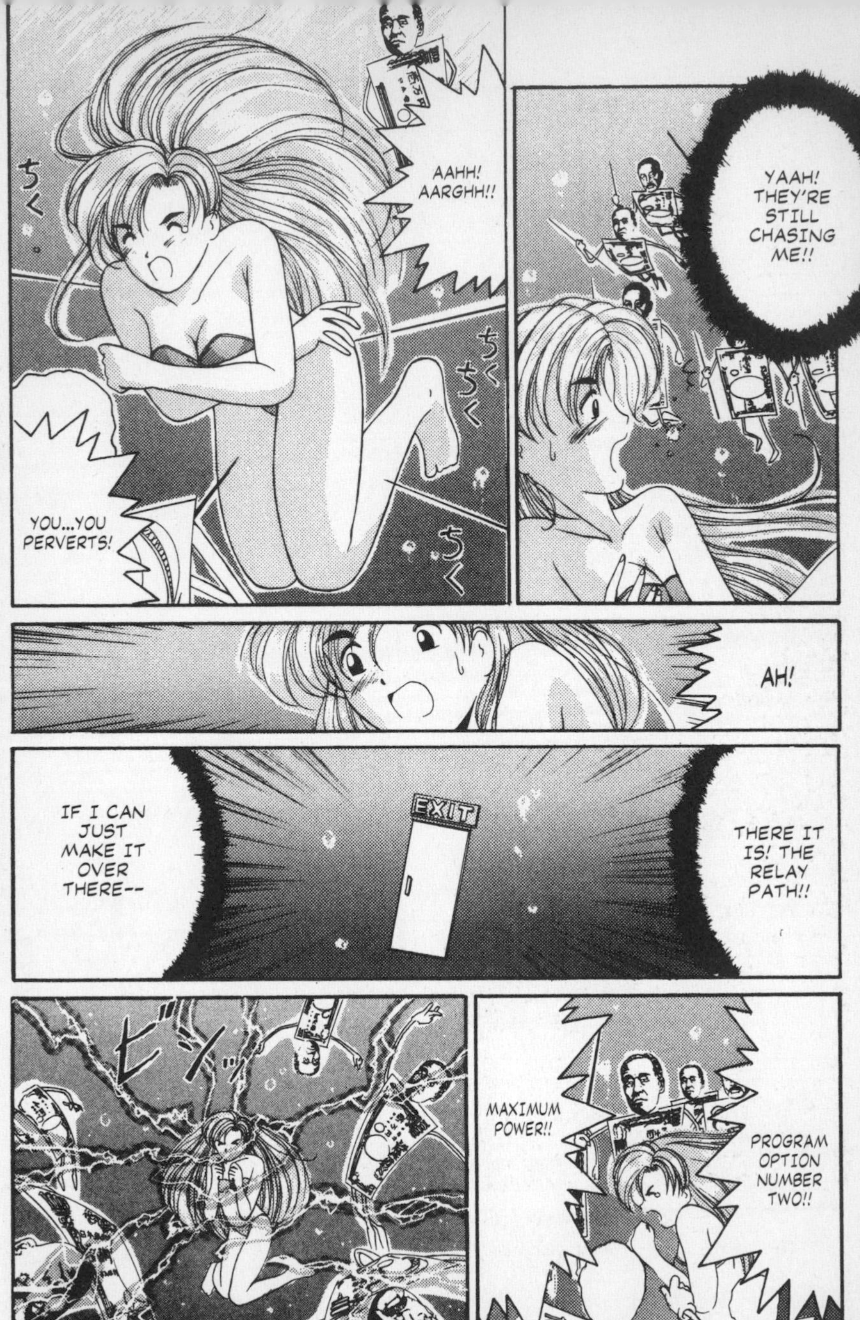
YAAH! THEY'RE STILL CHASING ME!!
AAHH! AARGHH!!
ちく。
ちく ちく
ちく
YOU...YOU PERVERTS!
AH!
THERE IT IS! THE RELAY PATH!!
IF I CAN JUST MAKE IT OVER THERE--
EXIT
PROGRAM OPTION NUMBER TWO!!
MAXIMUM POWER!!
ビジッ

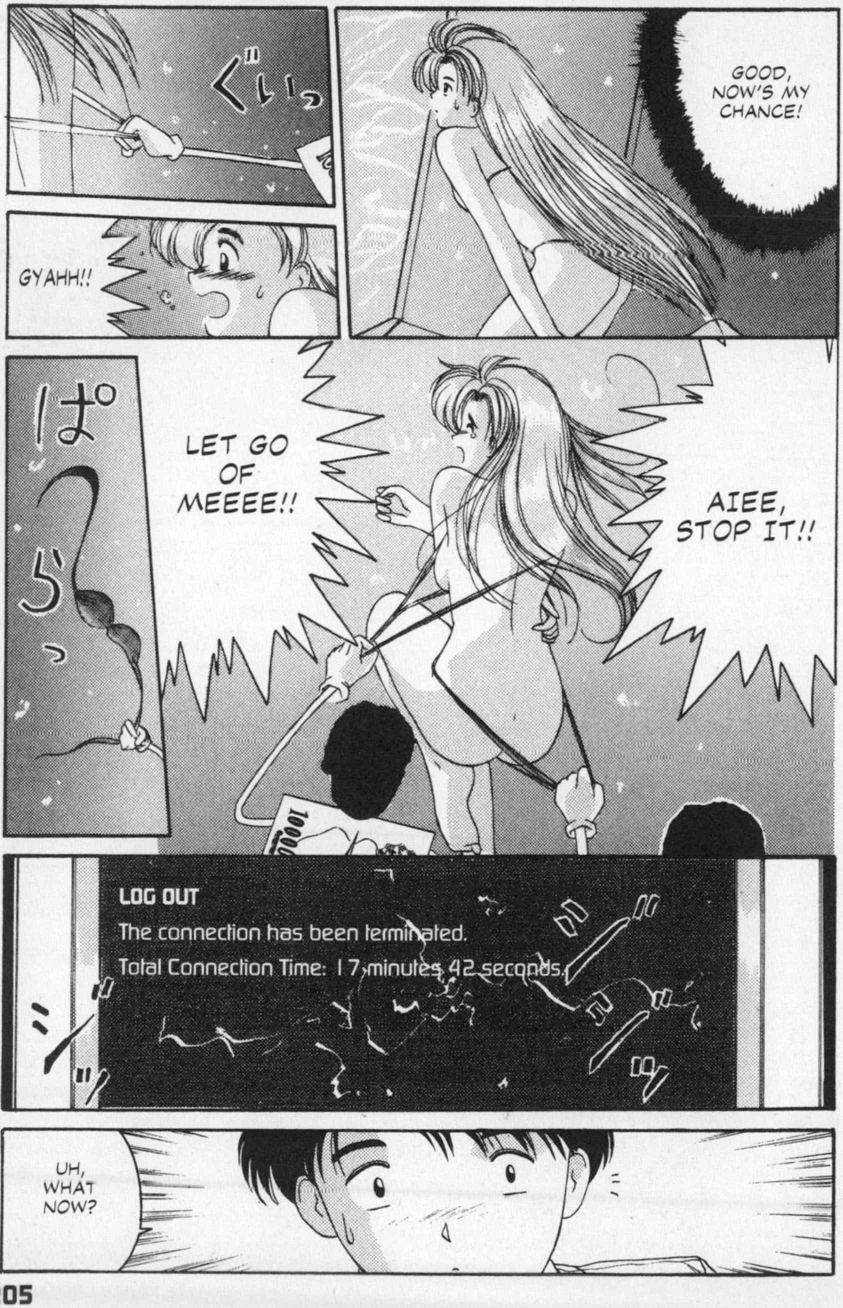
GOOD, NOW'S MY CHANCE!
ぐいっ
GYAHH!!
AIEE, STOP IT!!
LET GO OF MEEEE!!
ぱらっ
LOG OUT
The connection has been terminated.
Total Connection Time: 17 minutes 42 seconds.
UH, WHAT NOW?

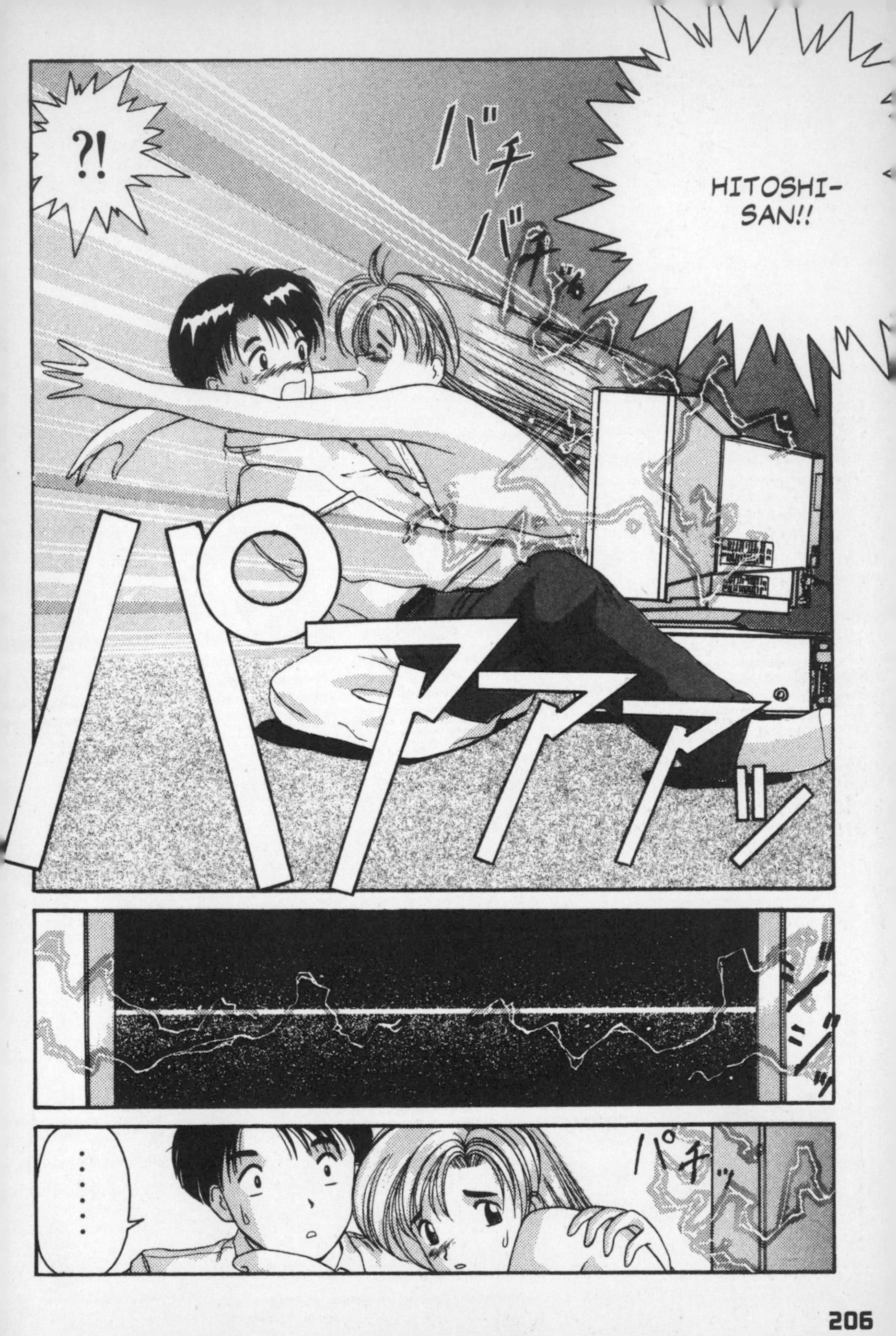
HITOSHI-SAN!!
?!
バチバチッ
パアアアッ
パチッ
......

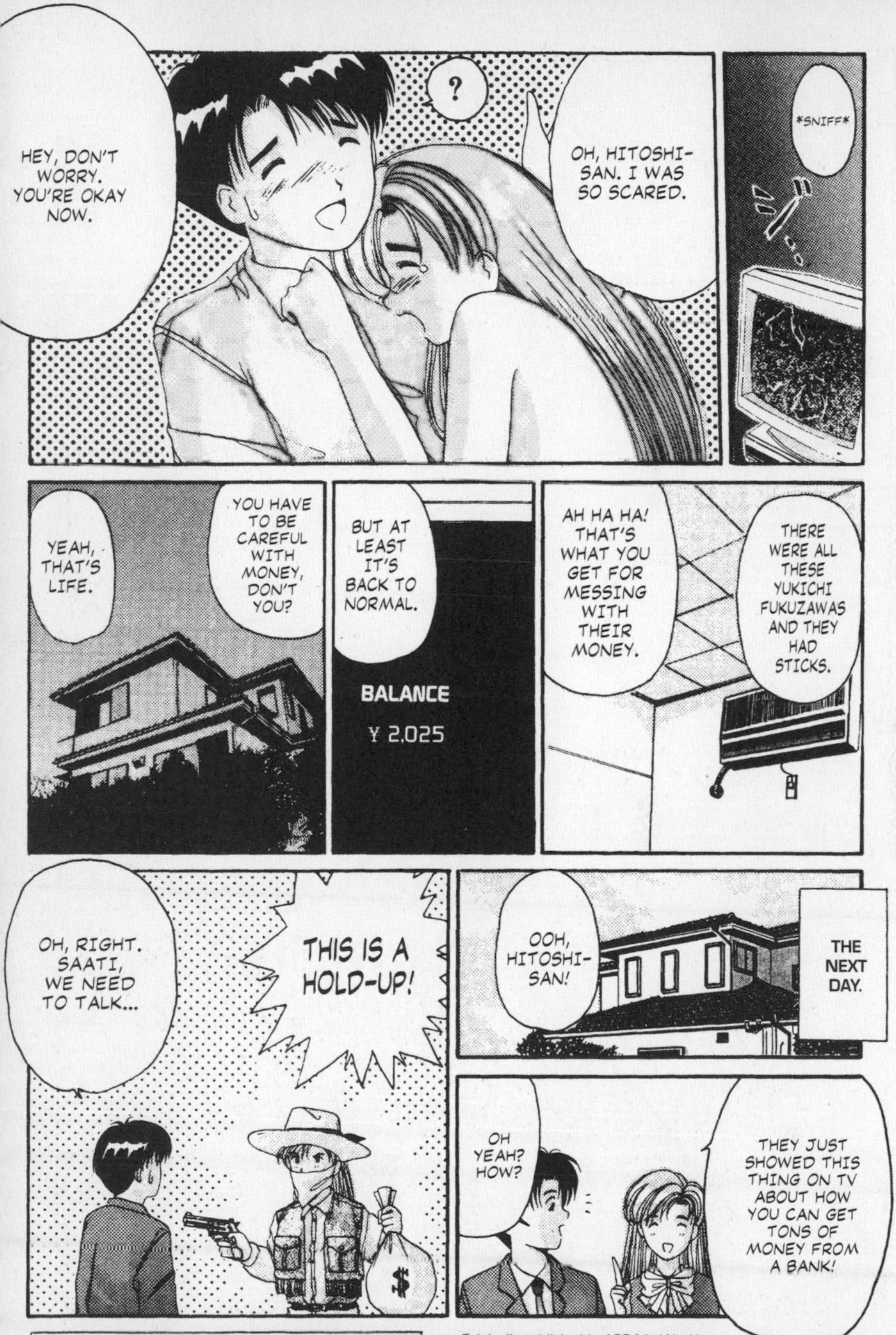
SNIFF
OH, HITOSHI-SAN. I WAS SO SCARED.
?
HEY, DON'T WORRY. YOU'RE OKAY NOW.
THERE WERE ALL THESE YUKICHI FUKUZAWAS AND THEY HAD STICKS.
AH HA HA! THAT'S WHAT YOU GET FOR MESSING WITH THEIR MONEY.
BUT AT LEAST IT'S BACK TO NORMAL.
BALANCE
¥ 2,025
YOU HAVE TO BE CAREFUL WITH MONEY, DON'T YOU?
YEAH, THAT'S LIFE.
THE NEXT DAY.
OOH, HITOSHI-SAN!
THEY JUST SHOWED THIS THING ON TV ABOUT HOW YOU CAN GET TONS OF MONEY FROM A BANK!
OH YEAH? HOW?
THIS IS A HOLD-UP!
OH, RIGHT. SAATI, WE NEED TO TALK...

▶To Be Continued

Originally published in 1994 in Weekly Shonen Magazine issues 18 through 25.

(No.30)

SAATI WAS DESIGNED AND BUILT USING THE PROGRAMMING LANGUAGE KNOWN AS C, WHICH IS A VERY DIFFICULT LANGUAGE TO CREATE ANYTHING THAT CAN THINK OR LEARN ON ITS OWN. ON SECOND THOUGHT, IT'S PRETTY MUCH IMPOSSIBLE! STILL, SOMETIMES WHEN I'M DRAWING SAATI, I'M REMINDED OF NARU FROM LOVE HINA (LAUGHS). THE LENGTH AND STYLE OF THEIR HAIR IS ALMOST EXACTLY THE SAME. OH, AND TRY COVERING UP SAATI'S EYEBROWS–YOU'LL SEE...(LAUGHS). (SAATI FIRST APPEARS IN VOLUME 1).

PROGRAM No.30

3 SIZE DATA

B:82

W:58

H:85

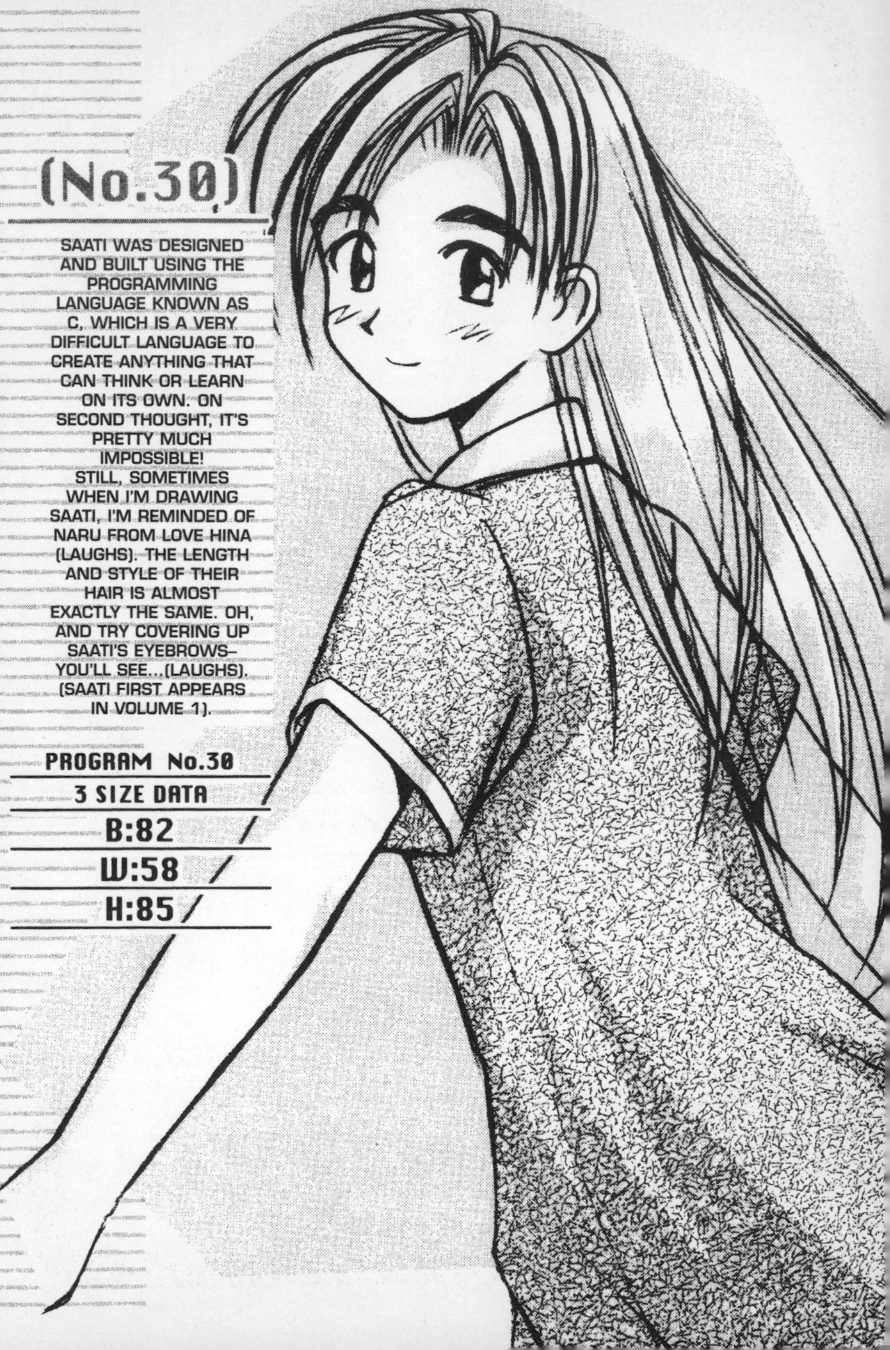

THE ORIGINAL COVER ART FROM THE FIRST RELEASE OF VOLUME 4

W/108/B90
B80?
NR7/NR1
R470
W/PB755.

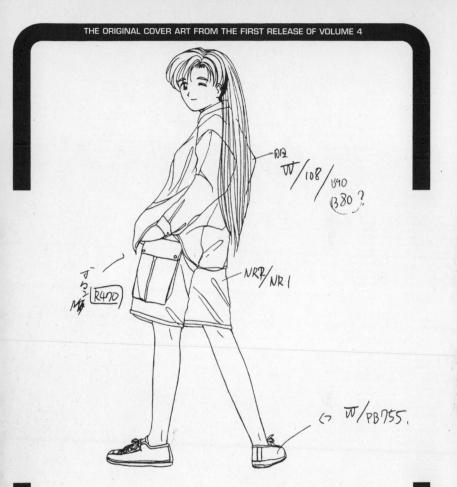

A.I. LOVE YOU: THE ANIMATION CEL COLORING METHOD

THE MAJORITY OF THE COVER ILLUSTRATIONS FOR A.I. LOVE YOU WERE DONE USING "CEL ANIMATION," THE SAME METHOD ONCE WIDELY USED IN MAKING ANIME. THE ORIGINAL LINE ART IS PHOTOCOPIED ONTO A CLEAR SHEET OF PLASTIC AND IS THEN COLORED WITH A SPECIAL TYPE OF PAINT.
THE NUMBERS ABOVE, SUCH AS "R470," ARE A NOTHING MORE THAN CODE FOR SPECIFIC PAINT COLORS. BY FOLLOWING THIS CODE, THE EXACT COLORS CAN BE REPRODUCED EVERY TIME. IN RECENT YEARS, "COLOR TONER" HAS BECOME MORE FREQUENTLY USED IN MANGA, BUT THE COVERS HAVE ALMOST ALWAYS BEEN DONE USING TRADITIONAL CEL ANIMATION.

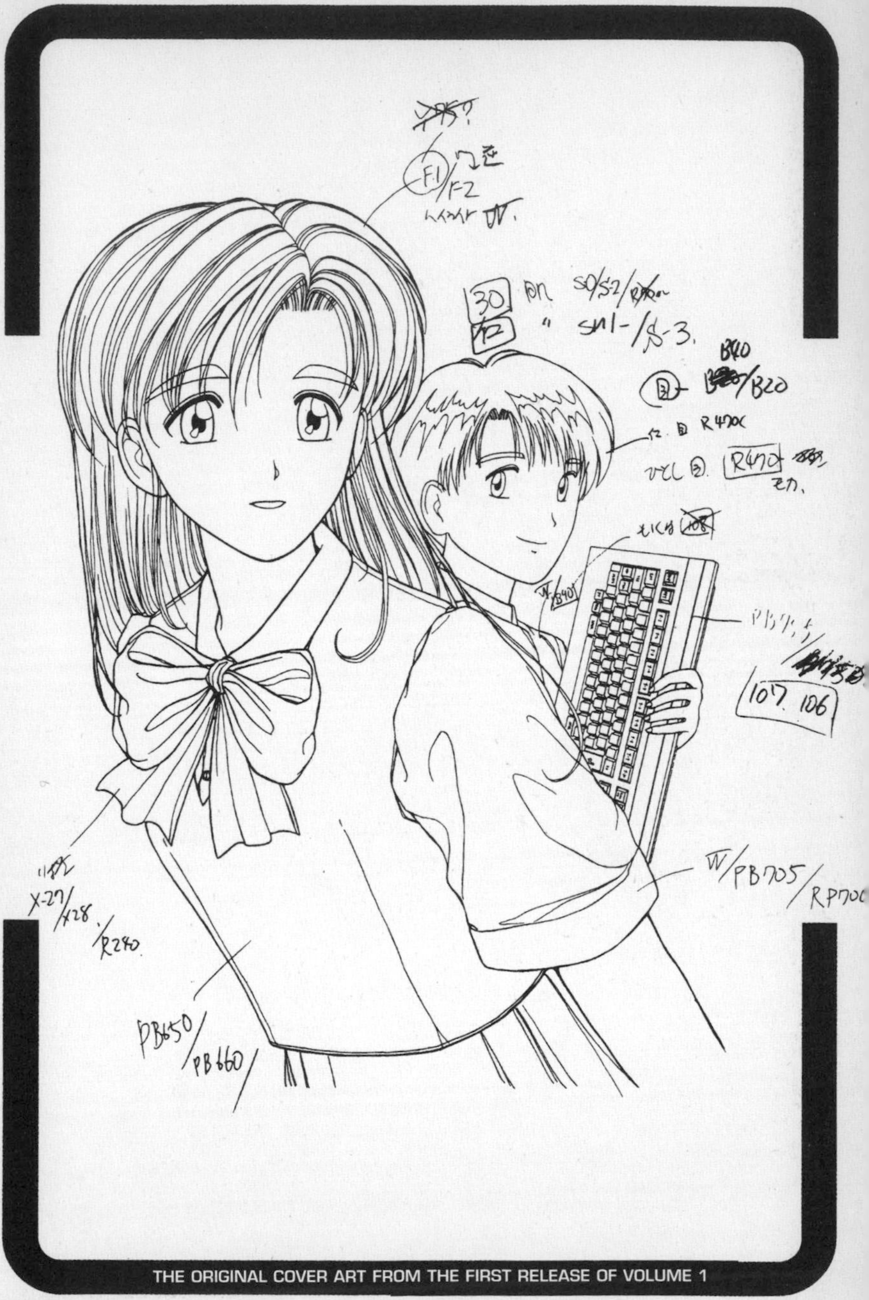
F1
F2
B40
B20
R470
107. 106
PB705
X-27/X28
R240
PB650
PB660

THE ORIGINAL COVER ART FROM THE FIRST RELEASE OF VOLUME 1

THE ORIGINAL COVER ART FROM THE FIRST RELEASE OF VOLUME 3

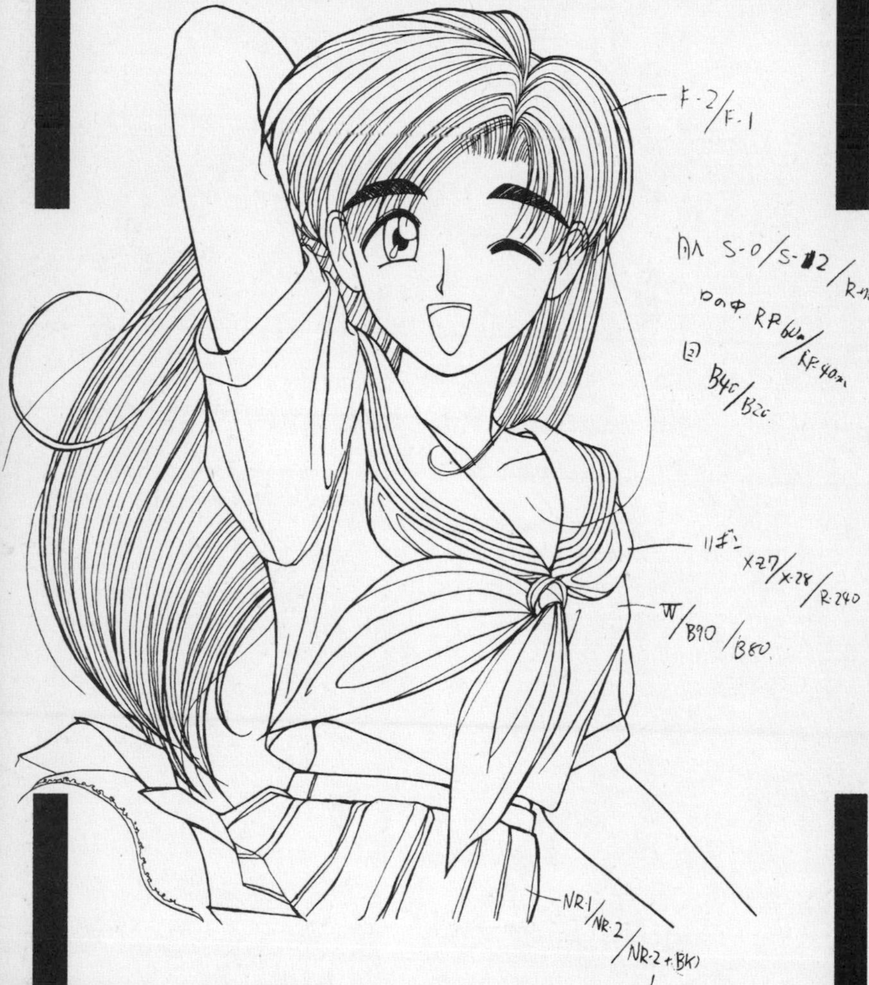
F-2/F-1
B40/B20
X27/X-28/R-240
B90/B80
NR-1/NR-2/NR-2+BK)
X166

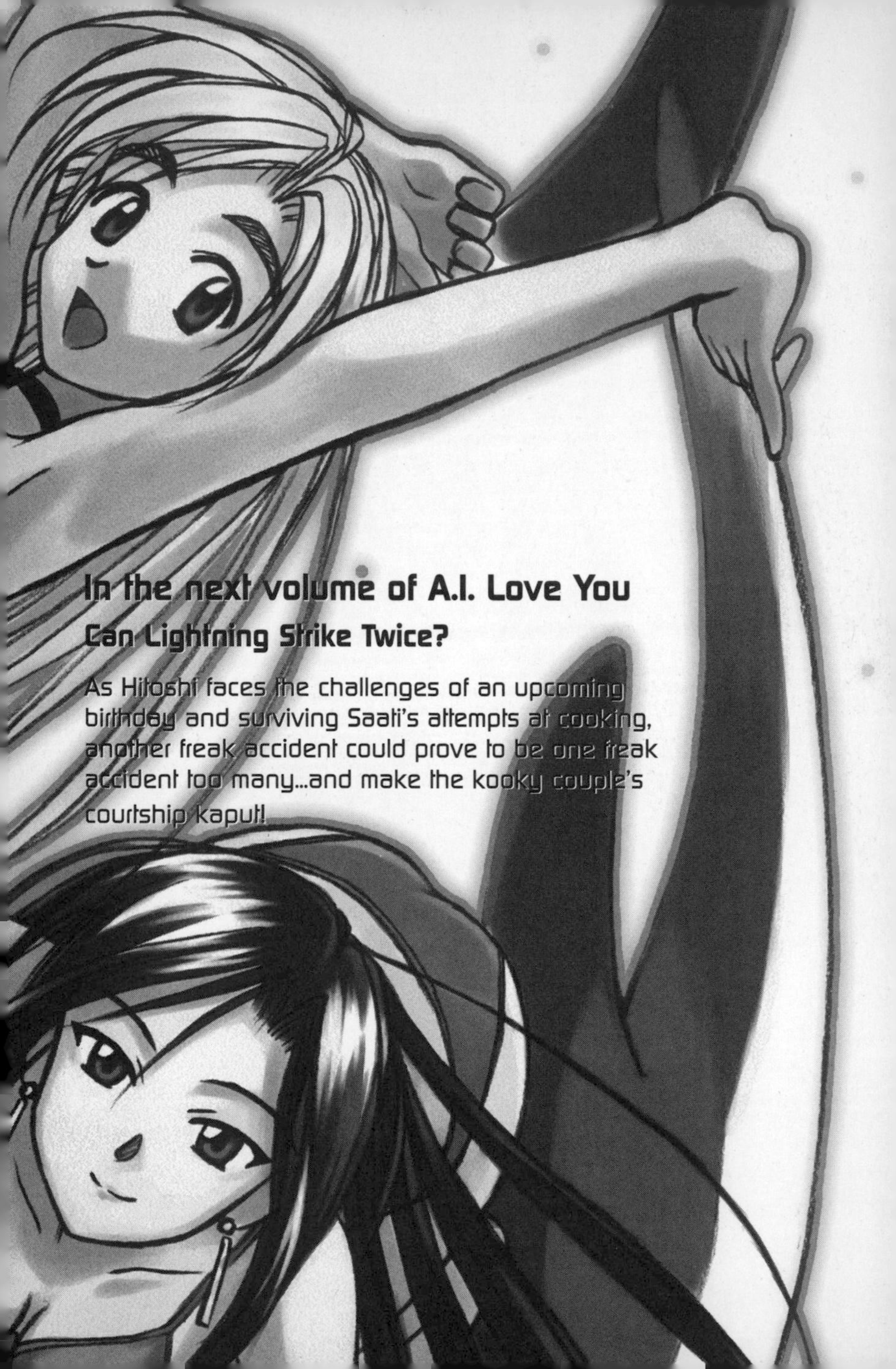

In the next volume of A.I. Love You

Can Lightning Strike Twice?

As Hitoshi faces the challenges of an upcoming birthday and surviving Saati's attempts at cooking, another freak accident could prove to be one freak accident too many...and make the kooky couple's courtship kaput!

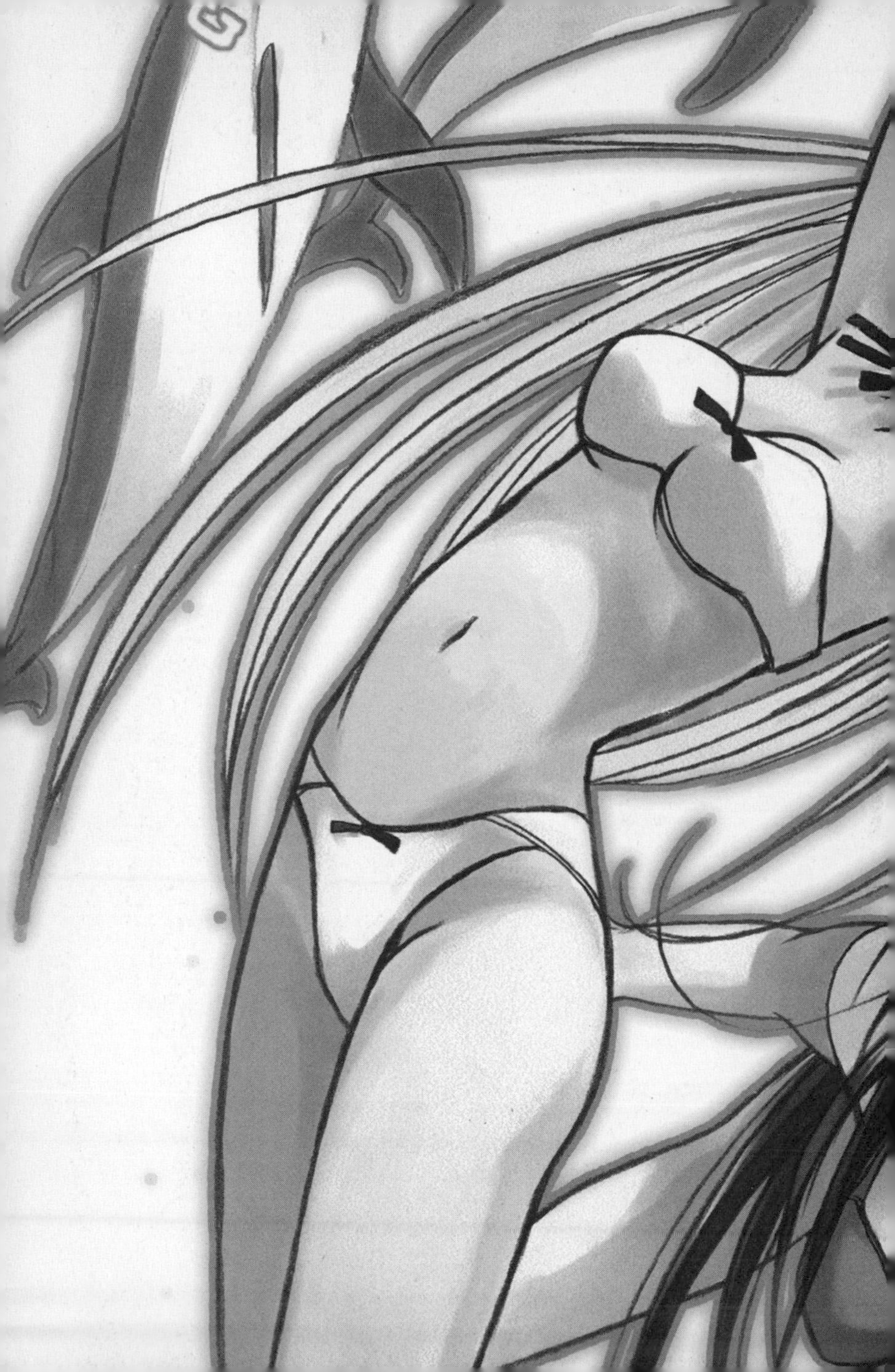

ALSO AVAILABLE FROM TOKYOPOP

MANGA

.HACK//LEGEND OF THE TWILIGHT
@LARGE
A.I. LOVE YOU
AI YORI AOSHI
ANGELIC LAYER
ARM OF KANNON May 2004
BABY BIRTH
BATTLE ROYALE
BATTLE VIXENS April 2004
BRAIN POWERED
BRIGADOON
B'TX
CANDIDATE FOR GODDESS, THE April 2004
CARDCAPTOR SAKURA
CARDCAPTOR SAKURA - MASTER OF THE CLOW
CARDCAPTOR SAKURA AUTHENTIC May 2004
CHOBITS
CHRONICLES OF THE CURSED SWORD
CLAMP SCHOOL DETECTIVES
CLOVER
COMIC PARTY June 2004
CONFIDENTIAL CONFESSIONS
CORRECTOR YUI
COWBOY BEBOP
COWBOY BEBOP: SHOOTING STAR
CRESCENT MOON May 2004
CYBORG 009
DEMON DIARY
DEMON ORORON, THE April 2004
DEUS VITAE June 2004
DIGIMON
DIGIMON ZERO TWO
DIGIMON SERIES 3 April 2004
DNANGEL April 2004
DOLL - HARDCOVER May 2004
DRAGON HUNTER
DRAGON KNIGHTS
DUKLYON: CLAMP SCHOOL DEFENDERS
ERICA SAKURAZAWA WORKS
FAERIES' LANDING
FAKE
FLCL
FORBIDDEN DANCE
FRUITS BASKET
G GUNDAM
GATE KEEPERS
GETBACKERS
GHOST! March 2004
GIRL GOT GAME
GRAVITATION
GTO
GUNDAM WING

GUNDAM WING: BATTLEFIELD OF PACIFISTS
GUNDAM WING: ENDLESS WALTZ
GUNDAM WING: THE LAST OUTPOST (G-UNIT)
HAPPY MANIA
HARLEM BEAT
I.N.V.U.
IMMORTAL RAIN June 2004
INITIAL D
ISLAND
JING: KING OF BANDITS
JULINE
JUROR 13 Coming Soon
KARE KANO
KILL ME, KISS ME
KINDAICHI CASE FILES, THE
KING OF HELL
KODOCHA: SANA'S STAGE
LAMENT OF THE LAMB May 2004
LES BIJOUX
LOVE HINA
LUPIN III
MAGIC KNIGHT RAYEARTH I
MAGIC KNIGHT RAYEARTH II
MAHOROMATIC: AUTOMATIC MAIDEN May 2004
MAN OF MANY FACES
MARMALADE BOY
MARS
MINK April 2004
MIRACLE GIRLS
MIYUKI-CHAN IN WONDERLAND
MODEL May 2004
ONE April 2004
PARADISE KISS
PARASYTE
PEACH GIRL
PEACH GIRL: CHANGE OF HEART
PEACH GIRL: AUTHENTIC COLLECTORS BOX SET May 2004
PET SHOP OF HORRORS
PITA-TEN
PLANET LADDER
PLANETES
PRIEST
PSYCHIC ACADEMY March 2004
RAGNAROK
RAVE MASTER
REALITY CHECK
REBIRTH
REBOUND
REMOTE June 2004
RISING STARS OF MANGA
SABER MARIONETTE J
SAILOR MOON
SAINT TAIL

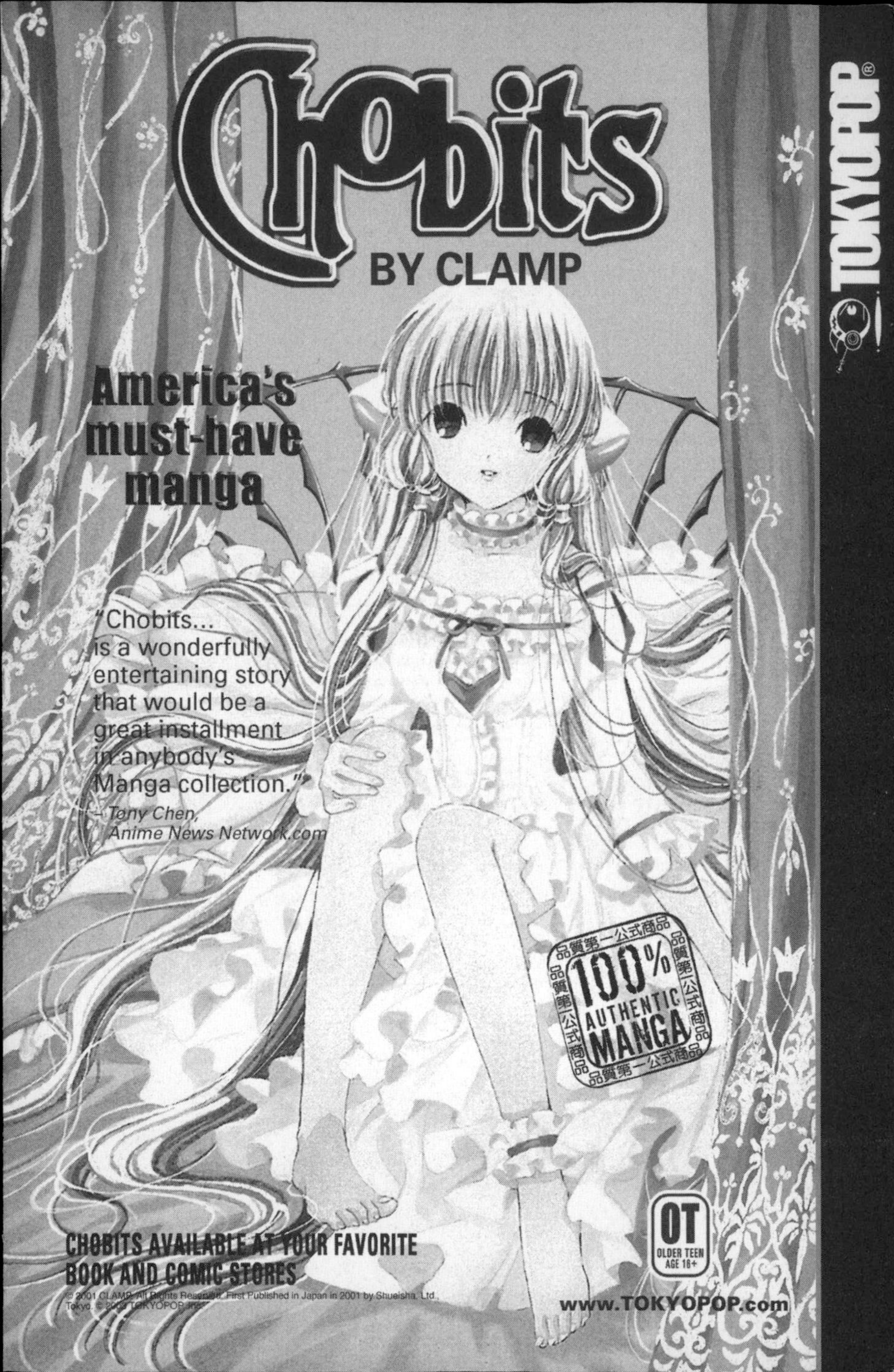
Chobits
BY CLAMP
TOKYOPOP®
America's must-have manga
"Chobits... is a wonderfully entertaining story that would be a great installment in anybody's Manga collection."
–Tony Chen, Anime News Network.com
100% AUTHENTIC MANGA
OT
OLDER TEEN AGE 16+
CHOBITS AVAILABLE AT YOUR FAVORITE BOOK AND COMIC STORES
© 2001 CLAMP. All Rights Reserved. First Published in Japan in 2001 by Shueisha, Ltd., Tokyo. © TOKYOPOP Inc.
www.TOKYOPOP.com

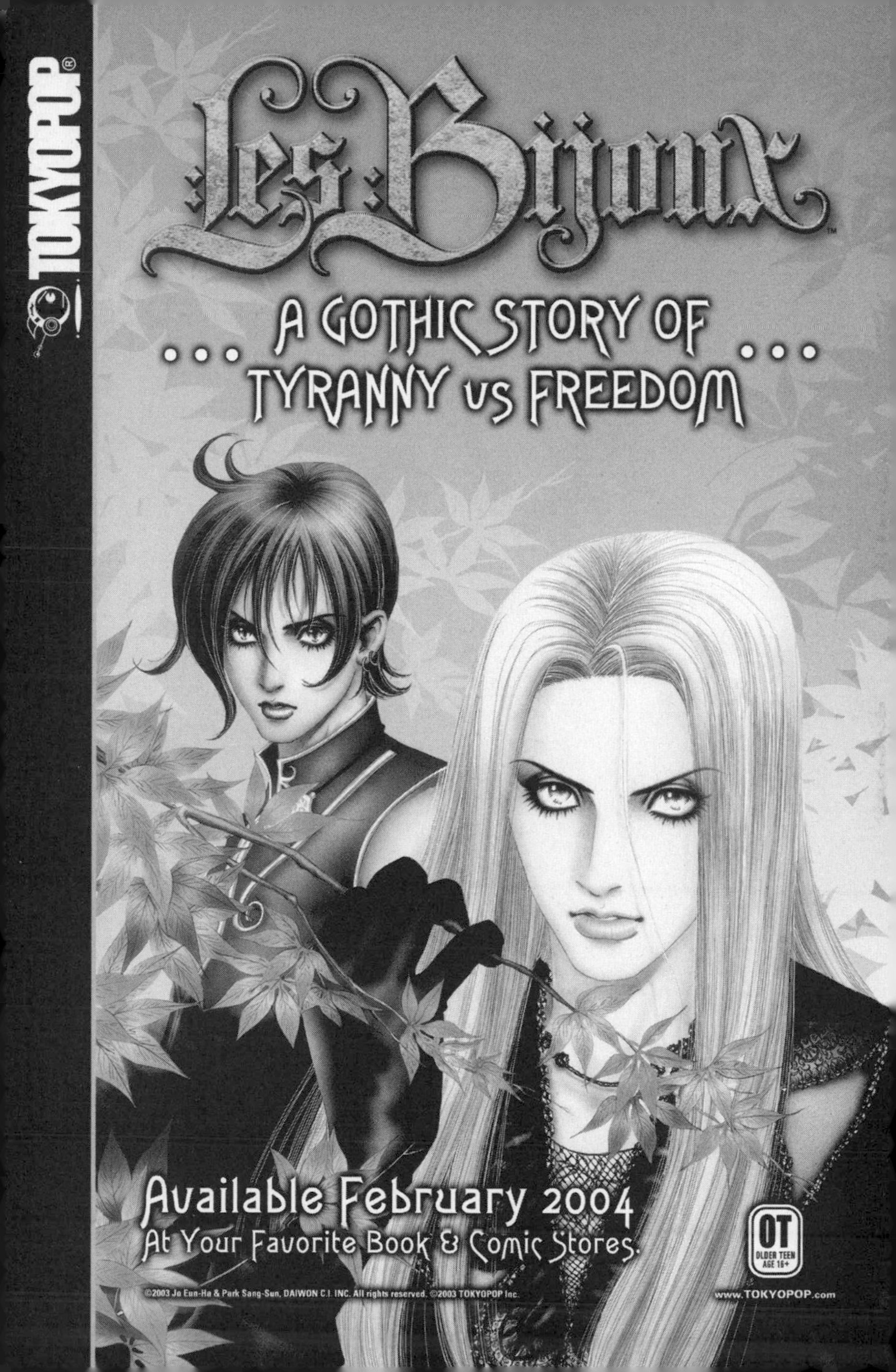
TOKYOPOP
Les Bijoux™
...A GOTHIC STORY OF TYRANNY vs FREEDOM...
Available February 2004
At Your Favorite Book & Comic Stores.
OT
OLDER TEEN AGE 16+
©2003 Jo Eun-Ha & Park Sang-Sun, DAIWON C.I. INC. All rights reserved. ©2003 TOKYOPOP Inc.
www.TOKYOPOP.com

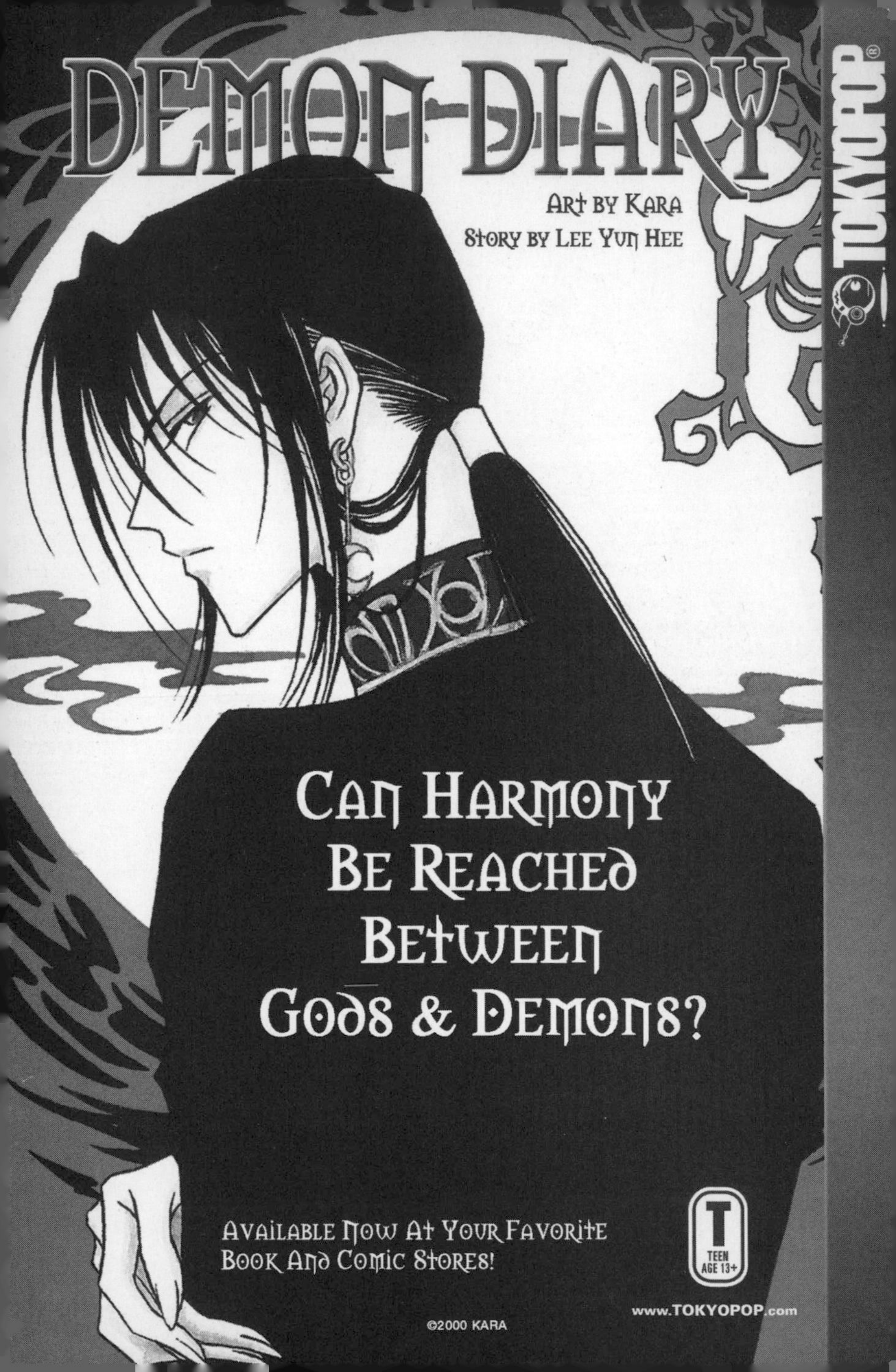
DEMON DIARY
ART BY KARA
STORY BY LEE YUN HEE
TOKYOPOP®
CAN HARMONY BE REACHED BETWEEN GODS & DEMONS?
AVAILABLE NOW AT YOUR FAVORITE BOOK AND COMIC STORES!
T TEEN AGE 13+
www.TOKYOPOP.com
©2000 KARA

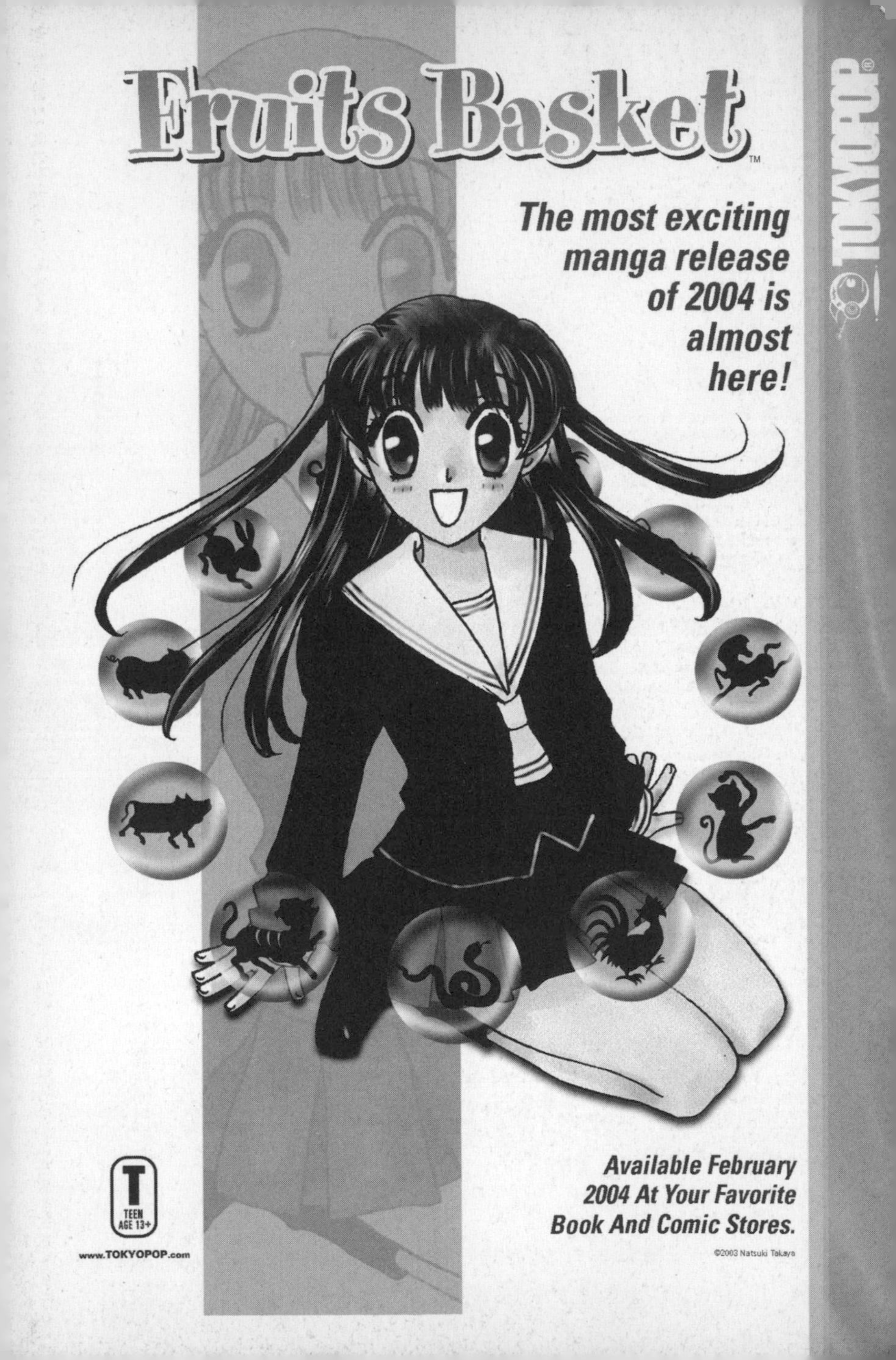
Fruits Basket™
The most exciting manga release of 2004 is almost here!
TOKYOPOP®
T TEEN AGE 13+
Available February 2004 At Your Favorite Book And Comic Stores.
www.TOKYOPOP.com
©2003 Natsuki Takaya

STOP!

This is the back of the book.
You wouldn't want to spoil a great ending!

This book is printed "manga-style," in the authentic Japanese right-to-left format. Since none of the artwork has been flipped or altered, readers get to experience the story just as the creator intended. You've been asking for it, so TOKYOPOP® delivered: authentic, hot-off-the-press, and far more fun!

DIRECTIONS

If this is your first time reading manga-style, here's a quick guide to help you understand how it works.

It's easy... just start in the top right panel and follow the numbers. Have fun, and look for more 100% authentic manga from TOKYOPOP®!